WOMEN
IN
MINISTRY

BIBLICAL & HISTORICAL
PERSPECTIVES

AD HOC COMMITTEE ON WOMEN'S ORDINATION

Michael Bernoi
Walter B. T. Douglas
Jacques B. Doukhan
Roger L. Dudley
Jon L. Dybdahl
Jo Ann Davidson
Richard M. Davidson
Robert M. Johnston

Jerry Moon
W. Larry Richards
Russell L. Staples
Peter M. van Bemmelen
Nancy Jean Vyhmeister
Randal R. Wisbey
Alicia A. Worley

WOMEN —IN— MINISTRY

BIBLICAL & HISTORICAL PERSPECTIVES

Special Committee, SDA Theological Seminary
EDITOR, NANCY VYHMEISTER

Andrews
University
Press

©1998 Andrews University Press
213 Information Services Building
Berrien Springs, MI 49104-1700
616-471-6915

ISBN 1-883925-22-3
Library of Congress Catalog Card Number 98-87693

Cover Design   Randy Siebold
Typesetting   Jennifer Minner Payne

TABLE OF CONTENTS

PROLOGUE

Why This Book?

Utrecht, 5 July 1995. Emotions ran high as the delegates to the 56th session of the General Conference of Seventh-day Adventists voted 1,481 to 673 to deny the request of the North American Division to be permitted to ordain women pastors within its territory. There was no way to know for sure how many delegates had voted "No" because they were convinced that the Bible does not allow a woman to be ordained, how many had voted "No" because of the customs of their lands, or how many voted "No" because they were concerned over allowing one division to break ranks with the rest of the world field. Neither was there any way to know what had moved those who voted "Yes" to do so.

Because of the wording of the motion, the question of whether or not a female Seventh-day Adventist pastor might properly be ordained to the gospel ministry was not answered at Utrecht. Less than one month after the Utrecht vote, several union presidents of the North American Division met with the faculty of the Seventh-day Adventist Theological Seminary, still asking the same question: May a woman legitimately be ordained to pastoral ministry? If so, on what basis? If not, why not? What are the issues involved—hermeneutics? Bible and theology? custom and culture? history and tradition? pragmatism and missiological needs? And furthermore, how could all these facets of the issue be presented in a logical, coherent manner? Would the Seminary faculty please address these questions and provide answers?

How Did This Book Come into Being?

At the next meeting of the Dean's Council, the decision was made to put together a study group to investigate the multiple issues surrounding ordination. Early in January of 1996 each department of the Seminary nominated two persons to an Ad hoc Committee on Hermeneutics and Ordination. Two students were added to the group. A chair was appointed. In February the committee met to discuss its task and the best way to go about it. After several prayerful discussions, the 15 committee members agreed on the need to investigate various aspects of the ordination question and present the findings in a book. This book would explore the question of the ordination of women to the gospel ministry in the Adventist Church in biblical, theological, and historical perspective. There would be no attempt to relate the findings of the study

1

to the empirical circumstances of the church in any place, nor would our research deal with the cultural constraints and accepted customs that might make the ordination of women inadvisable in many countries. Furthermore, there would be a studious avoidance of any attempt to tell individuals or churches what to do, or of any involvement in the official decision-making process regarding women in ministry. The study was to be driven by a desire to study the biblical, theological, historical understanding of church and ministry, ordination, and women. The final purpose was to provide data to facilitate informed decision making.

By May of 1996 the outline of the book and guidelines for the chapters were complete and the authors—most from the committee itself—had agreed to write. As the chapters began to come in, we gave copies to each committee member to read and critique. These were then returned to the author with suggestions for rewriting; a second version was then presented to the committee. In September of 1996 the committee commenced regular meetings every other Monday afternoon for two hours. These meetings always began with prayer, often several prayers—pleading with God for wisdom and understanding, love and firmness, but most of all for God's leading that His will might be done in the meeting and in the book. While the discussions were at times animated, a spirit of camaraderie developed. Sensitivity to the positions of others, both for and against women's ordination was evident. Yet, the firm desire to be true to Scripture was obvious. This was a group of dedicated Christians seeking to clarify an unclear issue, to do what was right.

Eventually, all the chapters were written, rewritten, and approved by the committee. After editing, the chapters were put together and given to outside readers for review. Their comments were taken into consideration in the final drafting of the book.

What Is the Hermeneutical Stance of the Authors of This Book?

The name given to this group—Committee on Hermeneutics and Ordination—suggested that if only we would clarify our hermeneutics we would be able to decide whether the ordination of Seventh-day Adventist women ministers was acceptable. However, as the committee prayed, studied, and discussed, it became clear that the issue of women's ordination hinged on more than the hermeneutical approach to certain passages of Scripture. Hence, the search was broadened and several chapters on history had to be included.

Nevertheless, the committee realized that in interpreting biblical stories and injunctions, the book's authors followed hermeneutical principles of which the reader would need to be aware. Rather than having a section on hermeneutics in each chapter containing biblical material, the group decided that one presentation, in the introduction, should be sufficient. Thus, the principles of interpretation described here apply to all chapters on biblical materials. The principles applied are time-honored approaches; similar rules appear in recognized Adventist publications.[1]

The following principles, considered basic by the authors and committee, undergird the interpretation of Scripture in this book.

In agreement with the first of the 27 fundamental beliefs of Seventh-day Adventists, we accept that all of the canonical Scriptures are divinely inspired. An indivisible blend of human and divine, the Bible is the authoritative rule of faith by which Christians are to direct their lives. Although it was first given to those who lived in an ancient Near Eastern or Mediterranean context and is couched in language best understandable to those readers and hearers, the Bible's message transcends its cultural backgrounds to present God's word for all people in all times.

Scripture must be allowed to interpret itself. One part of the Bible interprets another. The clear illumines the dark; the simple explains the complex. Because of the intrinsic unity of the Bible, the whole of the Bible message must be taken into account. Scripture must be compared with Scripture to find the true meaning of any passage: difficult texts must be studied in the light of clearer ones. Thus, doctrine cannot be construed on the basis of one text alone.

On matters on which Scripture is silent, one must search for biblical principles that relate to the situation and apply them with sanctified reasoning. For example, the Bible does not prohibit smoking, but it does admonish us to care for the body temple. Church organization is not spelled out in the Bible. In the 1850s and 1860s Adventist pioneers agonized over whether or not to organize the little flock. James White put forth his position: "All means which according to sound judgment, will advance the cause of truth, and are not forbidden by plain scripture declarations, should be employed."[2] While some Christians have taken the position that whatever Scripture does not specifically command is prohibited, Seventh-day Adventists have followed James White's thinking. Our committee did likewise.

While readers of the Bible can and do profit from a simple reading of a given passage, understanding is enhanced by a study of the context of a passage, both literary and historical. At the same time external interpretations cannot be imposed on the Bible. For example, the way things are today cannot be used to explain how things were in Bible times. A careful analysis of the text and its context leads today's readers to better understand the meaning of the passage for its original readers. It also helps modern Christians to apply Scripture to the life of the church.

To understand Scripture one must approach it in faith, with a heart willing to learn and obey. Without the aid of the Holy Spirit, Scripture cannot be correctly interpreted; thus prayer requesting God's gracious gift must precede and accompany the study of Scripture.

Finally, the committee recognized that absolute uniformity of understanding was not possible or desirable. We took note of the following paragraph from Ellen White:

> We cannot then take a position that the unity of the church consists in viewing every text of Scripture in the very same light. The church may pass resolution upon resolution to put down all disagreement of opinions, but we cannot force the mind and will, and root out disagreement. These resolutions may conceal the discord, but they cannot quench it and establish perfect agreement. Nothing can perfect unity in the church but the spirit of Christlike forbearance.[3]

How Is This Book Put Together?

The twenty chapters of this study fall into five different categories. The first looks at priesthood, ministry, and the laying on of hands in the Bible. The second concentrates on ordination, considering its meaning, both theological and historical. The third section reviews the contribution of women to ministry and leadership through the Bible and in Adventist history. In the fourth section, biblical concepts and injunctions, together with an Ellen White quotation, all considered as impediments to the ordination of women, are elucidated. Finally, various issues, especially urgent in the North American setting, are considered.

Each chapter was written by a different author and retains the writer's individual style. In fact, careful readers will notice slight differences of opinions between chapters. Our agreement was on the big picture.

Each author chose the Bible version he or she would use. As might be expected of a group of academics, references were considered vital. Yet in deference to readers who would feel that footnotes are burdensome, these references have been relegated to endnotes. Research language and the use of biblical languages were kept as unobtrusive as possible.

What Do We Hope This Book Will Do?

The Seminary Ad hoc Committee on Hermeneutics and Ordination prayerfully submits this book, not as the final answer to whether or not the Seventh-day Adventist Church should ordain its women in ministry, but rather as a resource tool for decision making. While recognizing that good decisions are based on hard facts, we are also cognizant of the fact that at times clear evidence may be lacking, thus making necessary the use of sanctified judgment and imagination to resolve questions and issues.

Naturally, this volume represents the understanding of the Seminary Ad hoc Committee on Hermeneutics and Ordination. We do not claim to speak for others, either at the Seminary or in church administration. Some may disagree with our findings. That is their privilege. We welcome their responses and invite them to dialogue.

We hope and pray that this volume may assist individuals, leaders, and the community of faith at large in deciding how to deal with the issue of ordination and, more specifically, the relationship of ordination to women. We believe that the biblical, theological, and historical perspectives elaborated in this book affirm women in pastoral leadership. As Seventh-day Adventists we have a mission, a task to accomplish: the sharing of a unique message of hope with a dying world. Let us all use all our energies to that end.

Nancy J. Vyhmeister
Committee chair and editor

Endnotes

1. Among these are: "Principles of Biblical Interpretation," *Problems in Bible Translation* (Washington, DC: General Conference of Seventh-day Adventists, 1954), 79-127; Gordon Hyde, ed., *A Symposium on Biblical Hermeneutics* (Washington, DC: Biblical Research Committee, 1974), especially 163-262; Gerhard Hasel, *Biblical Interpretation Today* (Washington, DC: Biblical Research Institute, 1985), 100-113; "Methods of Bible Study," report approved at the Annual Council of the General Conference of SDA, Rio de Janeiro, 1986, and published in the *Adventist Review*, January 22, 1987, 18-20; and Lee J. Gugliotto, *Handbook for Bible Study* (Hagerstown, MD: Review and Herald, 1995).

2. James White, "Making Us a Name," *Review and Herald*, 26 April 1860, 180; cf. idem, "A Complaint," *Review and Herald*, 16 June 1859, 28.

3. *Manuscript Releases*, 11:266.

PART ONE: MINISTRY IN THE BIBLE

Part One explores the theological meaning of the different forms of priesthood and ministry among God's people throughout the Bible. From the gates of Eden onward, patriarchs offered animal sacrifices in worship. At the Exodus, the priestly ministry was restricted to physically perfect, male descendants of Aaron. In the New Testament, the priesthood of all believers becomes normative for God's new-covenant people (chap. 1). Chapter 2 explores reasons for the exclusion of women from the sacrificial aspect of the priesthood while they were permitted to function as judges and prophets. The forms of New Testament ministry (chap. 3) were varied, yet might be subsumed under the idea of servant-hood—individuals gifted for service. The meaning and importance of the biblical rite of laying on of hands in setting apart for ministry are discussed in chapter 4. Together these four chapters paint a picture of the form and substance of ministry throughout the Bible.

CHAPTER 1

ALL
THE PRIESTHOOD OF∧ BELIEVERS

RAOUL DEDEREN

In a passage that deserves more attention than we seem to have granted it, the apostle Peter writes:

> Come to him, to that living stone, rejected by men but in God's sight chosen and precious; and like stones be yourselves built into a spiritual house, to be a holy priesthood, to offer spiritual sacrifices acceptable to God through Jesus Christ. For it stands in Scripture: "Behold, I am laying in Zion a stone, a cornerstone chosen and precious, and he who believes in him will not be put to shame." To you therefore who believe, he is precious, but for those who do not believe, "The very stone which the builders rejected has become the head of the corner," and "A stone that will make men stumble, a rock that will make them fall"; for they stumble because they disobey the word, as they were destined to do.
>
> But you are a chosen race, a royal priesthood, a holy nation, God's own people, that you may declare the wonderful deeds of him who called you out of darkness into his marvelous light. Once you were no people but now you are God's people; once you had not received mercy but now you have received mercy (1 Pet 2:4-10, RSV).

In these verses, Peter's own statement (vv. 4-5) is followed in vv. 6-8 by the quotation of three Old Testament texts (Isa 26:16; Ps 118:22; Isa 8:14, 15) mingled with a few explanatory comments. In vv. 9 and 10 Peter uses three additional texts (Isa 43: 20, 21; Exod 19:6; Hos 2:25), not quoted as directly as the first Old Testament references.

In his remarks on the nature of the church the apostle uses imagery common to early Christian believers: for instance, Jesus as the stone, cornerstone, and stone of stumbling, as well as members of the Christian community as stones forming a building. These were concepts commonly accepted in early Christianity (cf. Eph 2:19, 20; Rom 9:33; Mark 12:10, 11; Eph 2:20-22). The same is true of Jesus as rejected (Mark 8:31; Luke 17:25), and Jesus as elect (cf. Luke 9:35; 23:35). House, building and temple are terms commonly applied to the church in the New Testament (Matt 16:18; 1 Cor 3:9, 16-17; 1 Tim 3:15). So are the idea of sacrifices acceptable to God (Rom 12:1; 15:16; Heb 13:15,16) and the concept of those who were not a people becoming God's people (Rom 9:25; 11:17-24).

In 1 Pet 2:4-10, the apostle is moving in a circle of ideas that were shared among early Christians. Its center was faith in Christ and the concept of the church as the continuation of Israel. His was not an isolated stance, but reflected a common perspective of major significance.

In the conclusion of his argumentation (vv. 9 and 10) Peter carefully set forth the affirmation that Christians are "a chosen race, a royal priesthood, a holy nation, God's own people," that they may declare the wonderful deeds of God who called them out of darkness into his marvelous light. In these verses one finds the Old Testament concept of priesthood merged with part of Exod 19:5, 6: "Now therefore, if you will obey my voice and keep my covenant, you shall be my own possession among all peoples; for all the earth is mine, and you shall be to me a kingdom of priests and a holy nation."

This review of Peter's statement on the priesthood of all believers, however brief, will follow several steps. We shall first seek to bring together the basic elements of the Aaronic-Levitical priesthood. We will then inquire about the basis of Jesus' high priesthood as continuation and fulfillment of the Levitical priestly model. That will be followed by an examination of the New Testament concept that all born-again believers belong to the priesthood intended by God, its basic implications, and some of its most striking misunderstandings. Finally, we shall sketch a few words of conclusion, emphasizing the practical purpose of the biblical doctrine.

The Levitical Priesthood

At the heart of Old Testament religion was relationship with God. In Israel, the covenant, the temple, worship, and every facet of life were as many expressions of this relationship. Prophets and priests were the guardians and servants of this life of relationship. Their functions can best be understood in that context.[1]

Of Aaron, Priests, and Levites

While after the Sinai covenant some non-Levites performed priestly functions on occasion, as for instance Gideon (Judg 6:24-26), Manoah of Dan (Judg 13:19), Samuel (1 Sam 7:9), David (2 Sam 6:13-17), and Elijah (1 Kgs 18:23, 37-38), the office of priesthood was vested in the tribe of Levi .[2] All priests were Levites, but by no means were all Levites priests. The priesthood itself was restricted to the family of Aaron and his descendants (Exod 28:1, 41, 43; Num 3:10). They undertook the sacrificial duties. Aaron himself was "the priest who is chief among his brethren" (Lev 21:10), thus fulfilling an office described as that of "high priest" (Num 35:25, 28; Josh 20:6), "the priest" (Exod 31:10), or "the anointed priest" (Lev 4:3, 5, 16). Like that of the other priests, his office was hereditary and passed on to his eldest son (Num 3:32, 20:28; 25:10-13). The high priest bore the names of all the tribes of Israel on his breastplate into the sanctuary thus representing all the people before God (Exod 28:19). While his duties were similar in principle to those of the other priests, he had certain exclusive responsibilities, the clearest of which was his ministry on the annual Day of Atonement (Leviticus 16). To the Levites, whom he had assigned "as a gift to Aaron and his sons" (Num 8:19), God committed the supervision of the minor duties of the tabernacle (Num 1:50; 3:28, 32, 8:15, 31). They helped the priests (Num 3:6, 8; 18:2) and served the congregation in various capacities (Num 16:9; 8:19).

A Priest-People, A Kingdom of Priests

The high priest, the priests, and the Levites, all descending from Levi, represented the nation's relationship with God. They took the place of the first-born who belonged by right to God (Exod 13:1-2, 13; Num 3:12-13, 45), apparently reflecting God's original desire that his whole people should be a priestly people, a "kingdom of priests" (Exod 19:4-6; cf. Num 15:40). With the establishment of the theocracy at Sinai and the erection of the tabernacle, due to the failure of his people at the time of the golden calf apostasy (Exod 32:26-29; Deut 33:8-11), God appointed the tribe of Levi to its service instead of the first-born (Num 3:5-13; 8:14-19). In the background, however, the vision of the priest-people remained, waiting to become the "priesthood of all believers" under the one New Testament High Priest, the Lord Jesus Christ.

Basic Priestly Functions and Responsibilities

As noted earlier, at the heart of the Hebrew religion was one's relationship with God, a relationship disrupted by sin. The necessity of maintaining this relationship made the priests and their ministrations immensely important. Theirs was the role of mediators between God and Israel. They attended to the solemn task of approaching God on behalf of the people. Priests did so not because they were innately better or holier than the rest of the nation but because that was the task that God, in his mercy, had entrusted to them. Their functions and responsibilities were evidence of the mercy of God toward his people and of the importance of maintaining an acceptable relationship with God.

The elaborate seven-day consecration ceremony of Aaron and his sons (Exod 29:1-37; Leviticus 8) set the Hebrew priests apart from the people as holy persons, chosen of God, consecrated to God, and representatives of the people before God as well as representatives of God to the people. As representatives of the people they were to offer various acceptable sacrifices and officiate in the prescribed services as instituted by God through Moses. Representing God before Israel, the priest taught the people the law of the Lord (Lev 10:11; Deut 33:10), administered justice (Deut 17:8-13; 19:16, 17), watched over the physical health of the nation (Leviticus 13-15), and judged ritual cleanness (Leviticus 13). Other duties were shared with the Levites in general.

Representing Israel before God, the priests were primarily concerned with ministering at the altar and offering sacrifices (Deut 33:8-10). On the assumption that Israelites were sinners standing in need of a mediator, the essential duty of the priest was to represent Israel to God. This particular function was inherent to the priesthood; the others were additional responsibilities. The New Testament Epistle to the Hebrews emphasizes this Godward aspect of the priesthood as its very essence (Heb 6:20; 7:25; 9:24). This representation of sinners to God was an admission of the sinfulness of the human race, of the holiness of God, and of the need of conditions in one's approach to God. It also carried with it the right of access to God and the possibility of abiding in the presence of God.

Christ Jesus, the Ever-Living High Priest

A Continuation of the Old Testament Priestly Ministry

While early Jewish Christian believers continued to praise God in the temple at Jerusalem (Acts 2:46; 3:1; 21:27; 22:17), their understanding of the priesthood had undergone a radical change. The gospel they received and proclaimed had led them to understand that in Christ Jesus God had provided an ever-living Mediator. His life and death on the cross had an expiatory dimension. What in the past had been undertaken by priests and Levites on a continuous basis had now been fully achieved once for all in Jesus Christ, whose priesthood was seen as a continuation of the Old Testament priestly ministry. The priesthood of the Levites and of Christ were knit together as preparation with fulfillment, as provisional with ideal (Heb 8:5; 9:23-28). In the Epistle to the Hebrews one finds the application to Christ of the terms "priest" and "high priest."[3] Although Christ's priestly and mediatorial functions connected with sacrifice and intercession pervade the whole New Testament (Matt 20:28; John 1:29; Rom 8:34; 1 Cor 5:7; Eph 2:13-14, 18: 1 Pet 1:18, 19), in Hebrews the priesthood of Christ finds its fullest expression.

Redeemer and Priest

One may wonder why Christ's priesthood is so strongly brought forward in the Epistle to the Hebrews. It seems that its author was concerned about the spiritual degeneration (5:11-4), and backsliding, if not apostasy (6:1-9; 10:35), of its intended readers. A personal experience of the priesthood of Christ would bring back spiritual steadfastness, growth, and assurance. These Hebrew Christians knew Jesus as Savior and had an elementary knowledge of the truths of redemption (6:1) but may not have realized what it meant to have Christ as Priest. The distinction between the two is not without importance.

Centuries earlier the Levitical priesthood was established at Sinai *after* the redemption of God's people from Egypt and the crossing of the Read Sea. At Sinai Israel should have realized that God had brought them to himself (Exod 19:4) and that, beyond deliverance, their true relation to God and God's relation to them was his dwelling among them (Exod 19:4-6; 25:1-8). The priesthood was appointed to provide the means of access to God, without fear, on the basis of an already-existing redemption.

Likewise, Hebrew Christians knew Christ as Redeemer. They were now to discern the possibility, the power, and the joy of constant and free access to God through Christ, in full assurance and without fear (Heb 4:14-16). There is indeed a major difference between knowing Christ as Savior and as Priest. This is one of the central distinctions between the teachings of Romans and Hebrews. While Romans is concerned with redemption which makes access to God possible (Rom 5:1, 2), Hebrews is concerned with access made possible by redemption. The epistle's constant appeal is to "draw near" (Heb 10:22), not to "shrink back" (10:39) but to "go on" (6:1).

Christ's Qualifications

To the question, "What is it, exactly, that constitutes the representative character of Christ's priesthood"? or "Why did God appoint Christ and no other"? the Epistle to the Hebrews submits several answers. To begin, the priesthood of Christ is a continuation and fulfillment of the Old Testament priestly ministry. This is the basis of Christ's priestly qualifications. The epistle explains that Christ has been appointed by God (Heb 5:5-10) "to act on behalf of men in relation to God" (5:1). His perfect humanity involves oneness with men and women for whom he acts, having undergone, as they do, the discipline of suffering and temptation (Heb 2:9, 14-18; 4:15). In personal character Christ was holy and guileless (Heb 7:26, 27; cf. 1 Pet 3:18), thus having no need to be purged of sin as did the sons of Aaron (Heb 7:28) who had to offer sacrifices for themselves as well as for God's children (Heb 5:2, 3; 7:27, 28; 9:7). Being subject to death, Old Testament priests could not continue their ministry forever, but Jesus is sinless, a perfect and eternal High Priest (Heb 4:15; 5:7-10; 7:23-28; 9:14) who can fully "sympathize with our weaknesses (Heb 2:14-18; 4:15).[4]

In contrast to the imperfect sanctuary of the old covenant (Heb 9:1-5) with its repeated rituals (Heb 9:6-10) "which cannot perfect the conscience of the worshiper" (Heb 9:9; cf. 10:4), Christ, who paradoxically is both Priest and offering (Heb 9:11, 14, 26), entered the "greater and more perfect tent" (Heb 9:11) of which Moses' tabernacle was but "a copy and shadow" (Heb 8:1-7). He took his own blood and became the Mediator of a new and better covenant (Heb 9:11-15), making constant intercession (Heb 7:25). "Symbolic for the present age" (Heb 9:9), the Aaronic way into the sanctuary was standing "until the time of reformation" should come (Heb 9:10).

Christ's Priesthood and Melchizedek's

One of the most remarkable features of the discussion in Hebrews is the association of Christ's priesthood with that of Melchizedek,[5] a priesthood that not only surpasses that of Aaron's (Heb 7:11) but reaches back to the days of Abraham. Melchizedek is mentioned three times in the Scriptures and each time the reference is of particular significance. In Genesis 14 he appears in history in connection with Abraham and is called "priest of God Most High" (v. 18). In Psalm 110 he is mentioned in a psalm generally regarded as Messianic, which Christ applied to himself (Matt 22:44). He appears a third time in Hebrews, which not only takes the Genesis 14 account as it stands, but uses it to typify some of the aspects of the priesthood of Christ.

God had promised that the Messianic king would also be "a priest forever, after the order of Melchizedek" (Ps 110:4). Such a promise suggested the imperfections of the Aaronic order (Heb 7:11-14). The mere assertion of another priesthood at all is rather striking. Besides, the position of Melchizedek as king indicates the *royalty* of Christ's priesthood. The fact that in Genesis 14 Melchizedek "has neither beginning of days nor end of life" is used in Hebrews to typify the perpetuity of Christ's priesthood, unbroken by genealogical beginning or end (Heb 7:3; cf. 7:15-19). Melchizedek's order is also superior to Aaron's since Levi, in Abraham's loins, paid tithe to the king of Salem, the lesser to the greater (Heb 7:4-10). The priesthood exercised by Christ is unquestionably greater than that exercised by the Aaronic-Levitical priests.

The fundamental use of the Melchizedek's priesthood in the Epistle to the Hebrews has to do with the person of the priest-king rather than with his functions and responsibilities. The priestly person rather than the priestly work is underlined in the Melchizedek priesthood. Unlike Aaron, Melchizedek was a *royal* person, an *abiding* person and a *unique* person. The personal superiority of Melchizedek in these areas over the priesthood of Aaron is emphasized in Hebrews. No comparison is being drawn between Melchizedek and Christ, but Melchizedek is used to symbolize, to typify the personal superiority of Christ over all other priests, of his priesthood over that of Aaron. Christ's priesthood is inherent in his person as Son of God. First and foremost, it is this uniqueness as Son of God that gives Christ his qualifications for priesthood.

Christ's Priestly Functions

Since no characteristic priestly functions are recorded for Melchizedek, it was necessary to denote Christ's priestly functions in connection with those of Aaron. The contrast is shown, among other things, by the recurring word "better" (Heb 7:19, 22; 8:6; 9:23). The essence of the Levitical priesthood is representative offering. "Every high priest chosen from among men," writes the author of Hebrews, "is appointed to act on behalf of men in relation to God, to offer sacrifices for sins" (5:1). This is the essence of priesthood. The priest exercises his priesthood by making an offering to God (Heb 8:3). Having offered Himself as a sacrifice for sin (Heb 7:27), Christ presents his blood within the veil (Heb 6:20; 8:3 9:7, 24) after the daily and annual patterns of the Aaronic priesthood. By virtue of his sacrifice on the cross Christ has become "the mediator of a new [or "better"] covenant" (Heb 8:6; 9:15; 12:24), its "surety" or guarantee (Heb 7:22), and carries on his present work as Priest. As paradoxical as it may seem, Christ is set forth as offering and priest at the same time (Heb 9:14, 26, cf. 7:27).

As representative of the people in their approach to God, one of the high priest's tasks was to intercede. This aspect of Christ's ministry is explicitly set forth in the epistle (Heb 7:25, 26; 2:17, 18; 4:15, 16; cf. Rom 8:34). To Christ's function as Mediator and Intercessor, the epistle adds the work of sanctification (Heb 2:11; 10:10, 14; 13:12), once more connecting this aspect of his priestly ministry with his death on the cross. He did not merely make an offering once for all on the basis of which sinners may come to God, Christ also pursues a sanctifying work in his people. All these functions are part of the present activity of our High Priest.[6]

In the context of his priestly ministry Hebrews refers to Christ's second coming. He appeared "once for all" to put away sin by his death on the cross (Heb 9:26) and "to bear the sins of many" (v. 28), but "will appear a second time, not to deal with sin but to save those who are eagerly waiting for him" (v. 28). Christ's high-priestly ministry will go on "for ever" (Heb 7:24) till it be completed when he comes again.

The Priesthood of Believers

One more major dimension to the biblical concept of priesthood needs to be addressed. This is the New Testament concept that all born-again Christians belong to the priesthood. This teaching is often referred to as the priesthood of all believers.

The Testimony of Scripture

One may identify five specific New Testament references to the priesthood of believers. Three are found in the Book of Revelation which speaks of Christ who "made us a kingdom, priests to his God and Father"

(Rev 1:5,6), "a kingdom and priests to our God" (Rev 5:10), and of the redeemed who "shall be priests of God and of Christ" (Rev 20:6). Best known is Peter's statement exhorting fellow Christians to come to Christ "to be a holy priesthood, to offer spiritual sacrifices acceptable to God through Jesus Christ" (1 Pet 2:4, 5), followed by his conclusion: "But you are a chosen race, a royal priesthood, a holy nation, God's own people, that you may declare the wonderful deeds of him who called you out of darkness into his marvelous light" (v.9).

Baptism, the Sign of Our Universal Call

Risen from the dead and ascended on high, our High Priest is engaged in continuous intercession, so that day by day his presence, power, and prayer are made available to us. More than that, he has "made us a kingdom, priests to his God and Father," as we just noted. Buried with Christ in baptism, we have also been raised together with him through faith (Col 2:12; 3:1; cf. Rom 6:1-4). Through repentance and faith we have been admitted to God's covenant of grace and have been made participants in the priestly ministry of Christ, our Lord. Baptism is the anointing and consecration of every born-again believer as priest of Christ. It is the sign of our universal call. It signifies a new identity. Ellen White concurs.[7]

By virtue of our union with Christ we partake of a priesthood that is derived from his. His priestly standing before God is imputed to every Christian believer. By calling us "priests unto God,"[8] not only does John remind us that Jesus Christ is Mediator of the new and better covenant, but also that we, as a priestly, sacrificial body, are enlisted in a royal ministry through which Christ wants to redeem the world. The two titles, king and priest, place upon us a high calling and serious obligations, a commitment to the priestly work of Christ.

Offering Spiritual Sacrifices

What does God expect from those who lay claim on the scriptural doctrine of the priesthood of believers?[9] To do the true work of priests. The concrete content of this mandate is most impressively set forth by Peter. To begin with, as "a holy priesthood," we are "to offer spiritual sacrifice acceptable to God through Jesus Christ" (1 Pet 2:5).

Peter does not specify the content of these "spiritual sacrifices," but the context suggests that one's manner of life is in mind, as is stressed throughout the epistle (1 Pet 1:15-18; 2:12, 14-15, 20; 3:1-2, 6, 17; 4:19). Elsewhere in the New Testament the nature of these sacrifices is more specifically spelled out. The sacrifices of Christians include their praises and confessions of Christ's name: "Through him [Christ] then let us continually offer up a sacrifice of praise to God, that is the fruit of lips that acknowledge his name" (Heb 13:15). No longer the fruit of crops or the offsprings of animals, but "the fruit of lips." Next, deeds of charity and fellowship performed by Christians are sacrifices in which God delights: "Do not neglect to do good and to share what you have, for such sacrifices are pleasing to God" (Heb 13:16). The same is true of material gifts and offerings which, for instance, Paul received from the Philippians by the hand of Epaphroditus and describes as "a fragrant offering, a sacrifice acceptable and pleasing to God" (Phil 4:18).

Paul adopts an image from sacrificial rituals to describe his own self-giving in the work of ministry. One may see here an allusion to the prospect of his martyrdom: "Even if I am to be poured out as a libation upon the sacrificial offering of your faith, I am glad and rejoice with you all" (Phil 2:17). Then, the converts made by the missionary efforts of the church are regarded as a sacrifice offered to God and part of the priestly work (Rom 15:16). The early church considered converted Gentiles as the "first fruits" of the harvest of the world, gathered at Christ's request (Rev 14:4).

Paul probably reaches the high point of the Christian concept of sacrifice when he exhorts Roman believers to present their "bodies as a living sacrifice, holy and acceptable to God," their "spiritual worship" (Rom 12:1). The bodies of Christians are "members of Christ" (1 Cor 6:15), temples of the Holy Spirit (1 Cor 6:19). Because they are at every moment presented to God in Christ, Christians must endeavor to be what they already are by faith: holy, pure, without blemish. This sacrificial living is achieved through the power of Christ's resurrection and heavenly intercession.

The Missionary Obligation

Believer priests are not only called to be a holy priesthood, offering spiritual sacrifices acceptable to God through Jesus Christ, they are also to "declare the wonderful deeds of him who called them out of darkness into his marvelous light" (1 Pet 2:9).

According to Exod 19:5,6, which is at the root of Peter's statement, the sons and daughters of Israel were to be priests to God because of all nations he had chosen them for a special mission of service. They were called to offer to God the sacrifice of worship and obedience which the nations around them would not render, and to offer to the world the witness of grace God wanted to display though them. Their vocation was that of a priestly people, chosen and set apart for devotion to God and for the task of bringing God to all nations (cf. Gen 12:3; Isa 49:6; 53:3-5; 56:6-8; Gal 3:8). "If you will obey my will and keep my covenant, you shall be my own possession among all peoples; for all the earth is mine" was God's appeal to Israel through Moses (Exod 19:5; cf. v.3).

God had elected Israel not because he had no interest in the other nations but precisely because of his concern for "all the earth." Israel as a nation had been set apart as a priesthood with a mediatorial work vis-à-vis God and the world. It was a priesthood pointing forward to the coming Priest, Prophet, and King Messiah. Peter clearly calls the Christian believers—those who had received mercy and been made a "royal priesthood, a holy nation"—to proclaim that the "stone which the builders rejected" had "become the head of the corner" (1 Pet 2:7-10, quoting Ps 118:22). God has thus called the Christian church, as heir of the commission originally given to the Jewish nation, to represent him to all nations and the needs of all nations to God.

So this is what Christians are: a kingdom of priests. This is not an honorific title bestowed to boost our self-esteem, nor is it a regal claim to privilege. As Israel of old, besides offering our sacrifices to God, we are to be witnesses of his presence, reminders of his grace, unfolding God's loving presence in the world through lives shaped by his grace. As believer priests, a missionary obligation is placed on all of us. We are to introduce those we encounter to the nearness of God. We can no longer isolate ourselves from the sins and woes and cares of the world in which we live. We are to see our priesthood in the light of Christ's. As he was sent into the world to fulfill a priestly mission for sinners so also are his believer priests commissioned to fulfill the mission entrusted to them. He conceived of his mission in terms of service (Mark 10:45) and taught his disciples that they also were servants (Matt 10:24, 25; John 15:20): servants of the Servant of God, offering to all nations and peoples redemption through Christ's death on the cross and priestly ministry in heaven (Eph 1:7; Heb 9:15, 11-12).

It remains possible for us, however, to receive everything from God and still be the means of impeding his redemptive activity in the world. We need to guard against the temptation to selfishness and to be satisfied with spending our time talking to ourselves. We are not called to be priests to ourselves or to go to the altar alone.

A Corporate Priesthood

The priesthood about which the New Testament speaks is a corporate priesthood, a priesthood of the whole Christian church. Though spiritual gifts are granted individually to born-again Christians (1 Cor 12:4-11; 1 Pet 4:10), the priesthood is viewed in a collective sense as belonging to the whole body of believers. In every instance, whether in 1 Peter or Revelation, the words "priest" and "priesthood" are used collectively. The community of Christian believers, not just the individuals, is priestly. This is particulary plain in 1 Pet 2: 5 and 9 where the apostle uses "a body of priests (*hierateuma*)," in parallel with "a spiritual house," "a chosen race," and "God's people."

Thus, all members of the church have both an individual and a corporate responsibility. The full intention of priesthood, its ultimate meaning, is negated if priesthood is perceived only in individualistic terms—*my* access to God, *my* intercessory ministry, *my* right to interpret God's word. The church is a fellowship of believer priests, of gifted believer priests, who all have received from the Holy Spirit spiritual gifts for the good of the church as a whole (1 Cor 12:7; 1 Pet 4:10). Corporately, the church is the sacrificing priesthood instituted by God Himself so that men and women around the world may learn about God, have access to Him, and in turn offer spiritual sacrifices.

Of Misunderstandings and Abuses

Unlikely Callings

Since the gifts of the Spirit are granted to all Christian believers, each has a definite ministry, a priesthood, to fulfill. All have equal access to God. All may "with confidence draw near to the throne of grace" (Heb 4:16). All may "enter the sanctuary" and "draw near to God" (Heb 10: 19-22). All, according to their measure, share the priesthood of the ascended Christ from whom the church derives its character as a royal priesthood.

This intimation of equality that we are all priests demands that we take seriously the call of God to each believer priest. It requires that we take seriously some unlikely callings. Some whom God calls may have few of the traditional qualifications of respectability. Some may speak the wrong language or have the wrong skin color or be of the wrong gender.

Ordained Believer Priests

At the same time, the priesthood of believers does not imply that the church leaves no room for a separated ministry. While no priesthood existed belonging to a particular order of believers, the New Testament church recognized that in the exercise of its corporate life and responsibilities, special qualifications were required for the discharge of special duties and thus acknowledged the principle of representative selection.

Every born-again Christian is called to and capable of ministry. A "lay member" in the New Testament sense is a member of the *laos theou*, or "people of God" (Heb 4:9; cf. 1 Pet 2:9; Acts 15:14; Tit 2:14), is certainly not a church member who has no priestly responsibility, one who has handed over his or her functions of pastoral care or evangelism to certain professional believers who have been ordained and are paid to perform them. All the "laity," members of the *laos theou*, when we use the term in the biblical way, are priests and ministers in the church, and all those we today call "ministers" are equally "lay people."

Yet as priests of God and because they are priests, the Spirit calls some to specific ministries, including positions of leadership or oversight among God's people. Some are called and set aside, ordained to the sole occupation of stewards in the household of God and shepherds of his flock. They are gifts of God to the church. They are believer priests chosen by God and recognized by the church as endowed with the appropriate gifts for leading God's people in fulfilling the commission entrusted to the whole body (Eph 4:11-16). They hold no priesthood different in kind from that which is common to the Lord's people. These ordained believer priests are not placed above the body of Christ, but in it, in the fellowship of all believer priests. The difference is one of degree, not of kind.

Calling for an End to Ordination?

Because God welcomes the ministry of all believer priests, some have been calling the church to abolish the practice of ordination and to encourage God's people to function according to the gifts the Spirit has granted them, without regard to office. There is little doubt that in certain respects our current ordination practices have gone beyond what one finds in the Scriptures. Still, the laying on of hands, setting apart of believers, and commissioning them to special ministries is the custom plainly established in the Scriptures.

In the New Testament the laying on of hands is often connected with blessing (Matt 19:13-15), healing (Matt 9:18; Mark 6:5; 7:32; Luke 4:40; Acts 9:13, 17), and the reception of the Holy Spirit (Acts 8:16-17; 19:4-7). In the Old Testament it is associated with blessing (Gen 48:8-20) and ordaining or commissioning. Thus Moses set apart Joshua and commissioned him to lead the people of Israel (Num 27:18-23; cf. Deut 34:9). Returning to the New Testament we learn that Jesus "appointed" the Twelve "to be with him, and to be sent out to preach" (Mark 3:13, 14). Luke simply states that he chose them and named them apostles (Luke 6:13). No reference is made here to a particular ceremony.

The seven, in Acts 6:6, were set apart for a specific task by the laying on of hands. Paul and Barnabas, likewise, were commissioned in the same fashion at Antioch (Acts 13:1-3), as was Timothy (1 Tim 4:14; 2 Tim 1:6). The same thing occurred in numerous other early Christian congregations (cf. Acts 14:23). One should add that Paul expected Timothy to ordain others to leadership positions in the church since he exhorts him not to be hasty in the laying on of hands (1 Tim 5:22). This admonition shows that this commissioning, which we usually call "ordination," is always a solemn affair.

From these instances we may infer that ordination-commissioning was practiced by the apostles in the early church, starting with the case of the seven deacons. The essential rite appears to have been the laying on of hands along with prayer. In several instances it is related to specific gifts already granted by the Spirit, and marked by an act of public acknowledgment and commissioning (Acts 6:3-5; 13:3). As set forth in the New Testament it is embedded in the Spirit's universal calling of all believers to participate in the ministry of the whole church. It does not elevate some Christians above others but commissions them to a special ministry for the sake of leading the whole church of God "in the work of ministry" (Eph 4:12). Rather than ending the practice, what may be called for is further reflection on the meaning and role of ordination in the light of the priesthood of all believers.[10]

Ordaining Women to Ministry?

In the context of this article one cannot skip the matter of the propriety of ordination of women to special ministries, including the pastoral ministry. Some oppose full participation of women in church leadership on the basis that in the church God calls men to provide leadership or headship and women to assist them, particularly in the areas of worship and shepherding. Ministry in the church is regarded as a priesthood from which women are excluded.[11]

Males functioned as priests in the days of the biblical patriarchs as well as after God's covenant with Israel at Mount Sinai. With the move from Israel to the Christian church, however, a radical transformation occurred. A new priesthood is unfolded in the New Testament, that of all believers. The Christian church is a fellowship of believer priests. Such an ecclesiology, such an understanding of the nature and mission of the church, no longer poses roadblocks to women serving in any ministry. It in fact demands a partnership of men and women in all expressions of the ordained ministry. The recognition of the priesthood of all believers implies a church in which women and men work side by side in various functions and ministries, endowed with gifts distributed by the Holy Spirit according to his sovereign will (1 Cor 12:7-11).

Did Paul ever indicate that some gifts are bestowed upon men and others upon women? Is there any attempt on his part, or on Peter's, to distinguish between gift and role, between the Spirit gifting and the exercise of ministry by one particular gender? In the Christian church distinctions of race, social position, economic status, and gender are no longer valid considerations in ordering the church's ministry. We are all ministers within Christ's fellowship.

Misplaced Individualism

One more misunderstanding of the priesthood of believers needs to be pointed out. If this New Testament teaching does not imply that the church has no room for a separated ministry, if it does not object to seeing men and women serving side by side in all expressions of the priesthood, neither does it justify the attitude that a Christian may believe whatever he or she may choose and still be considered as a loyal and faithful member of the priesthood. While in their interpretation of the priesthood of all believers the sixteenth-century reformers intended to impress on their contemporaries that each of them could and must go directly to God, one may still wonder if any of them would have expected the kind of defiant individualism so common today.

Peter did not envision solo believers claiming that nobody could tell them what to believe, that "Jesus and I" was all that was needed. He insisted on the priesthood of *all* believers, emphasizing equality, not aloneness. Among early Christian believers, from what the New Testament tells us, it was in communities that the apostolic writings were read and interpreted (cf. Col 4:16). Such writings were usually sent to communities of believers, "to all of God's beloved in Rome" (Rom 1:7), "to the church of God which is at Corinth" (1 Cor 1:2; 2 Cor 1:1), "to the churches of Galatia" (Gal 1:2), to the Ephesian "saints who are also faithful in Christ Jesus" (Eph 1:1) and to "all the saints in Christ Jesus who are at Philippi" (Phil 1:1). So was Peter's first epistle addressed "to the exiles of the dispersion in Pontus, Galatia, Cappadocia, Asia and Bythinia" (1 Pet 1:1). It was in communities of believers that the ordinances were shared and violations of discipline dealt with (1 Corinthians 10 and 11; 5:1-5; cf. 2 Cor 7:9-12). It was in communities of believer priests that questions were asked and debated (1 Thess 5:19-21; 1 John 4:1), and that Christians rallied to care for each other in times of adversity (Acts 2:45; 4:32-37).

As the body grew and developed, churches united under the leadership first of the apostles then of overseeing elders appointed in every city (Acts 14:23; 20:28; Heb 13:17). While one can immediately observe various stages of spiritual and structural development, certain organizational principles appear basic to the New Testament church. Common customs characterized Christian congregations (1 Cor 11:16). Letters of recommendation were sent from one community to another (Acts 18:24-28). Collections were gathered and sent from one congregation to another in the name of the church (Rom 15:26; 1 Cor 16:1-4; 2 Cor 8:6-9). In times of discussion and disputation over the content of the Christian faith representatives of churches came together, reached a decision under the guidance of the Spirit, and the then shared them "for observance" with the congregations visited by the apostles (cf. Acts 15:1-29; 16:1-5). Churches depended on each other in a bond of unity in the same way that members in a local congregation did.

All believers have a unique and unalienable right of direct access to God. Quickened by his grace, they are fully capable of responding to him directly. Yet priesthood of believers does not mean "I am my own priest; I can believe anything I want to." It means, rather, that as one priest in a community of believer priests I must be alert to keep the body of Christ from drifting from "the faith which was once and for all delivered to the saints" (Jude 3). It means that in the community of saints God has so tempered the body that we are all priests to each other. Adherence to the truths of Scripture does not violate the priesthood of believers. This universal priesthood does not negate religious liberty, but neither is it a license for doctrinal irresponsibility. There is need for a proper balance between individual responsibility and theological integrity. In the very statement we have been considering (1 Pet 2:4-10) the apostle does not press for religious individualism but for its exact opposite, the reality of the church as a community.

Here is another of the church's delicate tasks. We can err either by drawing the boundaries too tightly or by refusing to draw them at all. It is the role of a proper biblical theology to help both the church and each believer to know the difference.

Conclusion

The doctrine of the priesthood of all believers is in its fullest sense a biblical doctrine (Exod 19:4-6; 1 Pet 2:4-10). No more than other churches has ours been able to express in its everyday life the richness of this teaching. Its content, indeed, is far richer than what it is usually taken to mean, that as priest, every individual Christian man and woman has, through Christ, direct access to God apart from the office of any human intermediary. The biblical view is much more profound than this. It means fundamentally that as Christ's body and as his new Israel the church is anointed to a priesthood in the world, a mediatorial ministry that declares the will of God "to every nation and tribe and tongue and people," and bears human needs before God's throne in prayer and intercession.

Yet this teaching is not to be confined to a doctrinal formula but must continuously find expression in the active life of the church. It should be decisive and determinative in shaping the course of the Advent Movement in years to come. As such it is a protest against the use of priesthood exclusively as a call addressed to a few. Nor is it to be limited to a particular race, gender, or social class. Every function of every member of Christ's body is called to be a priesthood, a ministry to be exercised in various spheres of life, whether in the church or in a "secular" context.

The practical purpose of the truth of this biblical doctrine is what must ever be kept in view. It is by means of our personal experience of Christ's heavenly priesthood that as Christians we may come out of spiritual infancy into spiritual maturity (Heb 6:1). This practical character is most clearly seen in the various exhortations in Hebrews having to do with our daily lives: "We have," "therefore let us." Having a great High Priest, let us hold fast (Heb 4:14). Having a sympathizing High Priest, let us draw near God's throne with boldness and confidence (Heb 4:15, 16).

Having boldness of access, let us draw near with faith (Hebrews 11), hold fast our hope (Hebrews 12), and consider one another in love (Hebrews 13). Having received a kingdom, let us be grateful and offer to God acceptable worship, with reverence and awe (Heb 12:28). As Jesus suffered, let us go forth to Him, bearing abuse for him (Heb 13:12, 13). Seeking the lasting city, the one that is to come, let us continually offer up a sacrifice of praise to God (Heb 13:14, 15). It might be summed up in the exhortation pointed out earlier, "Draw nigh," Hold fast," "Do not shrink back." We still need a Mediator, Jesus our Lord.

As we realize this privilege of nearness and respond to these exhortations to draw near and keep near, we shall find that element of boldness and confidence (*parresia,*) to be one of the essential character-istics of a dedicated Christian life. It is this boldness that the priesthood of Christ is intended to produce and develop in believer priests. This truth of priesthood, both of Christ as taught in Hebrews, and of believers as found in 1 Peter and the Book of Revelation, is essential to a vigorous life, a mature experience, and a joyous testimony.

Endnotes

1. It is not possible in this brief chapter to go into the technical historical and critical questions related to the Old Testament priesthood raised by the Graf-Wellhausen approach to the history of the Levitical system. Working from the basis of an evolutionary view of history, various critical scholars have claimed that the traditional functions of the Old Testament priesthood did not emerge until the days of the monarchy, or even until the close of the seventh-century B.C. The biblical account places the origin of Israel's priesthood in the days of Moses, in connection with ministry in the tabernacle (Exodus 25-40).

2. Priestly functions of sacrifice had been carried on from the earliest patriarchal times by heads of clans. The activities of Noah (Gen 8:20-24), Abraham (Gen 12:7; 13:4, 18; 22:1-13) and Job (Job 1:5) are illustrative of the patriarchal functions of fathers of households. Prior to the Hebrew priesthood established at the time of the Sinai covenant, the Old Testament tells of the priesthood of Melchizedek (Gen 14:18), of the Egyptians (Gen 41:45; 46:20; 47:22, 26), and of the Midianites (Exod 2:16; 3:1, 18:1). The priests mentioned in Exod 19:22, 24 are probably priests in Israel prior to the Levitical priesthood.

3. Though at times Christ is referred to as "priest" in the Epistle to the Hebrews (5:6; 7:11, 15; 8:4), the usual terminology is "High Priest" (2:17; 3:1; 4:14, 15; etc.) While in this essay we are more particularly concerned with Christ's priesthood, one should not forget that in the New Testament he is not only our Priest or High Priest. He is Prophet, Priest and King. As King he shares God's throne and all authority is given to him in heaven and on earth (Matt 28:18; Acts 2:33; 1 Cor 15:25; Heb 1:3, 13; Rev 3:21; etc). The same New Testament regards him as the prophet par excellence, *sent* from God as were the Old

Testament prophets (2 Chron 36:15, 16; Jer 25:4; 26:4-5; 29:19), "the prophet who is to come into the world" (John 6:14; cf. 1:21; 7:40), the fulfillment of the prophecy of Deut 19:15, 18. His high priestly ministry is more carefully investigated in this essay.

4. For a valuable discussion of Christ as Priest and High priest, see Oscar Cullmann, *Christology of the New Testament* (Philadelphia: Westminster, 1959), chap. 4.

5. Six times Christ's priesthood is compared to that of Melchizedek in Hebrews, (5:6, 10; 6:20; 7:11, 15, 17). One should not lose sight of the fact that Melchizedek was "resembling the Son of God" (Heb 7:3). His priesthood is not to be taken as the standard, thinking of Christ's as conforming to that pattern. It is the other way around: Christ's priesthood is definitive. Melchizedek helps us to understand it better.

6. Regarding the twofold priestly ministry of Christ, see, for instance, Frank B. Holbrook, *The Atoning Priesthood of Jesus Christ* (Berrien Springs, MI: Adventist Theological Society Publications, 1996), chaps. 1, 6, and 7.

7. Ellen G. White, *Desire of Ages*, 822.

8. The English word "priest" is a contracted transliteration of the Greek *presbyteros* and the Latin *presbyter*, "elder," from which it has derived by a process of compressing several syllables into one.

9. The priesthood of all believers has been a major concept in Protestantism. As urged first by Martin Luther, it denoted the duty of every Christian to hear the confession of fellow Christians, grant forgiveness to them, and sacrifice the self to God (Paul Althaus, *The Theology of Martin Luther* [Philadelphia: Fortress, 1966], 313-318). It has come to mean the right of all Christians to approach God without a priestly mediator, to interpret the Scriptures for themselves, or to preside at worship activities. All of these, however in harmony with Scripture, are applications of the Petrine statement rather than the result of exegesis.

10. Although through the centuries "the rite of ordination by the laying on of hands was greatly abused" and "unwarranted importance was attached to the act, as if a power came at once upon those who received such ordination" (*Acts of the Apostles*, 162), Ellen G. White early exhorted Seventh-day Adventists to "lay hands upon those who have given full proof that they have received their commission of God, and set them apart to devote themselves entirely to his work. This act would show the sanction of the church to their going forth as messengers to carry the most solemn message ever given to men" (*Early Writings*, 101).

11. It is beyond the scope of this essay to discuss the pros and cons of this view. Each side has been amply set forth. We shall limit ourselves to a few remarks from the perspective of the universal priesthood of believers.

CHAPTER 2

WOMEN PRIESTS IN ISRAEL: A CASE FOR THEIR ABSENCE

JACQUES B. DOUKHAN

Introduction

Despite the centrality of priesthood to worship in ancient Israel, scholarly studies on the specific topic of this chapter have been strangely scarce and wanting in comparison to other religious specializations.[1] In fact, the recent debate on the issue of women's ordination has awakened interest and triggered research in this domain.

Indeed, any reflection on the issue of ordination starts with a reference to the priest in Israel.[2] Thus, the argument about the ordination of women by those who are for it or against it has been built largely around the discussion of priesthood in Israel.[3] More specifically, the denial of pastoral ordination to women, consciously or not, has often been based on the observation that there were no women priests in ancient Israel.[4]

The question of whether one may or may not ordain women depends in part, then, on one's understanding of the Israelite priesthood and on the reasons given to explain the absence of women from this institution. This is the question I wish to address in this study: Why do we not find women among the priests in Israel? And, by implication, does the institution of the Israelite priesthood allow or forbid the ordination of women in our church?

Because I am approaching this issue with an ecclesiological concern—What should the church do?—I have chosen to treat the biblical data from an ecclesiological perspective; that is, as an authoritative document which speaks to the believers in its final form and within its canonical context.[5] For that matter, all the critical questions concerning the genesis and the possible development of the Israelite priesthood and the complex and often speculative reconstruction of its report in the Bible become irrelevant in our discussion.[6]

The method followed is that of exegetical research; I will not move from *a priori* definitions or from theological positions. I will not deal with all the problems, but I intend to seek an answer to my question by listening to the biblical word in regard to its historical and theological contexts as it describes and signifies the institution of priesthood. I will first analyze the structure of priesthood through the qualifications of the priest and then try to apprehend the profound meaning of the priesthood in its messianic and even ecclesiological applications.

Qualifications for Priesthood

The qualifications for priesthood were determined from the outside through divine appointment and cultural factors, and from the inside through the very functions of the priests.

External Factors

Divine appointment. Not anyone could qualify to be a priest in Israel. The right to priesthood was maintained exclusively for a special group of the Levite tribe, namely, the family of Aaron (Exod 28:41). The origin of the selection of the Levite tribe is traced to their special devotion to Yahweh at the time of the great apostasy of the golden calf (Exod 32:25-29; Deut 33:8-11).[7] No reason is given, however, for the selection of Aaron as the founder of a hereditary priesthood, but the "house of Aaron" was identified as the only legitimate priestly line (1 Chron 6:49-52; Ezra 7:1-3). His appearance on the biblical scene and his introduction to the events of Exodus were due only to his relationship to his brother Moses (Exod 4:14-16), to whom he was subordinate. He was Moses' spokesman to Israel (Exod 4:15-16) and to Pharaoh (Exod 7:1-2). In the ten plagues and in the events that followed, as well as in the organization of the cult, Aaron remained genuinely a passive associate of his brother. Even the divine instructions relative to the priestly duties were given to Moses and not to Aaron (Lev 6:1, 12, 17).

This subordinate role of Aaron to Moses suggests that in Israel even priesthood was dependent on prophecy. The sons of Aaron did not owe their priestly appointment to their Levitical origin. In fact, the call of the tribe of Levi came later, following that of Aaron.[8] The text emphasizes this sequential occurrence through an interesting pun which plays on the word Levi. "Also bring with you your brethren of the tribe of Levi, the tribe of your father, that they may be joined [*lāwā*] with you" (Num 18:2; cf. v. 4). In contrast to the ancient Near Eastern practice in which priests were appointed by the king to serve as his delegate functionaries,[9] the right to priesthood "is seen in the Bible basically as divine grace extended to a chosen tribe or part of it."[10] This divine appointment of the Israelite priesthood should prevent us from any definitive classification based solely on natural inherited qualities.

Cultural contingencies. In contrast to other ancient Near Eastern cultures, in Israel the priesthood was strictly reserved for males. This feature was all the more striking as it was probably a unique case in the ancient Near East.[11] As John Otwell put it: "Since other peoples in the ancient Near East worshipped in cults which used priestesses, their absence in the Yahwism of ancient Israel must have been deliberate."[12] This "radical break with the nature of priesthoods in the history of the ancient world"[13] was all the more conscious and intentional as the neighboring Canaanite, Ugaritic, and even Babylonian languages shared much of the same priestly vocabulary. The two key terms used to qualify the priest, *kōhēn* (from *kūn*: to stand[14]) and *qdš* (holy), are common in these cultures. In the Canaanite language, however, the word *khn* is also used to designate priestesses and even high priestesses (*rb khnm*); likewise, the word *qdš*, traditionally associated with priesthood in the Bible,[15] is also found in Ugaritic alongside *khn* to designate the sacred prostitute (*qdšh*).[16]

Indeed, the Israelite institution stood out against the ancient Near Eastern world with definite polemic intention. The reason for this "deliberate" distinction has been attributed to the fact that the ancient Near Eastern cults, and especially that of the Canaanites, who were the closest to Israel, involved goddess-worship fertility rituals.[17] There are then strong reasons to think that the exclusion of the Israelite women from the office of priesthood "became stricter as a reflex of defense against Baalist contaminations,"[18] in order to prevent Canaanite syncretism with all it implied of sacred prostitution[19] and sexual immorality.[20]

The Functional Factor

The "essential function" of the Israelite priesthood was "to assure, maintain and constantly re-establish the holiness of the elect people of God (Exod 28:38, Lev 10:17, Num 18:1)."[21] Besides the requirement of high moral and physical qualities (Leviticus 21), this function implied specific duties, some of which were allowed to men as well as to women, and others of which by their very nature were restricted only to men.

The three duties of priesthood. The functions of the priests were not only concerned with cultic (here meaning/related to the worship services) activities. On the basis of Deut 33:8-10, three types of duties may be distinguished.[22]

1. Didactic and administrative functions carried out in the daily civil life of Israelite society. The priests participated in judging; they are mentioned working together with judges (Deut 17:9; cf. 19:17). Also, Deuteronomy stipulates that "every controversy and every assault shall be settled" by the priests (Deut 21:5). Their involvement in jurisprudence qualified them to serve also as teachers of the law (Deut 33:10; cf. Mal 2:6-7; Jer 18:18).

2. Prophetic functions concerned especially with the mystery of the future and the making of a decision through the revelation of the divine will. Oracular techniques included the use of the Urim and the Thummim (Num 27:21), one of the three legitimate means—along with dreams and prophecy—of obtaining God's answers (1 Sam 28:6). In similar situations Ahab and Jehoshaphat consulted a seer or prophet[23] (1 Kgs 20:13ff.; 22:6; 2 Kgs 3:11).

3. Cultic functions such as dealing with the service in the temple, the treatment of impurities and diseases, and the atonement for sin. This function revolved mostly around the offering of sacrifices (Leviticus 1-16).

Duties allowed to women. Two of the three functions of the priest in Israel, prophecy and administration, were allowed to women. Indeed, the Bible attests to the presence of women among the prophets:[24] Miriam (Exod 15:20; Mic 6:4); Deborah (Judg 4:3-6); and Huldah (2 Kgs 22:14-20) The prophet Joel does not hesitate to use the technical verb "prophesy" (*nb'*) in referring to women (Joel 2:28). Also, against the cultural patterns in the ancient Near East, Hebrew society allowed women to hold offices of leadership: a judge (Judg 4:4), a queen (2 Kgs 11:3), and above all, numerous "wise women" (Judg 5:28-30; 2 Sam 14:2ff.; 20:16ff., etc.), "a special class" who by their sagacity and their counsel exerted "an active influence on the course of events."[25]

Furthermore, recent anthropological studies have shown that along with traditional patriarchal trends in the biblical society, one can find strong evidence of matriarchal tendencies.[26] These last findings suggest that in biblical times more women held positions of power and authority than a mere surface reading of the texts may suggest.

On the basis of these observations, one may conclude that it was neither the prophetic nor the headship functions that prevented women from being ordained priests.[27] Even in the cultic sphere, women were not totally excluded, since the biblical sources included women in religious gatherings (Neh 8:2, 13; 12:43) and also among those who ministered at the entrance to the tent of meeting (Exod 38:8; 1 Sam 2:22) or served as singers in the temple (Neh 7:67; Ezra 2:65; Ps 68:24-25).

Duties barred to women. In fact, the only function which seems to have been barred to women was the performance of the sacrificial rites.[28] And even here, the Bible never explicitly forbids women to perform the sacrifice. Besides, women participated in the sacrificial meals (Num 18:8-19; Deut 12:12; 14:22-29; 15:19-23; 16:9-15; 1 Sam 1:4) and were physically present at the ceremony of the sacrifice (1 Sam 2:19). It is significant, nevertheless, that in spite of the fact that the slaughter of sacrificial animals was not reserved to priests and could be performed by anyone, there is no biblical evidence for a woman actually slaughtering the sacrifice.[29] In any case, offering sacrifices was perhaps the only religious domain that was denied to women, a prohibition which seems to have been peculiar to Israel.[30]

The Bible gives no reason for this possible exclusion of women from the sacrificial act. It has been suggested, however, that this is essentially due to "'her ritual uncleanness and sexual nature as a woman.'"[31] More specifically, Mary Evans explains: "The ineligibility of women to become priests may have been . . . because of regular ritual uncleanness, or because of the heavy work involved in moving dead animals, etc."[32]

In fact, this restriction may well reflect a Hebrew attitude toward women, who were, from Eve on, traditionally associated with the giving of life.[33] And since the woman stands for life, she should be exempt from the act of sacrificing that stands for death. This principle may be recognized in the command, "You shall not boil a young goat in its mother's milk" (Exod 23:19; cf. 34:26; Deut 14:21). This common practice in the Canaanite cults of fertility was forbidden in Israel not only to keep Israel from falling into the trap of Baalist syncretism,[34] but also—and perhaps for a more profound theological-ethical reason—because it would be incongruous to associate the milk of the mother, carrier of life to the kid, with the death of the very kid. The same principle lies behind another commandment forbidding to "eat flesh with its life, that is, its blood" (Gen 9:4).[35] Because of her physiological nature as a provider of life, the woman could not be involved in the cultic act of taking life implied in the ritual of sacrifice. On the other hand, biblical tradition rooted in Gen 3:15 seems to situate the woman's religious and cultic duty precisely in her physiological faculty to channel the messianic seed until the coming of the Messiah.[36] Not only by nature, because she was created with the ability to generate life, but also by destiny, because she was the recipient of God's first promise of salvation through the incarnation of the Messiah, the woman, as messenger of life and hope in her flesh, was allowed, even required, to fulfill her "priestly" duties outside the sphere of blood, violence, and death. And this understanding of the role of women in regard to priesthood makes even more sense as we realize that the ultimate purpose of the Israelite priesthood was to point to the Messiah.

Messianic Priesthood

The divine appointment of the Israelite priesthood as expressed through its qualifications shows that this institution was not only designed to work in the present sphere; it was not a mere mechanical-magical means to achieve the immediate adequate relationship with the divine. It also contained prophetic elements which were read as signs of God's presence, and hence as omens of hope pointing to messianic salvation.

Sign of God

The essential concept underlying priesthood in the ancient world, especially in Israel, was that of mediatorship between the divine and human. By virtue of their divine appointment, their various functions as messengers of God, and the active performance of sacrifices offered to deity, the priests were viewed as the channel par excellence between the two orders. Certainly, this awareness pervaded the daily life of the cult. The priest was considered as God's representative, whose sanctity found expression in the requirement that he should be free from any physical defect (Lev 21:6-24) and keep himself pure from contact with death or impurity (Lev 21:1; 22:4-6). The absence of the priests was likened to the very absence of God Himself (2 Chron 15:3; cf. Hos 3:4-5). It is significant that the mere evocation of the precious priestly oil running down on the beard of Aaron (Exod 29:7; Lev 8:12) was enough to suggest feelings of hope and happiness (Ps 133:1-2), for the perfume of this oil was associated with the experience of God's presence. The priest was sensed as the physical sign of God's invisible presence among His people.

Type of Messiah

No wonder, then, that in the wake of the Old Testament, Jewish rabbis as well as Christian apologetes referred to the Israelite priesthood to express their idea of the saving Messiah. In the Old Testament, Psalm 110 is a classic example of this identification. There the ideal King of Zion, who will ultimately "rule in the midst of your enemies" (110:2) and participate in the ultimate judgment of the kings and nations (110:5-6), is described as a priest "according to the order of Melchizedek" (110:4). Likewise in the book of Daniel, Michael, a heavenly being who will participate in the eschatological war and bring ultimate victory and salvation (12:1), is dressed as a priest (10:5, 13). Even the suffering servant of Isaiah 52-53, who will rule with the great (53:12; cf. Ps 2:8), displays priestly features. He bears "the vessels of the Lord" and should keep himself from touching any "unclean thing" (52:11-12; cf. Lev 22:2). Like the priest, he "sprinkles" (Isa 52:15; cf. Lev 16:14), carries the iniquity of the people (53:6; cf. Lev 16:16, 17), and intercedes for their transgressions (53:12; cf. Joel 2:17). Zechariah also associates his vision of the high priest Joshua with that of a royal Messiah (Zech 3:8-9)[37] who will judge the house of God and have access to the heavenly council (3:7). In this clearly eschatological passage,[38] the prophet uses the two metaphors of "branch" and "stone" to refer to the Messiah, whom he sees as both king and priest. Later in Judaism, in the Dead Sea Scrolls,[39] the *Testament of the Twelve*,[40] and even in the Talmud[41] and the Midrash,[42] the Messiah is consistently identified as a priest.

Type of Jesus Christ

The New Testament follows the same tradition when it applies to Christ the Messiah the role and function of a priest. The conception is already expressed in Christ's own interpretation of his priestly mission to serve and give his life as a "ransom for many" (Mark 10:45), and more specifically in his explanations of the "new covenant" associated with his institution of the Eucharist (Luke 22:14-23).

As a secondary feature of Christ's priesthood, one finds the doctrine of Christ's mediatorship in the letters of Paul and Peter (Gal 3:20; 2 Cor 5:19; 1 Pet 1:1-2, 18-19; 2:24). In the book of Revelation (1:13-15), Jesus Christ is dressed with the garment of the high priest, reminiscent of the description of Michael in Daniel 10.

In the letter to the Hebrews this doctrine is fully elaborated. Jesus

Christ is presented as a sinless High Priest who was typified by the Old Testament figure of Melchizedek (Gen 14:18; cf. Psalm 110). Interestingly, the author of the epistle sees one of the most salient messianic features of this personage in the fact that he is "without father, without mother, without genealogy" (Heb 7:3). In other words, what makes this priest an appropriate type of the Messiah is that he transcends the contingencies of human birth—another way of suggesting his divine origin, "made like the Son of God . . . a priest continually." The same idea has already been recognized in the Aaronic priesthood, whose appointment also transcends birth. The rationale for this principle lies essentially in the fact that the priest represents the eternal God above, who is beyond any human category of birth, race, class, or gender.

Kingdom of Priests

A corollary of the biblical view of priesthood is its application to the whole community of believers. This view is typical of the Hebrew principle of corporate personality.[43] In fact, in biblical thought the priest represents God's union with humans.

In Eden

In the Garden of Eden priesthood was first evoked, related to both man and woman. To the Fall and the tragic prospect of death, God responded in two manners: (1) in a prophecy, God promised salvation through the messianic "seed" of the woman (Gen 3:15; see above); and (2) in a dramatic gesture, God came down and dressed Adam and Eve (Gen 3:21). This specific operation has direct bearing on the call for priesthood. The rare occasions when God dressed humans in the Old Testament always concerned the dressing of priests either directly by God himself (Ps 132:16; 2 Chron 6:41) or through Moses (Exod 28:41; 29:8; 40; Lev 8:13). And in our passage, the verb describing the act of dressing (*lbš*) in its *hiphil* form is the very technical term which is normally used for the dressing of the priests (Exod 28:41; Lev 8:7; Num 20:28; etc.).[44] In addition, the Hebrew word for "tunic" (*kᵉtōnet*) is the same that designates the priestly garment (Exod 28:39; 39:27). Adam and Eve were, indeed, dressed as priests, with one difference, however: instead of the fine linen that characterizes the priestly garment (Exod 28:39), God chose animal skin. This specification not only implies the killing of an animal, the first sacrifice in history, but by the same token, confirms the identification of

Adam and Eve as priests, for the skin of the atonement sacrifice was specifically set apart for the officiating priests (Lev 7:8).[45] By bestowing on Adam and Eve the skin of the sin offering, a gift strictly reserved to priests, the Genesis story implicitly recognizes Eve as priest alongside Adam.

In Ancient Israel

From the very beginning of the history of Israel, the whole nation is called to be a "kingdom of priests," and, therefore, a "holy people" (Exod 19:6; Lev 11:44ff.; Num 15:40). This promise is repeated by the prophets: "You shall be named the Priests of the Lord, men shall call you the Servants of our God" (Isa 61:6). The same thought is found in Ps 132:9, a messianic Psalm which identifies "the saints"[46]—that is, the whole religious community—as God's priests.[47] Now, that a special group is set apart as "priests," and that the people as a whole are also seen as a "kingdom of priests," should not be read as a contradiction. The two realities stand together in tension. The priests, the "saints," are set apart within Israel as a constant reminder of God's ideal and His call for His people.[48]

Under the New Covenant

This ideal is also attested in the New Testament doctrine of priesthood. The tension, however, is carried differently there, since the Christian community does not have priests anymore. Indeed, nowhere in the New Testament is the title of priest used to designate any individual member or order of ministry in the Christian community.[49] Christians do not need to have priests anymore, because they are all potential priests in Christ.[50] For as the church is one with Christ, so the church shares in the holiness of its Lord. Just as Christ was "a living stone," his followers are also to be "living stones" and "a holy priesthood" (1 Pet 2:4-5; cf. v. 9). The theme is again emphasized in the book of Revelation: Christ the lamb in heaven has "made us kings and priests to his God and Father" (Rev 1:6; cf. 5:10).

In the New Jerusalem

In the eschatological vision, the saved ones are not merely *called* "priests"; they *are* priests. It is no more a mere ideal to be pursued; it is now an actual living reality. Like the priests, "they are before the throne of God, and serve Him day and night in His temple" (7:15; cf. 1 Chr 9:27,

33); like the priests, they are clothed with a white robe (6:11; 3:4; 7:9; cf. Lev 16:4; Exod 39:27-29). Like the priests, their dressing implies God's direct intervention. Their robe is "given" to each of them. In heaven, in the Kingdom of God, just as in Eden, in the Garden of God, man and woman are in effect priests of God, an ideal which is sung by the Hebrew prophets and the Christian apostles as well.

Conclusion

To the question, "Why not a woman priest in Israel?" two basic answers may be given. The first is historical. The absence of women in the Israelite priesthood, an exceptional case in the ancient Near East, where priestesses abounded and were often associated with sacred prostitution, is to be understood as a reaction to pagan syncretism and sexual perversions. The second is theological. The Bible does not record any woman priest in Israel, not because the office of priesthood implied prophetic functions (there were women prophets in Israel), or because it implied leadership or teaching functions (there were women judges and "wise" women in Israel), but rather because of the sacrificial function, the only priestly act denied to women (there is no biblical evidence of women performing sacrifices in Israel). This absence may be explained by the incompatibility of the sacrifice, normally associated with death and sin, and the physiological nature of the woman traditionally associated in the Bible with life and messianic pregnancy.

It is noteworthy, however, that the cultural factor, namely, the presence of priestesses in pagan cults, did not play the determining role in keeping women from the priesthood. For, in spite of the powerful polemic concern, women were still allowed in the worship arena; only sacrificial rites were denied them. This made the typological element of priesthood certainly the most decisive factor in preventing women from becoming priests in Israel. Thus, the main reason for the absence of women from the priesthood was not in essence a negative one—reaction to pagan practices or because of something inherently lacking in women. Instead, the exemption of women from the priesthood has to be understood in positive terms—because of something inherently present in women, namely, the sign of life and promise.

Had it not been for these two factors, the ancient Near Eastern cults and more decisively the sacrifices, women might well have been priests in Israel.[51] This assumption is further supported by the Bible—implicitly in the messianic view of the priest as transcending the contingencies of birth (gender, class, race) and explicitly in the recognition of women in the priesthood both in the Garden of Eden and in the redeemed community. These contexts are both free from the threat of ancient Near Eastern cults and from the ceremonial slaughter of sacrifices.

Thus biblical identification of woman as priest in Eden and the redeemed community complements biblical approval of women's anointing as prophet and judge. In this context, and in reflection upon ordination to pastoral ministry, there is no case for women's exclusion.

Endnotes

1. On the reasons for this deficiency, see Lester L. Grabbe, *Priests, Prophets, Divine Sages: A Socio-Historical Study of Religious Specialties in Ancient Israel* (Valley Forge, PA: Trinity, 1995), 41.

2. Albert Vanhoye, *Old Testament Priests and the New Priest: According to the New Testament*, trans. J. Bernard Orchard (Petersham, MA: St. Bede's Publications, 1986), 19.

3. See, for instance, on one side, Stanley Atkins, "The Theological Case Against Women's Ordination," in *The Ordination of Women: Pro and Con*, ed. Michael P. Hamilton and Nancy S. Montgomery (New York: Morehouse-Barlow, 1976), 19; Lawrence Maxwell, "One Chilling Word," *Adventists Affirm* 9 (Spring 1995), 39ff.; Samuele Bacchiocchi, *Women in the Church* (Berrien Springs, MI: Biblical Perspectives, 1982), 36, 39; and on the other, Georges Barrois, "Women and the Priestly Office According to the Scriptures," in *Women and the Priesthood*, ed. Thomas Hopko (Crestwood, NY: St. Vladimir's Seminary Press, 1983), 52-60; John E. Toews, Valerie Rempel, and Katie Funk Wiebe, eds., *Your Daughters Shall Prophesy: Women in Ministry in the Church* (Winnipeg: Kindred, 1992), 64.

4. See, for instance, Atkins, 19; John A. Grindel, "The Old Testament and Christian Priesthood," *Communio: International Catholic Review* 3 (Spring 1976): 16-38; Raymond Holmes, *The Tip of an Iceberg: Biblical Authority, Biblical Interpretation, and the Ordination of Women in Ministry* (Wakefield, MI: Adventists Affirm and Pointer Publications, 1994), 76; cf. Bacchiocchi, 38-39.

5. See especially Brevard S. Childs, *Old Testament Theology in a Canonical Context* (Philadelphia, PA: Fortress, 1985), 15-16.

6. It suffices to note that the critical view that explains the development of the biblical material concerning Priesthood (so-called *P* source) against the background of the Second Temple period can no longer stand, considering the "increasing information about the cult of the peoples of the Ancient Near East" (Moshe Weinfield, "Pentateuch," *Encyclopaedia Judaica*, [Jerusalem: Keter Publishing House, n.d.], 13:240); cf. Yehezkel Kaufmann, *The Religion of Israel: From Its Beginnings to the Babylonian Exile*, trans. and abridged Moshe Greenberg (Chicago: Univ. of Chicago Press, 1960), 13ff.

7. The self-consecration of the Levites (Exod 32:29) did not qualify them for priesthood; they deserved, at the most, a simple blessing.

8. Even then, the appointment was not natural. Their ancestor Levi was not the firstborn; they were selected as the substitute for the firstborn to represent the people of Israel (Exod 32:25-29; Deut 33:8-11). Note the biblical pattern of the practice, which favors the younger son (Abel/Seth instead of Cain, Isaac instead of Ishmael, Jacob instead of Esau, etc.).

9. Bergman, 62-63; kings were also chief ministers of the cult.

10. *Encyclopaedia Judaica*, s.v. "Priests and Priesthood"; cf. Umberto Cassuto, *A Commentary on the Book of Exodus*, trans. Israel Abram (Jerusalem: Magnes, 1969), 259.

11. See Roland de Vaux, *Ancient Israel: Its Life and Institutions*, trans. John McHugh (London: Darton, Longman & Todd, 1961), 183-184.

12. John H. Otwell, *And Sarah Laughed: The Status of Woman in the Old Testament* (Philadelphia: Westminster, 1977), 155.

13. Carol Meyers, "The Roots of Restriction: Women in Early Israel," *Biblical Archaeologist* 41 (September 1978): 100.

14. See Deut 10:8.

15. See Lev 21:6, Num 8:14; Deut 10:8, 1 Sam 7:1, etc.

16. See B. A. Levine, "Priests," in *Interpreter's Dictionary of the Bible, Supplement* (Nashville: Abingdon, 1976), 688.

17. On the struggle in Israel against goddess worship, see Lacocque, 11.

18. Barrois, 53; cf. "When so many of the priestesses . . . have a sexual function as seems to be the case in Babylon, then it is not at all surprising that in Israel, at least when the Yahweh religion was in control, women were excluded from the priesthood; cf. Dt. 23:18f. (17f.)" (Clarence J. Vos, *Woman in Old Testament Worship* [Delft: Judels & Brinkman, 1968], 194).

19. See Samuel L. Terrien, *Till the Heart Sings: A Biblical Theology of Manhood and Womanhood* (Philadelphia: Fortress, 1985), 78.

20. A hint regarding this may be recognized in the specific warning concerning the clothing of the priests, who should be careful not to expose their nakedness (see Exod 28:42-43). This concern was all the more justified as pagan priests often performed naked precisely because of the sexual involvement implied in their office (see I.E.S. Edwards, C. J. Gadd, and N.G.L. Hammond, eds., *The Cambridge Ancient History*, 3d ed., vol. 1, part 2 [Cambridge: Cambridge Univ. Press, 1971], 672); cf. "Early pictorial representations showing that priests were often naked when performing their duties" (Linköping J. Bergman, "*kōhēn*," *Theological Dictionary of the Old Testament*, [Grand Rapids: Eerdmans, 1974-], 7:63).

21. R. Abba, "Priests and Levites," *Interpreter's Dictionary of the Bible*, 3:877-878.

22. Grindel, 27; cf. *Encyclopaedia Judaica*, 13:1076; and Edmond Jacob, *Théologie de l'Ancien Testament* (Paris: Delachaux et Niestlé, 1968), 200.

23. The linguistic relation of the Hebrew and Arabic term *kâhîn* may even suggest that "the offices of the priest and seer were once identical" (Ismar J. Peritz, "Woman in the

Ancient Hebrew Cult," *Journal of Biblical Literature*, part 2 [1898]: 143).

24. The example of Rebekah also shows that women were accustomed to inquire of the oracles (Gen 25:22ff.); also, perhaps, Rachel (Gen 31:19, 30, 34). "It is interesting to note," writes Phyllis Bird, "that the only two narrative references to *teraphim* in the Hebrew Bible place them in women's hands" ("Gender and Religious Definition: The Case of Ancient Israel," *Harvard Divinity Bulletin* 20 [1990]: 13). See also the chapter by Jo Ann Davidson.

25. Jacob, 203.

26. See, for instance: Gen 2:24, which enjoins a husband to follow his wife and not the reverse; Gen 24:67, which records a wedding ritual of the groom taking his bride to his mother's tent; Gen 28:2-5, which states repeatedly that Jacob should "go to the home of his mother's brother, a kinship reference indicative of matrilineality" (Savina J. Teubal, *Hagar the Egyptian: The Lost Tradition of the Matriarchs* [San Francisco: Harper & Row, 1990], 27). See also R. K. Harrison, "The Matriarchate and Hebrew Regal Succession," *The Evangelical Quarterly* 29 (1957): 29-34. Other clear signs of matriarchy may be detected in Cant 3:4 (cf. Ruth 1:8), which refers to the "house of my mother"; see also Song 3:11, which describes Solomon's mother as the one who "crowned him" (see Manes Kartagener, "Über Spuren und Reste des Matriarchats im Judentum," *Zeitschrift für Religions und Geistesgeschichte* 29 [1977]: 141). The biblical traces of matriarchy do not denote, however, goddess worship, as some have argued (see Gerda Weiler, *Das Matriarchat im Alten Israel* [Stuttgart: Verlag W. Kohhammer, 1989], 118ff.). This phenomenon should rather be explained on anthropological grounds: matriarchal trends are, indeed, often present in nomadic societies. Since nomadism was an important fact of life in biblical times, one would expect the biblical society to be saturated with matriarchal traditions. This connection (rather than the goddess-worship connection) is all the more correct as the observation holds across various cultures and is still valid today (see Thomas S. Barfield, *The Nomadic Alternative* [Englewood Cliffs, NJ: Prentice Hall, 1993], 15, 146).

27. Women were probably ordained already as prophets or judges, as both functions seem to have required ordination (see Num 27:22; Deut 34:9; 1 Kgs 19:16).

28. The passage of Lev 4:27-29, which seems to imply women as well as men in the neutral word *nepeš* (feminine) to designate the sinner in verse 27, shifts, however, from the feminine to the masculine subject in verses 28-29 when it comes to the actual performing of the sacrifice. Although the word *nepeš* may sometimes take a third-person masculine (see Lev 2:1), it seems here that the masculine is, indeed, intended under the masculine usage, implying thereby that the sacrifice was offered by the man on behalf of the woman (see Num 5:15). At any rate, one could hardly defend the view that women were performing the sacrifices on the unique basis of this verse and considering the ambiguity of the word *nepeš*; all the more so as this understanding would go against the general picture of the Hebrew Bible.

29. Referring to the woman medium of Endor who slaughters a calf (1 Sam 28:24), Gruber challenges the general view that women never performed sacrifices (Mayer I. Gruber, "Women in the Cult According to the Priestly Code," in *Judaic Perspectives on Ancient Israel*, ed. Jacob Neusner, Baruch A. Levine, and Ernest S. Frerichs [Philadelphia: Fortress, 1987], 46). Yet, this is an exceptional case in the Bible of a woman who stands

outside the "orthodox" track. Besides, the butchering of the calf serves the secular purpose of providing food.

30. Considerable archaeological evidence shows that women all over the ancient Near East engaged in sacrifices (see Ilse Seibert, *Women in the Ancient Near East*, trans. Marianne Herzfeld [New York: Abner Schram, 1974]; cf. Bernard Frank Batto, *Studies on Women at Mari* [Baltimore: Johns Hopkins Univ. Press, 1974], 128-129).

31. Sister Vincent Emmanuel Hannon, *The Question of Women and the Priesthood: Can Women Be Admitted to Holy Orders?* (London: Geoffrey Chapman, 1967), 60; cf. "the possibility exists that the menstruation of the woman was considered something of a compound of the holy" (Vos, 85); and cf. O. J. Baab, "Woman," in *Interpreter's Dictionary of the Bible*, 4:866.

32. Mary J. Evans, *Woman in the Bible: An Overview of All the Crucial Passages on Women's Roles* (Downers Grove, IL: InterVarsity, 1983), 30.

33. For the biblical etymology of Eve (*hawah* from *hayyim*, life), see Gen 3:20.

34. See especially Godfrey R. Driver, *Canaanite Myths and Legends* (Edinburgh: T. & T. Clark, 1956), 121: 6-14; H. Kosmala, "The So-Called Ritual Decalogue," *Anual of the Swedish Theological Institute* 1 (1962): 5056.

35. Cf. Lev 17:11: "For the life of the flesh is in the blood." On the rationale for this "ethical" prohibition, see Jacob Milgrom, *Leviticus 1-16*, Anchor Bible, vol. 3 (New York: Doubleday, 1991), 705ff.

36. See André Dumas, "Biblical Anthropology and the Participation of Women in the Ministry in the Church," in *Concerning the Ordination of Women* (Geneva: World Council of Churches, 1964), 69-70.

37. Cf. Jer 23:5; 33:15; Isa 11:1.

38. See especially the conclusion of the passage, with its classic eschatological association of the vine and the fig tree (Zech 3:10; cf. Mic 4:4); see Ralph L. Smith, *Micah-Malachi*, Word Biblical Commentary, vol. 32 (Waco, TX: Word, 1984), 201.

39. *Manual of Discpline*, 1QS 9:11; *Damascus Document*, CD 12:23; 4 Q175.

40. *The Testament of Levi*, chaps. 8 and 18.

41. Babylonian Talmud. *Sukkah* 52b.

42. *Canticle Rabba* 2:29.

43. See Abba, 877.

44. See Gordon S. Wenham, *Genesis 1-15*, Word Biblical Commentary, vol. 1 (Waco, TX: Word, 1987), 84; cf. Nehamah Leibowitz, *New Studies on the Book of Exodus* (Hebrew) (Jerusalem: World Zionist Organization, Department for Torah Education and Culture, 1994), 383.

45. See Kenneth A. Mathews, *Genesis 1-11:26*, The New American Commentary, vol. 1A (Nashville: Broadman & Holman, 1996), 255.

46. The same word (in Aramaic, though) is used in Daniel to designate the redeemed (Dan 7:18).

47. Cf. Ps 132:16; 149:1-2, 5.

48. The same phenomenon can be recognized on the level of space as well as on the level of time. Although the Bible sets apart holy moments (Lev 23:2; Hos 9:5) or holy places (Exod 40:10; 1 Kgs 9:3), it also affirms the presence of God at all times, always (Ps 102:12, 24) and everywhere (Ps 33:18). For this tension between particularism and universalism in biblical thinking, see Jacques B. Doukhan, *Hebrew for Theologians: A Textbook for the Study of Biblical Hebrew in Relation to Hebrew Thinking* (Lanham, MD: University Press of America, 1993), 215-216.

49. According to M. H. Shepherd, Jr., the first Christian writers to use the technical term for "priest" (*hiereîs*) for the church's ministers were Tertullian (*On Baptism*) and Hippolytus (*Preface to Refutation of All Heresies*); see "Priests in the NT," *Interpreter's Dictionary of the Bible*, 3:891. See chapter by Daniel Augsburger.

50. On the theological meaning of this "new" order of priesthood, see the chapter by Raoul Dederen.

51. A literal application of the biblical text without taking into consideration its theological and cultural context may well bring along conclusions in contradiction to its spirit. The very fact that various interpreters come to opposite conclusions on the issue of women's ordination, although on the whole they hold the same high regard of Scriptures and agree on the historical meaning of the biblical text, confirms this dynamic of the biblical principle. As Krister Stendahl writes: "The problem must be one of application. The problem is not exegetical in the strict sense of the word, but lies in opposite, or in any case different, principles of application and interpretation. Thus it is a problem of hermeneutics rather than of exegesis" (*The Bible and the Role of Women; A Case Study in Hermeneutics*, trans. Emilie T. Sander [Philadelphia: Fortress, 1966], 9).

CHAPTER 3

SHAPES OF MINISTRY IN THE NEW TESTAMENT AND EARLY CHURCH

ROBERT M. JOHNSTON

T he ministerial role of any group in the early decades of the Christian church cannot be considered apart from an investigation of the nature of ministry[1] in general and the dynamics that shaped it. In our study it will be convenient to distinguish between two types of ministry, based on the mode of reception, even though the distinction was not always a sharp one.[2] One type of ministry was that to which a person was called directly by Christ or his Spirit; since it was marked by the bestowal of a spiritual gift (Rom 12:3-8; 1 Cor 12:4-11, 28; Eph 4:11-13; 1 Pet 4:10, 11) we shall refer to it as charismatic ministry since the Greek word for gift is *charisma*. The other type is that to which a person was appointed by the church; we shall call it appointive ministry.

The Charismatic Ministry: Apostles

In the beginning Jesus called and appointed twelve men "to be with him, and to be sent out to preach and have authority to cast out demons" (Mark 3:14, 15).[3] The parallel in Matt 10:1 calls the Twelve "disciples," while that in Luke 6:13 adds that Jesus named them "apostles." The term "disciples" reflects Mark's remark that they were "to be with him," while "apostles" was an appropriate title for those who were "to be sent out," since the Greek *apostolos* (plural, *apostoloi*; the word comes from the verb *apostellō*, to send out) literally means "one who is sent out." Luke is apparently using the term technically as a title, for Jesus is said to have "named" them thus.[4] Both Matthew and Luke, immediately after the report of the calling of the Twelve, describe their being sent out on a missionary journey. Mark reports this mission in his sixth chapter and uses the title "apostle" in 6:30.

Origen's definition holds: "Everyone who is sent by someone is an apostle of the one who sent him."[5] Such a person represents the sender, and comes with the authority of the sender to the extent that he/she faithfully fulfills the mission that is committed to him/her. In John 13:16 Jesus says: "Truly, truly, I say to you, a servant is not greater than his master; nor is he who is sent greater than he who sent him." The Twelve were sent out by Jesus as his representatives with the assurance, "He who receives you receives me, and he who receives me receives him who sent me" (Matt 10:40).[6]

In harmony with Origen's definition, we later find *apostoloi* of churches, as in 2 Cor 8:23 (where the RSV translates the term as "messengers"). When used in this sense, apostleship might have become something more like an appointive office than a charismatic one, but we do not know how such *apostoloi* may have been chosen. It may well be that a church merely ratified the Holy Spirit's choice revealed through prophets, as in Acts 13:1-3 (cf. 1 Tim 4:14).

The Twelve chosen by Jesus were the apostles *par excellence*. The number twelve was significant, corresponding to the twelve Patriarchs and twelve tribes of Israel (Matt 19:28; Rev 21:12-14). They were clearly not the only disciples that Jesus had, but they occupied a special place in the scheme of things.

So important was the number twelve in the thinking of the infant church that they felt it necessary to fill the vacancy left among the twelve apostles by the defection and death of Judas Iscariot (Acts 1:15-26). "The Twelve" was so firmly established as a synonym for the original group of apostles that Paul referred to them thus even when they had become only eleven (1 Cor 15:5)! Furthermore, it was important that the office not be seen as bestowed by human choice or appointment, so the vacancy was filled by casting lots after prayer (Acts 1:23-26). But Peter did lay down special qualifications that must be met even to be considered as a candidate: an apostle must have been an eyewitness to the resurrection of Jesus (Acts 1:21, 22; cf. 2:32).[7] The lot fell on Matthias, about whom we read nothing more in the New Testament.[8]

It is understandable, then, that the earliest Christians in Palestine, largely Jews for whom the twelve were especially significant, were unwilling to concede that anyone other than the Twelve could be a legitimate apostle. But this limitation was shattered by Paul, in a development that was vehemently resisted. Paul needed constantly to defend his apostleship. In 1 Cor 9:1, 2 he did so by insisting on his qualifications: he was an eyewitness to the risen Lord (a claim supported in 15:8 and by Acts 9:3-5 and 22:6-11) and had done the work of an apostle. In Gal 1:11-19 he argued that by revelation he received his commission directly from the Lord, so that his apostleship was in no way inferior to that of the Twelve.

With Paul as the "point man," as it were, for expanding the apostolate, the number soon increased. Both Paul and Barnabas are called apostles in Acts 14:14, 4.[9] The list that can be compiled from the New Testament also includes at least Apollos (1 Cor 4:6, 9), Silvanus and Timothy (1 Thess 1:1; cf. 2:6), Titus (2 Cor 8:23, Greek), and Epaphroditus (Phil 2:25).[10]

A Female Apostle

An especially interesting case is presented in Rom 16:7, amidst a series of greetings Paul sends to friends and acquaintances in the church in Rome. The significance of this verse is usually missed because of the difficulty of translating it into English. However the various versions may deal with the verse, the correct translation is as follows: "Greet Andronicus and Junia my relatives and fellow prisoners, who are outstanding among the apostles, and who were in Christ before I was." The main problem[11] revolves around the second name, which is commonly taken to be Junias. Both Junias, a masculine name, and Junia, a feminine name, are first-declension nouns, easily distinguishable in the nominative case but indistinguishable in the accusative case, used here as direct object of the verb "greet." It is therefore impossible to determine on the basis of grammar alone whether the name should be Junias or Junia. We are not without further recourse, however. It is possible by computer or more laborious means to trace the usage of words and names in Greek and Latin documents through the centuries. When this is done, we discover that the male name Junias does not occur until some dubious references in the Middle Ages, but the female name Junia was well known in New Testament times.[12] It is most reasonable to conclude, therefore, that we are dealing here with a female apostle named Junia.[13] We can probably agree with ancient commentators that Andronicus and Junia were husband and wife, forming an apostolic team.

Other Charismatic Ministries and Their Implication

As noted at the beginning of this chapter, in three of Paul's letters and in 1 Peter we find lists of spiritual gifts (*charismata*). In three of the lists (1 Cor 12:28; 12:29-30; Eph 4:11) apostles stand at the head; in the remaining lists apostleship does not occur. By placing apostleship among the charismatic gifts Paul completes its "democratization," making it available to anyone to whom the Holy Spirit should choose to distribute it. These gifts are not limited to one gender: "It is the same God who inspires them all in every one. . . . All these are inspired by one and the same Spirit, who apportions to each one individually as he wills" (1 Cor 12:6, 11). Indeed this is explicitly the case with another of the gifts, prophecy, which along with apostleship and teaching is mentioned more widely than most of the other gifts. Peter's Pentecost sermon quotes Joel's prophecy that in the last days "your sons and your daughters will prophesy" and God will pour out His Spirit on His "menservants and maidservants" (Acts 2:17, 18). We know that women publicly prophesied at Corinth, where Paul directed that they should do so with their heads covered (1 Cor 11:3-10).[14] Philip the evangelist had "four unmarried daughters, who prophesied" (Acts 21:9).

It seems reasonable to assume that what was true of one spiritual gift was true of them all. The Holy Spirit distributed them as he willed, untrammeled by any artificial human limitation, and women received them also. It was God who called men and women to charismatic ministry.[15]

The Appointive Ministry

Acts 6 reports that administrative questions threatened to distract the twelve apostles from their ministry of preaching and teaching (6:1, 2). The Hellenistic Jewish Christians were complaining that their widows were not receiving what they should in the daily distribution of supplies to the needy. The apostles directed that the believers elect seven men, "of good repute, full of the Spirit and of wisdom," to this work (6:3). This was done and, judging from the Hellenistic names of the seven, they were chosen from among those who had complained; indeed, one was a proselyte. The seven stood before the apostles, and they[16] prayed and laid their hands on them (6:6). This was the beginning of the appointive ministry, leaders selected by the people and given authority by the laying on of hands.[17] Giles's understanding of the act has some plausibility:

The people set apart in this way are explicitly depicted as Spirit-filled leaders, who have already had a significant ministry. The laying on of hands by those assembled therefore does not signify the bestowal of a ministry, or of the Spirit, but rather that from now on their ministry is no longer an individual one: they are from this point on representatives of their community. What they do, they do not undertake in their own name, but in the name of the community that has set them apart as its representatives.[18]

What was the office assigned to the seven men of Acts? The office is not named. It has often been assumed that they were deacons.[19] They have equally often been called elders.[20] It is necessary to lay aside conceptions and distinctions that developed later, sometimes much later.[21] It is true that in Acts 6:2 we find the verb *diakonein*, cognate with the noun *diakonos*, whence the English word deacon. But this by itself is not conclusive, for in Acts 1:25 we find *diakonia*, belonging to the same word group, applied to apostleship. The words mean, respectively, to serve, a servant, and service. Equally satisfactory synonyms are to minister, a minister, and ministry.

Significantly, the word *diakonos* never occurs in the book of Acts, but *presbyteros*, meaning "elder," is frequent and used as a title for a church officer. The first occurrence of the word with the latter meaning is in Acts 11:30, where we are told that the famine relief for the Judaean believers that Barnabas and Paul brought was delivered over to the elders. In other words, the kind of work for which the seven were appointed in Acts 6 is said to be done by the elders in Acts 11:30.[22] Their method of appointment in the churches, reported in 14:23, resembles somewhat that of Acts 6. In Acts 15 we hear of only two offices in Jerusalem, those of apostle and elder. We must conclude that the church at this early stage knew of only one appointive ministry, which Luke designated "elder."[23]

The Gordian knot can be cut if we recognize that to begin with there was only one appointive ministry that could be called either *diakonos* (suggested by *diakonein* in Acts 6:2), a word describing function, or *presbyteros*, a word describing dignity. Only later did this one ministry divide into two levels, and the two terms came to be used to designate the two levels of ministry.[24] A similar branching into two ranks took place still later, between bishop[25] and elder, terms which were earlier interchangeable. The final result, in the time of Ignatius, was a three-storeyed ministry of bishops, elders, and deacons.[26]

The first indication of a distinction between elder and deacon is in the salutation of Phil 1:1, mentioning "bishops and deacons."[27] This is a two-tiered ministry, indicating that "bishop" was still synonymous with "elder." This synonymity is also exhibited in Acts 20, where the same people who are called elders (*presbyteroi*) in verse 17 are called *episkopoi* in verse 28. See also Titus 1:5-7, where Paul speaks of appointing elders and then immediately lists the qualifications of "bishops," and 1 Tim 3:1; 4:14; 5:17, 19.[28] The distinction between deacon and elder/bishop is hardened in the pastoral epistles, especially in 1 Tim 3:1-13.[29]

The lists of qualifications for bishop and deacon in 1 Timothy 3 call for some comment, for there is much about them that is problematic. Dibelius and Conzelmann list some of the more general questions: "Why are 'bishops' (*episkopoi*) and 'deacons' (*diakonoi*) described in very similar ways? In the catalogue of their duties, why are particular requirements for office not specified, but instead qualities which for the most part are presupposed for every Christian?"[30]

Of particular interest is an item in the list of qualifications for both bishop and deacon, "the husband of one wife" (verses 2 and 12; cf. Titus 1:6; note also the parallel expression, "having been the wife of one husband," 1 Tim 5:9). Interpreters have long debated whether this means "married only once," the traditional explanation, or "married to only one wife (at a time)," the explanation advanced by fathers of the Antiochene school. Some recent interpreters have suggested that the words are a prohibition of polygamy, while A. T. Hanson and others argue that it is a prohibition against remarrying after divorcing a previous wife.[31]

What is of particular interest to us is the use of this clause by some to rule out female ministers, since obviously a woman cannot be the husband of one wife.[32] Several considerations militate against such a conclusion. First of all, and most obviously, the same qualification is mentioned for both *episkopos* and *diakonos*, but Rom 16:1 proves incontrovertibly that the early church had female *diakonoi*, as we shall note below. Though this verse clearly destroys the contention in view, the question remains why the qualification is stated in such a way as to seem to exclude what Romans 16 supports.

At this point we need to review some philological considerations. Greek is an Indo-European language that possesses grammatical gender, as do also the Semitic languages. In such languages, when one has a group of mixed gender in view, or a person who could be of either gender, one must perforce use the masculine.[33] Were we not to read the Bible thus, the tenth commandment of the Decalogue (Exod 20:17) does not forbid a woman to covet her neighbor's husband, and Jesus's warning in the Sermon on the Mount not to look at a woman lustfully (Matt 5:28) leaves a woman free to lust after a man. But such a construal of these passages would be both hermeneutically and morally absurd. The application of the clause "husband of one wife" that we have been considering is in the same class.

If the twofold ministry of elder/bishop and deacon—as well as the subapostolic threefold ministry of bishop, elder, and deacon—exhibits a branching out from one original ministry that could at first be called interchangeably either deacon or elder, and if one single ministry eventually divided into two and then three ranks, a logical consequence results: at least in the earliest period, what can be said of "deacon" also applies to "elder." Both were ministries which in the beginning were one, and they likely remained one in many places for several decades. Even in the pastoral epistles, Timothy is called a *diakonos* (which the RSV translates "minister") in 1 Tim 4:6, though he had a charismatic gift that was somehow associated with prophetic designation and the laying on of hands (1:18, 4:14).

A Female Appointive Minister

Rom 16:1 contains Paul's commendation of a woman named Phoebe, who is designated as *diakonos*,[34] a word used for both genders. The New Testament makes no distinction between deacons and deaconesses. English translations of *diakonos* in Rom 16:1 vary: The KJV, NASB, and NIV read "servant," while the RSV has "deaconess." None of them bring out the fact that Phoebe occupies the same position as the deacons of 1 Timothy 3. Paul requests that she be given the same kind of reception as his other representatives, the same kind of support and respect that Paul enjoins for Titus and the other *apostoloi* (Titus in 2 Cor 8:24; Timothy in 1 Cor 16:10). Such a letter of commendation was the only kind of credential that the early church could offer.

If there could be one female minister there could as well be many, and this is confirmed by a letter sent by Pliny the Younger to the emperor Trajan about A.D. 108.[35] As governor of Bithynia, he arrested and interrogated Christians to find out what he could about their worship. He wrote: "I thought it the more necessary, therefore, to find out what truth there was in this by applying torture to two maidservants, who were called *ministrae*."[36] These women were apparently officers in their churches.

Translators and commentators are divided about the meaning of the women in 1 Tim 3:11. Are these the wives of the deacons that are discussed before and after this verse, or are they female deacons? The verse is as puzzling as its placement is awkward.[37]

That there were women in the appointive ministry implies something about that ministry that logically should have remained true even after it began to be differentiated into two and then three levels, just as the qualities of a piece of clay remain the same even when it is divided in two. But at some unknown point in history it ceased to be true, and women were squeezed out, at least from certain levels.

Other Developments

We also know that at some point, during New Testament times, ministry became professional. In 1 Pet 5:1-4 elders are warned to tend the flock of God "not by constraint but willingly, not for shameful gain but eagerly, not as domineering over those in your charge, but being examples to the flock." Among the unworthy motives for serving is the desire "for shameful gain." There would be no need to warn against this motive if the ministers were not paid. Paul, in 1 Cor 9:4-15, insists on the gospel worker's right to remuneration, but he himself chooses not to exercise that right. In Paul's argumentation he cites Deut 25:4, "You shall not muzzle an ox when it is treading out the grain." He alludes (in v. 14) also to the Lord's instruction, recorded in Matt 10:10. The same Scripture and saying of the Lord are cited in 1 Tim 5:17, 18, where it is laid down that "the elders who rule well, . . . especially those who labor in preaching and teaching," should be considered worthy of double pay.[38]

Conclusions

This survey may serve as a warning against what has been called "structural fundamentalism," the idea that one pattern of church organization and ministry was laid down once and for all time. In fact, we have seen the ministry of the early church change and develop before our very eyes. The apostolate changed from a small and exclusive circle of twelve men to an ever-expanding circle that ultimately included at least one woman. Before Acts 6 there was no appointive ministry, but in that chapter it begins, and it later develops ranks.

These changes did not occur all at once, nor did they occur without resistance. But they were generally natural developments dictated by necessity and determined pragmatically. A careful comparison of the ecclesiology of the various New Testament writings, as well as early sub-apostolic writings, reveals that the changes did not occur uniformly in every place. A Christian traveling around the Roman Empire early in the second century would encounter a twofold appointive ministry in some places and a threefold ministry in others. In some places he would find that apostles and prophets were cherished, and in others they were in disrepute and being replaced by appointive ministers, especially bishops.[39]

We do not know at what point and in what places women came to be squeezed out of the ministry. Sociology suggests that as revolutionary movements become institutionalized, women play a decreasing role in their leadership. In the early period, at least in the churches that Paul knew, that had not yet happened. How the change took place is not something to be explained theologically, but rather sociologically.

Two women in Romans 16, Junia—representing the charismatic ministry of the apostolate, and Phoebe representing the appointive mini-stry—stand at the gate of history and hold open today the door for women to ministry. If "ordination" simply means credentialing, Junia and Phoebe clearly had it, for Paul's commendations of them are explicable on no other grounds.

Furthermore, if one of the functions of laying on hands was to bestow the gift of the Holy Spirit (cf. Acts 8:17 and 1 Tim 4:14), we cannot pray for the outpouring of the Holy Spirit and at the same time deny the laying on of hands to any, man or woman. "And in the last days it shall be, God declares, that I will pour out my Spirit upon all flesh, and your sons and your daughters shall prophesy" (Acts 2:17).

Endnotes

1. The word "ministry" has come to denote a special privilege in the church, in the sense that one who has it is somehow a cut above those who do not have it. Ministry is indeed a privilege, but the correct connotation can be perceived only if we understand that its proper synonym is "service." A minister is a servant.

2. In 1 Pet 4:10, 11 the spiritual gifts are connected with the verb *diakonein*, related to *diakonos*, deacon. Hans Küng makes the point, "Charisma and diakonia are correlative concepts" (*The Church* [New York: Sheed and Ward, 1967], 393-394; cf. Kevin Giles, *Patterns of Ministry among the First Christians* [Melbourne: Collins Dove, 1989], 54).

3. Unless otherwise noted, biblical quotations in this article are taken from the Revised Standard Version (RSV). Important manuscripts insert into Mark 3:14 a second clause, "whom he also named apostles," but this looks like a case of harmonization, influenced

by Luke. It is also possible that the variant reading is authentic and the source of Luke's statement, but the Marcan verse exhibits considerable textual confusion.

4. Judaism also had functionaries called apostles (in Hebrew *shaliach*, in Aramaic *sheliach*). These were sent out from Jerusalem on various missions and errands to the Jewish communities scattered throughout the Roman empire and beyond. They also collected funds for the support of the temple, and generally kept the network of worldwide Judaism together (cf. Acts 28:21). Saul of Tarsus (Paul) was a Jewish apostle before he became a Christian apostle (cf. Acts 9:2). The term is used for Ezra as an emissary of the king of Persia in Ezra 7:14.

5. *Commentary on John* 32.17.

6. In harmony with Origen's definition and Christ's declaration, Mishnah *Berakoth* 5:5 says, "A man's *shaliach* is as himself."

7. This clearly only meant being an eyewitness to the risen Lord, able to give personal testimony to seeing Jesus alive after he died, since none of the Twelve had actually seen the resurrection itself occur. Only angels and perhaps some Roman soldiers saw that. The first witnesses afterward were two women, "Mary Magdalene and the other Mary." See Matt 27:65-28:15.

8. That nothing more is heard of Matthias in the New Testament is not unusual, for the same can be said of the majority of the Twelve. Nevertheless, it has often been maintained that the 120 brethren under the leadership of Peter who filled the vacancy with Matthias made a mistake and should have kept the place open for Paul (who, of course, had not been converted yet). A typical expression of this view is by G. Campbell Morgan: "Casting lots was wholly out of place, and was never resorted to after the coming of the Spirit. That the action was a mistake is revealed in that in His own time and way God found and fitted an apostle. It is to be noted how in consequence of this initial blunder, Paul had constantly to defend his right to the place of apostleship" (*An Exposition of the Whole Bible* [Westwood, NJ: Fleming H. Revell, 1959], 450).

9. Ellen White regards the commissioning of Paul and Barnabas by the Antioch church as an ordination and remarks: "Paul regarded the occasion of his formal ordination as marking the beginning of a new and important epoch in his life-work. It was from this time that he afterward dated the beginning of his apostleship in the Christian church" (*Acts of the Apostles*, 164-165). Paul was called and appointed by God in Acts 9, as reported also in Acts 22, but that calling needed to be recognized and ratified by the church. In other words, he needed credentialing. There is no hint here, however, of anything like the later doctrine of "apostolic succession," and it appears that the laying on of hands and commissioning were an act of the whole congregation. Not even the presence of one of the Twelve is mentioned. Paul, in fact, insisted that those "who were of repute added nothing to me" (Gal 2:6).

10. In the case of Epaphroditus it can be argued that *apostolos* is not used in the same way as elsewhere, but only in the sense of one sent by a congregation and representing it.

11. An additional question concerns the understanding of the phrase "among the apostles" (*en tois apostolois*). Does it mean merely that the reputation of Andronicus and Junia has come to the knowledge of the apostles, or that they are to be numbered among the apostles? The phrase is somewhat ambiguous, but the second option is the more probable

for the following reasons: (1) It is the most natural way to take the Greek; (2) Ancient commentaries, when not ambiguous, such as that of Chrysostom, understood it that way (see note 15, below); (3) Paul, who was always anxious to defend his apostleship, would not have spoken of the apostolic opinion in such a way as to seem not to include himself; (4) The first option is not usually taken when the person in question is thought to be a man named Junias. See Stanley J. Grenz, *Women in the Church: A Biblical Theology of Women in Ministry* (Downers Grove, IL: InterVarsity, 1995), 93; Richard S. Cervin, "A Note Regarding the Name 'Junia(s)' in Romans 16.7," *New Testament Studies* 40 (1994): 470.

12. See lexica, s.v. *Iounias*. Arndt and Gingrich list the name *Iounias* but note that it is not found elsewhere, other than Rom 16:7, and conjecture—without evidence—that it is probably a short form of Junianus. (The normal masculine name corresponding to Junia would have been Junius.) They further assert: "The possibility, fr[om] a purely lexical point of view, that this is a woman's name *Iounia, as, Junia*. . . is prob[ably] ruled out by the context" (William F. Arndt and F. Wilbur Gingrich, *A Greek-English Lexicon of the New Testament and Other Early Christian Literature* [Chicago: Univ. of Chicago Press, 1957], 381). The "context" is the fact that the two people named in the verse are numbered among the apostles. But such an argument is obviously circular. Since a woman could not have been an apostle Junia/Junias must not be a woman, which is begging the question. These lexicographers are apparently unmoved by a fact that they note: "Ancient commentators took Andr. and Junia as a married couple." The decisive facts, therefore, are these: (1) The feminine name Junia is grammatically possible; (2) The feminine name Junia is lexicographically and historically probable; (3) Ancient commentators whose mother tongues were Greek and Latin understood the person to be a woman. For these and other reasons Peter Lampe without hesitation identifies Junia as a woman and female apostle (*Anchor Bible Dictionary*, 3:1127; see bibliography there). Not until the twelfth century do we encounter the view that the person was a male, no doubt prompted by the same logic that influenced Arndt and Gingrich.

John Piper and Wayne Grudem, in *Recovering Biblical Manhood and Womanhood: A Response to Evangelical Feminism* (Wheaton, IL: Crossway, 1991), 79-81, argue against this, appealing to their computer search using the CD-ROM database *Thesaurus Linguae Graecae*. They found only three certain occurrences of the name Junia/Junias in Greek literature outside the New Testament: one in the first-century pagan writer Plutarch, one in Epiphanius, and one in John Chrysostom, the latter two fourth-century church fathers. In Plutarch the reference is clearly to a woman, Junia the sister of Brutus and wife of Cassius. The other two references are to the person in Rom 16:7. The Epiphanius reference speaks of Junias, a man who became a bishop. The Chrysostom reference understands the person to be a woman, Junia. Piper and Grudem conclude from this that the church fathers were divided and that therefore no argument can be made from Greco-Roman usage, but somewhat more weight should be given to the Epiphanius reference.

Piper and Grudem here make two blunders. The first is that their Epiphanius source, *Index discipulorum*, is spurious, probably from the twelfth century and therefore pseudepigraphical (Luci Berkowitz and Karl A. Squitier, *Thesaurus Linguae Graecae: Canon of Greek Authors and Works* [New York: Oxford Univ. Press, 1990], 152). It can be characterized as a late attempt to masculinize what had originally been feminine. Piper and Grudem themselves note that this eccentric source even designates Prisca (Priscilla) as a man (*Recovering*, 479, n. 19)!

The second blunder is that Piper and Grudem limited their search to Greek literature, though Junia is a Roman name, derived from the name of the Roman goddess Juno, the queen of the gods and Jupiter's sister and wife, divine protectress of women and goddess of childbirth. Junia meant "one belonging to Juno." In the Latin sources, again with the aid of the computer, we find more occurrences of the name (e.g., *Scriptores Historiae Augustae Maxim.* 27.5.5; Suetonius *VC.Cal.* 11.1.12; 12.1.7; Tacitus *Annals* 12.4.3; 13.19.3; 14.12.14; Velleius *History* 2.88.1.3). These references are all to women. For further evidence, see Cervin, 464-470; see also James Walter, "Phoebe and Junia(s)—Rom. 16:1-2, 7," in *Essays on Women in Earliest Christianity*, ed. Carroll D. Osburn (Joplin, MO: College Press, 1993), 1:167-190.

13. The first writer of record to comment on this verse was Origen, whose commentary on Romans survives only in a Latin translation by Rufinus. In it Origen understands the person to be Junia (feminine): "Therefore Paul himself, after considering the sum of the most transcendent mystery, identifies both Andronicus and Junia as some of his fellow prisoners in this world, and well known among the apostles" (*Ita ergo et Paulus tale aliquid de se et Andronico, ac Junia, secundum occultioris sacramenti intuens rationem, concaptivos eos sibi in hoc mundo nominat, et nobiles in apostolis* [*Patrologia Graeca* 14:1280]). It is true that Piper and Grudem find in the same work a passage where Origen/Rufinus refers to the person as Junias (*Patrologia Graeca* 14:1289): "Andronicus and Junias and Herodion, all of whom he calls relatives and fellow prisoners" (80). This discrepancy in the same author was probably introduced by later copyists. In the light of medieval tendencies to change Junia to Junias, we may apply the textual critical rule that the more difficult reading is to be preferred and conclude that the version which was more offensive to the sensibilities of later copyists is probably the original one.

The other ancient interpreters who commented on the verse understood the reference to be to a woman named Junia. Thus Chrysostom exclaimed: "Oh! how great is the devotion [*philosophia*] of this woman, that she should be counted worthy of the appellation of apostle" (*Homily 31 on Romans*, Nicene and Post Nicene Fathers, first series, 11:555). A footnote in the Nicene and Post Nicene Fathers by George B. Stevens, the translator and editor, disagrees with Chrysostom's interpretation on the grounds "that a woman should have been an apostle is out of the question"! This sort of circular reasoning lies behind many modern commentaries and translations.

14. The fact that women prophesied in the public service must be placed alongside Paul's injunction against their speaking in church (1 Cor 14:33b-36). Since their prophesying was obviously a speaking in church, the prohibition was clearly not absolute. Paul's reasoning at several points in 1 Corinthians 14 is rather convoluted and calls for sophisticated exegesis.

15. Paul's language in 1 Cor 11:4-7 seems to suggest that the Spirit's distribution of the gifts is not limited to any special class of believers.

16. "They" were presumably the apostles, but the Greek also permits the interpretation that the people, or everyone present, laid hands on the seven.

17. This is the first of the references in the book of Acts commonly taken to refer to "ordination." The actual expression is "laying on of hands" (here and in 13:3; in 14:23 the compound verb *cheirotoneō* is used, usually meaning to elect by raising hands). Elsewhere in the New Testament laying on of hands is performed also for various other purposes, such as bestowal of the Holy Spirit on new believers (Acts 8:17), blessing on children

(Matt 19:13, 15), and healing (Mark 6:5; 8:23, 25; Luke 13:13; Acts 28:8). In Acts 9:17 it seems to effect two purposes simultaneously. See chapter by Keith Mattingly.

18. Kevin Giles, *What on Earth Is the Church? An Exploration in New Testament Theology* (Downers Grove, IL: InterVarsity, 1995), 95. The laying on of hands in these situations has been traditionally designated "ordination," but that term is not used in the New Testament. Rather we find the expressions "laying on hands" and "appoint." The problem with "ordination" is that it carries some medieval baggage that gets retrojected anachronistically into the New Testament. Giles's understanding comes close to the meaning of "credentialing," which is probably the right concept.

19. Thus chapter 9 in Ellen White's *The Acts of the Apostles* is entitled, "The Seven Deacons" (87-96). It is to be noted, however, that the chapter titles are mostly the work of the editors. The term "deacon" does not occur in the text itself. Mrs. White simply calls them "officers" (89).

20. Thus, for example, Giles, 95.

21. Various denominations use these two terms quite differently. Among Baptists, for example, a deacon is equivalent to what Seventh-day Adventists call an elder.

22. In considering the role and function of the seven it is also necessary to consider that Acts goes to some length in reporting the activities of two of them—Stephen and Philip—and their ministry in chapters 6-8 is the preaching of the word, the very work that the apostles assigned to themselves while shifting the administration of relief to the seven!

23. There was a somewhat analogous office and term in Judaism. The New Testament reports elders of local synagogues and elders who were dignitaries of national stature (e.g., Acts 4:5).

24. Gordon Fee approaches my conclusion when he says, "It is altogether likely that *both* 'overseers' and 'deacons' come under the larger category *presbyteroi* ('elders')" (G. D. Fee, *1 and 2 Timothy, Titus*, New International Bible Commentary [Peabody, MA: Hendrickson, 1988], 22). Schreiner argues against this that "the New Testament nowhere identifies 'elders' and 'deacons' so that the latter could be construed as a subcategory of the former" (Thomas R. Schreiner, in Piper and Grudem 505, n. 15). Here Schreiner at best makes an overstatement, for we have shown that the book of Acts makes such an identification when the only title it uses for those who did the work of the seven was elder (Acts 11:30) and never uses the term "deacon."

25. "Bishop" comes from the Greek *episkopos*, which means literally overseer or supervisor. Thus originally "bishop" described function and "elder" described dignity. In secular usage *episkopos* meant a financial officer.

26. Ignatius, writing about A.D. 108, promoted the threefold ministry with such vehemence that we must infer that it was a relatively new development. Typical statements from his seven authentic epistles are *Smyrnaeans* 8:1, "See that you all follow the bishop, as Jesus Christ follows the Father, and the presbytery as if it were the Apostles. And reverence the deacons as the command of God"; *Trallians* 3:1, "Likewise let all respect the deacons as Jesus Christ, even as the bishop is also a type of the Father, and the presbyters as the council of God and the college of the Apostles"; and *Magnesians* 6:1, "Be zealous to do all things in harmony with God, with the bishop presiding in the

place of God and the presbyters in the place of the Council of the Apostles, and the deacons, who are most dear to me, entrusted with the service of Jesus Christ." The twofold ministry, however, was still the pattern when Clement of Rome wrote to the church of Corinth about A.D. 95 (*1 Clement* 42.4) and for the communities represented by the early church manual called the *Didache* (15:1, 2).

27. It has been pointed out that there is no definite article in the Greek of this verse, so that while two classes of people are referred to, they are not exactly clear-cut groups.

28. The term "elder" (*presbyteros*) probably came from the synagogue, while "bishop" was borrowed from secular Greek usage. Hermann Beyer notes, "There is no closely defined office bearing the title *episkopos* in the LXX," and the term was not used technically in Judaism (*Theological Dictionary of the New Testament* 2:608-622). The Christian usage of *episkopos*, at first as a synonym for elder or pastor, was apparently unique.

29. The qualifications of a deacon here are quite different from the qualifications of the ministers in Acts 6. Cf. Giles, 263, n. 51.

30. Martin Dibelius and Hans Conzelmann, *The Pastoral Epistles*, Hermeneia (Philadelphia: Fortress, 1972), 50.

31. A. T. Hanson, *The Pastoral Epistles,* TNCBC (Grand Rapids: Eerdmans, 1982), 77, 78. Hanson provides a brief but useful excursus on the clause. Dibelius and Conzelmann show that in the Greco-Roman world "special esteem is accorded the person who was married only once," whether man or woman, and point out that "in either case we are not dealing with a special instruction for bishops" (*The Pastoral Epistles*, 52).

32. Such a reading of the verse would also rule out unmarried men.

33. A modern illustration can be drawn from Spanish. *Padre* is father, and *madre* is mother; but the word for both parents together is *padres*. As will be seen, the modern feminist move to reform the English language into a "gender-inclusive" language (e.g., "Each person must bring their own spoon") undercuts correct understanding of biblical passages such as the one we here deal with.

34. The English distinction suggests not only difference but also inferiority. In the Seventh-day Adventist Church it has been the practice to ordain deacons, but not deaconesses.

35. *Epistles* 10.96.7, 8.

36. *Ministrae* is the plural of the Latin word *ministra*, feminine form of *minister*. It is the exact equivalent of the Greek *diakonos* and the origin of the English word "minister."

37. Barry L. Blackburn finds compelling evidence for reading "female deacons" ("The Identity of the 'Women' in 1 Tim 3:11," in *Essays on Women in Earliest Christianity*, 1:302-319).

38. The word used here is *timē,* which can mean either pay or honor (cf. English "honorarium"). Most translations read "honor," but the citation of Deut 25:4, as well as the Lord's saying in Matt 10:10 ("The laborer deserves his wages") would indicate that pay is meant.

39. At some point the bishops came to be regarded as successors to the apostles.

CHAPTER 4

LAYING ON OF HANDS IN ORDINATION: A BIBLICAL STUDY

KEITH MATTINGLY

One of the responses given to the suggestion that deaconesses receive the same laying on of hands as their deacon counterparts is, "I don't need laying on of hands in order to accomplish what I need to do; I am doing quite fine without it." The same sentiment is often carried into discussions on laying hands on women elders or pastors. Men may have the same attitude. Recently a man elected as deacon seven months earlier said he had no desire to receive laying on of hands, because, after all, he "really didn't do that much." My own experience indicates that the Seventh-day Adventist Church, as a whole, appears to place little emphasis on the topic. I received the laying on of hands in ordination twice, once as an elder and once as a minister. In both situations I received no instruction about the meaning of laying on of hands nor about the reason for laying on of hands. Yet, the church maintains the practice.

Of Protestant churches that deny that ordination is a sacrament of the church, Marjorie Warkentin asks, "Just why do we find it necessary to lay hands on one person in public?"[1] In this paper I will attempt to answer the question by reviewing pertinent biblical evidence that applies directly to the subject of ordination. My emphasis will be on the Old Testament, upon which the New Testament ordination texts are obviously firmly grounded. I will then draw conclusions that will answer the question, "What is a biblical understanding of laying on of hands?"

Laying on of Hands in General

It is not surprising that "hand" plays a significant symbolical role in the Old Testament and the Ancient Near East. Body parts were actually thought of "as seats of various attributes, even as the seat of life itself,"[2] or as "vehicles of the life inherent in the whole body."[3] Old Testament writers used the hand in a wide variety of ways to characterize a person. Aubrey Johnson points out that the hand indexed feelings, was associated with power, indicated purpose, reinforced or gave effect to the written and spoken word, carried magical or religio-magical implications, took on personal responsibility or engaged in some form of personal behavior, was subject to moral judgment, and, with a suffix, became an emphatic form of the personal pronoun.[4]

Such symbolism richly colors and complicates any interpretation of laying-on-of-hands symbolism. Yet, in nonbiblical texts, the laying on of hands as ordination or transfer of authority only occurs when Tutmose I transfers leadership to his daughter Hatshepsut.[5] The Hebrew noun for hand, yād, denotes individuality, ability, possession, power, authority, and creativity. The use of the word in the phrase "laying on of hands" could symbolize that the recipient of the gesture was in the hand layer's possession or power or that power and authority were passed on to the recipient. Yahweh spoke, gave commandments, acted, and ordained by the hand of human agents. Thus, "hand" became symbolic of agency, a symbol of the Lord's visible presence.

The Old Testament phrase for laying on of hands, sāmak yād, literally "he laid [his] hand," appears 25 times in a variety of contexts. Eighteen times hands are laid on animals for sacrifice or the scapegoat,[6] five times on people,[7] once on an inanimate object (a wall, Amos 5:19), and one use describes the Lord's support of one who stumbles (Ps 37:24). That 23 of the 25 texts occur in a cultic or worship setting leads to the conclusion that the two-word phrase "implies a technical term, by which a ceremony or ritual is depicted."[8]

The word sāmak suggests leaning, a gesture by which by which pressure is applied to the recipient.[9] David Daube compares laying on of hands using the verb sāmak with the same gesture using śîm (to put) and shîth (to place), used regarding laying on of hands in blessing. He proposes that sāmak signifies a "vigorous leaning" and that śîm and shîth refer to a force of a much "gentler character.[10] More recently, Wright has argued that this distinction is "hard to sustain on the meager evidence" and that the verb sāmak "may be only idiomatic and not indicate that pressure is applied."[11] In fact, sāmak indicates more than a mere "leaning" and includes very strongly the concept of sustenance and support. A combination of the symbolism of the hand and the leaning results in a picture of either a hand that powerfully leans on something or supports it, or hand as agency passing on power or support.

Various scholars have proposed that the number of hands makes a difference in the meaning of laying on of hands. This conclusion is based on the observation that the use of one hand was limited to sacrificial rites, while two hands were used in nonsacrificial rites.[12] A review of the broad range of the meanings of "hand" in the Old Testament does not support drawing a fine line of distinction between the meaning of one or two hands. Laying on of hands shares common ground between sacrificial and nonsacrificial rites. Sacrificial laying-on-of-hands ceremonies were closely associated with the ordination of Aaron and his sons (Exod 29:10, 15, 19; Lev 8:14, 18, 22), indicating a similar underlying meaning and no difference between the meaning of one or two hands. Scholarly conclusions as to which event is one-handed and which is two-handed appear arbitrary and contrived. Furthermore, three experiences of Moses illustrate that to the ancient mind the number of hands used was not as important as the fact that hands were used. The battle against the Amalekites went well when Moses held up his hand (singular); Israel lost when his hands (plural) were lowered (Exod 17:11, 12). In the descriptions of Moses' carrying the tables of stones, the Hebrew uses three different expressions: "his hand" (singular, Exod 32:15), "his hands" (plural, Deut 9:15, 17, and "my two hands" (Deut 10:3). In the passage describing the ordination of Joshua, the instructions for the ritual use the singular while its execution uses the dual (Num 27:18, 23).

In the Old Testament, only two instances of laying on of hands can be classified as ordination rituals. These are the laying on of hands of the Levites and the ordination of Joshua.

Levites and the Laying on of Hands

The ceremony of ordination of the Levites, recorded in Num 8:5-26, commenced with a divine command to "take" the Levites from among the other Israelites. The command further instructed Moses that after purifying them through a process that included sprinkling with the water of cleansing, shaving, and washing, he was to summon them to a public ceremony to be held in front of the tabernacle. "All the congregation of the children of Israel" were then to "lay their hands on the Levites." Having received the laying on of hands, the Levites were to lay their hands on bulls used for a sin offering and a burnt offering to make atonement for themselves. Aaron then presented the Levites to the Lord as a wave offering. They were "set apart" from the rest of the Israelites and dedicated to God that they might work in the tabernacle in the place of the firstborn males and make atonement for the whole congregation.

The significance of hand laying on the Levites can be organized into five categories: identification, setting apart, transfer, substitution, and appointment to office. First, laying on of hands identified or designated the Levites as the specified ones to become an offering of the whole congregation.[13] Or, through the laying of hands, the people identified with the Levites or their service.[14] Timothy Ashley suggests that laying on of hands identified the Levites with the people.[15] Second, the hand-laying rite distinguished the participants from the rest of the community. The Levites experienced an act of consecration in which they were set apart from the rest of the congregation in order to be completely dedicated to the sanctuary and its service.[16] Third, by laying hands on the Levites, the congregation of Israel symbolically transferred to the Levites their obligations in connection with the tabernacle service, including authority to act in behalf of the whole nation.[17] Fourth, as a direct result of transfer, hand-laying also expressed an act of substitution, indicating that the Levites substituted for and represented the rest of the congregation, in particular the firstborn.[18] Fifth, the hand-laying rite marked an appointment to office, that of exclusive work in the tabernacle.[19]

Joshua and Laying on of Hands

Joshua's ordination by Moses has been interpreted as the prototype of all later ordinations. Two texts describe the laying on of hands in the installation and ordination of Joshua: Num 27:12-23 and Deut 34:9. The instructions in Num 27:18-20 read:

> Take Joshua son of Nun, a man in whom is the spirit, and lay your hand on him. Have him stand before Eleazar the priest and the entire assembly and commission him in their presence. Give him some of your authority so the whole Israelite community will obey him.

In the Hebrew, the command "take" is syntactically linked to the following four verbs: "lay" your hand, have him "stand," "commission" him, and "give" him some of your authority. The imperative "take," along with the following four verbs, concludes in a "so that" clause. All actions were intended to have a specific result: Israel was to obey Joshua.

Instructions

One of the extended meanings of the Hebrew word for "take" (*lāqaḥ*) is "select" or "summon." The Hebrew imperative (literally, "take to yourself") demands personal involvement; this was a deliberate and selective act on the part of Moses. Further, often the imperative "take" (*lāqaḥ*) designates an initiative for subsequent action. Hebrew syntax in vv. 18-20 indicates a series of verbs that describe the intended subsequent actions: "lay," "stand," "commission," and "give." Laying on of hands answers both elements; as one of the intended subsequent actions it provided a physical means by which Moses became personally involved in the selection of Israel's next leader.

The Lord, "God of the spirits of all flesh," commanded Moses to lay his hands on Joshua, a man in whom there was spirit (Num 27:16, 18). Joshua's history reveals a man who had a careful and close walk with his God. It was no common individual who received laying on of hands. Not only was Joshua a man with an indomitable and courageous spirit, but the Lord had given him a special gift of the Spirit that changed him and endowed him for leadership. Hand laying is thus associated with a spirited man as well as a man filled with the Spirit of Yahweh.

The laying on of hands was to come together with the formal presentation of Joshua to Eleazar and the congregation. This presentation had the purpose of giving him to the congregation in a legal setting, thus also giving forensic precedence to hand laying. Jacob Milgrom suggests that the Hebrew places the laying on of hands after the formal presentation.[20] Thus the order of ceremony for Joshua's ordination appears to commence with the double presentation. As a second implication of "stand before," hand laying was associated with the physical gesture of standing that communicated two kinds of acceptance: (1) the one presented indicated acceptance of his responsibilities; and (2) the congregation, by allowing him to be presented, communicated its acceptance of Joshua. Third, religious usage of the term "stand before," reinforced by its association with the terms "priest" and "congregation," demonstrate hand-laying as part of a cultic and covenantal event. The term "stand before" also shows where Joshua's ordination ceremony was to take place. Presentation to priests and meetings of the congregation generally occurred at the tent of meeting. Thus, Joshua's ordination ceremony most likely took place at the courtyard gate of the tabernacle.

An analysis of the Hebrew syntax provides two further observations about laying on of hands: (1) it is more important than the other actions and (2) it happens before the other actions in the ordination ceremony. The sense of the imperative of v. 18, "take," continues with each of the verbs syntactically connected to it. At the same time a hierarchy is established: (1) lay, (2) stand, (3) command or charge, and (4) give. Each command becomes contingent on the previous. Hence, the primary action of this series of commands is the laying of Moses' hand on Joshua.

Hebrew syntax also indicates that each of the clauses syntactically connected with the imperative describes concomitant circumstances that coordinate with each other. In this case, Moses' laying his hand on Joshua would take place concurrently with having Joshua stand, giving him a charge, and giving him some of Moses' honor. However, even though all activities may take place concurrently, the activity listed first, the laying on of hands, retains primary significance in the hierarchy of activities.

In the divine instructions, hand laying is associated with a commission, which is spelled out in three parallel passages to Num 27:12-23: Deut 3:21-28; Deut 31:1-8, 14, 23; and Josh 1:1-9. First, Moses spoke words of encouragement to strengthen Joshua and make him resolute in his leadership. Second, Moses spelled out Joshua's twofold task, to conquer the land and distribute it equitably to all the tribes. Third, Moses expressed assurance of divine aid: God would personally support him. Fourth, Moses exhorted Joshua to keep the law. Hand-laying was thus associated with a commission verbally spoken by a human but effected by the Lord.

Implementation

In the implementation of the Lord's orders (Num 27:22-23), Moses stood Joshua before Eleazar and the congregation, laid hands on him, and gave him a charge; but the narrative makes no mention of giving him honor or authority. Why not? An answer to this question leads directly to the laying on of hands. The divine command of v. 20 instructed Moses to place some of his honor on Joshua. The use of "on him" in the placement-of-honor command corresponds directly to the "on him" of the hand-laying instruction of v. 18. Moses thus established a physical conduit for the transfer of his honor, which is linked syntactically to standing Joshua before Eleazar and the congregation, as well as to giving him a charge. The combination of laying on of hands with public presentation and giving a charge effectively passed some of Moses' honor to Joshua.

Joshua's reception of hand-laying, along with the critical elements of public presentation, commissioning, and a gift of some of Moses' honor was to have an intended effect. Joshua was to receive something further: obedience from the whole community. However, receiving such recognition did not put Joshua on the same plane as Moses, nor did it remove from Joshua the need of continually seeking the Lord's will. Joshua was to seek the Lord by standing before the high priest, Eleazar, who in turn was to ask God's will through use of the Urim (Num 27:21).

Num 27:12-23 concludes by placing Moses' "hand" in juxtaposition with the word of the Lord: "YHWH spoke by the hand of Moses." Here Moses' hand is treated as a visible representation of the Lord's communication and power. Moses' hand enabled Israel to see the "word" of God. Thus Moses' act of laying his hands on Joshua became a visible enactment of the "word" of YHWH, bringing with it all its attendant concepts of power, ability to create, and to effect what it signified. It is not surprising that, in the list of actions Moses accomplished in Joshua's ordination, the laying on of hands carried primary significance.

The second text describing laying on of hands for Joshua is Deut 34:9: "Now Joshua son of Nun was filled with the spirit of wisdom because Moses had laid hands on him. So the Israelites listened to him and did what the Lord had commanded Moses." Again, the laying on of hands receives special prominence and importance. The passage is placed near the end of the concluding section of Deuteronomy, of which the last four chapters describe the presentation, commission, and ordination of Joshua as the last act of Moses, the greatest of all prophets. In Deut 34:9, laying on of hands is *the* gesture that summarizes and gives meaning to the entire ordination event. The chapter concludes by reminding the reader that Moses possessed a mighty hand.

Deut 34:9 accords further importance to laying on of hands by noting two results of Moses' laying hands on Joshua. Upon assumption of leadership, Joshua found himself in a position of need he had never experienced; thus, at his ordination, the Lord gave him a special outpouring of the spirit of wisdom, to provide the insight and administrative ability this new position demanded. This gift of the spirit was received from God through the mediation of Moses' physical touch. In addition, Joshua experienced the obedience of the people as a direct result of the gesture.

Interpretation

What happened when Joshua received the laying on of hands as presented in Num 27:12-23 and Deut 34:9? The answer to this question will be organized into three sections: (1) the procedure, (2) the symbolic implications, and (3) the tangible effects.

Procedure. The procedure Moses followed was similar to that used for the Levites. Both ceremonies took place before the tent of meeting and in the presence of the entire community. Moses' hands became the visible representation of the hands of God. But at the same time, Moses also represented the congregation in expressing its support of Yahweh's choice. Presentation before the entire congregation played the important role of informing all whom Joshua would lead and for reminding Joshua of whom he was to lead. Joshua was also presented to the high priest, to remind him that he was to work in close harmony with the one who could communicate with God. Joshua was not to forget his connection with God. The ceremony included a four-part commission: (1) words to encourage Joshua's resolution; (2) words describing Joshua's task; (3) words promising divine assistance, sufficiency, and companionship throughout Joshua's leadership; and (4) words exhorting Joshua to read, preserve, and carefully keep the law.

Meaning. The laying on of hands in Joshua's ordination carried important symbolic meaning. Through it Joshua was identified as dedicated to the Lord, and as the Lord's specific choice as the next leader of Israel. Identification resulted in confirmation. The hand-laying gesture was a public act confirming and ratifying the spiritual gifts God had already given Joshua. The gesture was an act of validation recognizing Joshua's God-given capacity for leadership. Thus hand laying confirmed an inner endowment by an external recognition.

Further, laying on of hands indicated initiation to office. The gesture set Joshua apart from the rest of the congregation and distinguished him from all other potential leaders, that he might be dedicated to the service of leadership without the complication of competition. The gesture also signified an official investiture of responsibility and authority, a dedication to leadership, and a conferral of formal and public appointment to office.

Additionally, hand-laying symbolically transferred to Joshua power to act in behalf of the Lord and of the nation. While Numbers notes that Joshua already possessed spirit, Deuteronomy clearly states that Joshua received the spirit of wisdom *because* Moses laid hands on him. A spirit indeed was transferred to Joshua, a spirit from Yahweh, which enabled him to function better as leader.

Finally, laying on of hands in no way established a dynasty or any other circumstance that could be interpreted as "apostolic succession." Moses may have laid his hands on Joshua, but Joshua's authority was rooted in the Lord who had worked through Moses. Joshua's authority was founded in his connection with Yahweh rather than with Moses. However, the Lord did choose to establish Joshua through the physical contact of Moses' hands.

Effects. By touching Joshua, Moses marked him as the one to receive the symbolic meanings of hand-laying. Moses' hands became the conduit by which the Lord chose to bless Joshua. Because the hand-laying gesture was rooted in a command from the Almighty, it had at least two tangible results: (1) Joshua's reception of the spirit of wisdom in leadership skills, and (2) the congregation's receptivity of and obedience to Joshua's leadership.

The laying on of hands was central to the essence and purpose of Joshua's ritual investiture. These permeated the procedures, the symbolic meanings, and tangible results of the gesture. While the other elements of the ordination were important, the laying on of hands was indeed the strong identifying mark which bound together the rest of the elements.

The New Testament and Laying on of Hands

The New Testament uses two phrases for laying on of hands: *epitithein tas cheiras*, which occurs 20 times, and *epitheseōs tōn cheirōn*, which occurs 4 times. Most usages occur in the context of healing (i. e., Mark 6:5; Luke 13:13; Acts 9:12) or blessing (Matt 19:13-15). At times laying on of hands is related to the reception of the Holy Spirit (Acts 8:17-19) or spiritual gifts (1 Tim 4:14). For this study, the five most interesting are those that deal with commissioning.

Five texts (Acts 6:6; 13:3; 19:6; 1 Tim 4:14; 5:22; 2 Tim 1:6) speak of commissioning or installation in office; these have traditionally been tied to ordination. When commenting on these texts, T. F. Torrance notes that "the laying on of hands with prayer is the only ceremony that is taken over from the Old Testament by the New Testament church for the consecration and ordination of its ministry."[21] When introducing his study of these texts, Eduard Lohse comments that "hands were laid on the office-bearer to equip him with divine power."[22]

The laying on of hands recorded in Acts 6:1-6 was that of the "seven," often considered to be deacons, but never called that. Speaking of this event, Everett Ferguson points out that "verbal echoes indicate that Luke was deliberately alluding to the Old Testament episode" of Joshua's ordination as rendered in Num 27:12-23 by the Septuagint.[23] Luke follows the same basic sequence in Acts: a command to select someone filled by the Spirit, to be appointed to a responsibility, in a public ceremony, by the laying on of hands. Like Joshua, the seven were well known to be full of the Spirit (and wisdom) before the laying on of hands.

An ambiguity in the Greek text presents the possibility of drawing a comparison between hand-laying on the seven and on the Levites. Acts 6:6 allows either the apostles or the congregation to conduct the actual laying on of hands. Like the Levites, the seven were separated from the congregation in order to fulfill a function required of the congregation. Considering this comparison, the congregation probably did the hand-laying. If not, the apostles functioned as representatives of the congregation. In either case, prayer accompanied the laying on of hands. This ceremony authorized the seven to act as representatives of the people in the distribution of the food.

The setting apart and consecration of Paul and Barnabas (Acts 13:1-3) is even more similar to the case of the Levites. In both narratives the choice was divinely made. Paul and Barnabas were chosen to the "work to which [God] called them," as the Levites were to "work the works of the Lord." Paul and Barnabas were separated from the rest to be dedicated to a special work for the Lord, as the Levites were separated from the Israelites for a special work for the Lord in the sanctuary. The form and terminology of ordination are clearly present, thus indicating that this was indeed an ordination experience. Laying on of hands indicated congregational support as well as a setting aside to a specific missionary task.

The third laying on of hands in ordination or installation was that of Timothy, referred to in 1 Tim 4:14 and 2 Tim 1:16. T. F. Torrance refers to this ordination as the "most important instance of ordination by laying on of hands in the New Testament."[24] Marjorie Warkentin treats Paul and Timothy's relationship as analogous to that of Moses and Joshua.[25] As Moses laid his hands on Joshua, so Paul laid his on Timothy. Joshua's public presentation enabled congregational as well as priestly blessing on Moses' action. Timothy's reception of laying on of hands had the approval of the church as represented by the council of elders, with Paul no doubt acting along with them. Timothy, too, had the blessing of the Lord, a special spiritual gift, which was given to him by prophecy and laying on of hands, equipping him for his unique role. Paul admonished him to "not neglect the gift" that was in him, which had been given him by prophecy with the laying on of hands," and urged him to "stir up the gift of God" which was in him through the laying on of Paul's hands" (1

Tim 4:14; 2 Tim 1:6). Like Joshua, who was given the spirit of wisdom because Moses laid hands on him, Timothy received his gift formally through the act of laying on of hands, which authorized him as an accredited teacher and minister. Timothy needed this authority so that his youth would not hinder his work. God used the laying on of hands to impart to him a spiritual gift. Lohse notes in this connection that the laying on of hands "is not merely an accompanying sign. It also serves to pass on the gift with which God equips the office-bearer."[26]

It has been argued that laying on of hands on the seven was only for a specific task and not for an office, that laying on of hands on Paul and Barnabas was for a specific mission tour and not for an office, and that Timothy received a specific gift through laying on of hands, not necessarily an office. However, Ferguson maintains that "the earliest attested action for installation into church office is the imposition of hands."[27] Indeed, each of the hand-laying experiences resulted in installation to a church office: the seven to the office in charge of food distribution, Paul and Barnabas to the office of missionary, and Timothy to the office of teacher and minister.

Was grace received through the laying on of hands? Timothy received a special gift with (1 Tim 4:14) and through (2 Tim 1:6) the laying on of hands. Ferguson argues that usage of the words "with" and "through" communicate the idea of accompaniment and not means.[28] In other words, laying on of hands comes at the same time as reception of the gift; it is not the means of receiving the gift. On the other hand, Warkentin notes that "through" is used with the genitive of the person, generally used in the New Testament to indicate agency or mediation. She suggests that an honest interpretation of 2 Tim 1:6 "demands that we accept that Timothy's gift was received through the agency of the hands of Paul." We must, however, recognize that in the final analysis it is the hand of God that equips his servants.[29]

Conclusion

Hand symbolism plays an important role in developing an interpretation of biblical laying on of hands. God evidently has privileged his servants to perform signs and wonders in his behalf through physical contact. Warkentin notes that "when hands are laid on a person in an ecclesiastical setting they express the will of God through human agency. The imposition of hands makes a very serious statement indeed about the activity of God."[30] Hands become a symbol of God's visible presence.

What does Scripture teach that the laying on of hands accomplishes? I suggest five accomplishments. First, laying on of hands is an act of identification, establishing horizontal as well as vertical communication. Vertically, God identifies through his human representative a Spirit-filled individual chosen by himself. Horizontally, a congregation identifies through the hand gesture an individual it recognizes as chosen by God.

Second, laying on of hands sets an individual apart from the community in order to be completely dedicated to a specific task. In keeping with the meaning of support attributed to the Hebrew phrase, hand-laying also becomes a physical gesture by which the congregation and God indicate a pledge of support to the one on whom hands are laid.

Third, laying on of hands mediates a transfer to the individual from both God and the ecclesiastical community. To Joshua, God transferred a spirit of wisdom. To Timothy, God transferred a special gift of the Spirit. To both, God transferred authority to function in his name. The community, on the other hand, transferred authority to act in its behalf.

Fourth, as a direct result of transfer, hand-laying indicates that an individual represents the community. As Israel needed the Levites to fulfill religious obligations in its behalf, so the spiritual community needs individuals to fulfill its obligations. As Joshua substituted for Moses and filled the void of leadership created by his death, so the spiritual community needs to replace its leaders. Hand-laying indicates the one who becomes the representative or delegate of the community.

Fifth, laying on of hands identifies an individual as appointed to office, indeed, to a variety of offices including priesthood, distribution of food, mission, or the leadership of a nation or church. Therefore, laying on of hands can be to more than one office.

From this study I find five important features of the laying-on-of-hands ceremony. (1) The ceremony must be public, before the congregation and before God to remind the individual to whom he or she is accountable. (2) The public place should be carefully selected; both the Levites and Joshua received the gesture at the door to the sanctuary, thus indicating the importance of a place dedicated to the worship of God. (3) Hands must be physically placed on the individual; the one actually accomplishing the gesture represents both the congregation and God. The congregation should find some method to indicate its involvement in the physical act, perhaps by raising their hands or by each one placing a hand on the person in front, forming a chain connected directly to the individual receiving laying on of hands. (4) A four-part charge must be given to the candidate: words of encouragement based on past experience with God, description of the task for which the individual is being set aside, assurance of divine aid, and an exhortation to keep God's law. (5) Prayer should accompany the gesture.

Laying on of hands is to have an intended result, that of obedience. Joshua was to obey the voice of God in his leadership; the people, after Joshua received the hand-laying gesture, were to obey him. Young Timothy appeared to have problems with older believers; Paul reminded him of the authority granted him through the laying on of hands.

I return to Warkentin's question, "Just why do we find it necessary to lay hands on one person in public?" I would suggest two answers: First, laying on of hands declares that the individual receiving the gesture can act in the name of the community, in a way that he or she could not without first receiving the gesture. Second, laying on of hands is God's chosen means to pass on new gifts of the Spirit that enable the recipient of the gesture to better perform duties.

Thus, laying on of hands is as necessary for accomplishing certain God-given tasks as baptism is for salvation. Baptism provides no magic and neither does laying on of hands, yet both are required in order to accomplish the will of God.

I have often heard that a call to "the ministry" is the "highest calling." Laying on of hands affirms this highest of callings. Laying on of hands designates who has been filled by the Spirit and who is being inducted into this high calling; it provides a visible pledge of support from both God and the community of believers and places the individual in a special category which gives a unique authority. This is not an authority of position, but of servant leadership.

Should women receive the laying on of hands? Most definitely. The withholding of the laying on of hands may well be a refusal to recognize heaven's call and the individual's appropriately positive response. As Warkentin points out, we must "be careful lest in a misplaced zeal for the sovereignty of God we remove the human features from His revelation and in that moment remove ourselves from God."[31] In Acts 8:12-14 both men and women received the Holy Spirit by the laying on of hands. When denying an individual the laying on of hands, the church misses the opportunity of validating the Spirit's work and collaborating with the Almighty. Furthermore, to place a woman in the position of pastor or elder is to affirm that she is indeed called by God to ministry. Without laying on of hands, she lacks an important biblical authorization to fulfill her responsibilities. Laying on of hands identifies her before the congregation as its minister, sets her apart from the congregation, empowers her to be a representative of the congregation, and appoints her to office. Finally, the argument that one can perform God-given duties without the laying on of hands is usually made when arguing against the need for women to receive the gesture. While the argument certainly contains truth, it overlooks the fact that the laying on of hands is an important biblical principle and that male Seventh-day Adventist pastors see the gesture as an important part of their ordination. If the gesture is important at all, it should be equally important to pastors of both genders.

Endnotes

1. Marjorie Warkentin, *Ordination: A Biblical-Historical View* (Grand Rapids: Eerdmans, 1982), 179.

2. Foster Roland McCurley, "A Semantic Study of Anatomical Terms in Akkadian, Ugaritic, and Biblical Literature" (Ph.D. dissertation, The Dropsie College for Hebrew and Cognate Learning, 1968), 6-7.

3. Ernst Cassirer, *The Philosophy of Symbolic Forms* (New Haven, CT: Yale Univ. Press, 1953-57), 2:159.

4. Aubrey R. Johnson, *The Vitality of the Individual in the Thought of Ancient Israel* (Cardiff: Univ. of Wales Press, 1964), 52-64.

5. Keith Mattingly, "The Laying on of Hands on Joshua: An Exegetical Study of Numbers 27:12-23 and Deuteronomy 34:9" (Ph.D. dissertation, Andrews University, 1997), chap. 2, "Hands and Status in the Ancient Near East."

6. The use of one hand, 8 times: Lev 1:4; 3:2, 8, 13; 4:4; 4:24, 29, 33; and the use of 2 hands, once: Lev 16:21. The use of one or two hands, 9 times: Exod 29:10, 19; 29:15; Lev 4:15; 8:14; 8:18, 22; Num 8:12; 2 Chron 29:23.

7. Three passages refer to Moses laying hand(s) on Joshua (Num 27:18, 23; Deut 34:9); one passage refers to the children of Israel laying hands on the Levites (Num 8:10); and one refers to the congregation laying hands on a blasphemer (Lev 24:14).

8. B. J. Van der Merwe, "The Laying on of Hands in the Old Testament," in *New Light on Some Old Testament Problems: Papers read at the 5th Meeting held at the University of South Africa, Pretoria*, ed. A. H. van Zyl (Pretoria, South Africa: Ou Testamentiese Werkgemeenskap in Suid-Afrika, 1962), 36. Ps 37:24 and Amos 5:19 are the non-cultic verses.

9. Jacob Milgrom, *Numbers Bemidbar*, The JPS Torah Commentary (Philadelphia: The Jewish Publication Society, 5750/1990), 235. "The rabbis state explicitly that the act of *samakh* must be 'with all one's strength.'"

10. David Daube, *The New Testament and Rabbinic Judaism* (New York: Arno, 1973), 224-226.

11. D. P. Wright, "Hands, Laying On Of," *Anchor Bible Dictionary* (1992), 3:47. Also note that *śîm* and *shîth* do not always denote gentleness; they may also indicate taking things by force (1 Kgs 20:6), an arrest (2 Kgs 11:16; 2 Chr 23:15), compelling settlement of disputes (Job 9:33), and YHWH's judgment on the nations (Ezek 39:21). In addition, *sāmak* carries overtones other than "vigorous pressure," such as a gentle leaning against a wall, or support and sustenance, as well as reliance and stability.

12. René Péter, "L'imposition des mains dans l'Ancien Testament," *Vetus Testamentum* 27 (1977): 48-55; David P. Wright and J. Milgrom, *"sāmak," Theologische Wörtbuch Altes Testaments* (1986), 5: 884-888; Angel Rodriguez, "Substitution in the Hebrew Cultus and in Cultic-Related Texts" (Ph.D. dissertation, Andrews University, 1979), 196-198. Roy Gane, professor of Old Testament at Andrews University, argues that in sanctuary ritual the high priest laid two hands only on the scapegoat, while in all other sacrifices the offerers laid only one hand. This would distinguish between what is laid on Christ (vicariously borne sin) and what is laid on Satan (his own sin). For me the picture is not so clear.

13. M. C. Sansom, "Laying of Hands in the Old Testament," *Expository Times* 94 (1983): 325; Martin Noth, *Numbers*, Old Testament Library, trans, James Martin (Philadelphia: Westminster, 1968), 67-69.

14. J. Sturdy, *Numbers*, Cambridge Bible Commentary (London: University Press, 1976), 67; John Joseph Owens, "Numbers," Broadman Commentary (Nashville: Broadman, 1970), 2:106; James Philip, *Numbers*, Communicator's Commentary (Waco, TX: Word, 1986), 107-109; R. B. Allen, "Numbers," Expositor's Bible Commentary (Grand Rapids: Zondervan, 1990), 766-777; F. B. Huey, Jr., *Numbers*, Bible Study Commentary (Grand Rapids: Zondervan, 1981), 34; Arno C. Gaebelein, C. *Gaebelein's Concise Commentary on the Whole Bible* (Neptune, NJ: Loizeaux, 1985), 135.

15. Timothy R. Ashley, *The Book of Numbers*, New International Commentary on the Old Testament (Grand Rapids: Eerdmans, 1993), 170.

16. B. Maarsingh, *Numbers: A Practical Commentary*, trans. J. Vriend (Grand Rapids: Eerdmans, 1987), 31-32: Out of all the nations, the Lord had set apart Israel; out of all the Israelites, he had set apart the Levites; out of all the Levites, he had set apart the priests; out of all the priests, he had set apart the high priest. And he appointed Moses to set apart the Levites from the rest of the people. Other scholarly language describing the significance of laying on of hands for the Levites includes: "solemnly set apart" (R. Winterbotham, *Numbers*, PC [Grand Rapids: Eerdmans, 1977], 71; Robert Jamieson, A. R. Fausset, and David Brown, *A Commentary Critical, Experimental and Practical on the Old and New Testaments* [Grand Rapids: Eerdmans, 1945], 1:533-534; Huey, 34); "dedicated" (Ashley, 170); "completely dedicated" (Baruch A. Levine, *Numbers 1-20: A New Translation with Introduction and Commentary*, Anchor Bible [New York: Doubleday, 1993], 273-274); "ordained" (Walter Riggans, *Numbers*, Daily Study Bible [Philadelphia: Westminster, 1983], 65); "consecrated" (Paul Galtier, "Imposition des mains," *Dictionnaire de théologie catholique*, [1927], 7: 1304; Jamieson, 533-534).

17. Transfer obligations in connection with the tabernacle service: Philip, 107-109; *Seventh-day Adventist Bible Commentary*, 1:852; Matthew Henry, *Matthew Henry's Commentary on the Whole Bible* (Old Tappan, NJ: Fleming H. Revell, n.d.), 1:595-596; F. C. Cook and T. E. Espin, *The Fourth Book of Moses Called Numbers*, The Holy Bible According to

the Authorized Version (London: Murray, 1877), 679. Transfer blessing and authority: R. K. Harrison, *Numbers, An Exegetical Commentary* (Grand Rapids: Baker, 1992), 152. No transfer of power or spirit, J. K. Parratt, "Laying of Hands in the New Testament: A Reexamination in Light of Hebrew Terminology," *Expository Times* 80 (1969): 212-213.

18. Leonard Elliott Binns, *The Book of Numbers*, Westminster Commentary (London: Methuen & Co., 1927), 50; Gordon J. Wenham, *Numbers*, Tyndale Old Testament Commentaries (Downers Grove, IL: InterVarsity, 1981), 96-97; Allen 766-767; Ashley, 170; Sturdy, 67; *Seventh-day Adventist Bible Commentary* 1:852. As a direct result of all that was transferred, the Levites became the people's representatives (Philip J. Budd, *Numbers*, Word Biblical Commentary [Waco, TX: Word, 1984], 93).

19. Laying hands was a symbol of appointment to office, (Julius H. Greenstone, *Numbers, with Commentary* [Philadelphia: Jewish Publication Society, 1948], 80-83); Jamieson, 533-534. It was not an appointment to office (Parratt, 212-213).

20. Milgrom, *Numbers*, 235.

21. T. F. Torrance, "Consecration and Ordination," *Scottish Journal of Theology* 11 (1958): 235.

22. Eduard Lohse, "*Cheir,*" *Theological Dictionary of the New Testament*, 9:433.

23. Everett Ferguson, "Laying on of Hands in Acts 6:6 and 13:3," *Restoration Quarterly* 4 (1960): 250. (1) In Acts 6:3, the people are commanded to "look about for" (*episkepsasthe*, a relatively rare term); in Num 27:16, Moses asks God to "look about for" (*episkepsasthō*) a man to lead the people. (2) In Acts 6:3 the men are to be "full of the Spirit and of wisdom"; in Num 27:18 Joshua is a man "in whom there is spirit," and in Deut 34:9 Joshua is filled with the spirit of wisdom. (3) In Acts 6:3 the appointment is *epi tēs chreias tautēs*, "over this duty"; in Num 27:16 the appointment is *epi tēs sunagōgēs tautēs*, "over this assembly." (4) In Acts 6:6 the men were "made to stand" (*estēsan*) "before" (*enōpion*) the apostles; in Num 27:19 Joshua "shall stand before" (*stēseis enanti*) the people. (5) In Acts 6:6, they laid their hands on them (*epethēkan autois tas cheiras*); in Num 27:18,23 Moses laid his hands on him (*epithēseis tas cheiras sou ep'auton*).

24. Torrance, 238.

25. Warkentin, 136-142.

26. Lohse, 9:433.

27. Everett Ferguson, "Ordination in the Ancient Church, IV," *Restoration Quarterly* 5 (1961): 141.

28. Ibid., 140.

29. Warkentin, 174.

30. Ibid., 110.

31. Warkentin, 110.

PART TWO: ORDINATION IN EARLY CHRISTIANITY AND ADVENTISM

In relatively few centuries servant ministry by all believers in the New Testament gave place to a clear distinction between laity and clergy. Tracing this modification serves to highlight the unbiblical character of clergy privilege (chap. 5). At the birth of the Advent Movement, forms of church polity and pastoral leadership developed as the young church had need, often borrowing from other Christian bodies (chap. 6). For Seventh-day Adventists no theological study would be complete without an analysis of the writings of Ellen G. White on the topic; chapter 7 explores her understanding of ordination. Taking the Bible, history, and Ellen White into consideration, a Seventh-day Adventist theology of ordination is developed and set forth in chapter 8.

CHAPTER 5

CLERICAL AUTHORITY AND ORDINATION IN THE EARLY CHRISTIAN CHURCH

DANIEL A. AUGSBURGER

The study of the evolution of the concept of ordination is highly relevant at a time when traditional church institutional paradigms are under attack. The knowledge of the history of ordination and of the rise of ecclesiastical power can show whether those paradigms go back to the primitive church or reflect later and perhaps foreign religious influences. On another level, knowing the development of the idea of ordination can help us better understand the forces that shape and modify our rituals. For young Christians, weary of being spectators and eager to be involved in the church, a study of the development of church authority and ordination will show the degree to which laypeople in the early centuries participated in all aspects of church life.[1]

In the development of clerical authority we find three main stages. The first was a period of great involvement of all members in the service of the church, when baptism rather than ordination was the real license for work in the church. In a second stage, the bishop became monarchical and ordination expressed the legitimacy of his appointment and confidence in his orthodoxy and morality. With the imperial church and Augustine came the third stage, when ordination acquired a sacramental *character indelibilis*, "an indelible mark," attached forever to the person who had been ordained. With that third stage, clericalism, with its sharp distinction between ministry and laity, triumphed in the church. The clergy was considered to be endowed with a unique spiritual gift that set it totally apart from the laity, now looked upon as ignorant and morally unworthy. At that point ordination became a jealously guarded privilege that conferred immense prestige and authority.

The Nonclerical Climate of the Primitive Church

For the first generations of Christians, clericalism was out of the question because it conflicted with their view of the church, their concept of the ministry, and the role of the laypeople in the activities of the church. The church was a divine, not human, institution. It was Jesus' church and he was the authority. The term they chose to describe it, *ekklēsia*, designated in classical Greek the formal gathering of the people of a city as they exercised their rights as citizens. As used by the Jewish translators of the Old Testament, *ekklēsia* referred to the assembly of the people of God before their Lord, when they experienced the reality of being the Chosen People.

The adoption of the same term for their community revealed, as A. J. Mason says, "the audacity of their faith," that in Jesus a radically new Israel had been chosen.[2] They were the *ekklēsia tou theou*, the true people of God. Their community did not exist because of a blood relationship but because of a unity in the Spirit. A favorite metaphor was the body, of which Christ was the head and in which every member had equal importance. The *ekklēsia* was governed by the Spirit (see Acts 20:28). With that concept of a church there was little place for leaders endowed with institutional authority.

The True Christian Priesthood

The early Christians felt no need for human priests. They cherished the thought that their true high priest was Jesus Christ, who interceded for them in heaven and was far better than Jewish high priests. Polycarp (died ca. 156), for instance, referred to Christ as "the eternal and Heavenly High Priest."[3] Clement of Rome (bishop ca. 88-ca. 97) called Jesus "the High Priest who offers our gifts, the patron and helper in our weakness."[4]

There was, therefore, no need for sacrificial offerings. Justin Martyr (died ca. 163) summarized the feelings of the early Christians by saying that God "has no need of bloody sacrifices, libations, and incense. But we praise Him to the best of our power by prayer and thanksgiving for all our nourishment."[5] Irenaeus (ca. 115-ca. 202) told his readers that "God did not seek sacrifices and holocausts from them, but faith, and obedience, and righteousness because of their salvation." He explained, "The sacrifice to God is an afflicted heart, a sweet savour to God is a heart glorifying him who formed it."[6]

This rejection of the need for a human priesthood had important consequences for the early attitude toward ordination. By liberating themselves from the Old Testament pattern of worship, Christians were not tempted to copy the elaborate priestly ordinations of the Old Covenant. Without priests ordination became less significant.

The Priesthood of Believers

Because all Christians, Jews or Gentiles, could offer spiritual sacrifices, they were all priests. Justin Martyr wrote:

> Having been set on fire by the word of his calling, we are now of the true priestly family of God, as He Himself testifies, when He says that in every place among the Gentiles pure and pleasing sacrifices are offered up to Him. God receives sacrifices from no one, except through His priests.[7]

Irenaeus stated: "All who are justified through Jesus Christ have the sacerdotal order."[8] At the same time, the priesthood of believers was not a major topic of discussion in early Christianity.[9] The doctrine was probably taught most clearly in the writings of the Alexandrian Church Fathers, who derived their teaching from 1 Peter. "We have become a consecrated offering to God for Christ's sake," said Clement of Alexandria (ca. 160-215); "we are the chosen generation, the royal priesthood, the holy nation, the peculiar people, who once were not a people, but are now the people of God."[10]

Lay Participation in the Activities of the Church

The involvement of the lay people in the earlier days of the church was remarkable.[11] They were not passive spectators but participated in the liturgy, responding to the presiding minister and singing. They also brought gifts to the altar. Lay members also had a part in the teaching of orthodox doctrine. In the beginning, Ambrosiaster (late fourth century) tells us that before the bishops grasped for themselves the magisterial function of the church "everyone taught" the faith that was his.[12] *The Apostolic Constitutions* instructed: "Even if a teacher is a laic, still if he be skilled in the word and reverent in habit, let him teach."[13] In the late-second or early-third century, according to the *Apostolic Tradition*, a three-year process of religious instruction was prescribed. It ended with a laying on of hands, "whether the teacher be an ecclesiastic or a layman."[14]

Early Christians saw no objection to laypersons' baptizing. In the fourth century Ambrosiaster, author of the first Latin commentary on the Pauline epistles, stated that in the early days "everyone baptized."[15] Jerome, the translator of the Vulgate, affirmed that in his time (ca. 347-420), in remote places, laypeople often baptized.[16] However, as Tertullian (ca. 160-ca. 212) said, although believers had the right to baptize, it was unwise for laypeople to "assume functions that should be reserved to members of the clergy."[17] While laypersons might baptize, there is no evidence that they led out in the Eucharist.

Both the *Apostolic Tradition* and Cyprian (ca. 200-258) tell us how important the role of the laity was.[18] Until Constantine the laics elected the clergy. They also participated in church discipline. Polycarp of Smyrna believed that the laity and their presbyters had the right to discipline an unworthy presbyter.[19] Cyprian spoke of the role of the laity in the strongest terms; he had to persuade them, even "extort" from them the readmittance of separated schismatics.[20]

Laypeople actively shared their faith. Origen (ca. 185-ca. 251) described them in his work against Celsius, the pagan critic of Christianity, as going from village to village to spread the gospel at their own expense. Both men and women were engaged in witnessing.[21]

The ordination of the laypeople was their baptism. Tertullian explained what happened: "As we come forth from the laver, we are anointed with the holy unction, just as in the Old Dispensation priests were anointed with oil from the horn of the altar."[22]

Lack of References to Ordination in the Earliest Times

One must have in mind the foregoing picture of the spirit of the Early Church to understand the lack of references to ordination in those early centuries. As Catholic scholar Joseph Lécuyer writes,

> The data concerning the ritual of ordination of the ministers is extremely scarce in the first Christian generations. Especially the conviction of a unique relationship between the ritual—the laying on of hands—and a special gift from the Holy Spirit is essentially absent.[23]

The first Christian manual of church order, the *Didache*, gives information concerning church life in Syria at the end of the first century. Besides providing guidance for conducting baptism, the Lord's Supper, and Lord's Day worship, the *Didache* gives much attention to the treatment of traveling apostles and prophets. To them were to be given the first fruits of barns and fields, "for they are your high priests." The local congregations were urged to elect qualified bishops and deacons, "for their ministry to you is similar with that of the prophets and teachers."[24] Obviously the bishop was not the most prominent official and there is no reference to ordination in the *Didache*. There is no representation of ordination in early Christian art.[25]

Likewise, the Alexandrians did not put too much significance on ritual ordination. Clement of Alexandria, for instance, distinguished between two levels of hierarchy: a visible hierarchy that is manifested by the laying on of hands (*cheirotonia*) and the real hierarchy, that of holiness, of those who follow in the steps of the apostles to live in the perfection of righteousness according to the gospel.[26] Origen notes the dignity of ecclesiastical orders, but affirms that true dignity consists in being virtuous.[27]

There are no references to the ordination of clergy in documents where it would be most natural to expect them. For instance, Clement, bishop of Rome at the end of the first century, wrote to the church at Corinth, where some laypeople had rebelled against their bishop. Clement rebuked their lack of concern for proper church order by reminding them that nature and Scriptures teach that order is indispensable; the apostles themselves had appointed bishops and deacons. At that point it would have seemed proper to remind the Corinthians of the special badge of authority given to those leaders by ordaining them, but nothing is said.

The concern for church order is a key theme in the letters of Ignatius of Antioch, written to the churches of Asia Minor in the early-second century. The essence of the church was unity, which reflected the unity between Father and Son, and between Christ and his apostles. On earth the instrument of that unity was the bishop. In a well known passage of his *Letter to the Smyrnaeans*, Ignatius goes so far as to say: "You should all follow the bishop as Jesus did the Father. Follow, too, the presbytery as you would the apostles; and respect the deacons as you would God's law."[28] Here ordination could well have been mentioned, but it is not. Hans von Campenhausen states: "In all the first three centuries of the Church not a single bishop appealed to his consecration to claim for the clergy a privileged position as priests as against the laity."[29]

The idea of the chain of faithful transmitters of the truth appealed to Irenaeus, who was linked to the apostle John through Polycarp, the martyr. In his discussion of apostolic succession, Irenaeus states that the tradition from the apostles could be discovered in every church and that it was possible to reckon those who were instituted bishops by the apostles and their successors down to his own times. Yet there is not the least suggestion that the "secure gift of truth" was passed on by a continuity of ordinations.[30]

Ordination at the End of the Second Century

Tertullian

Tertullian, who wrote at the end of the second century, did not provide a description of ordination but showed that there was already a ministerial class, an *ordo*, a term that he liked because it expressed the idea of the holiness and majesty of the ministerial office. In his attempt to keep *ordo* and *plebs* within their proper realms, Tertullian thundered against the heretics who did not recognize the distinction between catechumens and baptized members, and between baptized members and clergy.

From his criticisms of the ordinations of the heretics we can deduce some of the characteristics of the ritual in his time in North Africa.

> Their ordinations [of the heretics] are hasty, irresponsible and unstable. Sometimes, they appoint novices, sometimes men tied to secular office, sometimes renegades from us. . . . So one man is bishop today, another tomorrow. The deacon of today is tomorrow's reader, the priest of today is tomorrow a layman.[31]

This passage suggests that appointments to office in the orthodox churches were not temporary and that novices could not be included in the ministerial ranks. It brings out the difference between the charismatic approach of the heretics and the orderly decisions of the orthodox.

Tertullian's insisted on monogamy for the *ordo sacerdotalis*. If a priest remarried after his wife died, he lost his place in that *ordo*.[32] Ordination could be revoked for breaking the rules of the church.[33] There was no indelible mark, an important aspect of ordination in later times.

The Apostolic Tradition

Around the beginning of the third century, detailed instructions for the ordination service appear in the *Apostolic Tradition* of Hippolytus (ca. 170-236).

In his *Refutation of All Heresies*, Hippolytus affirmed that the gifts of the Spirit had been passed on from the apostles "to men of orthodox belief." He said: "We are their successors, and share in the same gifts of high priesthood and teaching; we are numbered among the guardians of the Church, and for that reason we neither close our eyes nor keep silent as to the right teaching."[34] Although the argument of the superiority of the orthodox ministry is identical to that of Irenaeus or Tertullian, the tone of the third-century Father is different. The emphasis on *we*, with the claims of knowledge and authority, is quite different from the emphasis found previously. Hippolytus compared himself to the high priests of Israel and included himself among the guardians of the church.

Gregory Dix states that "it is now generally recognized that the *Apostolic Tradition* of St. Hippolytus is the most illuminating single source of evidence extant on the inner life and religious polity of the early Christian Church."[35] The ordination ritual in the *Apostolic Tradition* shows that the eucharistic service had become the heart of the priestly function. The *cheirotonia*, the laying on of hands, was now strictly reserved for those who participated in the eucharistic service. This is apparent in the instructions for the institution of the widows.

> Let the widow be instituted [*kathistatai*] by word only and then let her be reckoned among the [enrolled] widows. But she shall not be ordained [*cheirotonetai*] because she does not offer the oblation nor has she a [liturgical] ministry [*leitourgia*]. . . . But the ordination [*cheirotonia*] is for the clergy [*kleros*] on account of the liturgical ministry.[36]

The *katastasis* allowed for the widows came from the traditional Greco-Roman ceremony for investing a public official. No pagan equivalent of the *cheirotonia*, laying on of hands, can be found in the classical world. It was derived from the ordination of Jewish priests and implied the endowment of a special grace that enabled a priest to perform his service.

The term *leitourgia* in classical Greek described the performance of a special honorific service for the state, such as, for instance, outfitting a warship or providing a choir for a theatrical performance at a major ceremony. The honor dimension was important to that term. By the second century B.C. the word was used in popular language for priestly service in the worship of the gods. In the Septuagint it was used for the Hebrew *sharath* to designate participation in the divine worship, either as a officiant or as an worshiper. While in the New Testament the more common term for serving is *diakonia*, by Hippolytus' time *leitourgia* and *munus* were the accepted terms for the performance of Christian worship, especially the Eucharist. These words conveyed the idea of the prestige of the one who could officiate in the church service.[37]

The ordination of the bishop was much more elaborate than that of the presbyters or deacons and included several important steps. First was the election and confirmation of the new bishop, who was chosen by "all the people." Later the choice was confirmed "by all the people being assembled on the Lord's day together with the presbytery and such bishops as may attend." In the ordination prayer that followed, however, the bishop was clearly "the one whom Thou didst choose." Thus it was taken for granted that the decision of all the people was the expression of the divine will.[38]

Under the guidance of the Holy Spirit the bishop was elected and confirmed by the whole community; he was God's gift to his people in a particular location. The bishop was the living witness to the orthodox tradition, and bound the church to its roots, the apostles and Christ. A bishop gave his whole life to one congregation and his transfer to another church was extremely rare and raised much criticism.

The collective selection of the bishop by all the people found a ritual expression in the laying on of hands by the participating bishops, while the congregation in absolute silence was to pray "in their hearts for the descent of the Spirit." After studying the topic carefully from the linguistic and historical standpoints, Everett Ferguson concludes that

> the basic idea in early Christian laying on of hands was not creating a substitute or transferring authority, but conferring a blessing and petitioning for the divine favour. Blessing, of course, in ancient thought was more than a kindly wish; it was thought of as imparting something very definite (as in the patriarchal blessings of the Old Testament). "Hand" in biblical usage was symbolic of power. The laying on of hands accompanied prayer in Christian usage. It was essentially an enacted prayer, and the prayer spelled out the grace which God was asked to bestow. As an act of blessing, it was considered to effect that for which the prayer was uttered.[39]

The conferring of episcopal authority was made effective by another laying on of hands by the bishop who offered the consecration prayer. In it the duties of the bishop were delineated.

> Father who knowest the hearts, grant upon this Thy servant whom Thou hast chosen for the episcopate to feed Thy holy flock and serve as Thine high priest, that he may minister blamelessly by night and day, that he may unceasingly propitiate Thy Countenance and offer to Thee the gifts of Thy holy Church.
>
> And that by the high priestly Spirit he may have authority to forgive sins according to Thy command, to assign lots according to Thy

bidding, to loose every bond according to the authority Thou gavest to
the Apostles, and that he may please Thee in meekness and a pure heart,
offering to Thee a sweet saving savour.[40]

This prayer presents the bishop as a shepherd and priest. As a shepherd
the bishop represented God in the church, but as a priest he represented
the people, propitiating the divine countenance and offering to God the
gifts of the congregation. This insistence on the priestly duties of the
shepherd is significant. The document contains no reference to
administrative responsibilities or teaching ministry of the bishop. The
ordination centered around his liturgical functions, especially the offering
of the Eucharist and his penitential authority.

By Hippolytus' time the bishop was believed to be related to the
apostles, not by a succession of people who taught the truth but by the
transmission of the gift of a princely Spirit. The ordination prayer
implored God: "Pour forth that power which is from Thee, of the princely Spirit which Thou didst deliver to Thy beloved child Jesus Christ,
which He bestowed on Thy holy Apostles who established the church."[41]

These functions of the bishop in the *Apostolic Tradition* reflected
the deep changes that had come into Christianity: the metamorphosis of
the Eucharist into a sacrifice offered by the bishop and the transformation
of the *episkopos* (overseer) into a priest. The Eucharist took on a new
significance; no longer a supper, it became a sacrifice offered to God.[42]

Of course, this transformation of the congregational leader into a
priest contradicted the early Christians' boast that they had broken away
from the Jewish sacrificial system, that their high priest Jesus was far
superior to the Jewish high priest, and their spiritual sacrifices of prayer
and good works far better than the carnal offerings of the Jews. Eventually, however, they would draw relationships between their ministers
and the Israelite priesthood. Just as the high priest was the head of the
religious establishment, so now the bishop as a priest was the head of the
local church.[43]

The ordination prayer reflected the importance of the disciplinary
duties of the bishop. In the beginning, when utter rigorism ruled, there
was only one chance of repentance after baptism. Later, as the penitential
system developed, the bishop needed special authority to assign the
penance and to determine when the penance had been completed and the
sin could be forgiven. Apostolic succession became the handing down
from generation to generation of bishops, of the power that Jesus had
given Peter to bind and loosen. The power of the keys of the kingdom

now took on its full importance and gave the bishops immense prestige.

Language reflected this change. In the vocabulary of the apostolic age there was no specific term to designate those who had sacred rights.[44] Only in the third century did the word *clerus* (clergy) come into use (as contrasted with *plebs*), as a neologism from the Greek *kleros*, with a clear Levitical connotation.[45] Also in the same period the term *sacerdos* (priest), in the early period reserved for Christ, was applied to the clergy.

The *Apostolic Tradition* also gave instructions for the ordination of presbyters and deacons. At a presbyter's ordination the bishop had the leading role in the laying on of hands, but the other presbyters also placed their hands on him. The first part of the ordination prayer for a bishop was used but the second part, describing the responsibilities of the bishop, was replaced by a request for "the spirit of grace and counsel," that the presbyter might "share in the activities of the presbyterate and govern the people with a pure heart."[46]

The next paragraph refers to the setting apart of presbyters. They were to be "fellow counselors" who shared in the "Spirit of greatness" common to all the clergy. The *Apostolic Tradition* made it clear that the presbyters could not give holy orders. Hands were laid on a new presbyter, not to receive him into the clergy, but merely to bless while the bishop ordained.[47]

At his ordination, only the bishop laid hands on the deacon. The *Tradition* justifies the difference by stating that the deacon was not ordained for the priesthood but to serve the bishop. His function was to report to the bishop on the members who were sick so that he might visit them, to be the custodian of the property of the church, and to report what should be done. The ordination prayer requested for him "the Spirit of grace and earnestness and diligence."[48] This emphasis on different spirits given the bishop, the presbyters, and the deacons shows ordination was to a function rather than for the reception of a unique grace.

Special treatment was given confessors. Section 10 of the *Apostolic Tradition* states that there is no need to lay hands on a person who has been in chains for the name of Jesus, "for he has the office of the presbyterate by his confession. But if he be appointed bishop, hands shall be laid on him."[49] Hands need not be laid on a person who demonstrated the gift of healing,[50] the evident spiritual gift made ordination unnecessary. Thus we may conclude that an important aspect of ordination was the legitimatization of the authority of the bishop.

The Exclusion of Women from Ordination

One might expect that Christians would have treated women quite differently than did their contemporaries. On several occasions Jesus had shown the spiritual capacities of women and, under inspiration, the apostles uttered principles that should have revolutionized relations between men and women. In practice, however, the early Christians found it difficult to allow the lofty ideals of their faith to overcome the blinding power of their cultures. They shared the negative stereotypes and prejudices of their Jewish and pagan neighbors, which they often bolstered by erroneously applied biblical references.[51] Without notable exceptions, they believed that women were inferior beings, sensual and incapable of resisting temptation. Tertullian waxed eloquent about woman's guilt: "You are the devil's gateway; you are the violator of the tree; you are the first deserter of God's law. You are the one who duped him whom the devil was not powerful enough to assault."[52] Irenaeus argued that Eve was not made in the image of God but in the image of man. She was the cause of death.[53]

Celsus, to whom Irenaeus addressed his defense of Christianity, could not have found a more disparaging thing to say than that it was a women's religion. According to Celsus, Mary Magdalene, a hysterical woman who said that she saw Jesus after the resurrection, was the true founder of that faith.[54]

Pagans were especially hostile to women who had abandoned the public state religion and were active in private cults. Private religious cults, it was believed, were cesspools of immorality. In his *Golden Ass*, Lucius Apuleius, a North African Latin writer of the early-second century, described what most critics think is a Christian woman, revealing how pagans felt toward them. This description is put in the mouth of an ass:

> The baker who purchased me was otherwise a good and very modest man but his wife was the wickedest of all women and he suffered extreme miseries to his bed and his house so that I myself, by Hercules, often in secret felt pity for him. There was not a single vice which that woman lacked, but all crimes flowed together into her heart like into a filthy latrine: cruel, perverse, man-crazy, drunken, stubborn, obstinate, avaricious in petty theft, wasteful in sumptuous expenses, an enemy to faith and chastity, she also despised the gods and instead of a certain [traditional] religion she claimed to worship a god whom she called "only." In his house she practiced empty rites and ceremonies and

she deceived all men and her miserable husband, drinking unmixed wine early in the morning and giving her body to continual whoring.[55]

Christianity was seen as a woman's religion because in the house churches the women in whose homes the new congregations met assumed much of the leadership of those communities. This was normal since the house was the proper realm of the wife in Greco-Roman society, but it conflicted with the strong conviction that wives should share the religion of their husbands. With such biases toward women it is not surprising that to respect what was thought to be the will of God and nature, and in order not to scandalize the pagan neighbors, the church eliminated women from leading in the *leitourgia*. Obviously ordination could not even be considered.

Cyprian and Ordination

The middle of the third century was difficult for the church. In the early part of the century several emperors had shown favor to Christianity. This resulted in a rapid growth of the church and the influx of members who did not have the staunch commitment to Christ of previous generations of Christians. But the climate changed. In April 247, the empire celebrated its one thousand years. This event aroused a great deal of nationalism and xenophobia, in particular against the foreign beliefs that competed with traditional religion. Christians who, as could be expected, had abstained from the pagan patriotic festivals were treated with hostility.

A year later the Gothic invasions began, leading to a greater need for soldiers. As the Christians did not serve in the army, they became an extra burden in the struggle. After his victory over the Goths, the emperor Decius (249-251) passed an edict requiring everyone to sacrifice to the gods of the empire and obtain a *libellus* or certificate of completed sacrifice. As the Christians refused to comply, Decius launched a systematic persecution. Questions were also raised about the validity of baptism and ordination they performed after returning to the church but before being officially reconciled.

Valerius, successor of Decius, was even more severe. He forbade Christian worship meetings and singled out the clergy for execution. Some bishops fled; others yielded to government demand. Some, trying to soothe their consciences and save their lives, bought certificates from venial officials. All those who yielded in some way were called *lapsi*.

After the persecutions, throngs of *lapsi* returned to the church, begging to be readmitted. The problem was especially grave with bishops, whose apostasy raised questions concerning the validity of their previous ordination.

In this difficult context Cyprian's writing on ordination was mainly concerned with the validity of ordinations. His was a juridic perspective. As Lécuyer says, he thought in terms of rights and legitimacy.[56] Cyprian's attitude is stamped in expressions such as: "We say that heretics and schismatics anywhere have neither the authority nor the right to baptize."[57] For Cyprian, ordination was the visible expression of the approval of a bishop by the church. For that reason participation of the whole church, including the lay members, in the ordination service was indispensable as a guarantee of legitimacy. His *Epistle 67* tells us how elections were conducted:

> For which reason you must diligently observe and keep the practice delivered from divine tradition and apostolic observance, which is also maintained among us, and almost throughout all the provinces; that for the proper celebration of ordination all the neighbouring bishops of the same province should assemble with that people for which the prelate is ordained. And the bishop should be chosen in the presence of the people who have most fully known the life of each one as respects his habitual conduct.[58]

Priests who had received ordination and later apostatized could, if they repented, be readmitted only as lay people. They could no longer exercise their ministry.[59]

While ordination was most important, it is clear that for Cyprian it bestowed no indelible character on the recipient and could be lost.

Ordination at the Council of Nicea

At the Council of Nicea (325), ordination was a burning issue because the assembly had to deal with several heresies, the best known of which was Arianism. Because the Arians reordained orthodox priests and rebaptized church members who joined them, the problem of rebaptism and of the validity of ordination loomed large.

The council took the position that a bishop who returned to the church had to be reordained. The ordination of schismatics was valid, but orthodox ordinations took precedence. Thus a reconciled Arian bishop could not claim his position in a church where there was already an orthodox bishop; he had to be satisfied to be a priest.

Canons 15 and 16 prohibited a member of the clergy from moving from one church to another. In fact, a cleric who refused to return to his own church should be excommunicated. If a bishop ordained someone in the diocese of another bishop without the latter's permission, the ordination was not valid.

Canons 1, 2, 10, 17 shed light on the delegates' understanding of ordination. They all deal with the fate of clerics deposed because of moral turpitude. A clergyman who was a usurer lost his position. Voluntary eunuchs and gross sinners were excluded for life from the service of the church. Once again we find no hint of any indelible mark left by ordination.[60]

Dynamic Concept of Ordination

The Council of Nicea did not silence the controversies about the nature of Christ. To make things worse, because of the imperial involvement in the debates, what was heresy one day became accepted doctrine the following. Thus bishops were deposed and banished. The most famous of these was Athanasius (ca. 296-373), whose career was a sequence of banishments and returns to the episcopal throne. This, of course, gave a new urgency to the issues of baptism administered by heretics and the validity of their ordination. Thus, in the fourth century a dynamic understanding of ordination became quite common: ordination gave the cleric a spiritual power different from the normal action of the Holy Spirit.

The Cappadocian Fathers

The problem of the validity of heretical baptisms and ordination was considered by the Cappadocian Fathers. All of them affirmed that ordination confers a spiritual capacity that transforms the person.

Gregory of Nyssa (335?-394?), younger brother of the famous Basil of Nyssa, presented a clear statement on the dynamic power of ordination. In his sermon, *The Day of Lights* or *On Christ's Baptism*, Gregory pointed out that baptismal water, which is the same as any other water, and the stones with which the altar is built, which are totally the same as any other stones, become different because they have been put to a sacred use. This was especially true of the bread and the wine of the Eucharist, not different from other bread and wine, but powerful agents when God has sanctified them. He then wrote:

It is the same power of the Word that makes the priest august and venerable, separated from the common people by his new blessing. Yesterday still, he was only one among many others; and now suddenly he is a leader, a president, a doctor of piety, an initiator to the hidden mysteries. This happens without any change to his appearance or his body. According to the external appearances he remains what he was but his invisible soul has been transformed by an invisible virtue and grace into an eminent individual.[61]

Ordination at Antioch

Toward the end of the fourth century Antioch also had to deal with a complex schism that raised the same questions concerning the validity of baptism and ordinations. The homilies of John Chrysostom (ca. 350-407), the eloquent orator, contain interesting views on ordination. In *Homily on Pentecost* he distinguished sharply between the human spirit and the divine agent that acts in the ordained minister:

If there were no Holy Spirit there would not be any pastors or doctors in the church for they become what they are by the power of the Spirit. . . . When you answer [the pastor's gift of peace] by "with your Spirit," you bring to your memory the fact that the one who is visibly present produces nothing, that the gifts that are present are not the result of human nature, but that it is the grace of the Spirit coming in and covering all with its wings that accomplishes the mystical sacrifice.[62]

This "mystical sacrifice" takes place at ordination when the grace of ordination is added to that of baptism. Speaking of Stephen, described as a person full of faith and Holy Spirit, John Chrysostom said: "Before [the laying on of hands] he did not perform any miracles . . . so that one might know that regular grace is not sufficient, but that you must also have the *cheirotonia* so that there is an increase of the Spirit. The Spirit that he had before, he had received it at his baptism."[63]

In his discussion of 2 Tim 1:6-7, Chrysostom emphasized that the fire kindled at the time of the ordination could be extinguished (1 Thess 5:19): "It is up to us that this charisma should burn out or that it should burn brightly. . . . By lazyness [*sic*] or negligence it burns out. By vigilance and attention it is revived."[64] Thus ordination does not provide an indelible character to the clergy.

In the *Apostolic Constitutions*, a Syrian ordination liturgy from around 380 attributes different aspects of the ritual to different apostles. The rules for the *cheirotonia* of the bishop are given by Peter; those for the *cheirotonia* of the presbyters by the apostle John. The *Constitutions*, emphasize that the ceremony goes back to Moses, was used for Jesus himself, and was employed by the Lord for his disciples. The different documents also agree in proclaiming that ordination involves more than an appointment to a function. It confers a charisma, a special gift of the Spirit.

A characteristic feature of the ordination of the bishop in the *Apostolic Constitutions* is that while the presiding bishop, assisted by two other bishops, offers the ordination prayer, the other bishops and the presbyters pray silently, as the deacons hold open divine Gospels over the head of the one who is ordained. Severian of Gabalda (died ca. 408) provides an explanation of what takes place. The apostles already had received a first ordination from Jesus, but the ordination on the day of Pentecost transformed them into high priests. That ordination ritual should also remind the bishop who was ordained that even after ordination he must submit to a higher authority.[65]

Ordination in Egypt

Because the bishops of Egypt, especially Cyril of Alexandria (died 444), were so involved in the struggle against Nestorius and Chrysostom, they were forced to consider the issues raised by ordination. Through his typological view of Scriptures, Cyril found in the Mosaic priesthood a typology of the Christian ministry. Commenting on the ordination of Aaron and his sons in Lev 8:6, Cyril stated:

> But our Lord Jesus Christ transformed the figures of the Law into the power of truth and [now] it is by himself that he consecrates the priests of the divine altars. For he is himself the victim who operates the consecration, by making participants of his own nature by the communication of the Spirit, and by reshaping in some way the nature of the man into the power and the glory that are far beyond man.[66]

The gift of a special spiritual power is underlined: "It is a rich gift of spiritual charismas that is given those who must lead the peoples."[67]

For Cyril of Alexandria the gift granted at ordination sharply distinguished clergy from laity. Yet this spiritual endowment could be lost, especially by falling into heresy. Both points can be seen in his retort to Atticus, patriarch of Constantinople (406-425), who had restored Chrysostom to his bishopric to please the people.

> How could you name a layman among the bishops or among the legitimate bishops he who is not? . . . It is absolutely improper to topple

from top to bottom the laws of the church by placing a layperson among those who belong to the ministry and to place on the same level of honor . . . him who has been deposed from the episcopate.[68]

We have ordination prayers from Egypt in a *Sacramentary* written by Athanasius' friend Serapion, bishop of Thmuis, in the Nile delta, about 339. The title is significant: *Laying on of Hands and Installation of the Deacons or the Presbyters or the Bishops.* In Egypt in the fourth century, because the laying on of hands was identified with the sacramental gift, the *installatio*, or formal granting of authority in a church, became very important. The prayer shows clearly the dynamic dimension of consecration:

> You who from generation to generation ordain (*cheirotoneō*) holy bishops; please, O God of truth, make this man a zealous bishop, a holy bishop who belongs in the succession of the holy apostles and give him the divine grace and spirit that you granted to all your true servants, and prophets and patriarchs; make him worthy of leading your flock and let him persevere without reproach and without damage in the episcopate.[69]

The reference to the place of the bishop in the succession of the apostles is significant. This succession is no longer made up of people who faithfully fought for the truth against heresy, but of people who have been bishops. By communicating to an individual divine grace and spirit, the unique spiritual endowment of bishops, ordination makes him worthy of his place in that succession.

Ordination as a "character indelibilis"

The ideas of Augustine of Hippo (354-430) regarding ordination were expressed in the context of the bitter controversy with the Donatists. In 312 Cecilianus, bishop of Carthage, was accused of having been ordained by a bishop who during the persecutions of Diocletian had been a *traditor*, one who surrendered the sacred writings to the persecutors. Although his opponents were not able to prove their charges, they loudly rejected him because of their belief that a bishop who had yielded during persecution had lost his ordination. The controversy grew heated and violent in North Africa and eventually led to terrorism. At a council in Rome in 313, Donatus, leader of the schism, was condemned.

Obviously influenced by Cyprian, whom he often quoted,

Augustine was concerned with the legitimacy aspect of baptism and ordination. His thesis was that a sacrament never loses its value. In his book *On Baptism*, written around 400, he stated his position clearly:

> And as the baptized person, if he depart from the unity of the Church, does not thereby lose the sacrament of baptism, so also he who is ordained, if he depart from the unity of the church does not lose the sacrament of conferring baptism. For neither sacrament may be wronged."[70]

In his *Reply to Parmenian*, written a few years later, he repeated the same ideas even more forcefully:

> One cannot give any reason why he who cannot lose his baptism can lose the right to give it. Both, indeed, are sacraments and both are given man by a special consecration [*consecratione*], whether when he is baptized or when he is ordained [*ordinatur*]. That is the reason why it is forbidden in the Catholic Church to repeat either. Indeed, if at times, even bishops who have returned from Donatism, after correcting their error of supporting a schism, were received to foster peace, even if it felt important that they exercise the same functions that they had performed, they were not re-ordained. Just like baptism, ordination in them remained intact. The flaw was in the separation, which the unity of peace has corrected, not in the sacraments which remain what they are wherever they are found. And when the church finds it expedient that their bishops, joining the Catholic unity, should not perform their tasks, the sacraments of ordination are just the same not withdrawn from them, but remain in them.[71]

Augustine used several illustrations of the indelible nature of baptism and ordination. He likened baptism to the mark that was imprinted upon the forehead of a Roman soldier[72] or the owner's mark on sheep.[73] In the *Reply to Parmenian*, Augustine speaks of a "royal sign" and the mark (*character*) of the army on the soldier's body, a term which eventually was included in the theological formula *character indelibilis*.[74]

Augustine's understanding of the permanence of the ordination sacrament must be seen in light of his understanding of the church. It was holy because of the holiness of Christ in which it participates. Therefore, its sacrament could never be defiled.

Conclusion

While this study is far from exhaustive, it brings out some important points. The first generations of Christians knew nothing about an essential spiritual distinction between clergy and laypeople. The laics were involved in all the activities of the church and the function of presbyters or bishops was to direct worship and keep order in the church. In the early days of house worship, the lady of the house had a prominent part in the leadership of the church that met at her place. The clergy was ordained, it seems, but little attention was given to ordination, even when polemics about apostolic succession would have warranted an appeal to the ordination of orthodox ministers. No language existed to express a difference between laypeople and clergy.

From the beginning of the third century, a clear distinction was made between church officers who offered the Eucharist and those who did not. Bishops and presbyters became priests: those who exercised the sacrificial function needed ordination.

The involvement of the laity in the choosing and ordination of clergy practically disappeared by the fourth century. In the *Apostolic Constitutions*, they merely repeated their consent three times. In the later *Testament of Our Lord,* laypeople only uttered the word "Worthy" three times. While lay participation lasted longer in the West than in the East—Augustine and Ambrose were both raised to the episcopacy by the acclamation of the people—there, too, it was lost. The triumph of clericalism reduced the laypeople to noninvolvement. The laity became spectators. The machine replaced the Spirit.

In the early centuries ordination was considered to give a special spiritual blessing, but that gift could be lost. It did not remain with the ordained person regardless of his conduct. Later, Augustine made ordination into a sacrament, an irrevocable gift that left an indelible mark on the one who received it.

The exaltation of ordination came together with radical changes in the church after the conversion of Constantine. The bishops now had immense prestige.

By the middle of the fourth century the clergy was identified publicly by distinctive vestments; by the end of that century the tonsure, inherited from the Egyptian monks, became the outward reminder of the laying on of hands on the ministers. The bishop's teaching chair in the cathedral turned into a veritable throne. The most exalted language was used for the priests. According to Chrysostom, priests were entrusted with the stewardship of things in heaven, and had received an authority which "God had given neither to angels nor to archangels." Narsai, head of the Nestorian school at Edessa (437-457), compared the experience of the priest who offered the Eucharist to that of Isaiah when he had his vision of the heavenly tabernacle. Narsai found the priest an object of awe even for the Seraphim, and described him as follows: "O corporal being, that carries fire and is not scorched! O mortal, who being mortal, does distribute life! Who has permitted thee, miserable dust, to take hold of fire! and who has made thee to distribute life, thou son of paupers."[75]

By mid-fourth century the bishops had taken over the power to preach and the authority to judge Christians. Eventually, after bitter conflicts, the clergy was freed from all secular control. Clericalism had triumphed.

What can the church learn from history? Ordination can easily become the expression of clericalism, which always brings impoverishment to the church. The more we distinguish between the clergy and the people, the less the people care about the well-being of the church. As long as church members talk about the church as "they' rather than "we," they put the whole burden of the fulfilment of the task upon the ministers. The church can be healthy only as long as all, laypeople and clergy, feel they are members of a body. The essential qualification for the task is the endowment of the Holy Spirit, not ordination.

There is no support in early Christian history for an ordination attached to the person of the minister rather than to his mission. Thus Adventist ordination that is valid worldwide reflects a later, Augustinian concept of ordination. If ordination is the expression of the church's confidence in a person selected for a mission, it can be given to all to whom the church entrusts a mission, women as well men. Ordination need not be limited to those who stand in the pulpit.

In its early-Christian sense, ordination cannot be considered a symbol of power. Instead, it is the symbol of spiritual empowerment and recognition by the church body. Any other understanding is not based on the New Testament or the early Christian Church.

Endnotes

1. "Ordain" and "ordination" are words derived from the Latin *ordinare* and *ordinatio*. The root of these two words is *ordo*. In the popular tongue, *ordo* belonged to the weaving trade. It designated the order of the thread in a woof. Thus at its very root it conveyed the notion of orderly arrangement. The term acquired a corporate sense, "the orderly grouping of people." The Senate was called *ordo amplissimus*. In religion it applied to the college of the priests of a temple. In Christian writing *ordo* referred to the members of the ministry and often was contrasted with *plebs*, "the common people," and *laicos*, "the

laypeople." *Ordo, ordinare and ordinatio* appear first in Tertullian. As he was the first Latin Christian writer, it is difficult to know whether he introduced the words into church language or whether they were already in use. Pierre van Beneden has carefully gathered and studied every use of those terms in Christian literature till 313 (Pierre van Beneden *Aux Origines d'une terminologie sacramentelle: Ordinare, Ordinatio dans la littérature chrétienne avant 313*, Spicilegium sacrum Lovaniense: Etudes et documents 38 [Louvain: Spicilegium Sacrum Lovaniense], 1974).

2. A. J. Mason, "Concept of the Church in Early Times," in *Church, Ministry, and Organization in the Early Church Era*, Studies in Early Christianity 13, ed. Everett Ferguson (New York: Garland, 1993), 7.

3. Polycarp *Martyrdom of Polycarp* 14.3.

4. Clement 1 *Clement* 36.1.

5. Justin Martyr *First Apology* 13.

6. Justin Martyr *Against Heretics* 4.17:2, 4.

7. Justin Martyr *Dialogue with Trypho* 116.

8. Irenaeus *Against Heresies* 4.8.3.

9. James L. Garrett, Jr., "The Pre-Cyprianic Doctrine of the Priesthood of All Christians," in *Church, Ministry, and Organization*, 253. See also I. Ryan, "Patristic Teaching on the Priesthood of the Believers," *The Irish Theological Quarterly* 29 (1962): 25-51.

10. Clement *Exhortation to the Heathen* 4; see also Origen *Homily on Leviticus* 9.3.

11. See George H. Williams, "The Role of the Laymen in the Ancient Church," in *Church, Ministry and Organization*, 271-304.

12. Ambrosiaster *Commentary on Ephesians*. 4.12.3. In the list of gifts in Eph 4, "doctors" are included. These were probably those who led in the prebaptismal teaching. According to the ordination manuals, these were not ordained; we have good ground to believe they were lay people. See A. Turck, "Aux Origines du catéchuménat," in *Conversion, Catechumenate, and Baptism in the Early Church*, Studies in Early Christianity 11, ed. Everett Ferguson (New York: Garland, 1993), 266-287.

13. *Apostolic Constitutions* 8.31 the source of this may have been as early as the first decades of the third century.

14. *Apostolic Traditions* 17.

15. Ambrosiaster *Commentary on Ephesians* 4.11.

16. Jerome *Dialogue against Lucifer* 9.

17. Tertullian *On Baptism* 17.

18. Hans von Campenhausen, *Ecclesiastical Authority and Spiritual Power in the Church of the First Three Centuries*, trans. J. A. Baker (Stanford, CA: Stanford Univ. Press, 1969), 273-275.

19. Polycarp *Martyrdom of Polycarp 44.*

20. Cyprian *Letter* 59.15.

21. Origen *Against Celsus,* 3.9.

22. Tertullian *On Baptism 7.*

23. Joseph Lécuyer, *Le Sacrement de l'ordination: Recherche historique et théologique,* Théologie historique, vol. 65 (Paris: Beauchesne, 1983), 21.

24. *Didache* 13, 15.

25. L. de Bruyne, "L'Imposition des mains dans l'art chrétien ancien," *Rivista di archeologia cristiana* 20 (1943): 119.

26. Clement *Stromata* 6 and 13, 106-107.

27. Quoted in Lécuyer, 34, 35.

28. Ignatius *To the Smyrnaeans* 8.1, 2.

29. Hans von Campenhausen, *Tradition and Life in the Church. Essays in Church History,* trans. A. V. Littledale (Philadelphia: Fortress, 1968), 222.

30. Irenaeus *Against Heresies* 3.3.1; 4.26.2.

31. Tertullian *Prescriptions against Heretics* 41.

32. Tertullian *Exhortation to Chastity* 7.2.

33. For a collection of ordination rituals of the early church, see Paul F. Bradshaw, *Ordination Rites of the Ancient Churches of East and West* (New York: Pueblo, 1990).

34. Hippolytus Preface to *Refutation.*

35. Gregory Dix, ed., *The Treatise on the Apostolic Tradition of St. Hippolytus of Rome* (London: S P C K, 1937), 1:11. The Greek original of the *Apostolic Tradition* has been lost, but the text is found in a Latin codex at Verona. Many of its provisions have been included in later documents. The *Egyptian Church Order* provides the best Eastern text of the *Apostolic Tradition.*

36. *Apostolic Tradition* 11. 4, 5.

37. Gregory Dix, *Le ministère dans l'église ancienne,* trans. A. Jaermann and R. Paquier (Neuchatel: Delachaux Niestlé, 1955), 26-29.

38. In the fourth-century *Apostolic Constitutions,* the people were asked three times whether the candidate was worthy to be a bishop (8.4.2).

39. Everett Ferguson, "Laying on of Hands: Its Significance in Ordination," in *Church, Ministry and Organization,* 148 There were six or seven laying on of hands during a baptism. Wrote Cyprian: "The baptized obtain the Holy Spirit by our prayers and imposition of hands" (*Epistle 72.9*). A laying on of hands was the final step of the reconciliation of the penitents, where it replaced rebaptism.

40. *Apostolic Tradition* 3.4, 5.

41. Jaroslav Pelikan, *The Emergence of the Catholic Tradition*, vol. 1, *The Christian Tradition: A History of the Development of Doctrine* (Chicago: Univ. of Chicago Press, 1971), 170.

42. Eventually the idea of sacrifice was more clearly defined by Cyprian who, according to J.N.D. Kelly was the first to clearly espouse that concept (J.N.D. Kelly, *Early Christian Doctrine*, 2d ed. [New York: Harper and Row, 1960], 215); cf. Pelikan, 169.

43. Willy Rordorf, "La théologie du ministère dans l'église ancienne," *Church, Ministry, and Organization in the Early Church Era* 97.

44. A. Michel, "Ordre, ordination," *Dictionnaire de Théologie Catholique* (Paris: Letouzey et Ané, 1923-1972).

45. "Order and Ordination," *Sacramentum Mundi*, 4:305-306.

46. *Apostolic Tradition* 8.2.

47. Ibid., 9.3, 4, 7, 8.

48. Ibid., 9.2, 3, 11.

49. Ibid., 10.1.

50. Ibid., 10.15.

51. J. Kevin Coyle, "The Fathers on Women and Women's Ordination," in *Women in Early Christianity*, Studies in Early Christianity, vol. 14 (New York: Garland, 1993), 117-167.

52. Tertullian *The Apparel of Women* 1.1.2.

53. Irenaeus *Against Heresies* 3.23.2; 3.22.4.

54. Origen *Against Celsus* 2.55; 3.55; Margaret Y. MacDonald, *Early Christian Women and Pagan Opinion* (Cambridge: Cambridge Univ. Press, 1996), 49-126. See also Ross S. Kraemer, *Her Share of the Blessing: Women's Religions among Pagans, Jews and Christians in the Greco-Roman World* (Oxford: Oxford Univ. Press, 1992).

55. Lucius Apuleius *Metamorphosis* 9.14. See also MacDonald, 67-73; Marcel Simon, "Apulée et le Christianisme," in Melanges d'histoire des religions, ed. Antoine Guillamont and E. M. Laperrousaz (Paris: Press Universitaires de France, 1974), 299-305.

56. Lécuyer, 44

57. Cyprian *Epistle* 69.1.

58. Cyprian *Epistle* 67.5.

59. Cyprian *Epistle* 72.2.1

60. See Charles Joseph Hefele, *A History of the Christian Councils*, vol. 1 (Edinburgh: T & T Clark, 1894), 375-435.

61. Gregory of Nyssa *Discours sur le jour des lumières*.

62. John Chrysostom *Homily on Pentecost* 14.

63. John Chrysostom *Homily on Acts* 15.1.

64. John Chrysostom *Homily on 2 Timothy 1:6, 7*.

65. Lécuyer, 99-101.

66. Cyril *Commentary on John* 12:20.

67. Cyril *Fragment on Luke* 12.41.

68. Cyril *Epistle 787 to Atticus*.

69. Prayer no. 28, *Didascalia et Constitutiones Apostolorum*, vol. 2, ed. F. X. Funk (Padeborn: Ferdinand Schoeningh, 1905), 188.

70. Augustine *On Baptism* 1.3.1.

71. Augustine *Reply to Parmentian* 2.13, 28.

72. Ibid., 1.6. 4-5.

73. Ibid., 23; a little later he uses "the stamp of the monarch," (10.10).

74. Augustine *On the Priesthood* 3.5.182-189.

75. *The Liturgical Homilies of Narsai*, ed. R. H. Connolly, *Texts and Studies*, vol. 8, no. 1 (Cambridge: The Univ. Press, 1909), 7, 67.

CHAPTER 6

EARLY SEVENTH-DAY ADVENTISTS AND ORDINATION, 1844-1863

GEORGE R. KNIGHT

Seventh-day Adventism was born in an antiorganizational milieu. Throughout 1843 and 1844 Millerite believers were increasingly disciplined by and cast out from their various denominations, largely because of their belief in the premillennial Second Coming of Jesus and their public agitation on that topic. The closer the predicted end of the world came, the more serious the problem became for both the churches and the Millerites.

By the summer of 1843 the issue had festered to such an extent that Charles Fitch published a pamphlet indicating that "whoever is opposed to the PERSONAL REIGN [i.e., Second Coming] of Jesus Christ over this world on David's throne, is ANTICHRIST," or Babylon. Fitch argued that by their high-handedness in opposing what the Millerites held to be a central biblical doctrine, the denominations—both Protestants and Catholics—had apostatized from the truth. Thus they had become a Babylon of confusion between Christianity and error. Many Millerites saw this as the fruit, not only of the insistence of the denominations on sticking to their inflexible creeds, but also of their church machinery— machinery that had been used to persecute God's Bible-believing people.[1]

The Babylonian Crisis

The upshot of their problem with the denominations was that large numbers of Millerites held ever more tightly that they would have no creed but the Bible. Another result was an aversion on the part of many to any form of church organization. Thus Fitch had a significant following when he called for his Advent brothers and sisters to come out of Babylon, or the organized churches.[2]

George Storrs took the logic implicit in Fitch's argument a giant step forward in February 1844. "Take care," he penned to his fellow believers, "that you do not seek to manufacture another church. No church can be organized by man's invention but what it becomes Babylon *the moment it is organized.*"[3]

Storrs' appeal bore prolific and widespread fruit among the post-Disappointment believers. In fact, of the several denominations that began to evolve out of the Millerite crisis in late 1844, none was able to create a formal organization before the late 1850s or early 1860s. Antiorganizational impulses were at the heart of their experience and imposed themselves on their practices.[4]

Unfortunately, those practices left believers with no defenses against the divergent beliefs and various forms of fanaticism that ran through the Adventist groups in the late 1840s and 1850s. Anybody who wanted to preach had more or less an opening to any group that considered itself Adventist. There were no checks on orthodoxy or even morality among large sectors of Adventism as it faced the crisis of a self-appointed ministry. Of course, some responsible ministers desired to create some standards, but their opponents merely charged their brethren with seeking to take away their God-given freedom through Babylon-like moves. And such accusations found a fertile field in disorganized and disoriented post-Disappointment Millerism.[5]

The problems facing Adventism in general also affected the Sabbatarian branch of the movement. By late 1853 the Sabbatarian leaders decided to raise the issue to a higher level of visibility among their adherents. As a result, in December, James White, while noting that God had been leading His people out of Babylon and "from the confusion and bondage of man-made creeds," also sought to call the Sabbatarians' attention to "gospel order" as set forth in Scripture.

> It is a lamentable fact that many of our Advent brethren who made a timely escape from the bondage of the different churches, who as a body rejected the Advent doctrine, have since been in a more perfect Babylon than ever before. Gospel order has been too much overlooked by them.
>
> The Advent people professed to take the Bible as their guide in doctrine and in duty. If they had followed this guide strictly, and had carried out the gospel principles of order and discipline, much confusion would have been saved. Many in their zeal to come out of Babylon, partook of a rash, disorderly spirit, and were soon found in a perfect Babel of

confusion. . . . God has not called any of his people away from the confusion of the churches, designing that they should be left without discipline. . . . To suppose that the church of Christ is free from restraint and discipline, is the wildest fanaticism.[6]

Ellen White was of the same mind as her husband. Late in 1853 she penned an article based largely on a vision she had experienced in September 1852. "The Lord," she wrote, "has shown that gospel order has been too much feared and neglected. That formality should be shunned; but, in so doing, order should not be neglected." There is order in heaven, and the church on earth had order both during Christ's sojourn and after his ascension. And in "these last days . . . there is more real need of order than ever before," since the conflict between Christ and Satan will intensify. It is Satan's aim, she argued, to keep order out of the church.[7]

At that point in her presentation, Ellen White made a crucial transition by raising the issue of the damage done by unqualified ministers who are "hurried into the field; men without wisdom, lacking judgment." She expressed the concern that men "whose lives are not holy, who are unqualified to teach the present truth, enter the field without being acknowledged by the church . . . and confusion and disunion [are] the result." Unfortunately, she noted, "these men, who are not called of God, are generally the very ones that are the most confident that they are so called." Such "self-sent messengers are a curse to the cause."[8]

"I saw," Mrs. White continued, "that the church should feel their responsibility, and should look carefully and attentively at the lives, qualifications, and general course of those who profess to be teachers," to see if God has called them to the preaching office. As did her husband, she appealed for the church to "flee to God's word, and become established upon gospel order which has been overlooked and neglected."[9]

She then pointed her readers back to the days of the apostles, when the church was also in danger of being deceived by false teachers. God's solution, she noted, was the setting apart of ministers by the laying on of hands. These leaders could then baptize and administer the ordinances of the Lord's Supper.[10]

Ellen White, as might be expected, advocated that the Sabbatarian Adventists follow the apostolic example set forth in the Bible. "Brethren of experience, . . . with fervent prayer, and by the sanction of the Spirit of God, should lay hands upon those who have given full proof that they have received their commission of God, and set them apart to devote themselves entirely to the work."[11]

Authority for Ordination

As noted above, Ellen White's concern for the need to ordain ministers was rooted in the teachings of the New Testament. That position was consistently set forth by James White, J. B. Frisbie, and other early Sabbatarian writers on ordination.

James White's 20 December 1853 article is quite representative of the general Sabbatarian treatment in terms of both logic and use of Scripture. He noted that Jesus "'ordained twelve . . . that he might send them forth to preach.' Mark iii, 14." These were commissioned to preach and baptize believers in his name (Matt 28:19-20). Then, basing his argument on Eph 4:11-16, White pointed out that the offices of preaching and evangelism would be a part of the church until the end of time.[12]

Other Sabbatarian writers, such as J. B. Frisbie, demonstrated from Acts and the Pastoral Epistles that the laying on of hands was continued throughout the early church period. Not only, Frisbie pointed out, was a replacement disciple chosen for Judas Iscariot (Acts 1:20-26), but Saul and Barnabas were also set apart by the laying on of hands by the church for the work of the ministry (Acts 13:1-4). In a similar manner, Paul and other early Christian leaders set qualified workers apart for the work of the church by the laying on of hands. To Frisbie, ordination "was the separating act by which grace was imparted to do the work and office of a bishop."[13]

In short, the Sabbatarian leaders by the mid-1850s had no doubt as to the biblical validity of ordination. Even those opposing James White in the organizing of a formal church structure, such as R. F. Cottrell, were clear on the biblical basis and necessity of ordination.[14] The Sabbatarian literature indicates no sources beyond the Bible used to justify the developing position on ordination. On the other hand, Sabbatarian leaders were obviously aware of what was being done in terms of ordination by other churches. After all, James White and others had been ordained in various denominations before their exit from "Babylon."

Beyond the biblical precedent and teaching on the topic of ordination, White set forth three objectives that could be met by ordination. First, those going out into "a cold world" to preach the Advent message might "know that they have the approbation and sympathy of ministering brethren and of the church." Second, ordination would have a uniting impact on the church that would forward its message, since "where there is not union of action, there is but little lasting interest, and but very little accomplished."[15]

These first two objectives that would be accomplished by ordination were important to White, but he gave the bulk of his space to his third point—"to shut a door against Satan." "In no one thing has the gospel suffered so much," he wrote, "as by the influence of false teachers. We can safely say, from the experience of several years, that the cause of present truth has suffered more in consequence of those who have taken upon themselves the work of teaching, whom God never sent, than in any other thing."[16]

Ordination for ministry, White held, was a pressing need of the hour. "Let those who are called of God to teach and baptize, be ordained according to the Word, and known abroad as those in whom the body have confidence. By this course the greatest cause of evils that has existed among us as a people, will be removed."[17]

Early Ordination

It is obvious that Sabbatarian Adventists went for several years without any means of setting apart new workers. But that does not mean that they lacked ordained ministers. To the contrary, several men had been ordained to the gospel ministry before becoming Adventists. James White had been ordained in the Christian Connection denomination. It seems that Frederick Wheeler and John Byington were ordained Methodist ministers, and A. S. Hutchins was ordained in the Freewill Baptist Church.[18] Undoubtedly there were others, but the problem was that the incipient denomination had no mechanism for certifying new ministers.

In the first decade of the Sabbatarian movement ministers who had been ordained in other denominations appear to have carried over their ordination into Adventism. Thus we read that in 1856 the Lord's Supper was being "regularly administered among Adventists, by the ordained ministers from all the various denominations composing the Advent ranks." But that would change by 1862, when it was officially voted by the recently established Michigan Conference of Seventh-day Adventists "that ministers of other denominations, embracing present truth, should give proof of being called to preach the [Advent] message, and be ordained among us, before administering the ordinances."[19]

Meanwhile, back in the early 1850s the Sabbatarians had begun to ordain church workers. It is impossible to determine the exact beginning of the practice or even who was the first to be ordained. J. N. Loughborough claims that his ordination at the hands of James White and M. E. Cornell was "the first service of this kind among Seventh-day

Adventists," but there is no contemporary evidence. Beyond that, Loughborough did not join the church until late 1852 and was apparently not ordained until 1854, at the age of twenty-two.[20]

The earliest known record of a Sabbatarian Adventist ordination was that of Washington Morse in July 1851. During a service in which six candidates were baptized, the *Review and Herald* reports that "our dear Bro. Morse was set apart by the laying on of hands, to the administration of the ordinances of God's house. The Holy Ghost witnessed by the gift of tongues, and solemn manifestations of the presence and power of God. The place was awful, yet glorious." Yet looking back from 1888, Morse dates his ordination to the "ministry" to the summer of 1853.[21]

Some have speculated that the 1851 ordination may have permitted Morse to function only in the administration of the Lord's Supper as a forerunner of what came to be known as a local church officer, while the later ordination was to the full gospel ministry. However, that conclusion does not seem correct for at least two reasons. First, there are other dating problems in Morse's 1888 article. That is quite understandable, given the fact that he is dealing with recollections of events that had taken place more than 35 years earlier. Second, Morse goes out of his way in the 1888 article to note that after his ordination to the ministry he had "received the most unmistakable evidences of the approbation of God." That remark certainly lines up with the 1851 report of Morse's ordination which "the Holy Ghost witnessed by the gift of tongues, and solemn manifestations of the presence and power of God."[22]

Thus Morse's 1851 ordination probably represents the first ordination to the gospel ministry by Sabbatarian Adventists of which there is any record. But even if Morse's later recollection that the event took place in the summer of 1853 is correct, his would still be the first ordination of which we have any contemporary records.

Ordination to gospel ministry did not become a general practice among Sabbatarians until the autumn of 1853. Earlier that year the leading ministers adopted a plan whereby approved Sabbatarian preachers received a card "recommending them to the fellowship of the Lord's people everywhere, simply stating that they were approved in the work of the gospel ministry." The cards were dated and signed by two ministers known by Sabbatarian Adventists to be leaders of the movement. The one given to Loughborough in January of 1853 was signed by James White and Joseph Bates.[23] The purpose of the cards, of course, was to make it more difficult for charlatans to prey upon the scattered believers.

Methods of Ordination

As noted in the previous section, the ordination of ministers did not find a significant place in Sabbatarian ranks until the autumn of 1853. At that point we begin to find frequent mention of such services.

The services seem to have been rather simple and straightforward. Their components are best seen in the accounts reported in the *Review*. In the September 20 issue we read: "'It seemed good to the Holy Ghost and to us,' to set apart out dear Bro. Lawrence to the work of the gospel ministry, to administer the ordinances of the church of Christ, by the laying on of hands. The church was of one accord in this matter. We hope our dear brother will be able to give himself wholly to the study, and the preaching of the word."[24]

Two months later James White reported that J. N. Andrews, A. S. Hutchins, and C. W. Sperry were set apart "to the work of the ministry (that they might feel free to administer the ordinances of the church of God) by prayer and the laying on of hands." As the service was being performed, the "Holy Ghost came down upon us. There, bowed before God, we wept together and rejoiced." The same article said that E. P. Butler, Elon Everts, and Josiah Hart were also ordained. "And while engaged in this most solemn duty, the presence of the Lord was indeed manifested. We never witnessed a more melting, precious season. The very atmosphere around us seemed sweet as heaven. How cheering to the Christian to *know* that his honest endeavors to do his duty are owned and blest of Heaven!"[25]

The form of ordination did not change in this early period. Thus we read in 1861 that "at the close of this meeting, Bro. D. T. Bourdeau was ordained by prayer and the laying on of the hands of preaching brethren present. The Holy Spirit fell sweetly and powerfully upon us, manifestly approving of the solemn and important step."[26]

The key elements of the ordination service in these reports and the many others provided by the *Review* were prayer and the laying on of hands by the other ministers. Thus there was nothing unique in the ordination service of Sabbatarian Adventists. They were quite in harmony with the practices of the evangelical churches of their time.

One point that probably stands out in the minds of those who today read about these setting apart services was the almost universal mention of the presence of the Holy Spirit. That presence was felt in various ways—all the way from the gift of tongues at the ordination of Morse to the sweet "melting" experienced at the setting-apart of E. P.

Butler—but it was nearly always mentioned. That experience was also largely shared by other denominations. The sweet "melting" on such occasions was a phrase especially used by the Methodists in their encounters with the presence of God. Another practice the Sabbatarians shared with the Methodists was a period of ministerial probation before a person was ordained.[27]

The year 1853 also saw the first reported ordination of deacons by the Sabbatarians. In December two men were set apart "by prayer and laying on of hands" as local officers of the churches in Fairhaven and Dartmouth, Massachusetts. The reason given for their selection was that the ministers had to travel and as a result there was no one to administer the Lord's Supper. The respective congregations believed such a move was in harmony with "gospel order."[28]

Thus by the end of 1853 the Sabbatarians had two levels of ordained individuals: the traveling preachers who performed the work of evangelists and administered the ordinances whenever available, and the deacons who appear to have been the only local church officers at that early period. Each church appears to have had one deacon ordained by the ministers. The Sabbatarians did not have church pastors as we know them today. Rather, the preachers were traveling elders, much like the Methodist circuit riders, except there were no circuits or coordination of the labor of the ministers at this period of Sabbatarian Adventist history. In the absence of a minister—which was most of the time—the deacon was in charge of the local congregation, combining the functions of both deacon and elder. As with the ministers, the ordination of deacons was repeatedly affirmed by the Holy Spirit.[29]

The Clarification of Roles among Ordained Sabbatarians

By January 1855 questions were being raised about a second category of officers being ordained for local churches. Thus John Byington queried the *Review* editor if both "Elders and Deacons [are] to be appointed in every Church" with sufficient number of members to utilize their talents. James White replied by citing Acts 14:21-23, where the "apostles that preached the gospel, returned and exhorted and confirmed the souls of the disciples, [and] ordained Elders in the churches."[30]

Two weeks earlier J. B. Frisbie had noted that there were "two classes of preaching elders in the churches" when Paul had written to Timothy. The class that included Paul, Silas, Timothy, and Titus "had the oversight of all the churches as evangelical or traveling elders. . . . Another class of local elders . . . had the pastoral care and oversight of one church." This twofold understanding of the eldership became the accepted position among Sabbatarian Adventists.[31]

A few months after these discussions we begin to find increasing mention of the ordination of local elders. Thus we read in the *Review* of 27 December 1855 that "it was . . . proposed to take into consideration the propriety of establishing further order in the churches in Central New York. Brn. Hiram Edson and David Arnold were then chosen, and afterwards set apart by prayer and the laying on of hands, to act as Elders in the church."[32]

In his January 1855 article, Frisbie also set forth the understanding of the duties of elders and deacons that came to be accepted by the Sabbatarians. "The office of elder and deacon," he penned, "were two different offices. One had the oversight of the spiritual, the other the temporal affairs of the church."[33]

The next year Frisbie raised the issue of the office of deaconess, in the process quoting Adam Clarke's commentary that these female deacons were also "'*ordained* to their office, by the imposition of the hands of the bishop.'"[34] In this area the early Sabbatarians did not follow the implications of Frisbie's presentations on church order.

A final issue to be settled had to do with the division of responsibility in the spiritual realm between the traveling elder or minister and the local elder. It seems that in many cases they had overlapping duties in the late 1850s. Thus Ellen White not only spoke both of "local and traveling" elders, but said that local elders had the responsibility in the absence of ministers (traveling elders) "to administer baptism if it is necessary, or to attend to the ordinances of the Lord's house." Both sets of elders had been "appointed by the church and by the Lord to oversee the church, to reprove, exhort, and rebuke the unruly, and to comfort the feeble-minded." The position of the overlapping duties of local and traveling elders as understood by Ellen White would be the one officially accepted by the organizing meeting of the Michigan Conference in October 1861.[35]

Elders and deacons were often ordained at the same service. That was especially true when new churches were being established.[36]

Ordination at the Time the Denomination Was Organized

On 5 and 6 October 1861, the Michigan churches united to form the Michigan Conference of Seventh-day Adventists. By that time the process and meaning of ordination had been pretty well hammered out by the young church. The organizing meetings were confirming rather than creative on the topic. The most important function of formal organization for the issue of ordination was to give official standing to many previously made decisions. At that meeting some significant decisions related to ordination were made: (1) It was the duty of those ministers recognized by the conference to ordain local officers for the churches. (2) Those persons holding the higher offices (in the rank order of minister, local elder, and deacon) could perform the tasks of the lower officers, but the lower could not perform the higher offices unless ordained to that higher office. (3) Local churches would assume the responsibility of issuing letters of commendation to traveling ministers who belonged to their congregations, so that "the churches in different places may not be imposed upon by false brethren coming into their midst, to whom they are strangers."[37]

The organizing meeting also voted that ministers be granted both certificates of ordination and credentials to be signed by the officers of the conference. Such credentials were to be renewed annually. Apparently the issue of false preachers infiltrating the churches was still a genuine problem to the Sabbatarian congregations.[38]

In the months after organization, James White was not above waving the benefits of organization and credentialing in the faces of those who were still resisting organization. "We have a State Conference," he proclaimed in the *Review* in September 1862, "from which our preachers receive credentials, to be renewed annually, and to which they are responsible. This saves our brethren from impostors, and from being divided by self-called, tobacco-eating, gift-hating preachers."[39]

The 1862 annual meeting of the Michigan Conference passed several resolutions that would affect the work of ordained ministers. First, it took a giant step forward when it decided that ministers would be assigned to their field of labor by the conference. Before that time every minister went where he thought he might be needed. The result was that some churches were consistently neglected while others at times had surplus leadership. Second, at the yearly meeting ministers would report their labors for each week of the year. And third, ordained ministers coming into the Adventist faith from other denominations would no longer automatically be able to perform ministerial functions in Adventist congregations. Such ministers would now have to "give proof of being called to preach the message, and be ordained among us."

That position was a radical shift from the one earlier held by the Sabbatarians.[40]

On 21 May 1863, the several state conferences organized into the General Conference of Seventh-day Adventists. This extension of Seventh-day Adventist organizational structure did not effect any changes in ordination or the role of ministers. What had been developed over the previous decade and had been institutionalized by the Michigan Conference became the pattern for all local conferences affiliated with the General Conference.[41]

Concluding Remarks

Between 1844 and 1863 the group that became the Seventh-day Adventist Church moved from a stance of radical antiorganization to one of conference organization that could guide the growing work of the church. At the forefront of the need to organize was the necessity of certifying which ministers were faithful to the Sabbatarian message. That necessity was met through both the issuing of certificates and ordination.

The Sabbatarian approach to ordination was pragmatic and eclectic rather than built upon a tightly-reasoned theology of ordination. The leaders of the movement, however, were concerned to justify their practices from the Bible. The function of ordination was to serve the mission of the church. The Sabbatarians' pragmatic approach to ordination was generally sufficient for their purposes, but it has left Adventism with some ambiguities, such as the rather confusing use (at least in some countries) of the term "elder" for both pastors and local officials. On the other hand, Sabbatarian Adventists appear to have been in harmony with the ordinational practices of the other evangelical churches of their day.

The Sabbatarians must have had some underlying idea of apostolic succession, since the ones performing the initial ordinations were those who had already been ordained in other Protestant denominations. Another point of interest is that in 1861 the newly organized Seventh-day Adventists had three forms of credentialing their pastors: (1) a letter of commendation from their home congregation, (2) credentials from their local conference, and (3) a certificate of ordination. That triple system would eventually be superseded by the dual system of recognition in practice today of certificates of ordination plus conference credentials.

By 1863 the Seventh-day Adventist denomination had its ideas and practice of ordination firmly in place. Outside of traveling elders becoming settled pastors in the early twentieth century, not much has changed in the way ministers are selected and credentialed or appointed to fields of labor. In short, the ordinational system established in the late 1850s and early 1860s appears to have worked satisfactorily for the mission of the church. Thus, until recently, there were no moves toward change or challenges to the way things were being done. In other words, ordination was something that Adventists did, not something to which they gave a lot of theoretical thought. That would all change in the 1970s and 1980s when women began to look toward ordained ministries. That stimulus has forced the denomination to take a new look at an old practice.

Endnotes

1. Charles Fitch, "Come Out of Her, My People" (Rochester, NY: J. V. Himes, 1843), 9-11, 16 (in George R. Knight, ed., *1844 and the Rise of Sabbatarian Adventism* [Hagerstown, MD: Review and Herald, 1994], 87-99); George R. Knight, *Millennial Fever and the End of the World: A Study of Millerite Adventism* (Boise, ID: Pacific Press, 1993), 141-158.

2. David Tallmadge Arthur, "'Come Out of Babylon': A Study of Millerite Separatism and Denominationalism, 1840-1865" (Ph.D. dissertation, University of Rochester, 1970).

3. George Storrs, "Come Out of Her My People," *Midnight Cry*, 15 February 1844, 238.

4. Clyde E. Hewitt, *Midnight and Morning: An Account of the Adventist Awakening and the Founding of the Advent Christian Denomination, 1831-1860* (Charlotte, NC: Venture Books, 1983), 264-287; Knight, *Millennial Fever*, 245-342; Arthur, "'Come Out of Babylon.'"

5. See J. N. Loughborough, *The Church: Its Organization, Order and Discipline* (Washington, DC: Review and Herald, 1906), 85-90, 101.

6. [James White], "Gospel Order," *Review and Herald (RH)*, 6 December 1853, 173. Cf. [James White], "Church Order," *RH*, 23 January 1855, 164. For a comprehensive account of White's contribution to SDA organizational development, see Andrew G. Mustard, *James White and SDA Organization: Historical Development, 1844-1881* (Berrien Springs, MI: Andrews Univ. Press, 1987).

7. Ellen G. White, *Supplement to the Experience and Views of Ellen G. White* (Rochester, NY: James White, 1854), 15; Arthur L. White, *Ellen G. White: The Early Years, 1827-1862* (Washington, DC: Review and Herald, 1985), 286.

8. E. G. White, *Supplement*, 15-18; J. White, "Church Order," *RH*, 23 January 1855, 164.

9. E. G. White, *Supplement*, 18, 19.

10. Ibid., 19.

11. Ibid.

12. [James White], "Gospel Order," *RH*, 20 December 1853, 188.

13. J. B. Frisbie, "Church Order," *RH*, 19 June 1856, 62, 63; 26 June 1856, 70, 71.

14. R. F. Cottrell, "What Are the Duties of Church Officers?" *RH*, 2 October 1856, 173.

15. [James White], "Gospel Order," *RH*, 20 December 1853, 189.

16. Ibid. Cf. [James White], "Eastern Tour," *RH*, 15 November 1853, 149.

17. [James White], "Gospel Order," *RH*, 20 December 1853, 189.

18. James White, *Life Incidents* (Battle Creek, MI: Seventh-day Adventist Publishing Assn., 1868), 104; Arthur Whitefield Spalding, *Origin and History of Seventh-day Adventists* (Washington, DC: Review and Herald, 1961), 1:295.

19. [James White], "The Rise and Progress of Adventism," *RH*, 29 May 1856, 43; Joseph Bates and Uriah Smith, "Business Proceedings of the Michigan State Conference," *RH*, 14 October 1862, 157.

20. J. N. Loughborough, *Miracles in My Life: Autobiography of Adventist Pioneer J. N. Loughborough*, ed. Adriel Chilson (Payson, AZ: Leaves-of-Autumn Books, 1987), 39; *Seventh-day Adventist Encyclopedia*, 2d rev. ed. (Hagerstown, MD: Review and Herald, 1996), 1: 960-961.

21. F. M. Shimper, "Dear Bro. White," *RH*, 19 August 1851, 15; Washington Morse, "Items of Advent Experience During the Past Fifty Years, No. 4," *RH*, 16 October 1888, 643.

22. *SDA Encyclopedia*, 2:254; Morse, 643; Shimper, 15.

23. Loughborough, *The Church*, 101.

24. James White, "Eastern Tour," *RH*, 20 September 1853, 85.

25. [James White], "Eastern Tour," *RH*, 15 November 1853, 148.

26. A. S. Hutchins, "Report of Meetings," *RH*, 25 June 1861, 40.

27. Shimper, 15; [James White], "Eastern Tour," *RH*, 15 November 1853, 148; Matthew Simpson, ed., *Cyclopaedia of Methodism* (Philadelphia: Everts and Stewart, 1876), 682.

28. H. S. Gurney, "From Bro. Gurney," *RH*, 27 December 1853, 199.

29. See, e.g., ibid.; S. B. Whitney, "From Bro. Whitney," *RH*, 20 May 1862, 199.

30. [James White], "Church Order," *RH*, 23 January 1855, 164.

31. J. B. Frisbie, "Church Order," *RH*, 9 January 1855, 155; R. F. Cottrell, "What Are the Duties of Church Officers?" *RH*, 2 October 1856, 173.

32. J. N. Loughborough, "Oswego Conference," *RH*, 27 December 1855, 101. Some have questioned whether this passage was referring to ordination to the local eldership or to the ministry (see *SDA Encyclopedia*, 1:494). Several reasons indicate that it is referring to the

local eldership. First, the time was right. The year 1855 was the year the issue of local elders was first discussed. Before that time we find no one ordained as an elder, and no discussions on the topic. But from 1855 onward we find discussions of the difference in the jobs of elders and deacons and elders and ministers. Beyond that we find regular reports of the ordination of local elders. Second, invariably, both before 1855 and after, those being ordained are referred to as being ordained to the "ministry" or the "gospel ministry," not as elders. Third, the passage's context lends itself to the local elder interpretation.

33. J. B. Frisbie, "Church Order," *RH*, 9 January 1855, 155. Cf. J. B. Frisbie, "Deacons," *RH*, 31 July 1856, 102; R. F. Cottrell, "What Are the Duties of Church Officers?" *RH*, 2 October 1856, 173.

34. J. B. Frisbie, "Deacons," *RH*, 31 July 1856, 102.

35. E. G. White to Bro. and Sis. Scott, 6 July 1863; E. G. White to Bro. B., undated (B-20-1859); E. G. White, MS. 1, 1859; J. N. Loughborough et al., "Conference Address," *RH*, 15 October 1861, 157.

36. See, e.g., R. F. Cottrell, "A Short Tour Among the Saints," *RH*, 25 November 1858, 4; Wm. S. Ingraham, "From Bro. Ingraham," *RH*, 27 October 1859, 184; Jn. Bostwick, "Conference in Lynxville, Wis.," *RH*, 19 June 1860, 37; James White, "Western Tour," *RH*, 6 November 1860, 196.

37. J. N. Loughborough et al., "Conference Address," *RH*, 15 October 1861, 156-157.

38. Joseph Bates and Uriah Smith, "Doings of the Battle Creek Conference, Oct. 5 & 6, 1861," *RH*, 8 October 1861, 148.

39. [James White], "Organization," *RH*, 30 September 1862, 140.

40. Joseph Bates and Uriah Smith, "Business Proceedings of the Michigan State Conference," *RH*, 14 October 1862, 157.

41. "Report of General Conference of Seventh-day Adventists," *RH*, 26 May 1863, 204-206.

CHAPTER 7

ORDINATION IN THE
WRITINGS OF ELLEN G. WHITE

J. H. DENIS FORTIN

Beneath the sheltering trees of a mountainside, not far from the Sea of Galilee, Jesus privately gathered his twelve apostles. He desired to teach them in the sanctuary of nature, away from confusion and disturbing noises. In this setting of natural beauty, the first step was taken in the organization of the church.[1] "When Jesus had ended His instruction to the disciples," Ellen White writes, "He gathered the little band close about Him, and kneeling in the midst of them, and laying His hands upon their heads, He offered a prayer dedicating them to His sacred work. Thus the Lord's disciples were ordained to the gospel ministry."[2]

The simplicity of this first ordination service is startling, given its impact upon the future of the gospel proclamation. There is no costly temple, no dazzling rituals, no dignified guests in attendance. The order of service is unadorned and straightforward.

Although the ordination service as performed in the Seventh-day Adventist Church has kept some of the simplicity of this first service, the issue of ordination has become much more complex. For many years the Seventh-day Adventist Church has discussed the possibility of ordaining women to the gospel ministry. In the course of numerous conversations and arguments, it has appeared to me that much of the confusion within our discussions stems from our vague understanding of what ordination is. Hence our need to elaborate a Seventh-day Adventist theology of ordination.

As part of our construction of such a theology, we need to turn to the writings of Ellen G. White. Since we affirm the prophetic role and doctrinal authority of Ellen White, we believe that her understanding of ordination can help us clarify our theology of ordination. To this end we ask some questions: How does Ellen White define ordination? What does she say concerning the qualifications for ordination? What is the theological context in which she discusses ordination? Is it connected with church authority? And, who decides who is to be ordained?

Therefore, my purpose in this chapter is to study Ellen White's writings on the subject of ordination, without addressing directly the issue of the ordination of women, and come to some conclusions as to what ordination meant to her. Since ordination has traditionally been part of the doctrine of the church, we will consider her thoughts on ordination in the context of her overall understanding of what the church is and how it functions.

The Church as Representative of God on Earth

One of Ellen White's basic theological notions regarding the church is that it is the representative of God on earth.[3] Within the context of the great controversy theme, she believed that Christians and the church are instruments that God uses to witness to the universe that he is a God of love, mercy, and justice.[4] "God has made His church on the earth a channel of light, and through it He communicates His purposes and His will."[5] In this context, her comments emphasize the pragmatic functions of the church, its role and purpose, more than its ontological aspects.

Although ordained ministers, as servants of God and the church, are to act as God's representatives on earth,[6] they are not the only ones. Every Christian has a role to play within the great controversy and is a representative of Christ.[7]

The Priesthood of All Believers

In the Old Testament only certain men ordained to the priesthood could minister within the earthly sanctuary;[8] however, Ellen White believed that no one is ever restricted from serving God, even though one is not an ordained priest or minister. In her writings she indicated that all Christians, regardless of their walks of life, are servants of God. Even though, in her published writings, she never gave it that name, she nonetheless affirmed the Protestant concept of the priesthood of all believers.

Two passages of Scripture are foremost in her understanding of this concept. The first one is 1 Pet 2:9: "But you are a chosen race, a royal priesthood, a holy nation, God's own people, that you may declare the wonderful deeds of him who called you out of darkness into his marvelous light" (RSV).[9] The second is John 15:16: "Ye have not chosen Me, but I have chosen you, and ordained you, that ye should go and bring forth fruit, and that your fruit should remain: that whatsoever ye shall ask of the Father in My name, He may give it you." Many times she referred to or quoted parts of these passages in support of dedicated Christian service and to insist that all Christians are called or commissioned by God to serve him.[10]

This concept of the priesthood of all believers underlies her understanding of both Christian service and ordination. Throughout her ministry, Ellen White repeatedly appealed to church members to engage in wholehearted Christian service. She held that it is a fatal mistake to believe that only ordained ministers are workers for God and to rely solely on them to accomplish the mission of the church.[11] She stated that "All who are ordained unto the life of Christ are ordained to work for the salvation of their fellow-men."[12] "Those who stand as leaders in the church of God," she adds, "are to realize that the Saviour's commission is given to all who believe in His name. God will send forth into His vineyard many who have not been dedicated to the ministry by the laying-on-of-hands."[13] Thus, every Christian is a minister for God.[14]

Consequently, every Christian is ordained by Christ. Emphatically she asked, "Have you tasted of the powers of the world to come? Have you been eating the flesh and drinking the blood of the Son of God? Then, *although ministerial hands may not have been laid upon you in ordination, Christ has laid His hands upon you* and has said: 'Ye are My witnesses.'"[15] Thus, she noted, "many souls will be saved through the labors of men who have looked to Jesus for their ordination and orders."[16]

Church ordination, therefore, is not a prerequisite to serve God, because it is the Holy Spirit who gives fitness for service to Christians who in faith are willing to serve.[17] Humility and meekness are character traits that God looks for in his servants to qualify them for ministry; these are more necessary than eloquence or learning.[18] In fact, as in the case of Paul and Barnabas, ordination from above precedes ordination by the church.[19]

This is also, I believe, how she understood her own call to ministry. Although she was never ordained as a minister by the Seventh-day Adventist Church, she believed that God himself had ordained her to the prophetic ministry. In her later years, while recalling her experience in the Millerite movement and her first vision, she declared, "In the city of Portland, *the Lord ordained me* as His messenger, and here my first labors were given to the cause of present truth."[20]

From these passages we can draw a few initial conclusions concerning Ellen White's underlying thoughts on ordination. First, Ellen White's concept of the priesthood of all believers is the fundamental qualification for Christian service; every Christian is intrinsically a priest for God. Second, in a spiritual sense, every Christian is ordained by God to this priesthood. Third, church ordination is not a requirement to serve God.

The Meaning of "Ordain" in Ellen G. White's Writings

Before we proceed any further in this discussion, we need to explore what Ellen White meant by the verb "to ordain." In her published writings, this verb in its various forms appears nearly one thousand times. Although it may refer to the Christian rite of appointment to a church office by means of a laying-on-of-hands ceremony, "ordain" does not always refer to this ceremony. The basic root meaning of the word is "to order or organize." The word may also mean "to command or decree." These various shades of meaning of this verb appear in Ellen White's writings.

When she refers to John 15:16, as quoted above, to support a dedicated Christian service on the part of all believers, the verb "ordain" in the KJV does not seem to refer to a laying-on-of-hands ceremony, but instead has the meaning of decree or command. God decrees or commands that Christians should go and bring forth much fruit.

At the beginning of the chapter, "A Consecrated Ministry," in *Acts of the Apostles,* Ellen White states that the "great Head of the church superintends His work through the instrumentality of men ordained by God to act as His representatives."[21] Although in this chapter she clearly discusses the work and influence of the ordained minister, nowhere else does she allude to ordination; the verb "ordain" is used only this once and refers to God's appointment of some persons as his instruments. Her usage of the verb may also include the spiritual ordination we have just discussed. Her intent may be to emphasize that a minister's ultimate ordination is not from men but from God himself. The same shades of meaning are present in her statement about her call to the prophetic ministry, "the Lord ordained me as His messenger." Here the verb "ordained" has a primary meaning of "appointed to the office" but also suggests a secondary meaning: God himself ordained her or laid his hands upon her. I conclude from her comments regarding the concept of the priesthood of all believers that underlying Ellen White's use of the verb "ordain" is the idea that God is the one who ordains or appoints a person to be his servant and, consequently, it is also God who spiritually lays his hands upon this servant.[22]

Because of these various shades of meaning, I have limited my study of her writings on ordination to references where she clearly used the verb in the context of a laying-on-of-hands ceremony, a spiritual ordination by God, or the work of an ordained minister.

Ecclesiastical Organization and Ordination

The question may well be asked, If all Christians are priests and ministers for God, ordained by God to serve him, why does the church ordain officers? A look at how Ellen White perceived the development of the early Seventh-day Adventist Church organization or "gospel order," as it was called then, will provide some answers to this important question and will shed further light on her understanding of ordination. Within the context of the church, ordination is closely related to church organization. For her the ordination of deacons and elders in the New Testament and the ordination of ministers in the early Adventist movement were solutions, provided under the guidance of the Holy Spirit, to serious moments of crisis. Even though the early and elementary ecclesiastical structures (or lack thereof) of both movements did not provide for new ordained ministries, she believed that these structures were adaptable and allowed for the creation of new ministries (as in the case of the seven in Acts 6). These ordinations to ministry in the New Testament church and early Adventist movement, therefore, demonstrated the organizational principles of harmony, order, and adaptability.

Harmony and Order

Soon after the Millerite disappointment, the little flock of Sabbatarian Adventists was confronted with many divergent views which threatened its very survival. In a vision related in her 1854 *Supplement to "Experience and Views,"* Ellen White inquired of an angel as to how harmony could be brought within the ranks of this new fledgling group and how the enemy with his errors could be driven back. The angel pointed to God's Word and gospel order as the solution. These would bring the church into the unity of the faith and would secure the members from false teachers. But how would early Adventists do this, since they had no church organization? Scripture had the answer: they were to follow the example of the early Christian church.[23]

> I saw that in the apostles' day the church was in danger of being deceived and imposed upon by false teachers. Therefore the brethren chose men who had given good evidence that they were capable of ruling well their own houses and preserving order in their own families, and who could enlighten those who were in darkness.[24]

Thus, as the early church and the apostles had chosen qualified men to serve as leaders and ordained them, so the early Adventist church was to proceed. The solution to false teachings and anarchy was the ordination of able men who would supervise and look after the interest of the people.[25] Building upon the experience of the early church, and in the midst of disorganization and lack of structure, she counseled the brethren that God desired his people to follow the New Testament model in the ordination of its first ministers. Early Adventists were to select men "and set them apart to devote themselves entirely to His work. This act would show the sanction of the church to their going forth as messengers to carry the most solemn message ever given to men."[26] Harmony and order could then be preserved in the Adventist movement through the ordination of ministers.

Adaptability

Also building upon this biblical model for the ordination of church officers, Ellen White articulated the need for the structure of the church to be adaptable and at the service of the people.

She mentions in *Acts of the Apostles* that a moment of crisis in the New Testament church occurred as murmuring arose among Christians of Greek origin when they saw their widows neglected in the daily distribution of food (cf. Acts 6:1-6). As the rapid growth in membership brought increasingly heavy burdens upon those in charge,

> [Not] one man, or even one set of men, could continue to bear these burdens alone, without imperiling the future prosperity of the church. There was necessity for a further distribution of the responsibilities which had been borne so faithfully by a few during the earlier days of the church. The apostles must now take an important step in the *perfecting of gospel order* in the church, by laying upon others some of the burdens thus far borne by themselves.[27]

This *perfecting of gospel order* was accomplished when "the apostles were led by the Holy Spirit to outline a plan for the better organization of all the working forces of the church."[28] They gathered all the disciples together, explained the situation, and then suggested that seven men be chosen to oversee the daily distribution of food. This proposal pleased the whole assembly. They chose the Seven and presented them to the apostles, who in turn ordained them to their new ministry.[29]

Commenting on this service, Ellen White understands that

> [The] organization of the church at Jerusalem was to serve as a model for the organization of churches in every other place where messengers of truth should win converts to the gospel. Later in the history of the early church, when in various parts of the world many groups of believers had been formed into churches, *the organization of the church was further perfected*, so that order and harmonious action might be maintained.[30]

Her description of the events indicates that changes to the organizational structure of the church (as in the institution of a new ordained ministry) were made as the leadership realized new needs. This, in some sense, meant the "perfecting" of the structure the apostles had inherited from Jesus; it also meant that the early organizational structure of the church had not achieved a static rigidity. The earlier organizational structure could be "perfected" if, through the guidance of the Holy Spirit, the membership and the leadership thought it needed to be modified. This understanding of the adaptability, or the further "perfecting," of the organizational structure of the church, is an important clue to understanding how early Seventh-day Adventists viewed the development of their own model of church governance.

During the period of 1854-1860, as discussions and controversies occurred concerning the establishment of our early system of church organization and even the choice of a name, James White concluded that "we should not be afraid of that system which is not opposed by the Bible, and is approved by sound sense."[31] It may seem difficult to understand this comment from the leader of a movement which identified itself solely with Scripture. Yet Andrew Mustard argues in his dissertation that James White "had moved away, perhaps unconsciously, from the idea that the only valid principles of organization were those specifically indicated in the Bible, to a less restrictive view that any method of organization was acceptable if effective, provided that it was not specifically opposed by Scripture."[32] Thus some of our pioneers concluded, on the basis of the New Testament example, that church organization is at the service of God's people on earth and not vice versa.[33]

Consequently, with the theological understanding that church structures must reflect order and harmony and be adaptable to new needs, Seventh-day Adventists have been able, through the years, to set up new ministries and move forward solidly and unitedly in spreading the gospel.[34] We can also conclude from Ellen White's understanding of these two organizational principles that the church can determine, under the guidance of the Holy Spirit, which ministries are beneficial and who is to function as an officer in the church. Thus, as we will see, the ordination of officers becomes a function of the church.

Particular Ministries within the Church

A Functional Ministry

Since, according to Ellen White, the Lord himself instituted an ordained ministry, first with the ordination of his twelve apostles and later in guiding the early church to ordain deacons and elders,[35] we can assume that although all Christians are priests and ministers in the service of God, some are especially chosen by God to carry out specific functions within the church.[36] As we have seen, the ordained ministry in the Seventh-day Adventist Church has a God-ordained purpose.[37] For this reason Ellen White cautioned that individuals ordained to ministry in the church ought to be carefully selected.

A Word of Caution

Ellen White earnestly believed that a thorough investigation should be made before a person is ordained to the ministry, carefully following Paul's injunction to Timothy, "Lay hands suddenly on no man" (1 Tim 5:22).

> [Those] who are about to enter upon the sacred work of teaching Bible truth to the world should be carefully examined by faithful, experienced persons.
>
> After these have had some experience, there is still another work to be done for them. They should be presented before the Lord in earnest prayer that He would indicate by His Holy Spirit if they are acceptable to Him. The apostle says: "Lay hands suddenly on no man" [1 Tim 5:22]. In the days of the apostles the ministers of God did not dare to

rely upon their own judgment in selecting or accepting men to take the solemn and sacred position of mouthpiece for God. They chose the men whom their judgment would accept, and then they placed them before the Lord to see if He would accept them to go forth as His representatives. No less than this should be done now.[38]

Throughout her ministry, Ellen White repeatedly sounded this caution regarding the ordination of new ministers.[39] Her major concern was to raise "the standard higher than we have done hitherto, when selecting and ordaining men for the sacred work of God."[40] Haste in ordaining elders or ministers brings grievous trouble upon the church when the chosen persons are "in no way fitted for the responsible work—men who need to be converted, elevated, ennobled, and refined before they can serve the cause of God in any capacity."[41]

Qualifications for Ministry

Consequently, the qualifications for the ordained ministry are both spiritual and practical. Ellen White believed that those who bear responsibilities in the church must be trained for the task.[42] They must be people whom God can teach and honor with wisdom and understanding, as he did Daniel. "They must be thinking men, men who bear God's impress and who are steadily progressing in holiness, in moral dignity, and in an understanding of their work. They must be praying men."[43] Ordained ministers and elders need spiritual discernment,[44] should be distrustful of self, and should labor in humility.[45]

Beyond these spiritual qualifications, Ellen White considered the practical ones just as important. Ministers must live the truth they preach in the pulpit.[46] In this respect she urged a thorough investigation of a future minister's behavior before ordination.

> There are ministers who claim to be teaching the truth, whose ways are an offense to God. They preach, but do not practice the principles of the truth. Great care should be exercised in ordaining men for the ministry. There should be a close investigation of their experience. Do they know the truth, and practice its teachings? Have they a character of good repute? Do they indulge in lightness and trifling, jesting and joking? In prayer do they reveal the Spirit of God? Is their conversation holy, their conduct blameless? All these questions need to be answered before hands are laid upon any man to dedicate him to the work of the ministry.[47]

She also commented on the practice of health reform as a

prerequisite for ministry. "No man should be set apart as a teacher of the people while his own teaching or example contradicts the testimony God has given His servants to bear in regard to diet; for this will bring confusion."[48]

Ordination and Authority

If, as Ellen White contended, the Seventh-day Adventist Church first ordained ministers to ward off doctrinal errors, do ministers have some authority within the church? If so, where does this authority come from, and how is it related to ordination?

Ecclesiastical Authority

Roman Catholicism and other episcopal churches believe that

[by] the laying on of hands in the ceremony of ordination, the authority of the apostles has been transmitted down through history to the bishops of today. According to this theory, which is known as the theory of apostolic succession, modern bishops have the authority which the apostles had, authority which the apostles had in turn received from Christ.[49]

This view of apostolic succession closely associates ordination and authority. There is no ecclesiastical authority without ordination. Furthermore, ordination within the apostolic succession confers upon the recipient a sacramental power to perform the rites and ceremonies of the church. Without the proper ordination, the minister cannot perform efficaciously the sacraments of the church.

Ellen White's understanding of the purpose of ordination varies greatly from the episcopal model; her clearest comments on this are found in connection with the ordination of Paul and Barnabas.[50] These two apostles had seen their labors abundantly blessed by God during their early ministry in Antioch even though "neither of them had as yet been formally ordained to the gospel ministry."[51] But they had reached a point in their ministry when God desired to entrust to them the carrying of the gospel message to the Gentiles. For this purpose, and to meet the challenges of the task, "they would need every advantage that could be obtained through the agency of the church."[52]

Here Ellen White's concept of ordination suggests a close relationship between God and his church. As we have already seen, God commissions and ordains all Christians to ministry first; then, under the guidance of the Holy Spirit, the church recognizes the work of God through the laying on of hands on some chosen individuals. "The circumstances connected with the separation of Paul and Barnabas by the Holy Spirit to a definite line of service show clearly that the Lord works through appointed agencies in His organized church."[53] Before being sent forth as missionaries, Paul and Barnabas were dedicated to God by the church at Antioch, which, in this case, became God's instrument in the formal appointment of the apostles to their God-given mission.

According to Ellen White's description of this event, the ordination of Paul and Barnabas fulfilled five interrelated purposes. First, the church invested them with full church authority to teach the truth, perform baptisms, and organize churches.[54] Second, foreseeing the difficulties and the opposition ahead of them, God wished for their work to be above challenge and, thus, receive the sanction of the church.[55] Third, their ordination was a public recognition that they had been chosen by the Holy Spirit for a special work to the Gentiles.[56] Fourth, "the ceremony of laying on of hands added no new grace or virtual qualification;" it was the action of the church setting its seal of approval upon the work of God.[57] And fifth, hands were laid upon the apostles to ask "God to bestow his blessing upon them."[58] Thus we see that Ellen White's definition of ordination is altogether pragmatic: it is a public recognition of divine appointment and an "acknowledged form of designation to an appointed office."[59]

To come back to our introductory question, What is the relationship between ordination and authority? For Ellen White, the church grants authority to the ordained minister to preach the gospel, and to act in its name in the organization of churches. Her comments suggest that only the church can authorize an individual to perform its rites. Therefore, the church does confer authority upon some chosen individuals through the ordination ceremony. Here we find that the laying on of hands is a ceremony to serve the purpose of the church. It is also the church, under the guidance of the Holy Spirit, which ultimately decides who is to be given authority through ordination.

Divine Authority

Our understanding of the relationship of authority to ordination would be incomplete if we were to consider only the church's authority conferred upon a minister at ordination. Ellen White presented another aspect of authority which is shared by all Christians, and particularly ordained ministers. As a Christian, an ordained minister possesses not only ecclesiastical authority to perform duties for the church, but also *divine* authority to preach the gospel and serve as an ambassador of God. This divine authority is fundamentally related to the priesthood of all believers than to ordination.

Speaking about ordained ministers as Christ's ambassadors on earth, she affirms that from "Christ's ascension to the present day, men ordained of God, *deriving their authority from Him*, have become teachers of the faith. . . . Thus the position of those who labor in word and doctrine becomes very important."[60] She later adds, "He has ordained that there should be a succession of men who *derive authority from the first teachers of the faith* for the continual preaching of Christ and Him crucified. The Great Teacher has delegated power to His servants."[61]

Although, at first glance, the phrase "a succession of men who derive authority from the first teachers of the faith" may seem to validate a belief in episcopal apostolic succession, Ellen White did not say that ordained ministers receive their authority directly from Peter, through a direct succession of laying-on-of-hands ceremonies. Rather, she affirmed that the authority of God's servants is *derived* from God and the first teachers of the faith. This derivation of authority is based upon faithfulness to the Word of God and to truth.

Her comments in *Desire of Ages* concerning the apostolic succession are explicit.

> Descent from Abraham was proved, not by name and lineage, but by likeness of character. So the apostolic succession rests not upon the transmission of ecclesiastical authority, but upon spiritual relationship. A life actuated by the apostles' spirit, the belief and teaching of the truth they taught, this is the true evidence of apostolic succession. This is what constitutes men the successors of the first teachers of the gospel.[62]

As long as a servant of God (not only an ordained minister) is faithful to God and his word, this person has divine authority to "labor in word and doctrine." This ties in with what we have seen regarding the priesthood of all believers. This is what the church acknowledges when ordaining a person to ministry. The authority of an ordained minister is, consequently, derived from God and conferred by the church. The first gives authority to teach the faith; the second, to act for the church.

A Diversity of Ordained Ministries

Within the theological perspective I have outlined thus far, one that is founded on the priesthood of all believers and sees the organizational structure of the church as adaptable to new needs, we can understand why Ellen White allowed for the church to decide whether some people, other than ministers, should be ordained or set apart by the laying on of hands in other ministries. She earnestly believed that the ordained ministry alone was not sufficient to fulfill God's commission, that God is calling Christians of all professions to dedicate their lives to his service.[63] Since the church can branch out into different kinds of ministries to meet the needs of the people, she favored, for instance, the ordination of medical missionaries and women in ministry.

Ellen White considered the work of the medical profession as an effective means of proclaiming the gospel and, for this reason, believed medical missionaries ought to be ordained to God's service.

> The work of the true medical missionary is largely a spiritual work. It includes prayer and the laying-on-of-hands; he therefore should be as sacredly set apart for his work as is the minister of the gospel. Those who are selected to act the part of missionary physicians, are to be set apart as such. This will strengthen them against the temptation to withdraw from the sanitarium work to engage in private practice.[64]

In this passage Ellen White drew a parallel between the setting apart of the medical missionary and the minister of the gospel. To sacredly set apart a medical missionary is viewed as a form of ordination in which the church acknowledges the blessings of God upon the chosen individual and serves as a means of strengthening the dedication of the worker in his service for God.

Ellen White also favored women as laborers in the gospel ministry. In 1898, while in Australia, she recalled how God had impressed her with the injustice that had been done to some women, wives of ordained ministers. These women had been very active in gospel ministry, visiting families and giving Bible studies, yet without receiving any due recognition or financial compensation. She understood that these women were "recognized by God as being as necessary to the work of ministry as their husbands."[65] And, consequently, in agreement with the priesthood of all believers, she approved women laboring in the gospel ministry.[66]

In a similar context, she favored that women in gospel ministry be also set apart or ordained.

Women who are willing to consecrate some of their time to the service of the Lord should be appointed to visit the sick, look after the young, and minister to the necessities of the poor. They should be set apart to this work by prayer and laying-on-of-hands. In some cases they will need to counsel with the church officers or the minister; but if they are devoted women, maintaining a vital connection with God, they will be a power for good in the church. *This is another means of strengthening and building up the church. We need to branch out more in our methods of labor.*[67]

Ellen White's basic reason for supporting the setting apart of women and medical missionaries concurs with what we have already seen on the adaptability of church structures to meet new needs. Under the guidance of God, the church can and should branch out in its methods of labor by setting apart in ordination Christians serving in various ministries. But more importantly, I believe, Ellen White suggested here that God is leading the church in this direction, that it is God's will for the church to branch out, to be strengthened and built up.

Conclusion

Ellen White's concept of ordination can best be described within her understanding of God's purpose for the church and the priesthood of all believers. She supported the concept that all Christians are ministers of God, ordained by God (John 15:16) into the priesthood of all believers (1 Pet 2:9) to demonstrate to the world the mercy and love of God. In the organized church, however, some Christians are appointed to different kinds of functional ministry such as that of ordained ministers or church administrators. Church ordination, far from being a sacrament that adds grace or virtue, is a means of publicly recognizing God's will and call for an individual. Since the ordained minister is the foremost representative of God and his church, ordination to ministry in the Seventh-day Adventist Church is a serious matter and its ministers are to be carefully selected according to spiritual and practical qualifications.

Furthermore, Ellen White's theological understanding of ordination is related to her understanding of church organization and how she perceived the function of the church as the representative of God on earth. During the early developments of the Seventh-day Adventist Church organization she counseled the believers to follow the example of the New Testament church and to draw from it principles needed to establish the proper gospel order. In that context, ordination to ministry was needed to keep order and harmony in the church and demonstrated the adaptability of the church structures to meet the needs of the people. Thus, to better fulfill its mission, Ellen White believed the church needed to branch out in its methods of evangelism, allowing every Christian to have a part in spreading the gospel. Where the church sees fit, under the guidance of the Holy Spirit, ministries should be established and people ordained by laying on of hands to these ministries. Thus ordination, in Ellen White's thought, is a means used by the church to acknowledge God's will for his church and for individual Christians, both women and men.

Endnotes

1. Ellen G. White, *The Desire of Ages*, 290-291.

2. Ibid., 296.

3. Ibid., 290.

4. Ellen G. White, *Testimonies for the Church*, 6:12.

5. Ellen G. White, *Acts of the Apostles*, 163. Two chapters, in particular, clearly present her understanding of the purpose of the church: "God's Purpose in the Church," White, *Testimonies for the Church*, 6:9-13, and "God's Purpose for His Church," White, *Acts of the Apostles*, 9-16.

6. One good example of this is the chapter, "A Consecrated Ministry," in White, *Acts of the Apostles*, 359-371.

7. Indicative of her thoughts on this is the following passage in "A Preparation for the Coming of the Lord," *Review and Herald*, 24 November 1904. "Brethren and sisters, how much work have you done for God during the past year? Do you think that it is those men only who have been ordained as gospel ministers that are to work for the uplifting of humanity?—No, no! Every one who names the name of Christ is expected by God to engage in this work. The hands of ordination may not have been laid upon you, but you are none the less God's messengers. If you have tasted that the Lord is gracious, if you know his saving power, you can no more keep from telling this to some one else than you can keep the wind from blowing. You will have a word in season for him that is weary. You will guide the feet of the straying back to the fold. Your efforts to help others will be untiring, because God's Spirit is working in you."

8. See Ellen White's comments on the rebellion of Korah, *Patriarchs and Prophets*, 398-399.

9. Three centuries before Ellen White, Martin Luther also appealed to 1 Pet 2:9 to express his belief that every Christian is a priest for God. In a 1520 treatise, in which he invited the German princes to reform the church, he wrote, "The fact is that our baptism consecrates us all without exception, and makes us all priests" (*An Appeal to the Ruling*

Class of German Nationality as to the Amelioration of the State of Christendom, in John Dillenberger, ed., *Martin Luther: Selections from His Writings* [New York: Doubleday, 1962], 408).

10. Concerning 1 Pet 2:9 see, for example, Ellen G. White, *Testimonies to Ministers and Gospel Workers,* 422, 441; White, *Testimonies for the Church,* 2:169; 6:123, 274. For John 15:16 see, White, *Testimonies to Ministers and Gospel Workers,* 212-213.

11. Ellen G. White, "The Great Commission: A Call to Service," *Review and Herald,* 24 March 1910.

12. Ellen G. White, "Our Work," *Signs of the Times,* 25 August 1898.

13. White, *Acts of the Apostles,* 110.

14. Ellen G. White, "A Preparation for the Coming of the Lord," *Review and Herald,* 24 November 1904.

15. White, *Testimonies for the Church,* 6:444 (italics supplied).

16. Ellen G. White, "Words to Our Workers," *Review and Herald,* 21 April 1903.

17. White, *Acts of the Apostles,* 40.

18. Ellen G. White, Letter 10, 1899, to J. H. Kellogg, 14 January 1899 (*Manuscript Releases,* 2:32, 33).

19. Concerning these two apostles, Ellen White stated: "God had abundantly blessed the labors of Paul and Barnabas during the year they remained with the believers in Antioch. But neither of them had as yet been *formally* ordained to the gospel ministry. . . . Both Paul and Barnabas had already received their commission from God Himself" (*Acts of the Apostles,* 160, 161, italics supplied). In my opinion, her use of the adverb "formally" indicates that God had already ordained them to their ministry.

20. Ellen G. White, Letter 138, 1909, quoted in Arthur L. White, *Ellen G. White: The Later Elmshaven Years, 1905-1915,* 211 (italics supplied).

21. White, *Acts of the Apostles,* 360.

22. See footnotes 15 and 16.

23. *Early Writings of Ellen G. White,* 100, 101.

24. Ibid.

25. Ibid., 101,

26. According to Ellen White, ecclesiastical organizations should also follow the biblical principle that "God is not the author of confusion, but of peace" (1 Cor 14:33). This principle was the basis for the ordination of the seven (Acts 6) to a new ministry in the New Testament church. She argued, in reference to the ordination of the seven, that "[the] order that was maintained in the early Christian church, made it possible for them to move forward solidly, as a well-disciplined army, clad with the armor of God. The companies of believers, though scattered over a large territory, were all members of one body." (*Acts of the Apostles,* 95, 96). Worldwide unity and harmony of action are natural

and required consequences of a biblical ecclesiastical structure. God "requires that order and system be observed in the conduct of church affairs to-day, no less than in the days of old. He desires His work to be carried forward with thoroughness and exactness, so that He may place upon it the seal of His approval" (ibid., 96).

27. White, *Acts of the Apostles*, 88-89 (italics supplied).

28. Ibid., 89.

29. Here we find a pattern of change in organizational structure of the early church that is repeated in other places in the New Testament. First, the church encounters a need which may bring about a crisis; second, the church meets together to find a solution; third, the Holy Spirit guides the believers toward the best solution possible at the time; and, fourth, the apostles or the church approve of the decision.

30. White, *Acts of the Apostles*, 91-92 (italics supplied).

31. James White, "A Complaint," *Review and Herald*, 16 June 1859, 28; quoted in Andrew Mustard, *James White and SDA Organization: Historical Development, 1844-1881* (Berrien Springs, MI: Andrews Univ. Press, 1987), 131.

32. Mustard, 131. For further thoughts on the relationship between the development of New Testament ecclesiology and the Seventh-day Adventist organizational structure, see Raoul Dederen, "A Theology of Ordination," *Ministry*, February 1978, 24K-24P.

33. The *perfecting of gospel order* was a recurring principle in the development of the Seventh-day Adventist church structure. Mustard has well documented this development in his dissertation (ibid., 134, 171-172, 221-222, 231-232).

34. The implementation, in the 1860s, of systematic benevolence, which later became the tithe system, and the reorganization of the General Conference structure in 1901 and 1903 illustrate how we have "perfected" our own ecclesiastical organization through the years. This is also reflected in the institution of various credentials and licenses issued to church workers, such as commissioned ministers, commissioned ministers of teaching, missionaries, and literature evangelists.

35. See White, *Desire of Ages*, 290; White, *Acts of the Apostles*, 160, 161.

36. This, I believe, is in harmony with the lists of spiritual gifts in 1 Corinthians 12 and Ephesians 4, which mention different ministries within the church. In Paul's mind some of these ministries clearly have a higher rank or significance in the organized church. Luther also understood the work of the ecclesiastical ministry in the same light, "Every one who has been baptized may claim that he has already been consecrated priest, bishop, or pope, even though it is not seemly for any particular person arbitrarily to exercise the office. Just because we are all priests of equal standing, no one must push himself forward and, without the consent and choice of the rest, presume to do that for which we all have equal authority. Only by the consent and command of the community should any individual person claim for himself what belongs equally to all. . . . It follows that the status of a priest among Christians is merely that of an office-bearer" (*An Appeal to the Ruling Class*, in Dillenberger, 409).

37. Ellen White had a high view of the ordained ministry of the church. She believed the

ministry was "divinely appointed" (*Testimonies to Ministers*, 52) and "a sacred and exalted office" (*Testimonies for the Church*, 2:615). Furthermore, she affirmed that the "highest of all work is ministry in its various lines; . . . there is no work more blessed of God than that of the gospel minister" (*Testimonies for the Church*, 6:411).

38. White, *Testimonies for the Church*, 4:406.

39. She remarked that the "after history of Judas would show them [the disciples] the danger of allowing any worldly consideration to have weight in deciding the fitness of men for the work of God" (White, *Desire of Ages*, 294). "It would be well for all our ministers to give heed to these words [Titus 1:5-7] and not to hurry men into office without due consideration and much prayer that God would designate by His Holy Spirit whom He will accept" (White, *Testimonies for the Church*, 5:617).

40. Ellen G. White, "Danger in Rejecting Light," *Review and Herald*, 21 October 1890.

41. White, *Testimonies for the Church*, 5:617, 618.

42. Ibid., 549.

43. Ibid.

44. Ellen G. White, "Be Gentle Unto All Men," *Review and Herald*, 14 May 1895.

45. White, *Testimonies for the Church*, 4:407.

46. White, *Testimonies for the Church*, 5:530.

47. White, "Danger in Rejecting Light," *Review and Herald*, 21 October 1890.

48. Ellen G. White, Letter 23, 1896 (*Manuscript Releases*, 7:338). Ellen White based this strong advice on the fact that ministers speak to the people in Christ's stead and should therefore live according to the health reform. As the priests of Israel were required to make special ceremonial preparations before coming into the presence of God, she believed that ministers ought to remember "that the mighty God of Israel is still a God of cleanliness" (*Counsels on Health*, 82).

49. Millard J. Erickson, *Christian Theology* (Grand Rapids: Baker, 1983-1985), 1071.

50. Her concept of ordination is clearly nonsacramental and nonepiscopal. Writing about the ordination of Paul and Barnabas, she says, "At a later date, the rite of ordination by the laying-on-of-hands was greatly abused; unwarrantable importance was attached to the act, as if a power came at once upon those who received such ordination, which immediately qualified them for any and all ministerial work. But in the setting apart of these two apostles, there is no record indicating that any virtue was imparted by the mere act of laying-on-of-hands. There is only the simple record of their ordination, and of the bearing that it had on their future work" (White, *Acts of the Apostles*, 162).

51. White, *Acts of the Apostles*, 160.

52. Ibid.

53. Ibid., 162.

54. *Redemption: or the Teachings of Paul, and His Mission to the Gentiles*, 5. In *Early*

Writings Ellen White indicated that ordination in the early church conferred also the authority to perform the Lord's Supper (101).

55. Ibid., 6.

56. Ibid.

57. Ibid., 7.

58. Ibid.

59. Ibid., 6-7.

60. White, *Testimonies for the Church*, 4:393 (italics supplied).

61. Ibid., 4:529 (italics supplied).

62. White, *Desire of Ages*, 467.

63. Ellen G. White, *Medical Ministry*, 248-249.

64. Ellen G. White, *Evangelism*, 546.

65. Ellen G. White, MS 43a, 1898 (*Manuscript Releases*, 5:323).

66. Ibid. (*Manuscript Releases*, 5:325).

67. Ellen G. White, "The Duty of the Minister and the People," *Review and Herald*, 9 July 1895 (italics supplied).

CHAPTER 8

A THEOLOGICAL UNDERSTANDING OF ORDINATION

RUSSELL L. STAPLES

The focus in this essay is on the understanding of ordination to the gospel ministry in the Seventh-day Adventist Church. Its purpose is to uncover and explicate some of the major issues in the Adventist understanding of the church and its ministry as a contribution to an informed discussion of the ordination of women to the ministry.

The confluence of a broad range of factors is leading to a reassessment of the nature of ministry. Among these are church finances and the possibility of bivocational ministries, ministerial accountability, tension between conference appointment and congregational call of ministers, church renewal, issues related to church growth and decline, the increasing number of single-parent families in inner-city congregations, and ongoing transition from monocultural to multicultural communities.

No single issue, however, has served to focus attention on matters relating to ministry in the Adventist Church as has that of the ordination of women and their place in the ministry. It is probably fair to say that regardless of the outcome, the discussion this issue has generated will have served the useful purpose of forcing the church to come to grips with, and clarify, many important issues related to the church and its ministry.

The Christian church was brought into being by the acts of God in Jesus Christ. It is a community of grace and of the Spirit, but its mission is on earth, and it functions in many respects as a community fulfilling human needs. Many of the concerns giving rise to the conviction that women should be ordained are grounded in valid social/demographic issues and needs; however, solutions should ultimately be sought in theological understandings of the church and its mission.

A Pauline View of the Church

There are many images of the church in the New Testament. These include the salt of the earth, a letter from Christ, branches of the vine, the bride of Christ, ambassadors, a chosen race, a holy temple, the body of Christ, a new creation, citizens of heaven, the household of God, and a spiritual body. A broad reading of the letters of Paul reveals an understanding of the church which gathers these images together into two dominant foci, Christology and eschatology.[1] On this view, the church is conceived of as an ellipse with two foci. It is both the "body of Christ," the image most commonly used by Paul (1 Cor 12:12, 27; Col 1:18; Eph 1:22, 23; 4:12, 16), and an eschatological community (Phil 3:20, 21, "citizens of heaven") with a mission to perform (2 Cor 5:17-6:1, "Christ's ambassadors"). This relationship might be visualized as follows:

Christology	Eschatology
Defines the foundation of the church as the body of Christ	Defines the character of the church on earth and its mission

What the church is, its essential being, is grounded in Christology. It is the body of which Christ is the head (Col 1:18). Its function and the horizon of its work among the nations and in time are grounded in its eschatological identity (Matt 28:18-20). The interrelationship between these two foci has been highly determinative of understandings of the church. Four major patterns have emerged in the history of the church: conflation of the two foci, emphasis upon the body of Christ to the neglect of eschatology, emphasis upon eschatology to the neglect of the being of the church, and a balanced emphasis on the church as a divinely instituted community of faith with an eschatologically defined mission. Understandings of ministry and ordination have been typically different in each case.

1. Conflation of the Foci

When the two foci are conflated as in medieval Catholicism, an understanding of the church as *Christus prolongatus* (meaning the extension of the incarnation) swallowed up eschatology. The church was so closely identified with kingdom that traditional understandings of eschatology were displaced. This resulted in a view of the church as the intermediary between God and human beings, and of priests as performing sacraments that confer divine grace. Ordination came to be understood as the sacramental conferral of an indelible grace.

2. Emphasis on the Christological Focus

There have been communities of faith with a high concept of the church as the mystical body of Christ in which there is deep personal faith and devout and joyous celebration of the sacraments without any serious sense of mission. On this view, eschatology is reduced to a sense of personal salvation and all but divorced from the wider sweep of God's concern for all peoples of earth. Just as the church is regarded as the body of Christ instituted by the power of God, so also ordination is thought of as a downward flowing of grace from God and not merely as a setting apart for a religious vocation by the community of faith.

3. Emphasis on the Eschatological Focus

Eschatology defines the character of the church as a community of faith which seeks to actualize the principles of the kingdom in this present life while it works to hasten the day of Christ's coming. It is possible for an eschatological commitment to so preoccupy the church that the essence of its being as the corporate body of Christ is lost from sight. The church may be regarded primarily as an institution to be organized and directed in ways that enhance efficiency in spreading the good news. On this view, ministry is thought of in pragmatic terms, and ordination as a setting apart for a vocation of service. There is little that differentiates clergy from lay members other than clerical vocation and office.

4. Holding Both Foci in Balance

Christology and eschatology need to be held together as twin foci to avoid imbalance. For Paul, the missionary, the emphasis is on the church as the interim community of faith bearing a faithful witness to the world. But he also emphasizes the Christological foundation of the church, even to the extent of calling Christ the church (1 Cor 12:12). The corporate oneness of members in Christ is emphasized again and again in his letters. His delineation of the "works of the flesh" and "fruit of the Spirit" (Gal 5:19, 20, 22) concentrates precisely upon those vices and virtues that either disrupt or contribute to this oneness.

On this view, both the essential nature of the church as a divinely constituted community of faith and its responsibility to proclaim the coming kingdom are affirmed. There is a balance between what the church is and what it does. Ministers are not simply human agents selected because of personal capability, and ordination is more than the corporate act of a social community.

Ministry in the New Testament Church: No Priest

In 1 Pet 2:9, 10, the church is described as a "royal priesthood." However, while the priesthood of the entire community of faith is thus affirmed, no church officer of any kind is designated as a priest in the New Testament. The writer of Hebrews, in referring to the "better sacrifice" of Christ, which was offered "once and for all" (Heb 10:10-14), makes it clear that the priesthood of the Old Testament has been fulfilled and brought to an end. Christ, the new priest (Heb 7:15, 17), has taken up his office and is now the "one mediator between God and man, Christ Jesus" (1 Tim 2:5).

The significance of this is that while there remains a continuity in God's purposes for Israel and the church, priests of the Old Testament and ministers of the Christian church perform widely different roles. Neither the church nor any priest/minister stands in the position of a mediator between God and human beings. Christ is the unique priest and mediator, and all who believe have "access to God with freedom" through him (Eph 3:12). This is the basis for the Protestant doctrine of the priesthood of all believers. All Christians are priests in the sense that they have direct access to God.

Having established that ministers are nowhere in the New Testament called priests, or described as functioning as such, we come to a consideration of the ministry in the New Testament church. It is clear that in, addition to the variety of gifts given by God through the Holy Spirit (1 Cor 12:4-13; Eph 4:11-14), the church had a "set-apart" ministry which was called, commissioned, and consecrated. However, it is difficult, if not impossible, to extrapolate a set order of church polity, or structured pattern of relationships in the ministry from the New Testament records.[2] Newton Flew portrays both the vitality of the New Testament church and the fluidity of its structure under the guidance of the Holy Spirit:

There is nothing in the Greco-Roman world comparable to this community, conscious of a universal mission, governed and indwelt by an inner life, guided by the active divine Spirit to develop these ministries for the expression of its message to mankind. All the ministries are based on the principle of the universal ministry of all believers.[3]

Ordination in the New Testament

The English word "ordination," to which we have become so accustomed, derives not from any Greek word used in the New Testament, but from the Latin *ordinare* meaning to arrange, set in order, or regulate. "Ordain" is used in the King James Version (KJV) to translate almost thirty different Hebrew and Greek words with a wide range of meaning, including both divine and human acts of selecting, determining, establishing, appointing, and ordering in both religious and secular contexts.[4] One of the striking differences between the KJV and contemporary translations is that, in the latter, words that translate the original more precisely are used, and in some the term "ordination" hardly appears. For instance, "ordain" is used in the KJV in translation of the following Greek words:

Mark 3:14	"he [Christ] ordained twelve." *poieō*—means literally "he made twelve."
Acts 1:22	"ordained . . . a witness." *ginomai*—means "to become."
Acts 14:23	". . . ordained elders in every city." *cheirotoneō*—means to stretch out the hand, a raising of the hand in voting.
1 Tim 2:7	Paul "I am ordained . . . an apostle." *tithēmi*—means "I am placed."
Titus 1:5	"ordain elders in every city." *kathistēmi*—means to arrange.

The significance of this is that whereas the term "ordained" as used in the KJV gives the impression of a set order, a consideration of the Greek terms reveals the fluidity and breadth of practice in the New Testament church. In these and other passages we see the following: the direct action of the Holy Spirit in calling leaders, a process of selection by the church, and the function of the apostles in appointing leaders in every place.[5]

The Laying on of Hands[6]

The hand is a symbol of power and the laying on of hands is commonplace in the Old Testament in a variety of contexts. Hands were laid on in blessing, in the healing of the sick, and in induction into office. Moses gave Joshua his commission by the laying on of hands before the assembled congregation (Num 27:18-23). This is widely regarded as a model for the rabbinic practice of ordination.

There is frequent reference in the New Testament to the laying on of hands in connection with the healing of the sick (e.g., Jesus, Luke 4:40; Peter, Acts 3:7, Ananias, Acts 9:17, 18; Paul, Acts 28:7, 8). The laying on of hands at baptism was not uncommon and in two recorded cases was connected with the outpouring of the Holy Spirit (Peter and John and the Samaritans, Acts 8:16, 17; and Paul at Ephesus, Acts 19:1-6). These may be atypical examples signifying the bonding of the Samaritans to the Jerusalem church in the first case, and the Ephesians to the wider Christian community, in the second. The question in all of this is whether the laying on of hands is instrumental in the conferral of a blessing or gift of grace or whether it is an accompanying symbol of the grace bestowed in response to prayer, signifying in addition the oneness inherent in the body of Christ. The importance of this question is enlarged when it comes to a consideration of the significance of the laying on of hands in ordination to the ministry.

The laying on of hands has been an intrinsic part of appointment to church office since the days of the apostles. In four New Testament passages, laying on of hands is directly connected with appointment to a church office, commissioning to a special mission, and setting apart for ministry:

1. Acts 6:1-6. The election of "the seven" by the congregation in Jerusalem and their appointment to office by prayer and the laying on of hands.

2. Acts 13:1-3, 14:26. The commissioning of Barnabas and Saul, at the direct instigation of the Holy Spirit, for the missionary work to which God had called them, with fasting and prayer and the laying on of hands.

3. The most discussed and influential passages regarding the meaning of the laying on of hands in ordination are those contained in Paul's admonitions to Timothy regarding the cultivation of the "gift" (*charisma*) within him "by the laying on of hands" (*epitheseōs tōn cheirōn*) (1 Tim 4:14, 2 Tim 1:6).[7]

4. 1 Tim 5:22. "Lay hands on no man suddenly" is either an admonition to Timothy to exercise caution in the appointment of church officers or a warning of the danger of lightly rehabilitating repentant

sinners, lest he incur joint responsibility for their misdeeds. This passage adds little to our knowledge regarding the significance of the laying on of hands except that either interpretation signifies the gravity of the office of an elder and provides additional evidence of the universality of the practice.

In medieval Christianity, ordination, with the laying on of hands and prayer, came to be understood as the sacramental conferral of a grace which effected an indelible, lifelong change and empowered the ordinand to celebrate the sacraments. The development of this understanding of ordination was supported by ancillary theological developments, particularly an elevation of the doctrines of the church and the sacraments, but the scriptural base was the "gift . . . through . . . the laying on of hands" of 1 Tim 4:14 and 2 Tim 1:6.

The basic issue, therefore, confronting us is the meaning of the "gift" (*charisma*) conferred by the laying on of hands in ordination to ministry in the early church. There seems not to be consensus among New Testament scholars in this regard. E. Lohse speaks for those who interpret this as a gift, but not a sacrament, which equips for service. The content of the gift is determined by God's call and the designated mission. He writes,

> When prophetic voices pointed to Timothy as the selected office-bearer (1 Tim 1:18; 4:14) the divinely granted charisma which he needed to discharge his office was imparted to him by laying on of hands. Hence the *epithēsis tōn cheirōn* is not presented merely as an accompanying sign. It also serves to pass on the gift with which God equips the office bearer. . . . God's will to call and to send determines the content of the ordination by which the office-bearer is publicly authorised before the congregation, equipped with the charisma of office, and instituted into the office of proclaiming the Word.[8]

Everett Ferguson, on the other hand, emphasizes the enabling prayer of blessing, rather than the concept of a special gift.

> The basic idea in early Christian ordination was . . . conferring a blessing and petitioning for the divine favor . . . . The laying on of hands accompanied prayer in Christian usage. It was essentially an enacted prayer, and the prayer spelled out the grace which God was asked to bestow. As an act of blessing, it was considered to effect that for which the prayer was uttered.
>
> The idea of blessing or benediction, especially in the case of an efficacious sign, is the meaning which best explains all the varied

occasions when the rite was employed in the ancient church. . . . If there is any unifying conception it is in terms of a benediction. The kind of blessing would vary according to the occasion when used.[9]

Ferguson supports this position by referring to studies of early extra-biblical writers.

> When theologians came to reflect on the theological meaning of ordination, they put the emphasis on the prayer and interpreted the rite in terms of a benediction. This may be seen already in Hippolytus' comments on the role of presbyters in ordaining other presbyters. Their imposition of hands is interpreted as a benediction, or an act of 'sealing' what the bishop did.
>
> Gregory of Nyssa goes the farthest of any writer before Augustine in attributing to ordination the power to effect a sacramental change in a person, but he attributes this change to the benediction.[10]

With the growth of the church and the passage of time, developments in both doctrine and practice were in the direction of the enlargement of the office of the clergy and magnification of the gift bestowed by the laying on of hands. Eventually ordination was elevated to the status of a sacrament. Protestants, however, have generally maintained that the laying on of hands involves a spiritual element of blessing and enabling grace—difficult to define—which prepares for ministry. This is widely different from sacramental understandings of ordination.

Of greater significance to us is the question of how the Adventist Church has understood the function of the laying on of hands. Ellen White's most extensive comments on the laying on of hands relate to the commissioning of Barnabas and Paul at Antioch (Acts 13:1-3). She writes:

> Both Paul and Barnabas had already received their commission from God Himself, and the ceremony of the laying on of hands added no new grace or virtual qualification. It was an acknowledged form of designation to an appointed office and a recognition of one's authority in that office. By it the seal of the church was set upon the work of God.
>
> At a later date the rite of ordination by the laying on of hands was greatly abused; unwarrantable importance was attached to the act, as if a power came at once upon those who received such ordination, which immediately qualified them for any and all ministerial work. But in the setting apart of these two apostles, there is no record indicating that any virtue was imparted by the mere act of laying on of hands. There is

only the simple record of their ordination and of the bearing that it had on their future work.[11]

A question that arises is whether the commissioning of Barnabas and Paul to their mission of evangelism is an exact parallel to the ordination of Timothy. This seems not to be the case. The passages in Timothy referring to the "gift . . . through . . . the laying on of hands," on which the sacramental view of ordination is grounded, are not dealt with explicitly in Ellen White's published writings. The *SDA Bible Commentary*, however, states unequivocally "Timothy's gift of church leadership was not bestowed on him at the time of his ordination. No special power flowed through the hands of the 'presbytery.' Rather, the ordination service recognized Timothy's abilities and consecration and thus expressed the church's approval of his appointment as a church leader."[12] This interpretation presupposes a divine call and bestowal of gifts for ministry prior to the laying on of hands in ordination. It may also reflect a concern to move as far as possible from any sacramental concept of ordination.

The concept of ordination cannot be separated from the concept of a call. Christian ministry in its very essence is a sending by Christ. No person exercises a right in respect to either ordination or the practice of ministry. Even a cursory reading of the New Testament makes this abundantly clear. There is first of all the "inner call," but even when a person has experienced a call from God, the church has the responsibility of judging as best it can whether the call is genuine and whether the ordinand bears the fruits of the Spirit in his or her life and he or she has the gifts appropriate to the ministry to which he or she is called. This function of the church has come to be called the "outward call." The understanding of both an inward and an outward call has been maintained throughout the history of the church and is strongly affirmed by almost all Protestant churches.

In summarizing, the Protestant church, generally, has tended to connect ordination, by prayer and the laying on of hands, with a special blessing or even the bestowal of a gift. The Adventist Church has tended to give primary weight to the direct call of God and moves a little further in the direction of a setting apart to a vocation of ministerial service.

Historical Developments

The Reformers made the reformation of the hierarchical threefold order of ministry in the church a central concern. They soundly rejected medieval views of ordination and priesthood and affirmed, instead, the priesthood of all believers. They taught that every person has direct access to God through Jesus Christ, the one Mediator between God and humans. A single ordination by presbyters, with the laying on of hands on the basis of the "inward call" of God tested by the "outward calling" of the church, was practiced. The distance between clergy and laity was much reduced. Ordination conferred authority and responsibility to preach the Word and administer the sacraments. In general, as regards religious office, the dividing line was authority to administer the sacraments of baptism and the Lord's Supper.

Concepts of Ministry in the Adventist Church

The frequency with which Adventists use the term "movement" in book titles, addresses, and articles to describe the Adventist Church indicates a sense of identity that must be taken seriously. Adventism, from its inception, has been an eschatologically driven movement with a powerful sense of mission. The movement in the process of formation was composed largely of Methodists, Christianites, and Freewill Baptists. Members coming from the two latter groups were strongly anticreedal and antiformalist, with the conviction that theological and institutional developments after the age of the apostles had led to distortion of truth. Once the basic landmark doctrines of the Advent movement had been established, there was little concern regarding the niceties of theological definition. Besides, there was no time for such things. It was practical necessity rather than theological reflection upon the nature of the church that drove them to institute structures of church organization and patterns of ministry.

There was no necessity for early Adventists to define the priesthood of all believers.[13] Once the "shut-door" concept of limited access had been rejected, all members of the pilgrim band felt a zeal to invite their acquaintances to join them on the upward way to the heavenly city. And the ministers, called traveling preachers, functioned as evangelists more than as pastors. Because somebody was needed to administer the ordinances in the churches, ordained deacons were at first empowered to do so.[14] Fairly early, however, the different functions of deacons and elders were more clearly defined. Local elders were then ordained and authorized to celebrate the Lord's Supper and, on occasion, baptize. Ellen White refers to both the "traveling elder" or minister and "local elder" and their functions.[15] This arrangement, which made provision for the "overlapping duties of local and traveling elders as understood by Ellen White,"[16] was accepted as official policy at the organizational meeting of the Michigan Conference in 1861 and has remained so ever since.

The biblical basis for this pattern of ministry would appear to have been an extrapolation of the "elders in every place" (Titus 1:5) of the pastoral epistles and the example of the traveling ministries of persons like Paul and Timothy. The question of what, if anything, as regards religious status and function, constitutes the dividing line between clergy and elder seems not to have been a concern.

In the nineteenth century, the Methodist Church had an arrangement of traveling preachers (ordained ministers, called elders) and ordained local elders (laymen), who were authorized to perform the sacraments. This arrangement was developed to fulfill a practical need and enhance efficiency in ministry. The Methodist experience is cursorily described here because they have wrestled with the overlapping functions of two categories of elders. Methodist Bishop Cannon, former dean of the Candler School of Theology, writes:

> The ambiguity between an ordained layman and an unordained clergyman, for example, has hardly been recognized as such simply because the Methodist concern has not been with the nature of the doctrinal entities in a nice theological structure, but rather with effective functioning and satisfactory activity.
>
> The peculiarity of ministry in Methodism, which seems incapable of making a proper distinction between clergy and laity or at least providing a theological reason for such distinction when in practice it becomes apparent, inheres in the very origin of the ministerial office in the eighteenth century revival under the leadership of John and Charles Wesley.[17]

Most of the Methodist preachers in England during Wesley's lifetime, including several notable women, were not ordained. In appointing ministers to lead the church in America immediately after the War of Independence, Wesley ordained R. Whatcoat and T. Vasey as "elders" and Thomas Coke as "superintendent." He changed the Anglican titles "priest" and "bishop" to "elder" and "superintendent"; thus "elder" became a title commonly applied to ministers in America. The American Methodists, however, soon abandoned "superintendent" for "bishop."

The normal pattern of ministry in American Methodism was that of the "traveling preacher," who was an ordained "elder." This itinerant ministry left the churches without a resident minister; therefore, in contradistinction to Wesley's plan for frequent celebration of the Lord's Supper, it came to be celebrated quarterly. Apparently even this was not always possible and, partly in response to this need, the Methodists ordained local "elders" who nevertheless remained laymen, and conferred upon them the same sacramental privileges as ministers within their local sphere of authority.

In most Protestant churches ordination, which confers authority to celebrate the sacraments, constitutes a bright line differentiating clergy from laypersons. On this view, ordination to the ministry is more than an ecclesiastical endorsement of an inner call and appointment to an office in the church. It is regarded, in some indefinable sense, as the conferral of a special benediction or grace. Differentiation between clergy and laity in this respect did not exist in the Methodist Church prior to union with the Evangelical United Brethren in 1968, and neither does it exist in the Adventist Church.[18] Bishop Cannon's observation, quoted above, that the Methodist Church "seems incapable of making a proper distinction between clergy and laity or at least providing a theological reason for such distinction," would seem to apply with equal validity to the Adventist Church, and for precisely the same reasons.

Toward an Understanding of Ordination in the Adventist Church

It is extremely difficult to delineate understandings of ministry and ordination within the Adventist Church with exactitude and clarity. For the greater part, patterns of church organization and ministry have been developed pragmatically by an eschatologically driven movement rather than derived from a theological understanding of the ontology of the church. However, three fundamental concepts regarding the Adventist understanding of ordination are clear.

The first is that the primary basis of ministry in Adventism is the direct action of God in the inward personal call that attracts and drives a person to ministry. As we have seen, this is in accord with the biblical portrayal of the callings of God, in both the Old Testament and New Testament, to those He needed to fulfil His mission and lead His people. This is also in accord with the general Protestant understanding of the foundational basis of the Christian ministry. There are countless references to the callings of God in the writings of Ellen White and in the historical records of the Adventist Church. Note the dominant position of "a special calling" in the statement on ministerial ordination adopted by the General Conference in 1991.

The Gospel Ministry: A Special Call

While elders and deacons are appointed on the basis of spiritual experience and ability (Titus 1:5; Acts 6:3), the gospel ministry, Seventh-day Adventists believe, is a special calling from God. Regardless of the means by which the Lord initiates it, His call becomes an all-absorbing passion, a relentless drive that leads its possessor to exclaim: 'Necessity is laid upon me. Woe to me if I do not preach the gospel!' (1 Cor 9:16). The conviction becomes a 'fire in the bones' that will not be denied expression (Jer 20:9).

Ordination, an act of commission, acknowledges God's call, sets the individual apart, and appoints that person to serve the church in a special capacity.[19]

In most Protestant denominations the distinction between lay persons and ministers is authority to administer the sacraments. The statement above implies, however, that the distinction lies in the call of God. God's summons to a person to preach the gospel is foundational to the Adventist understanding of ministry.

The other side of this personal, inner call is that the call must be tested from the outside by the community of faith. This is an equally sacred responsibility exercised in stages by those involved in the ordinands' preparation for ministry, by the community of faith which they serve, and by the elders of the church.

Second, ordination is the public dedication by prayer and the laying on of hands of one who has demonstrated a calling to the lifelong vocation of ministry. One called by God, tested and approved by the church, is set apart for a holy vocation by ordination. But ordination is not regarded as the conferral of a divine gift which imparts a special element of grace. It is defined in the *SDA Minister's Manual* as "the church-at-large setting aside its ministerial leaders."[20] This is in keeping with Ellen White's commentary on the setting apart of Barnabas and Saul quoted above. Raoul Dederen, professor of theology at Andrews University, while stating that Adventists "have no elaborate doctrine of the ordination to the ministry," defines ordination "as the church's setting apart a person whom it believes God has called."[21] Adventists hold a view of ordination as a setting apart for service rather than as a conferral of grace. Ancillary to this is the view that a clergy person's ministry is valid only as long as it is effective. The functions of ministry are inseparable from the spiritual and moral experience of the person. Ordination is thus neither indelible nor irreversible in the Adventist Church; nevertheless, it does change the life of candidates deeply, for they thereby make a commitment to subordinate their lives to dedicated service of the church.[22]

The third important point regarding the Adventist understanding of ordination is that it makes no distinctive difference, that can be defined in theological and religious terms, between clergy and laypersons. Differences between ordained ministers and ordained elders (lay persons) are defined in the *Church Manual* in terms of office and sphere of authority, and not in terms of religious nature or substance.[23] For instance, the North American Division reserves only three functions for the ordained minister: organizing a church, uniting churches, and ordaining local elders and deacons.[24] Adventist polity in this respect is essentially the same worldwide.

There is, generally, within a given denomination, a compatibility between contingent theological concepts. High views[25] of Christology, the eucharist, church, ministry and ordination are usually associated together in mutually supportive contiguity. The opposite is equally true. Low views of Christology (an emphasis upon the human Christ), eucharist (an emphasis on symbolic representation rather than on a mystical or spiritual presence), church (emphasis on a functional rather than an ontological understanding), ministry (conceived of as heralding the gospel and exercising a pragmatic spirituality rather than as performing sacramental acts), ordination (understood more as a setting apart to a vocational status than as a sacramental bestowal of a spiritual gift) naturally belong together as mutually supportive elements of an integrated system of theological thought. If one applies this pattern of thought to the four paradigms of the church outlined at the beginning of this chapter, the incompatibility of low views of ministry and ordination with the first two paradigms, in which a high view of the church as the body of Christ is maintained, is obvious. On the other hand, the Adventist understanding of ordination described above more naturally fits the pragmatically driven church described in the third paradigm.[26]

The Ordination of Women

Having given consideration to the basic concepts of church, ministry, and ordination in biblical, theological, and historical perspective, and the way these have been understood in the Adventist Church, we now address the specific issue of the ordination of women to the ministry in the Adventist Church. The following argument in support of this practice is developed in four successive stages.

1. The position has been taken—on the evidence of Scripture, the witness of the Protestant churches, and the practice and stated understandings of the Adventist Church—that the most fundamental basis of ministry is the direct action of God in the "inner call." As a complement to this, the church has been given the responsibility of exercising the "outward call." If this is accepted, then the question may arise as to whether the church in its refusal to ordain one whom God has called and manifestly blessed in ministry may not be guilty of thwarting the purpose of God.

This is precisely the question the Methodists in America faced and which eventually led to the ordination of women to the gospel ministry. In 1853 Luther Lee[27] preached the sermon at the ordination of Antoinette Brown, said to be the first woman ordained to the ministry in the United States.[28] Subsequently Methodist women were ordained in a number of smaller Methodist churches. Phoebe Palmer, perhaps the most prominent holiness revivalist of the mid-nineteenth century, wrote the book *Promise of the Father* with the purpose of promoting a larger role for women in the spiritual leadership of the church.[29]

If the thesis is accepted that the primary basis of ministry is the inward call of God, then the Adventist Church now faces the issue of the ordination of women on precisely the same grounds as did the Methodists 150 years ago. This is a weighty spiritual issue that must be prayerfully weighed lest the church be found guilty of standing in the way of the purposes of God.

2. A second consideration relates to the line denominations draw dividing clergy and laity. On the one hand, ecclesiastical bodies with a high ecclesiology and an understanding of ministry as a priesthood standing between God and human beings make a wide distinction between the two. At the opposite extreme, where a low ecclesiology coincides with a radical view of the priesthood of all believers, no significant difference may be made between clergy and members. Ordination may be declined as in some Quaker and early Anabaptist groups. All were held to be ministers, with each serving according to the gift given to him or her by God. Of course, many positions are held between these two extremes, some closer to the high view with others

closer to the low view. The more usual position in Protestantism, even among those bodies which accept the priesthood of all believers, is that ordination confers authority to administer the sacraments and constitutes a clear line of differentiation between clergy and laity.

If Bishop Cannon is correct in describing Methodism as seemingly incapable of making a proper distinction between clergy and laity theologically, then Methodism endorses a low view of ordination. Analysis of the Adventist understanding and practice of ordination, as we have seen, would seem to place it in a similar category.

If there is, then, so little in any religious or theological sense dividing clergy and laity in the Adventist Church, what serious impediment can there be to the ordination of women? If laywomen, ordained as local elders, can perform all the functions of the minister, barring organizing and uniting churches, which together with geographical restriction are matters of polity rather than of religious function, then it would appear that the only religious/theological difference between them and ministers is the right to ordain elders and deacons. Inasmuch as women may administer the Lord's Supper and baptize, even this would appear to be more a matter of polity than of essential religious status. One can hardly avoid the conclusion that, given the Adventist understanding of both ministry and ordination, there is no theological basis for withholding ordination from women.

In the absence of any weighty, religiously-defined difference between ministers and elders (ordained laypersons), the matter of the ordination of women becomes one of evenhanded justice rather than of theological definition.[30]

3. Third, there is the matter of the silence of the Scriptures regarding the ordination of women. It is true that partisans on both sides of the issue claim support for their position from Scripture. But careful and impartial analysis serves to show, as many of the chapters in this book illustrate, that such arguments are based on indirect deduction and/or inference. There is simply no direct "Thus saith the Lord," either affirming or denying the ordination of women. How then does the church get beyond this impasse? Two positions have been taken. Most commonly one hears phrases derived ultimately from Thomas Campbell's famous "Declaration and Address" of 1809: "Where the Scriptures speak, we speak; where they are silent, we are silent."[31] In this case, silence simply means "No!" While this approach was commonplace among some of the groups, members of which joined the early Adventist

movement, this has not been the typical Adventist way. Adventists have not felt bound by the silences of Scripture. The most likely reason for this is that our forefathers, while following the Scriptures closely, also sought more directly applicable guidance from the Lord through Ellen White. As the movement grew, practical answers were sought that would protect the flock and enhance its effectiveness in proclaiming the message.[32] In addition, Ellen White encouraged the use of sanctified reason. Instead of indicating an unthinking No, the silences of the Scripture have been regarded in Adventism as invitations to careful study, prayer for guidance, and the use of sanctified reason.

In this particular case, then, it is time for the Adventist Church to calmly admit that the Scriptures are silent on the matter and that we have no direct word from the Lord either in Scripture or in the writings of Ellen White. This is an opportunity therefore for the exercise of prayerful study and sound judgment. It is our responsibility to seek divine guidance and make a decision as best we can in the light of the Adventist understanding of the church and its mission.

4. The fourth and final argument advanced builds on the previous three and is pragmatic, rather than directly theological. If the primary basis of ministry is the call of God, and if there is no substantive theological distinction in the Adventist understanding of ministry between ordained laypersons and clergy, and if the silence of the Scriptures on this matter is accepted, then an important and fundamental question facing the church in connection with this issue is that of the relationship between the ordination of women and the fulfillment of the mission of the church. The entire structure of the Adventist church and its patterns of mission and ministry have been built up in response to its self-understanding of mission. The ordination of women is one more issue that should be seen in this light.

Ellen White wrote at length about the fruitfulness of women in ministries of various kinds.[33] There is now an extensive body of literature on the contemporary experience of women in chaplaincy and ministry in many Protestant denominations indicating how much they enhance the ministry of the church in responding to the needs of persons in ways that complement what men are able to do.[34]

In the arguments for and against the ordination of women heard recently, the pragmatic issue regarding the tremendous contribution women can make to the church in the fulfillment of its mission has been largely swept aside as a second-order concern not worthy of serious consideration. This is false reasoning. The Adventist church was called into being by God to fulfill a mission, and if the three considerations outlined above are accepted as representing the Adventist understanding of ministry, then the function of ordained women in the fulfillment of the mission of the Church becomes a fundamental and important consideration in the issue of the ordination of women.

Patterns of ministry in the Adventist Church vary from place to place. The exercise of ministry by women in some places need not imply universality of practice. Where social circumstances and cultural constraints do not favor such roles for women there should be no feeling of necessity. But God is opening up wonderful opportunities for the advancement of the cause by the ministry of women in many countries of earth. Is this not, then, a challenge to all of us who seek to faithfully serve our Lord to prayerfully seek the guidance of the Holy Spirit in this matter in order that every avenue of witness might be fully employed in the proclamation of the Three Angel's Messages? Our Lord promised: "When he, the Spirit of truth, is come, he will guide you into all truth." (John 16:13). And Ellen White writes of our responsibility in the last days, "We are living in the most solemn period of the world's history. The destiny of earth's teeming multitudes is about to be decided. Our own future well-being, and also the salvation of other souls, depend upon the course we now pursue. We need to be guided by the Spirit of Truth. Every follower of Christ should earnestly inquire, 'Lord, what wilt Thou have me to do?' "[35] Let us then earnestly seek the guidance of the Holy Spirit in our search to understand the will of the Master for his church in these last days.

Endnotes

1. J. Christiaan Beker, *Paul the Apostle* (Philadelphia: Fortress, 1980), 303-318.

2. See the chapter by Robert Johnston.

3. R. Newton Flew, *Jesus and His Church: A Study of the Idea of the Ecclesia in the New Testament* (London: Epworth, 1938), 146, 147.

4. R. P. Lightner, "Ordain, Ordination," *Evangelical Dictionary of Theology*, ed. Walter A. Elwell (Grand Rapids: Baker, 1985), 801, 802.

5. For a fuller discussion of this, see V. Norskov Olsen, *Myth and Truth about Church Priesthood and Ordination* (Riverside, CA: Loma Linda Univ. Press, 1990), 121-125.

6. For more detailed discussions see Eduard Lohse, "*Cheir*," *Theological Dictionary of the New Testament*, ed. Gerhard Kittel and G. Friedrich (Grand Rapids: Eerdmans, 1964-1976), 9:424-434; Everett Ferguson, "Laying on of Hands: Its Significance in Ordination," *The Journal of Theological Studies* 26 (April 1975): 1-12. See also the chapter by Keith Mattingly.

7. That this is recorded as "through the laying on of the hands of the elders as a body" in the first epistle and "by the laying on of my hands" in the second (i.e., whether there were one or two ordinations) is not of consequence to this discussion, which is concerned with the significance of the laying on of hands rather than with the office to which Timothy was instituted. The consensus seems to be that these accounts refer to a single event and that the difference is adequately accounted for by the personal tone of the second letter.

8. Lohse, 433, 434.

9. Ferguson, 2, 6.

10. Ibid., 10.

11. Ibid., 162.

12. "1 Tim. 4:14," *SDA Bible Commentary*, 7:307.

13. See chapter by Denis Fortin.

14. See chapter by George Knight.

15. Ibid.; see also chapter by Jerry Moon.

16. See chapter by George Knight.

17. William R. Cannon, "The Meaning of the Ministry in Methodism," *Methodist History*, (October 1969): 3, 4.

18. Adventist and Methodist patterns of ministry are parallel in other respects as well. Methodists have steadfastly maintained a system of appointed rather than congregationally called ministry, and so have Adventists. There are also similarities in the conference system practiced by the two denominations (Cannon, 16).

20. *Seventh-day Adventist Minister's Manual* (Silver Spring, MD: General Conference of Seventh-day Adventists, 1992), 76.

20. Ibid., 83.

21. Raoul Dederen, "A Theology of Ordination," *Ministry*, February 1978, 24M, L.

22. The Adventist ordinand is required to take no vows of faithfulness to the Lord and his church, as are common in many communities of faith. Perhaps this is because vows in ordination have been regarded as remnants of prerequisites for a sacramental understanding of ordination as an indelible conferral of grace.

23. General Conference of Seventh-day Adventists, *Seventh-day Adventist Church Manual* (Silver Spring, MD: General Conference of Seventh-day Adventists, 1990), 58, 59.

24.   North American Division of Seventh-day Adventists, *Constitution, Bylaws and Working Policy of the General Conference of Seventh-day Adventists, North American Division* (Silver Spring, MD: North American Division, 1994-1995), 313.

25.   The categories, high and low, as used here do not at all imply superiority and inferiority. Rather, "high" signifies an emphasis upon the divine side of Christology, the church, etc.; whereas "low" emphasizes the human nature of Christ, the church, the ministry, and the natural elements in the eucharist.

26.   This paradigm, however, falls short of maintaining a balance between the being/essence and the eschatological/functional dimension of the church. The question therefore naturally arises as to whether predominantly functional understandings of ministry and ordination adequately take account of the work of the Holy Spirit and of the element of divine blessing manifest in the New Testament accounts.

27.   Together with Orange Scott and the Millerite preacher George Storrs, Lee was one of the founders of the Wesleyan Methodist Church

28.   The sermon has been reprinted in *Holiness Tracts Defending the Ministry of Women* (New York: Garland, 1985), 3-22.

29.   Phoebe Palmer, *Promise of the Father* (Boston: Henry V. Degen, 1859).

30.   This essentially is the position taken by Roger Dudley; see his chapter in this book.

31.   Thomas Campbell, *The "Declaration and Address,"* 1809; quoted in *American Christianity* (New York: Charles Scribner's Sons, 1960), 1: 578, 579.

32.   The compilation of Ellen White's writings entitled *Evangelism* is an illustration of this. Her writings contain a vast amount of information on many topics, and go far beyond what is directly available in the Scriptures.

33.   See the chapters by Jerry Moon and Michael Bernoi.

34.   Helen Beard, *Women in Ministry Today: A Positive Statement on the Role of Women* (Plainfield, NJ: Logos International, 1980); Mary E. Giles, *When Each Leaf Shines: Voices of Women's Ministry* (Denville, NJ: Dimension, 1986); Roberta Hestenes, *Women and Men in Ministry: Collected Readings* (Pasadena, CA: Fuller Theological Seminary, 1988); Kenneth R. Mitchell, *Multiple Staff Ministries* (Philadelphia: Westminster, 1988); Judith L. Weidman, ed. *Women Ministers: How Women Are Redefining Traditional Roles* (San Francisco: Harper & Row, 1981); Catherine Wessinger, ed. *Religious Institutions and Women's Leadership: New Roles Inside the Mainstream* (Columbia, SC: Univ. of South Carolina Press, 1996).

35.   Ellen G. White, *Great Controversy*, 601.

PART THREE:
WOMEN IN MINISTRY AND LEADERSHIP

Throughout the ages, women have served God in many ways. In spite of the patriarchal structure of their society, women occupied respected positions of leadership in Old Testament times; their contribution to the church in the New Testament was also visible (chap. 9). In the early years of the Seventh-day Adventist Church the work of women in ministry was approved by Ellen G. White (chap. 10) and carried out by notable women (chap. 11). The twentieth-century contributions of godly women in ministry and the movement toward the recognition of their gifts and calling are documented in chapter 12.

CHAPTER 9

WOMEN IN SCRIPTURE: A SURVEY AND EVALUATION

JO ANN DAVIDSON

Introduction and Orientation

Some Bible readers contend that the Old Testament illustrates and the New Testament admonishes that all women are to be under the authority of all men. Others insist that this is not the case. Thus, it becomes of utmost importance to evaluate meticulously the evidence Scripture exhibits. In past eras of church history, this has customarily been a masculine endeavor, as women were generally excluded from theological studies. After centuries of male-dominated scholarship, the contemporary feminist movement has sought to redress what they perceive as male bias in both the Scripture documents and their interpretation.

Other factors beyond feminist concerns have also been operative. Biblical interpretation during this century has been largely dominated by the historical-critical method, in which the biblical text is dissected and varying amounts either discounted or discarded. Subtle linguistical nuances have been either unrecognized or ignored, rather than considered essential to the interpretive process. For example, the characteristic repetitions in Hebrew narratives have often been attributed to sloppy later redactors rather than appraised for their value within the narration itself.

The last twenty-five years or so have spawned further interpretive developments. Renewed attention is being focused on the biblical text as it reads. Meanwhile, those stressing pluralistic concerns often accept the Bible canon but place it on a parity with sacred texts of other religious traditions. Thus detailed exegetical involvement with Scripture is usually not pursued. Other interpreters urge a closer reading of the text through rhetorical criticism and narrative analysis.[1]

Feminist authors mirror some of the same developments. One wing in feminism seeks to retain some vestige of importance for the Christian Bible. Others insist that any serious theological reflection must leave behind the Bible's perceived chauvinism if women are to have any prospect of ministry in the church.

Whether or not they accept some modicum of authority for Scripture, most feminists complain about what they perceive as its extensive and oppressive patriarchy.[2] As a result, some radical feminists seek to revise Scripture or to reconstruct its history.[3] Thus feminists seem to concur that Scripture, with its presumed male hierarchical posture, has been more of a curse than a blessing.

The modern feminist movement, though displaying many divergent currents,[4] insists that its authors are releasing themselves from forced domination of men throughout Judeo-Christian history. Their writing is often forceful and bitter, and many of the sentiments expressed are uncompromising.[5]

Included in their stance is a revulsion of much of the interpretation of Scripture by the Church Fathers and the myriad male-authored commentaries of both the Old and New Testaments.[6] Radical feminists scorn a wide-spread, long-held Christian conviction that all women must be submissive to all men. They deride this posture as being forged through the centuries by male-dominated theology. This, they insist, has denied them full citizenship in the Christian church.[7]

Some in the Seventh-day Adventist Church are concerned that feminist influences have subtly (or not so subtly) swayed many of those who are encouraging the ordination of women. Therefore, any movement in this direction demonstrates an obvious drift away from the eternal principles of Scripture which, they feel, instruct all women to be under the authority of all men.

However, other Seventh-day Adventists (SDAs) contend that the correct interpretation of Scripture reveals that women (when married) are under the headship of their husbands, but in the church men and women stand together in full equality under Christ. Still others argue that the Apostle Paul contradicts himself on this issue in his various New Testament writings and thus should be ignored—or that his counsel is outdated in this modern era.

Historically, SDAs have maintained that Scripture is an indivisible unit and, when properly understood, presents no contradictions among the various authors.[8] I hold this position and therefore do not allow that Paul can be inconsistent with himself. However, though not a "feminist," I do acknowledge the deplorable treatment of women throughout Christian history. I resonate with Mary Kassian's sentiments:

> I am a woman. I have experienced the scorn and prideful superiority with which men have, at times, treated me. I have listened to insults against my capabilities, my intelligence, and my body. I have burned with anger as I have wiped the blood from a battered woman's face. I have wept with women who have been forcefully, brutally raped—violated to the very core of their being. I have been sickened at the perverted sexual abuse of little girls. I have challenged men who sarcastically demean women with their "humor." And I have walked out of church services where pastors carelessly malign those whom God has called holy. I am often hurt and angered by sexist, yes, SEXIST demeaning attitudes and actions. And I grieve deeply at the distortion of the relationship that God created as harmonious and good. As a woman I feel the battle. I feel the sin. Feminism identifies real problems which demand real answers.[9]

Realization of such conditions has influenced many feminists to turn away bitterly from the church and Scripture. Recently, however, there have been a number of female scholars who have returned to the biblical text and drawn attention to many details there regarding women, details that had previously been overlooked or ignored.

One valuable consequence has been a more accurate comprehension of Old Testament patriarchy. New concentration on minute details of the Old Testament narratives is modifying previous negative bias toward them. As a result, even a number of male scholars have begun to provide a much-needed corrective to previous perceptions of women in Scripture.[10] What is now being increasingly comprehended is that throughout both the Old and New Testaments women served not only in home and family administration but also in public and religious spheres. The roles of women in Scripture are varied and vigorous.

At first glance, the male may appear to predominate by sheer numbers. However, even this fact must be understood with a correct evaluation of historical writing itself.

No history book is exhaustive. Each historical document includes certain events/people/ideas deemed by that historian as the most crucial affecting subsequent human life. Scripture, though including much historical material which spans multiple centuries, is not exhaustive, as seen in John 21:25 and Heb 11:32, 35, 36. One cannot help but observe time voids in the records.

Christians have long believed that the development of the canon has been superintended by God to include those people and events that, from the divine perspective, are the most decisive in salvation history. The historical panorama thus is lengthy yet basically narrow in scope. The reader is informed of patriarchs and matriarchs, kings and queens, prophets and prophetesses—couched between great gaps of information regarding other female and male personages and events throughout the many centuries connected by the biblical documents. In this light, it becomes more precarious to insist that males have *always* dominated women. This is not possible to substantiate from biblical history. Furthermore, new probing into the biblical text itself also suggests that this is not the case.

As Carol Meyers advises, patriarchy itself must be carefully defined in the light of its original context. Feminists often appear biased negatively against patriarchy in any form. But Meyers posits that perhaps they have not adequately informed their position from the biblical record. She even proposes that many of the details recorded in the Old Testament indicate a seemingly equitable situation between male and female up to the time of the Israelite monarchy. As a result of the establishment of the throne in Israel, she argues, great changes came to Israelite society, with the subsequent position of the female slowly diminishing.[11] She also carefully evaluates other factors contributing to the deteriorating status of woman, especially "the superimposition of Greco-Roman thought and cultural forms on the biblical world." She notes:

> Greco-Roman culture brought a dualistic way of thinking to the Semitic world: pairs such as body and soul, evil and good, female and male became aligned. Eve was the victim of this alignment: female was linked with body and evil. Relegated to a position of decreasing power as the household lost its prominence, she then became associated with negative aspects of life. The misogynist expansions of the Eden story in early Christian Jewish literature begin to emerge. A new concept of Eve associated with sin, death, and suffering is superimposed so indelibly on the assertive and productive figure of the Eden narrative that we can hardly see the original woman of Genesis 2-3.[12]

This paper proceeds on the basis of Meyers' basic assumption that women were more prominent in the Old Testament than past perception has generally acknowledged. Her reasoning appears valid in view of numerous intriguing features within the Old Testament narratives.

Beyond the Old Testament, Christ's treatment of women, in contrast with many in his society, was remarkable.[13] Furthermore, the Apostle Paul, whom feminists regard with scorn, mirrored Christ's own positive behavior toward women.

Old Testament Women

Women in Genesis

Eve. The discussion of biblical women rightfully begins with Eve, with careful consideration of the textual nuances regarding her before and after the Fall. Richard Davidson's contribution to this book, dealing with biblical headship, focuses extensively on this (see chapter 13).

Sarah. Abraham's life of faith has been extensively (and rightly) studied and admired. His wife, Sarah, though rarely acknowledged on a par with her husband, is equally remarkable.[14] Katheryn Darr invites one to ponder that

> as Sarai and Abram are approaching Egypt, he does not order her to comply with his planned deception. Rather, Abraham must ask her to say that she is his sister. He cohabits with Hagar because Sarah wants him to; and when she decides that Ishmael is a threat to her own son's inheritance, Sarah succeeds in expelling both mother and child. Indeed, God defends her demand; and this is not the only time that the Lord acts on Sarah's behalf. In Pharaoh's court, and within the household of Abimelech, God is concerned that Sarah be protected and returned to her husband.[15]

Janice Nunnally-Cox argues that, even within patriarchy, Sarah and Abraham were amazingly equal:

> She appears to say what she wants, when she wants, and Abraham at times responds in almost meek obedience. He does not command her; she commands him, yet there seems to be an affectionate bond between them. Abraham does not abandon Sarah during her barrenness, nor does he gain other wives while she lives, as far as we know. The two have grown up together and grown old together, and when Sarah dies, Abraham can do nothing but weep. Sarah is a matriarch of the first order: respected by rulers and husband alike, a spirited woman and bold companion.[16]

The narrator seems intent that Sarah be regarded as critical to the divine covenant as Abraham himself. For one finds the unwavering indication that it will be *Sarah*'s offspring who will fulfill the covenant promise—even when Abraham contends with God that he already has a son Ishmael (Gen 17:18-19; cf. Isa 51:1, 2).

This particular era in biblical history of patriarchs and matriarchs deserves renewed attention. Savina Teubal rightly insists:

In particular, women have traditionally been depicted as primitive and childish in their aspirations and generally lacking in vision. Fresh study of our female forebears, however, invalidates this view and shows us that the matriarchs were learned, wise women who were highly developed spiritually.[17]

Sarah's life itself demonstrates this:

1. When Abraham pleads with Sarah to misrepresent their marital relationship,

His plea sounds apologetic. Instead of being a proud and overbearing patriarchal figure, Abraham begs Sarah to lie for him. This appears uncharacteristic for a totally dominant patriarchal society. Is Sarah a completely submissive wife, or does she retain some right and control? The text does suggest that she maintained some sort of authority and that Abraham was not the absolute master figure that might be assumed even though the story is set within the patriarchal period.[18]

2. When offering hospitality, Abraham the patriarch is depicted as sharing in the preparations along with his wife. Sarah is summoned to prepare the bread (Gen 18:6); Abraham, along with his servants, is involved in the preparations for the meal (18:7-8).[19]

3. Jack Vancil comments further on Sarah's significance on this occasion:

The very first recorded utterance from the visitors after the meal was the question, "Where is Sarah your wife?" (v. 9), and then from v. 10 she is the leading subject.[20]

Hagar. She is the victim of a grave mistake by Abraham and Sarah. Yet the poignant details recorded in Genesis 21, after she and her son had been excluded from Abraham's family, show that this Egyptian slave woman was "more highly honoured in some respects than almost any other figure in the Bible."[21] For example, the "Angel of the Lord" appeared, for the first time in biblical history, to this rejected woman (Gen 21:17). Indeed, He even called her by name! Abraham and Sarah did not grant her this dignity but typically referred only to her status.[22]

God did not abandon Hagar or her son Ishmael in this devastating situation caused by human error. His word regarding the covenant through Abraham was eternal, yet he pointedly provided for mother and son. He promised to make Ishmael a great nation. In fact, his promise to Hagar and her son is arrestingly similar to the one they had been hearing for years in Abraham's household (Gen 16:10; 17:20). This is also the only time that a covenantal-type promise was announced to a woman.

Trevor Dennis evaluates this poignantly:

> How very surprising is the honour which is bestowed upon Hagar (and upon Ishmael too) in Genesis 16. For a start, annunciations are a rare commodity in the Bible. . . . In only three cases is the promise of a son made to the one who will be the mother of the child. In only four cases does God make the announcement himself. . . . Only two women in the entire Bible receive annunciations from God himself, Hagar and the unnamed wife of Manoah.[23]

It is also significant that she, a woman, chooses the wife for her son. Moreover, Hagar is the only woman in the Old Testament, the only person in all of Scripture, to give deity a name, "El-Roi" (Gen 16:13a). As Dennis points out:

> The name El-Roi occurs nowhere else in the Old Testament. It is Hagar's name for God, and Hagar's alone. It arises out of, and speaks eloquently of, her own private encounter with him. . . . Let no one underestimate how extraordinary this naming is. . . . Moreover, Hagar does not name her God as an aside, or declare his identity to herself after he has left the stage. She names him to his face: "*You* are the God who Sees Me." The phrase the narrator uses for the naming is the usual one in Hebrew narrative. It is the same as the one used, for example, when the man in the Garden named his wife Eve, or Eve herself named her third son Seth.[24]

Hagar is one of only three women to engage in dialogue with God in Genesis—and she a rejected slave woman.

Rebekah. The next matriarch[25] in Genesis also exhibits the same force of character as Sarah. Sharon Jeansonne compels us to consider that

> rather than minimizing Rebekah's contribution to the Israelite people, the narratives that introduce and develop the portrait of the second of the matriarchs are striking in the way she is depicted. Although she is described as being a beautiful wife for Isaac, she is not appreciated solely for her appearance. Like Abraham, her independence and trust are demonstrated by her willingness to leave her family and travel to a strange land.[26]

Furthermore, the Rebekah narratives are structured to portray her as an important character in her own right. According to Jeansonne, techniques such as dialogue, narrative pace, genealogical notation, and other literary features suggest the prominence of Rebekah in Israel's history.[27]

When Abraham directs Eliezer to find a wife for Isaac, one of the instructions he gives his servant is a significant allusion to a woman's status during the patriarchal era. Abraham declares that "if the woman is not willing to come with you, then you will be free from this oath of mine" (24:8). Jeansonne contends "that Abraham assumes the woman will have the final say in the matter."[28] And indeed, ultimately Rebekah herself chooses to go with Eliezer. In fact, in the lengthy narrative of Genesis 24, Rebekah affirms her determination to travel with Eliezer directly; it is not just recounted by the narrator (Gen 24:55-58).

Rebekah arranges for the hospitality of Eliezer herself. Her father says hardly a word throughout. Eliezer asks for a place in her "father's house" (v. 24), but the narrator speaks of Rebekah's "mother's house" (v. 28).

Most importantly, there is noticeable correspondence of key terms between Rebekah's narratives and Abraham's. They both leave behind "their country," "their kindred," and their "father's house." Both will be "blessed" and "become great." James Williams underscores this significance by suggesting, "With this blessing the narrator quietly moves Rebecca into the cycle of God's promises to the patriarchs."[29]

After Rebekah marries Isaac and becomes pregnant, she is anxious enough "to inquire of the LORD" and she does this herself (Gen 25:22). Mary Turner notes:

> The critical issue of this story comes into play as Rebekah suffers through her pregnancy. The children struggle within her and, presumably on the basis of her discomfort, Rebekah "inquires (darash) of the Lord." This phrase is of great importance in the Old Testament. Only the great prophets like Moses and Elisha and the greatest kings of Israel inquire of the Lord. . . . Rebekah inquires and, as a result, receives the oracle from Yahweh which destines her younger son to rule the older.[30]

The formula used to announce Rebekah's delivery, "And her days were fulfilled that she should give birth" (Gen 25:24), is used of only three biblical women: Elizabeth and Mary in the New Testament and Rebekah of the Old Testament.

Later, when her son Esau married two Hittite women, this was a "grief of mind to Isaac and Rebekah" (26:35). Turner suggests that this inclusion of Rebekah's distress regarding Esau's marriage to pagan women reveals that Rebekah was just as concerned about the covenant promise/line as was Isaac.[31]

After examining Rebekah's narratives, Jeansonne correctly argues that

> the characterization of Rebekah yields a deeper understanding of her significance. . . . All of these actions are given without a polemical context, and the narrator does nothing to indicate that these were unusual activities for a woman to take. . . . The presentation of Rebekah shows that women in Israel were viewed as persons who could make crucial decisions about their futures, whose prayers were acknowledged."[32]

The Genesis matriarchs were not "wall flowers"! It would be unfair to the portraits of Genesis women to argue that women within patriarchy bowed in submission to all men. Rather, though respectful of their husbands, they were intelligent, willful, and directive. Meyers is right to insist:

> Feminists who condemn or bemoan the apparent patriarchy of ancient or other societies may be deflecting their energies from what should be the real focus of their concern: the transformation of functional gender balance to situations of real imbalance. . . . If our position with respect to biblical or Israelite patriarchy is revisionist, this is not to idealize ancient Israel but rather to free feminist critics from a misplaced preoccupation with biblical androcentrism and allow them to search for the dynamics that led to the dichotomizing of gender attributes by early postbiblical times.[33]

Deborah. The first Old Testament Deborah appears in the patriarchal period. Gen 35:7-9 records Jacob's return to Bethel. There, Deborah, Rebekah's nurse, dies. This woman is mentioned only twice in Genesis (24:59, 35:8). Yet, surprisingly, her death and burial are included in the scriptural record. Ellen White movingly comments:

> At Bethel, Jacob was called to mourn the loss of one who had long been an honored member of his father's family—Rebekah's nurse, Deborah, who had accompanied her mistress from Mesopotamia to the land of Canaan. The presence of this aged woman had been to Jacob a precious tie that bound him to his early life, and especially to the mother whose love for him had been so strong and tender. Deborah was buried with expressions of so great sorrow that the oak under which her grave was

made, was called "the oak of weeping." *It should not be passed unnoticed that the memory of her life of faithful service and of the mourning of this household has been counted worthy to be preserved in the word of God.*[34]

Women at the Time of the Exodus

A notable roster of women appears at the opening of the book of Exodus.

Shiphrah and Puah. These two midwives bravely disobeyed Pharaoh's command to murder newborn Hebrew baby boys. That these two courageous women are named (even Pharaoh himself remains unnamed) is highly significant in Hebrew narrative. Also noteworthy is the fact that they have two separate audiences with Pharaoh.

Trevor Dennis rightly concludes of these midwives:

Of all the initiatives taken by human beings in Ex 1-14, it is those of the women, however, that display the greatest courage, invite our keenest admiration, and have the most powerful influence on events. . . . Shiphrah and Puah and the women of 2.1-10 together succeed in defeating the policy of genocide, and save Moses from drowning.[35]

Egyptian princess. Divine providence ironically enlisted strategic protection for Israel's future deliverer from the very Egyptian monarchy which issued the death decree! Ellen White describes how the daughter of the most powerful ruler of the world at that time was directed by angels to the basket with Moses in it.[36]

Danna Nolan Fewell and David M. Gunn are insightful:

The actions of this non-Israelite are presented in direct parallel to those of the God of Israel: 'She "comes down," "sees" the child, "hears" its cry, takes pity on him, draws him out of the water, and provides for his daily needs' (cf. 3:7-8). What she does for Moses, God is soon to do for Israel.[37]

Jochebed. Biblical history records the unusual means she devised to spare Moses' life in spite of Pharaoh's grim decree. Her husband, after the brief mention in Exod 2:1, is never referred to again except in genealogical notation. Instead, attention is focused on his wife.

Miriam. The daughter of Jochebed exhibited intelligence, diplomacy, and courage to speak to the Egyptian princess, cleverly suggesting a "nurse" for the baby in the basket.

Apparently Miriam never married. The Old Testament includes no record of a husband or names of any children for her as it does for Moses and Aaron. In Exodus the focus of attention often centers on her two brothers, Moses and Aaron. Any regard ever granted Miriam concentrates on her errors (Num 12:1-10). This single woman's position during the Exodus has perhaps been underestimated. However, Scripture includes an indicative genealogical mention of her. In 1 Chr 6:3 Miriam is listed among the sons of Amram; that she is mentioned in a chapter of fathers and male offspring confirms her prominence.

In the book of Exodus, she is presented as a prophet, the second person in the Pentateuch so identified (Exod 15:20). At the crossing of the Red Sea hers was a dual role: prophetess and musician at the side of her two brothers. Through Micah, God Himself insists:

> For I brought you up from the land of Egypt,
> I redeemed you from the house of bondage;
> And *I sent before you* Moses, Aaron, *and Miriam* (6:4, emphasis added).

Furthermore, as Rita Burns observes:

> First of all, the fact that Miriam's death and burial were recorded at all is striking. Whereas other figures in the wilderness community (Hur, Eldad and Medad, Moses' wife and father-in-law, etc.) disappeared without mention, the notice of Numbers 20:1b seems to be at least an implicit witness that Miriam was a figure of some significance. . . .
>
> It is noteworthy that Miriam is the only member of the wilderness community whose death is recorded without being explicitly connected with divine punishment (cf. Numbers 20:2-13, 22ff; Deuteronomy 32:48-52). . . . It can hardly be accidental that . . . the deaths of Miriam, Aaron and Moses coincide with the last three stops on the wilderness journey.[38]

Women during the Time of the Judges:

Ruth. Old Testament history records the history of a young, childless widow who chose to abandon her national identity, culture, and religion. She gave up all opportunity for wealth and security in her homeland to accompany her widowed mother-in-law.

Phyllis Trible suggests that Ruth's choice to serve the God of Heaven was just as radical a decision of faith as that of Abraham leaving Ur. While not minimizing Abraham's exceptional act of trust, one must take into account his circumstances: he traveled with his spouse, much wealth, and many household servants; he was sustained by a direct call from heaven and a divine promise. In this light, Ruth's radical decision to serve Naomi's God marks an extraordinary venture.[39]

Ruth's and Naomi's initiatives are evident in a book where men never assume major roles. Yet the narrator does not exhibit shock or distaste over such female enterprise. Naomi's name itself (meaning "my delight" or "my pleasantness"), given to her in such a time and culture where sons were often more welcome than daughters (Ruth 4:15), suggests that Naomi's parents were full of joy by the birth of their *daughter*.[40]

A close reading of this narrative discloses an even deeper meaning. Ruth is the epitome of abnegation. She acts in her mother-in-law's place in order to save an Israelite line from extinction, although she herself is a Moabitess. Veritable redeemer of an Israelite clan, her self-sacrifice is eventually revealed for what it is: a national salvation. The Moabitess is a vital link in the covenantal history between God and his people, not only with the Davidic king, but as an ancestor of the Messiah (Matt 1:4).[41]

Deborah. The book of Judges includes the narrative of the second Old Testament Deborah, described not only as wife and musician, but also as judge and prophet. Charme Robarts notes:

> Deborah is the only judge described as a prophet and, in the tradition of the other biblical prophets, she spoke the word of Yahweh. Her summons to Barak is couched in the command of Yahweh, and her prophetic competency is proved by the outcome of the battle and the extirpation of the enemy at the hand of a woman. In her song, Deborah proclaims the mighty acts of Yahweh.[42]

She is depicted as a military leader with the same authority as male generals, and a judge to whom other male Israelites turned for legal counsel and to settle court cases (Judg 4:5). She was a recognized political leader and one through whom God initiates a war. The narrative indicates that she arbitrated disputes, assembled people to combat, and was regarded as an oracle of the divine will.[43]

There seems to be no negative reaction to this woman, nor is she regarded as peculiar. She is merely introduced in the common Old Testament manner. No excuses or explanations are necessary that a woman should be in this prominent position. Vancil is correct to argue that "nothing in the narrative suggests that Deborah's gender improved or detracted from her status as judge/deliverer, nor is there indication that Yahweh had any reservations about her functioning in this role.[44]

Moreover, many have seen Deborah's narrative as the single positive episode in the otherwise dreary history of the other (male) judges in the Judges book. As Robarts observes,

With few (but significant) exceptions, the development of each major judge narrative leads to a decline, . . . even during the judge's lifetime. Typically, after becoming a leader of the people and eliminating the source of oppression, the judge leads the people away from Yahweh. . . . The exception . . . is Deborah.[45]

Women during the Time of the Monarchy

Hannah. In the pivotal transition from judges to monarchy, the key transitional person is a woman. The Samuel narratives commence with an extended account of his mother Hannah. Trevor Dennis alerts the sensitive reader that

> The Books of Samuel are primarily concerned with . . . just one man, with David, for Samuel comes to prepare the way for him, while the ac-count of the reign of Saul very soon becomes the story of David's own rise to power. . . . Hannah . . . appears right at the start of it all, when David is but a twinkle in the narrator's eye. Her story provides the be-ginning of this great chapter in Israel's story, just as Eve's began the whole work, and Shiphrah and Puah and the women of Exodus 2 pre-sided over the accounts of Israel's beginnings as a people in Egypt. . . . Hannah will begin a tale which will lead Israel into the ambiguities of monarchy.[46]

In these narratives, Hannah's vow (1 Sam 1:10-11) is her first recorded speech. After this, she speaks more than anyone else. In her initial prayer, she vows to dedicate the promised son as a Nazirite. According to Num 6, men or women normally took this pledge for themselves. When Samson's birth was announced, God declared that the child would be a Nazirite (Judg 13:4). However, on this occasion, Hannah took the initiative. As Dennis points out, "What God commands in Judges 13, she herself vows at Shiloh."[47] Hannah

> does not need Elkanah to pray for her. *She* prays, and in doing so becomes the first woman, indeed the *only* woman, in the entire Bible to utter a formal, spoken prayer, and have her prayer quoted in the text for us to read. . . . In the narratives of the Old and New Testaments Hannah's prayer is unique—and no other woman pays God such a vow as hers, either.[48]

Only after Samuel is weaned do we learn of Hannah's earlier vow regarding him. As the text suggests, "Hannah has not asked Elkanah to confirm her vow. . . . She presents her plan to dedicate Samuel as something already decided upon (1 Sam 1:22)."[49] Elkanah is not asked for his permission; he merely gives his blessing (1 Sam 1:23). Dennis notes:

> From now on he will have nothing to say, and nothing to do (he does
> not take any action in 2.20). Except for a few words of blessing from Eli
> in 2.20, all speech in the rest of Hannah's story will be put in her
> mouth, all the initiatives taken will be hers, all that is done . . . will be
> done by her.[50]

When Hannah brings Samuel to Shiloh in fulfillment of her vow
to God, the narrative focuses solely on her. Ellen White notes that she
travels with her husband; however, she takes all the initiatives (1 Sam
1:24).[51] This is significant, especially since Elkanah was a Levite (1 Chr
6:33-38) and Hannah's activities are generally thought of as belonging to
the male. As Dennis points out, when Hannah journeyed to the house of
the Lord with bulls, flour, and wine, she went

> expressly to perform her own vow. It is she who has come with such
> fine offerings for sacrifice, and, remarkably, with her own child to
> dedicate to the service of God. Hannah's offering of Samuel is without
> parallel in biblical literature.
>
> It is hard to respond adequately to such an act as Hannah's and Eli
> does not try. This time he does not answer her. Only Hannah herself
> can speak to what she has done. After noting that she left Samuel with
> Eli, the narrator takes us straight into her song. For the second time she
> pours out her soul to God.[52]

Hannah's exultant anthem is striking. One does not hear a gentle
lullaby; instead, she gives

> a vigorous shout of triumph, enough to make Peninnah and Eli and
> their like tremble. There is nothing ladylike about it!
>
> Indeed, it does not look like the song of a woman in Hannah's
> position at all. At one point it uses the imagery of war. It speaks of the
> shattering enemies, and closes with a prayer for the king. That final
> reference is significant, of course. In Hannah's day there was no
> monarchy. . . . [yet] Hannah sings *a king's song!*[53]

Many commentators see the glorious New Testament "Magnificat" of
Mary (Luke 1:46-55) as but an echo of Hannah's triumphant hymn!

Shunamite Woman. Continuing in the Old Testament, one finds
an extended narrative of a woman and her dying son (2 Kgs 4:8-37). The
father plays a very minor role in these verses, and nothing more is known
of the lad after the miracle of Elisha. He was not a son in the covenant
line and is never named.

Generally, when this narrative is recounted, the emphasis is on the prophet Elisha and the miracle God brought through him. However, the narrative focus remains centered on the many determined actions of this earnest woman in caring for her stricken son. She does not seek her husband's permission for her decisive actions, but rather takes full initiative. Such a detailed portrait of this vigorous person corresponds to the description of the "woman of strength" in Prov 31:10-31.

Huldah. This prophetess comes into the foreground as a chief religious authority at the time of an intense religious revival (2 Kgs 22:14f). The text expresses no surprise that the King of Judah sends Hilkiah the priest and Shaphan the scribe and several other prominent officials to this woman to ask her concerning the meaning of the discovery of the Book of the Law. As John Willis comments, "The biblical text does not suggest that seeking divine revelation from a woman was in any way unusual."[54]

The scroll of Deuteronomy, dealing with crucial moral and political issues, was found as the Temple was being repaired and refurbished. Thus the authority that the King recognized in Huldah is profound. Ellen White explains:

> At that time the prophetess Huldah was living in Jerusalem, near the temple. *The mind of the king*, filled with anxious foreboding, *reverted to her*, and he *determined to inquire of the Lord through His chosen messenger*, to learn, if possible, whether by any means within his power he might save erring Judah, now on the verge of ruin.
>
> *The gravity of the situation, and the respect in which he held the prophetess, led him to choose as his messengers to her the first men of the kingdom.*[55]

Some commentators have suggested that perhaps Huldah was consulted because there was no male prophet available at the time. However, no less a prophet than Jeremiah was already established in his prophetic office. Others have considered that the role was too important for a female and have suggested that Huldah might have been a man. However, the Hebrew text specifically states that Huldah was a wife (2 Kgs 22:14)!

Other Old Testament women could be considered, such as Abigail, who embarked on a mission of "solo diplomacy" during a volatile family situation, only later notifying her husband. There is also the "wise woman of Tekoa," who was enlisted to influence King David.[56] In addition, one could elaborate on other textual indicators sprinkled throughout the Old Testament, such as Ps 68:11, that hint to wider involvement of women in Old Testament religion than sometimes recognized: "The Lord gave the word; great was the host of those who proclaimed it;" (Ps 68:11) The Hebrew reveals this "host" to be a *female* company, but only a few translations indicate this.[57]

Moreover, as Alice Laffey comments on Deut 10:16 and 30:1-10,

> Buried in this text . . . is the directive: circumcise your hearts. The author here . . . thus transforms an essential sign of covenant partnership (cf. Gen 17:10-14; Ex 4:24-26) from one which can include only males to one which can include both men and women. . . . [Furthermore] verse 6 [of Deut. 30] transforms the phrase of Dt 10:16, "circumcise your hearts." It is now not they, the Israelites, who are to do it (an imperative), but rather the Lord who will do it for them. . . . Making circumcised hearts rather than circumcised bodies the appropriate sign of the covenant relationship with Yahweh [yields] that relationship more directly available to women.[58]

The Song of Songs represents full female equality in the marriage relationship. Meyers points to the situation there as

> one of relationships, and the primary orientation lies with the female of the pair. . . . There is no trace of subordination of female to male, and there is a presence of power images for the female and not the male.[59]

We turn now to the New Testament.

Women in the New Testament

Women in the Gospels

Matthew, Mark, Luke, and John contain rich narratives regarding women.

Elizabeth. When Luke records Zechariah's priestly lineage (1:5), he immediately indicates that "his wife Elizabeth was also a descendant of Aaron." This is one of the rare times when a priest's wife is named in Scripture. Such significant mention links with Luke's immediate insistence that "they were *both* righteous before God, walking in all commandments and ordinances of the Lord blameless" (1:6, emphasis added). Luke's pointed inclusion of the word "both" confers remarkable affirmation on Zechariah's wife.

Anna. At the time of Christ's birth, Luke refers to the widow and prophetess Anna (2:36-38). Perhaps Luke may be including her in this narrative of the presentation of the infant Jesus at the Temple because she was the second witness testifying of Jesus' significance. At that time the

Israelite injunction that in "the mouth of two or three witnesses the thing is established" (Deut 17:6; Matt 16:18) was taken very seriously. If so, Luke is thus assigning a vital position to this woman. Ellen White's passing comment seems to suggest this:

> Anna, also a prophetess, came in and *confirmed Simeon's testimony concerning Christ*. As Simeon spoke, her face lighted up with the glory of God, and she poured out her heartfelt thanks that she had been permitted to behold Christ the Lord.[60]

Luke also describes Anna as proclaiming the Incarnation in the city (Luke 2:38). Some have noticed a biblical pattern of God commissioning prophets to announce both the beginning and ending of timed prophecies. If so, near the end of the 490-year prophecy announcing the coming Messiah, God enlists a female prophet to draw attention to this climactic event in the city of Jerusalem.

In fact, three women prophets appear at this pivotal historical event. Anna is actually designated a prophet by Luke. However, Elizabeth and Mary also "prophesied" at this very time (Luke 1:41-45; 1:46-55).

Woman at the Well. Later, the Gospels include impressive portraits of Christ's dealing with women. The narrative in John 4 of the woman at the well in Samaria is a case in point. The conversation with her is the longest recorded discussion Jesus had with anyone—and she, a Gentile woman.[61] And yet, as Denise Carmody notes, "Jesus treated the woman as intelligent. He paid her the honor of assuming she could catch his drift. The more she pressed, the more forthcoming he was."[62]

Unfortunately, commentaries on John repeatedly classify this woman as the town slut at worst, or at least a woman of questionable reputation. True, as Jesus pointed out, she had had five husbands and her current relationship was not lawful. Yet, the narrative explicitly records that the men of the city returned with her to see Jesus when she recounted how he had "told her everything that she did (John 4:28-30)."

It is hard to imagine the male population of any city following a known harlot to see a person who could divine! It is unlikely that the men of a town would believe a prostitute's word about the Messiah or anybody, and go openly with her to see him. Perhaps this woman has not been given due credit for her true social position in Samaria. The narrative seems to indicate that she was a knowledgeable, informed woman. Her discourse with Christ reveals an intelligent familiarity with the foremost theological issues of the day. Commentators regularly attribute major significance to this lengthy dialogue, but not to this woman. However, she is the first person recorded in Christ's public ministry whose witness brought a group of people into a believing relationship with the Messiah (John 4:39-42). Ellen White recounts how once she

> found the Saviour, the Samaritan woman brought others to Him. She proved herself a more effective missionary than His own disciples. . . . This woman represents the working of a practical faith in Christ. Every true *disciple* is born into the kingdom of God as a missionary.[63]

Moreover, this narrative's position in the Gospel, immediately following that of Nicodemus (John 3), perhaps is not coincidental. Is the narrator seeking to contrast the weak faith of a prominent male Jewish religious leader with that of a Gentile woman?[64] See how she at once hastens to spread her conviction regarding the Messiah, whereas Nicodemus did not publicly align himself with Jesus until Christ's death.

Martha and Mary. The narratives of Mary, Martha, and Lazarus contain rich insights regarding Christ's attitude toward women. Lazarus is miraculously raised from the dead, the greatest and last of the "signs" John records leading up to Christ's Passion.[65] However, no direct speech of Lazarus is ever recorded. Rather, it is Martha, as Frank Wheeler notes, who

> makes one of the premiere confessions of faith in the New Testament, "I believe that you are the Messiah, the Son of God, the one coming into the world." . . . The confession by Martha in John 11 may be compared to the confession by Peter in the Synoptic Gospels at Caesarea Philippi. Martha's statement is very close to Matthew's account, "You are the Christ, the Son of the living God" (Matt 16:16). The parallel confessions of Martha and Peter, according to Raymond Brown, are part of the tendency of the Fourth Gospel to give to women roles normally associated with Peter in the other gospels.[66]

On another occasion Jesus coaxed Martha to accept her sister's priorities of opting to study rather than assist in the kitchen. However, Martha herself apparently had also been an avid pupil of the Messiah, to issue the penetrating statement of faith that appears in John 11:23-27.

Her sister Mary has always been perceived as an earnest student of the Messiah. Christ's affirmation of this was noteworthy:

> Mary's choice was not a conventional one for Jewish women. She sat at the feet of Jesus and was listening to "his word." Both the posture and the reference to Jesus' "word" seem to imply teaching, religious

instruction. Jewish women were not permitted to touch the Scripture; and they were not taught the Torah itself, although they were instructed in accordance with it for the proper regulation of their lives. A rabbi did not instruct a woman in the Torah. Not only did Mary choose the good part, but Jesus related to her in a teacher-disciple relationship. He admitted her into the "study" and commended her for the choice. A Torah-oriented role for women was not unprecedented in Israel . . . but the drift had been away from it.[67]

Mary was also the first to see the resurrected Jesus. And Christ gave her the commission to tell the disciples that he was ascending to the Father. She thus became the first to announce the resurrection.[68] Wheeler notes that "Mary's prominence among witnesses of the resurrected Jesus is significant for John's readers. Of the six resurrection appearances of Jesus in the Gospels, five of them include Mary."[69]

However, Wheeler is careful to suggest:

While the focus in John is not to argue for greater recognition of women in terms of discipleship and ministry, that certainly could have been one of the results within the early Christian community. The focus, rather, appears to be on discipleship and giving testimony to Jesus as Messiah. In the fourth Gospel, women are shown to be capable of fulfilling that role as well as men. . . . However unexpected it might have been socially or religiously, women had a profound impact at crucial points in Jesus' ministry.[70]

The Gospels record no evidence of the Messiah ever treating women as inferior to men, or urging all women to be in submission to all men. Yet, at this time, though the status of women in Judaism was complex, the position of the female is generally conceded to have been restrictive. First-century rabbi Eliezer wrote: "Whoever teaches his daughter Torah is like one who teaches her lasciviousness."[71] Women did not count for the minimum number required for worship. They could not bear witness. However, Jesus repeatedly rejected these customs.

He also refused to limit a woman's horizon to nurturing family and cooking. When a woman once called to Jesus from a crowd, "Blessed is the womb that bore you and the breasts you sucked," Jesus widened this feminine perspective by responding, "Blessed rather are those who hear the word of God and keep it" (Luke 11:27-28). And yet Christ never belittled the role of a mother. In fact, he likened himself to a mother hen seeking to gather her baby chicks under her wings (Matt 23:37).

In one trilogy of parables, all of which revealed a likeness of God, the Messiah placed in the center a woman seeking a lost coin.

Scholars, even feminists, have widely acknowledged that Christ treated both men and women with fairness and equality. But the question is often asked, Why did Jesus select twelve male apostles? One could respond, Why only *Jewish* men? Evelyn and Frank Stagg suggest:

> The twelve apostles included no women, nor did they include any Samaritans even though Jesus clearly repudiated the Jewish-Samaritan antipathy. Custom here may have been so entrenched that Jesus simply stopped short of fully implementing a principle that he made explicit and emphatic: "Whoever does the will of God is my brother, sister and mother (Mk 3:35). The Twelve could be offering a parallel to the twelve patriarchs or 12 tribes of Israel, each headed by a son of Jacob, and thus dramatize both the continuity with national Israel, now to include women, Samaritans and Gentiles. However, at this time this may have been an ideal awaiting its time of actualization. That Jesus did introduce far-reaching principles bore fruit even in a former rabbi who said "There is not any Jew nor Greek, not any slave nor free, not any male and female; for ye all are one in Christ Jesus (Gal 3:28).[72]

Women in the Epistles of Paul

In spite of Paul's explicit Galatians declaration (Gal 3:28, just above), he, of all the New Testament authors, receives the greatest scorn from feminists, especially for his supposedly extreme chauvinistic statements in 1 Timothy. Because of what they consider as Paul's sexist language these feminists often jettison all of Paul's teachings and many times the entire New Testament itself.[73]

However, it is very dangerous to construct any scriptural teaching from a single passage. Radical feminists and others seem to neglect to compare Paul's counsel to Timothy in Ephesus with numerous other Pauline passages portraying Paul's attitudes and dealings with women in churches in other cities. These varied details must be taken into account in the interpretation of 1 Timothy.[74]

Paul clearly acknowledges that in Corinth women pray and prophesy in church (1 Cor 11:5). He requires, however, that they do so appropriately dressed and coiffed, in a manner that would not bring dishonor to their husbands or to the church (vv. 5-15). If women are enjoined to refrain from speaking (1 Cor 14:34, 35), it is a ban on "disruptive verbal misconduct" of wives who were "giving free rein to 'irresistible impulses' to 'pipe up' at will with questions in the assembly.[75]

Paul's wish was that in the worship service all things should be done "decently and in order" (1 Cor 14:40).

Several studies on women in the Philippian church have appeared, arguing persuasively that "Philippi is perhaps the classic New Testament case study on the roles of women in the founding and developing of a local congregation."[76]

In Romans 16, Paul sends greetings to twenty-six people in the church at Rome. John Stott is instructive on this passage:

> Reflecting on the names and circumstances of the people Paul greets, one is particularly impressed by the unity and diversity of the church to which they belong. . . . The most interesting and instructive aspect of church diversity in Rome is that of gender. Nine out of the twenty-six persons greeted are women . . . Paul evidently thinks highly of them all. He singles out four (Mary, Tryphena, Tryphosa and Persis) as having "worked hard." The verb *kopiaō* implies strong exertion, is used of all four of them, and is not applied to anybody else on the list. . . . The prominent place occupied by women in Paul's entourage shows that he was not at all the male chauvinist of popular fantasy.[77]

Three names of Paul's roster in Romans 16 call for special attention: (1) *Phoebe* functions as Paul's emissary, as did Titus and Timothy. Her designation as "deacon" (the Greek word is not "servant") does not imply the modern "deaconess" but rather the same position as that of the church leaders designated in 1 Tim 3:8-10. (2) *Priscilla*, in verse 3 (and in three other New Testament verses) is named first before her husband (Acts 18:18, 26; 2 Tim 4:19). Whatever the reason behind this ordering, Paul recognizes her leadership and her sharing in the instruction of Apollos. (3) *Andronicus and (female) Junia*. Paul mentions four details about them: that they are his kinsfolk and at some time have been his fellow prisoners. They were converted before he was, and they *are outstanding among the apostles.*[78]

Moreover, Paul's positive attitude toward women in the church is implicit in many of his writings. For instance, John Stott notes that Paul, in Rom 12:1-2, entreats the believers in Rome to

> "Offer your bodies as living sacrifices, holy and pleasing to God—this is your spiritual act of worship" (1b). Paul uses five more and less technical terms. He represents us as a *priestly people*, who, in responsive gratitude for God's mercy *offer* or present our bodies as living sacrifices. These are described as both *holy* and *pleasing to God*, which seem to be

the moral equivalents to being physically unblemished or without defect, and a fragrant aroma [cf. Lev 1:3, 9].[79]

There is no differentiation here between men and women. All the believers are functioning in this "priestly" role.

Nevertheless, it is Paul's first letter to Timothy in Ephesus that the early Church Fathers and modern feminists cite most often as disparaging women in ministry. And because of this passage many feminists have forsaken Scripture and Christianity altogether, and many SDAs argue against women's ordination. But what if this particular perception of 1 Tim 2:9-15 has not taken account of the initial situation that Paul was addressing in Ephesus?[80]

It is now known that Ephesus was a major center for Mother Goddess worship ("Diana of the Ephesians," Acts 19:23-41), major tenets being that a female goddess gave birth to the world, that Eve was created before Adam, and that to achieve highest exaltation woman must achieve independence from all males and from child-bearing. Sharon Gritz suggests that such false teaching was endangering the faith of the new Christian converts in Ephesus. And Paul was likely counseling Timothy how to deal with such radical departure from the Christian faith.

Gritz argues persuasively that this seems to be behind Paul's counsel to Timothy.[81] Instead of exhibiting a negative attitude toward women, Paul is seeking to preserve their exalted position in biblical teaching.[82] Thomas Geer also concurs:

Paul's concern in 1 Tim 2:8-15 is not that women might have authority over men in the church but that certain assertive women in the church who had been influenced by false teachers would teach error. For this reason, he charges them to "be silent."[83]

It is significant that Paul wrote this singular counsel to Timothy in Ephesus. When Paul appealed to the churches in Philippi or Galatia, a different situation existed, and such issues were not addressed.

One wonders what might have been the case if the Timothy passage had thus been understood throughout the history of the church. The interpretation of 1 Timothy 2 suggested by Gritz and others enables all aspects of Paul's personal ministry (including the women-organized and -led Philippian congregation), along with his written counsels, to be held together without contradiction. Paul can even be seen following in the positive example of Christ, who himself treated men and women with equal dignity, while preserving the marriage union. Moreover this view also dovetails with the positive presentation of Old Testament patriarchal women as seen above.

Conclusion

Neither Old or New Testament women should be used to illustrate that "according to Scripture" all women must be in submission to all men. As we have seen, an entirely different situation exists in that women in Scripture are observed as functioning with competence and confidence in many different spheres, often including positions of leadership. Feminists have been right to force attention on the abuse of women inside and outside the church. But they have been wrong in their understanding of the Apostle Paul and Old Testament patriarchy.

Upon a closer reading of both Old and New Testament narratives, the entire canon can be seen to affirm women, whether in the home or in public ministry, or both.

Endnotes

1. Robert Alter's book, *The Art of Biblical Narrative* (New York: Basic, 1981), has been pivotal in showing how certain details within the narratives previously overlooked (such as who actually speaks in the dialogues, the amount of dialogue within a narrative, whether or not a person is named, the sequence of narratives, etc.) are critical in understanding the narrator's intention.

2. For example, Mary Daly affirms: "If God in 'his' heaven is a father ruling 'his' people, then it is in the 'nature' of things and according to divine plan and the order of the universe that society be male-dominated" (M. Daly, *Beyond God the Father: Toward a Philosophy of Women's Liberation*, 2d ed. [Boston: Beacon, 1985], 13). Carol P. Christ writes: "I left the church . . . because I concluded that patriarchy was deeply rooted in Christianity's core symbolism of God the Father and Son" (Aida Besancon Spencer, "Father-Ruler: The Meaning of the Metaphor 'Father' for God in the Bible," *Journal of the Evangelical Theological Society* 39 [September 1966]: 433).

3. Thus they postulate a period of glorious peace and harmony during the pre-patriarchy period of the Mother Goddess. See, for example, Riane Eisler, *The Chalice and the Blade: Our History, Our Future* (San Francisco: Harper & Row, 1987).

4. Mary Kassian describes the movement as grouped "according to their political theories or historical mentors." They are "enlightenment liberal feminists, cultural feminists, Marxist feminists, Freudian feminists, existential feminists, and radical feminists. One religious woman-studies text delineates them as biblical (evangelical), mainstream (reformist), and radical (revolutionary)" (Mary A. Kassian, *The Feminist Gospel: The Movement to Unite Feminism with the Church* [Wheaton, IL: Crossway, 1992], 219).

5. For example: "Every woman working to improve her own position in society or that of women in general is *bringing about the end of God*. All feminists are making the world less and less like the one described in the Bible and are thus helping to lessen the influence of Christ and Yahweh on humanity." Women in leadership will "change the world so much that He won't fit in anymore" (Naomi Goldenberg, *Changing of the Gods: Feminism and the End of Traditional Religions* [Boston: Beacon, 1979], 3, 10).

6. For example: "The infamous passages of the Old and New Testaments are well known. I need not allude to the misogynism of the church Fathers—for example, Tertullian, who informed women in general: 'You are the devil's gateway,' . . . or Augustine, who opined that women are not made in the image of God. I can omit reference to Thomas Aquinas and his numerous commentators and disciples who defined women as misbegotten males. I can overlook Martin Luther's remark that 'God created Adam lord over all living creatures but Eve spoiled it all'" (Mary Daly, *Beyond God the Father*, 3).

7. "Someplace along the line, the effects of the sacraments are going to have to be able to be manifested in the ministries, as much for a woman as for a man. There's either something wrong with the present theology of ministry, or there is something wrong with the present theology of all the sacraments. If women qualify for baptism, confirmation, salvation, and redemption, how can they be denied the sacrament of ministry" (Joan Chittister, "The Fullness of Grace," in *Cloud of Witnesses*, ed. Jim Wallis and Joyce Hollyday [Maryknoll, NY: Orbis, 1991], 186).

8. "As several writers present a subject under varied aspects and relations, there may appear, to the superficial, careless, or prejudiced reader, to be discrepancy or contradiction, where the thoughtful, reverent student, with clearer insight, discerns the underlying harmony" (Ellen G. White, *Great Controversy*, v, vi).

"There is not always perfect order or apparent unity in the Scriptures. . . . Those who take only a surface view of the Scriptures will, with their superficial knowledge, which they think is very deep, talk of the contradictions of the Bible, and question the authority of the Scriptures. But those whose hearts are in harmony with truth and duty will search the Scriptures with a heart prepared to receive divine impressions" (Ellen G. White, *Selected Messages*, 1:20).

9. Kassian, 242.

10. Trevor Dennis comments: "Looking at these texts consistently from the points of view of their female characters has for me been exhilarating and liberating, but it has shaken me and disturbed me more than I could have anticipated. It has put me in touch with my own sexism, with destructive stereotypes about women, and about men also, deep rooted within me. . . . Shall I conclude that God always gives his more important tasks to men? But that would be absurd. . . . Shall I believe that he calls men and not women to be the conspicuous bearers of his promises? But I for one have had more than enough of that belief in the Church, and wish to see no more of the great harm it does to those who hold to it, or of the greater harm it does to their victims" (Trevor Dennis, *Sarah Laughed: Women's Voices in the Old Testament* [Nashville: Abingdon, 1994], 176, 179).

11. "The rise of the state meant the gradual end of a society in which the household was the dominant social unit. The locus of power moved from the family household, with its gender parity, to a public world of male control. The establishment of a nation-state meant the growing prominence of the military and of state and religious bureaucracies controlling economic development. These institutions are typically public and male controlled; whenever they become an important part of a society's organization, female prestige and power recede" (A.D.H. Mayes, *Judges* [Sheffield, England: JSOT, 1985], 189-190).

12. Ibid., 196.

13. Even the most radical feminists, such as Mary Daly, speak with great appreciation of Christ's attitude toward women: "In the New Testament it is significant that the statements which reflect the antifeminism of the times are never those of Christ. There is no recorded speech of Jesus concerning women 'as such.' What is very striking is his behavior toward them. In the passages describing the relationship of Jesus with various women, one characteristic stands out starkly: they emerge as persons, for they are treated as persons, often in such contrast with the prevailing custom as to astonish onlookers" (Mary Daly, *The Church and the Second Sex: With a New Feminist PostChristian Introduction by the Author* [New York: Harper & Row, 1975], 37-38).

14. Savina Teubal has suggested that she may have been an early priestess. It is not possible or necessary to confirm that idea, but Teubal's assertion does draw attention to the exceptional portrait of Sarah that Genesis presents: Sarah is the only matriarch whose death age is recorded, her burial at Mamre receives great attention, and Isaac consummates his marriage to Rebekah in his mother's tent. Her theory could possibly help explain the interest Abimelech exhibited in Sarah though she was 90 years old (Savina Teubal, *Sarah the Priestess: The First Matriarch of Genesis* [Chicago: Swallow, 1984], 110-122).

Jack Vancil concurs regarding Sarah's importance: "Abraham's effort and negotiations to purchase a burial place for Sarah, as well as the site chosen raises more questions. . . . That an entire chapter would be devoted to her death and burial, and stressing such detail as it does has been observed by many commentators. . . . It is striking too, that after Sarah's death there is very little further told us about Abraham. The marriage to Keturah is told in order to mention Abraham's other descendants, but we do not even know where they lived" (Jack W. Vancil, "Sarah—Her Life and Legacy," *Essays on Women in Earliest Christianity*, ed. Carroll D. Osburn [Joplin: College Press, 1995], 2:61-63).

15. Katheryn Pfisterer Darr, *Far More Precious Than Jewels* (Louisville, KY: John Knox, 1991), 9.

16. Janice Nunnally-Cox, *Foremothers: Women of the Bible* (New York: Seabury, 1981), 9.

17. Teubal, xii.

18. Vancil, 48-49.

19. In Genesis there does not seem to be a distinct division of labor between men and women in the household. Either gender could be a shepherd. Rebekah and Laban shared farm chores and the particulars of family hospitality (Gen 24). Both sons of Rebekah knew how to cook (Gen 25:29).

20. Vancil, 56.

21. Dennis, 176.

22. Sarah does not use Hagar's name but refers only to her position: "Go, please, to my slave-girl" (Gen 16:2b). Up to this point only the narrator has given Hagar's name.

23. Dennis, 68.

24. Ibid., 71.

25. Keturah, Abraham's wife after Sarah's death, is mentioned without any of the impressive detail of Sarah's narratives.

26. Sharon Pace Jeansonne, *The Women of Genesis: From Sarah to Potiphar's Wife* (Minneapolis: Fortress, 1990), 53.

27. The genealogy in Gen 22:20-24 "presents the names of the children born to Abraham's brother Nahor and his sister-in-law Milcah. Nahor and Milcah's eight sons are listed, but the offspring of these eight sons, the third generation, are mentioned only in two cases. The offspring of Kemuel and Bethuel alone are deemed significant. The name of Kemuel's son, Aram, is given only in a parenthetical phrase. In contrast Bethuel's offspring is given greater attention. A separate phrase announces, 'Bethuel begat Rebekah' (22:23). Moreover, her name is arresting in this context because she is the first offspring who is mentioned." Even the placement of this genealogy after the account of the testing of Abraham (22:1-19) emphasizes the importance of Rebekah (Jeansonne, 54-55).

28. Ibid., 57.

29. James G. Williams, *Women Recounted: Narrative Thinking and the God of Israel*, Bible and Literature Series, vol. 6 (Sheffield: Almond, 1982), 44. Danna Nolan Fewell and David M. Gunn concur: "It is she [Rebekah], not Isaac, who follows in Abraham's footsteps, leaving the familiar for the unknown. It is she, not Isaac, who receives the blessing given to Abraham (22:17). 'May your offspring possess the gates of their enemies!' (24:60)" (*Gender, Power, and Promise: The Subject of the Bible's First Story* [Nashville: Abingdon, 1993], 73). See also Mary Donovan Turner, "Rebekah: Ancestor of Faith," *Lexington Theological Quarterly* 20 (April 1985): 43-44.

30. Turner, 44-45.

31. Ibid., 47.

32. Jeansonne, 69.

33. Meyers, 45.

34. Ellen G. White, *Patriarchs and Prophets*, 206, emphasis added.

35. Dennis, 114.

36. White, *Patriarchs and Prophets*, 243.

37. Fewell and Gunn, 93.

38. Rita J. Burns, *Has the Lord Indeed Spoken Only through Moses? A Study of the Biblical Portrait of Miriam*. SBL Dissertation Series, 84 (Atlanta: Scholars, 1987), 120.

39. Phyllis Trible, *God and the Rhetoric of Sexuality* (Philadelphia: Fortress, 1978). Denise Lardner Carmody reflects similarly on Ruth: "Her pledge itself is religiously remarkable, because in it Ruth completely throws in her lot with Naomi's faith. A Moabite, Ruth presumably had her own gods and religious ways. . . . So her dedication to Naomi is extremely radical. . . . By the grace of God, she had chosen to join the chosen people. . . . What an example she gave of daughterly devotion and religious discernment!" (*Biblical Woman: Contemporary Reflections on Scriptural Texts* [New York: Crossroad, 1989], 33-34).

40. Louise Pettibone Smith, "Introduction to Ruth," *The Interpreter's Bible* (Nashville: Parthenon, 1992), 829-832.

41. Andre LaCocque concludes: "In the book of Ruth, however, it must be noted that the genealogical motif, culminating as it does with the advent of King David, corresponds perfectly with the mention at the beginning of the story of Bethlehem, the home city of King David" (*The Feminine Unconventional: Four Subversive Figures in Israel's Tradition* [Minneapolis: Fortress, 1990], 111).

42. Charme E. Robarts, "Deborah—Judge, Prophetess, Military Leader, and Mother in Israel," *Essays on Women in Earliest Christianity*, ed. Carroll D. Osburn (Joplin: College Press, 1995), 2:74.

43. Fewell and Gunn rightly remark: "Deborah is introduced by the epithet *'eshet lappidot*, . . . wife of Lappidoth. We might expect her importance to the story to lie in her role as wife. Yet we soon discover that wifehood reveals little about Deborah. It is not her relationship to her husband that will prove significant, but her relationship to Israel and to her appointed commander" (Fewell and Gunn, 122).

44. Vancil, 80.

45. Robarts, 76.

46. Dennis, 115-116.

47. Ibid., 123.

48. Ibid., 124.

49. Ibid., 130.

50. Ibid.

51. White, *Patriarchs and Prophets*, 571.

52. Dennis, 132.

53. Ibid, 133.

54. John T. Willis, "Huldah and Other Biblical Prophetesses," *Essays on Women in Earliest Christianity*, ed. Carroll F. Osburn (Joplin: College Press, 1995), 2:112.

55. Ellen G. White, *Prophets and Kings*, 398, emphasis added. Duane Christensen argues that the narratives of Deborah in Judges 4 and Huldah in 2 Kings 22 frame the Deuteronomic history of life in the promised land, forming an inclusio:

A--Deborah: a "Prophetess" of YHWH alongside Barak (Israel)

    B--Jezebel: A royal advocate of Baal in Israel

    B'--Athaliah: a royal advocate of Baal in Judah

A'--Huldah" a Prophetess of YHWH alongside Josiah (Judah)

(D. L. Christensen, "Huldah and the Men of Anathoth: Women in Leadership in the Deuteronomic History," *SBL 1984 Seminar Papers* [Chico, CA: Scholars, 1985], 399-403).

56. Jacques Doukhan (see chapter 2) draws further attention to the whole tradition of Old Testament women in teaching functions, instructing males and females.

57. Jack Blanco's *The Clear Word* recognizes this: "You, our Lord, spoke and victories were won. The women spread the news and everyone knew" (Jack J. Blanco, *The Clear Word: A Paraphrase to Nurture Faith and Growth* [Hagerstown, MD: Review and Herald, 1994], 675). The *New Living Translation* also: "The Lord announces victory, and throngs of women shout the happy news" (*New Living Translation* [Wheaton, IL: Tyndale House], 605).

58. Alice L. Laffey, *An Introduction to the Old Testament: A Feminist Perspective* (Philadelphia: Fortress, 1988), 64-66.

59. Meyers, 180.

60. Ellen G. White, *Desire of Ages*, 55, emphasis added.

61. Another extended conversation was with the Syrophoenician mother (Mt 15:21-28; Mk 7:24-30). Ellen White writes of Christ's discussion with the Samaritan woman that it is the "most important discourse that Inspiration has given us" (*Testimonies for the Church*, 3:217).

62. Denise Lardner Carmody, *Biblical Woman: Contemporary Reflections on Scriptural Texts* (New York: Crossroad, 1989), 106.

63. White, *Desire of Ages*, 194-195, emphasis added.

64. The juxtaposition of narratives is increasingly seen as significant in the larger structure of biblical books.

65. Frank Wheeler notes: "The location of this story in the Gospel of John is significant. Just as the first sign was initiated by a woman, Jesus' mother, the last sign is initiated by women, Martha and Mary" (Frank Wheeler, "Women in the Gospel of John," *Essays on Women in Earliest Christianity* [Joplin: College Press, 1995], 2:215.

66. Ibid., 216, 217. He continues, "Martha's statement may also be compared to the confession of Thomas in John 20. . . . Actually, Martha's confession is more powerful than Thomas' for she had not yet seen Jesus' or even Lazarus' resurrection."

67. Evelyn Stagg and Frank Stagg, *Women in the World of Jesus* (Philadelphia: Westminster, 1978), 118.

68. It almost seems that the two disciples traveling to Emmaus are disparaging the fact that the "women" have been the only ones to proclaim the resurrection: "*Certain women of our company*, who arrived at the tomb early, astonished us. When they did not find His body, they came saying that they had also seen a vision of angels who said He was alive. And certain of those who were with us went to the tomb and *found it just as the women had said; but Him they did not see*" (Luke 24:22-24, emphasis added).

69. Wheeler, 219.

70. Wheeler, 223. He continues, "The Fourth Gospel may not have as much to say directly about the public or official roles of women in the church as one might like. Nevertheless, this Gospel does make it clear that the faith, testimony, and discipleship of women is equal to that of men and is equally as important to the Christian community. The value of women's discipleship and influence has been tremendously overlooked" (224).

71. Mishnah *Sotah* 3:4.

72. Stagg and Stagg, 123.

73. Carmody shows an example of outrage at Paul because of 1 Tim 2:11-15: "But the prejudicial, if not outrightly vicious, interpretation of Yahwist mythology we find in this text triggers my bile. How arrogant and self-serving! What a dangerous precedent, as generations of patriarchal Christian leadership have proved! . . . Among the biblical wrongdoers, he stands out as a paramount oppressor."

74. Nancy Vyhmeister deals extensively with this passage in chapter 16 of this book.

75. Carroll D. Osburn, "The Interpretation of 1 Cor 14:34-35," in *Essays on Women in Earliest Christianity*, ed. C. D. Osburn (Joplin, MO: College Press, 1993), 1:242. On the matter of women in the Corinthian church, see Larry Richards' chapter in this book. See also Willis, "Huldah and Other Biblical Prophetesses," 2:120-121; and William F. Orr and James Arthur Walter, *1 Corinthians*, Anchor Bible (Garden City, NJ: Doubleday, 1976), 263-264.

76. A. Boyd Luter, "Partnership in the Gospel: The Role of Women in the Church at Philippi," *Journal of the Evangelical Theological Society* 39 (September 1996): 411. See also: W. D. Thomas, "The Place of Women in the Church at Philippi," *Expository Times* 83 (1972): 117-120; F. X. Malinowski, "The Brave Women of Philippi," *Biblical Theology Bulletin* 15 (1985): 60-64; L. Portefaix, *Sisters Rejoice: Paul's Letter to the Philippians and Luke-Acts as Received by First-century Women* (Stockholm: Almqvist and Wikgren, 1988). Significant attention to the circumstances in Philippi is also found in such broader studies of New Testament women as E. M. Tetlow, *Women and Ministry in the New Testament* (New York: Paulist, 1980); B. Witherington, *Women in the Earliest Churches* (Cambridge: Cambridge Univ. Press, 1988).

77. John Stott, *Romans: God's Good News for the World* (Downers Grove: InterVarsity, 1994), 394-396.

78. Robert Johnston studies this significant detail and also the example of Phoebe in chapter 3 of this book.

79. Stott, 321.

80. Leon Morris reminds us that Paul's epistles were truly letters. "What Paul wrote was a series of genuine letters addressing specific situations in which he and his converts found themselves. He was not setting himself to produce literary works. Each of these missives was clearly written in the light of what was needed in a given situation; none was written with a view of adding to the stock of Jewish literature. They all focus on the situation confronting Paul at the time he wrote them" (Leon Morris, *Galatians: Paul's Charter of Christian Freedom* [Downers Grove, IL: InterVarsity, 1996], 13).

81. Sharon Hodgin Gritz, *Paul, Women Teachers, and the Mother Goddess at Ephesus: A Study of 1 Timothy 2:9-15 in Light of the Religious and Cultural Milieu of the First Century* (Lanham: University Press of America, 1991).

82. Angel Rodriguez reaches a similar conclusion through a New Testament word study of the terms Paul is using. He concludes: "Having examined the New Testament evidence, we can now take a closer look at 1 Timothy 2:11, 12. There is no doubt that Paul is concerned about controversies in the church. In verse 8 he exhorts men to pray 'without anger or disputing.' In the case of the women, the apostle is also concerned about behavior and attitudes that could be disruptive. . . . Why did Paul single out women? Possibly because some of them had become the target of false teachers and their instructions (2 Tim. 3:6). As a result, they were bringing controversies into the church. Paul forbids this type of controversial and divisive speech when he says that 'a woman . . . must be silent'" (Angel Manuel Rodriguez, "Women's Words," *Adventist Review*, 14 November 1996, 27).

83. Thomas C. Geer, Jr., "Admonitions to Women in 1 Tim 2:8-15," *Essays on Women in Earliest Christianity*, ed. C. D. Osburn (Joplin: College Press, 1993), 1:281-302.

CHAPTER 10

"A POWER THAT EXCEEDS THAT OF MEN":[1] ELLEN G. WHITE ON WOMEN IN MINISTRY

JERRY MOON

B
ecause Seventh-day Adventists have held from the earliest beginnings of their movement that the Bible and the Bible only is their rule of faith and practice,[2] the bulk of the monograph of which this article forms a part, is rightly devoted to an examination of the scriptural evidence regarding God's purpose for women in ministry.

However, the Scripture also teaches that the Holy Spirit has placed in the church the gift of prophecy,[3] not to add to the canon of Scripture, but to make authoritative application of the Scripture to specific situations in the ongoing, changing life of the church.[4] Seventh-day Adventists believe this gift was manifested in the life and ministry of Ellen G. White, and that "her writings are a continuing and authoritative source of truth."[5]

Furthermore, the divine choice, as Adventists believe, of a woman as a prophetic messenger to the modern church, raises provocatively the question whether it was God's intention to limit the other gifts of Eph 4:11, particularly that of pastor-teacher, to persons of the male gender. Consequently, the question of Ellen White's personal belief, teaching, and practice regarding women in ministry cannot be ignored or omitted from a Seventh-day Adventist consideration of this issue.

The purpose of this article is to examine the writings and practices of Ellen G. White with specific reference to the following questions: (1) How did Ellen White use the term "ministry" with reference to women? (2) Did she characterize women's participation in ministry as essential, or merely optional? (3) What roles did she envision for ministering women? (4) What are the implications for the question of ordaining women to ministry?

Ellen White's Use of the Term "Ministry" with Reference to Women

Ellen White used the terms "minister" and "ministry" to encompass a broad spectrum of meaning. Most basic, she used the term ministry to designate the calling and work of every Christian. In one of her most widely circulated works, *Desire of Ages*, p. 822, she explains:

The Saviour's commission to the disciples included *all* the believers. It includes *all* believers in Christ to the end of time. It is a fatal mistake to suppose that the work of saving souls depends alone on the *ordained minister*. *All* to whom the heavenly inspiration has come are put in trust with the gospel. *All* who receive the life of Christ are *ordained* to work for the salvation of their fellow men. For this work the church was established, and *all* who take upon themselves its sacred vows are thereby pledged to be co-workers with Christ.

"The Spirit and the bride say, Come. And let him that heareth say, Come." Rev. 22:17. Everyone who hears is to repeat the invitation. Whatever one's calling in life, his first interest should be to win souls for Christ. He may not be able to speak to congregations, but he can work for individuals. To them he can communicate the instruction received from his Lord. *Ministry* does not consist alone in preaching. Those *minister* who relieve the sick and suffering, helping the needy, speaking words of comfort to the desponding and those of little faith. Nigh and afar off are souls weighed down by a sense of guilt. It is not hardship, toil, or poverty that degrades humanity. It is guilt, wrongdoing. This brings unrest and dissatisfaction. Christ would have His servants *minister* to sin-sick souls [emphasis supplied].

Note her assertion that "all" Christians "are ordained to work for the salvation of their fellow men." Then she associates the terms "minister" and "ministry" with any kind of Christian service "to sin-sick souls." Thus her basic definition of ministry is the calling of all Christians "to work for the salvation of their fellow men."[6] Within this basic concept are two subdivisions, which I have arbitrarily labeled "category 2" and "category 3."

The second category of usage of the terms minister and ministry designates specific vocations that support and augment the "ministry of the word." Chief among these are "medical missionary work" and literature evangelism, the ministry of selling Christian literature house to house. Regarding the latter, Ellen White distinguished literature evangelism from "the ministry," but calls it "a part . . . of the ministry," and in "importance," "fully equal" to "the ministry."[7]

She describes "medical missionary work" in similar terms. The medical work is distinguished from "the ministry of the word," "the gospel ministry," yet it "must not be separated" from, but "connected with the third angel's message . . . and the ministry."[8] She writes further that "medical missionaries who labor in evangelistic lines are doing work of as high an order as are their ministerial fellow laborers. . . . The faithful physician and the minister are engaged in the same work."[9]

Category three in Ellen White's usage of "ministry" employs phrases such as "gospel ministry," "ministry of the word," or "ordained minister," and refers to the officially recognized clergy of the church.[10] While this three-part categorization may be an oversimplification of the range of Ellen White's usage of the terms "ministry" and "minister," nevertheless it is sufficient to give sharper focus to the study of women in ministry. It will be shown that Ellen White used the term "ministry" to designate the work of women not only in category one ("To all Christ has given the work of ministry"[11]), and category two ("men and women . . . should be . . . working as medical missionary evangelists, helping those engaged in the gospel ministry"[12]), but in category three as well: "There are women who should labor in the gospel ministry."[13]

Perhaps her most emphatic statement about women "in the gospel ministry" comes from MS 43a, 1898, "The Laborer is Worthy of His Hire," and has been reprinted in several sources.[14] Here Ellen White asserts unequivocally, "There are women who should labor in the gospel ministry."[15] Three paragraphs earlier she refers to the same group by a shorter expression, "women who labor in the gospel." She also speaks of women who do "work that is in the line of ministry," and who are "necessary to the work of ministry." The context of this statement is a question that "several" had asked Ellen White: "Should minister's wives adopt infant children?" To some of these she answered, "No; God would have you help your husband in his work." A few lines later she explains the reason for this "advice":

> There are women who should labor in the gospel ministry. In many respects they would do more good than the ministers who neglect to visit the flock of God. Husband and wife may unite in this work, and when it is possible, they should. The way is open for consecrated women. But the enemy would be pleased to have the women whom God could use to help hundreds, binding up their time and strength on one helpless little mortal, that requires constant care and attention.[16]

She quoted Isa 56:1-5, in which God promises the childless "a name better than [that] of sons and daughters," and then concluded, "This is the grand

and noble work that the minister and his wife may qualify themselves to do as faithful shepherds and guardians of the flock."

Thus, for some women who have special "ability" to "help to give the message," the work of the ministry could be a higher priority than child rearing. She made a similar point elsewhere when she recognized that a woman in ministry may sometimes need to put "her housework in the hands of a faithful, prudent helper," and leave "her children in good care, while she engages in the work."[17]

Ellen White also shows a clear preference for team ministry. Twelve times in five pages[18] she refers to husbands and wives working together, strongly implying that this is the ideal ministerial team. Nevertheless, she also refers to "young women" without reference to marital status being trained for this work, and widows of ministers continuing in this work,[19] showing that while a husband-and-wife team has many advantages, it is not the only setting in which women are called to ministry.[20]

In support of the essential role of women in ministry, she urged General Conference President A. G. Daniells to "study the Scriptures for further light on this point. Women were among Christ's devoted followers in the days of His ministry, and Paul makes mention of certain women who were 'helpers together' with him 'in the gospel.'"[21] The "elect lady" of 2 John 1 she believed to be one of the unnamed women leaders of the New Testament church—"a helper in the gospel work, a woman of good repute and wide influence."[22]

Elsewhere she reiterated, "Women helped our Saviour by uniting with Him in His work. And the great apostle Paul writes, . . . 'I entreat thee also, true yoke-fellow, help those women which labored with me in the gospel'" [Phil 4:3].[23] Following the citation from Phil 4:3, she paraphrased Paul's words about "women who labored in the gospel," appropriating the Pauline precedent in support of "modern women who should labor in the gospel ministry."[24]

The Need, Legitimacy, and Divine Mandate for Women in Ministry

The foundational premise that undergirds all of Ellen White's counsels about women in ministry is that neither men nor women can do alone the quality of work that the two can do together. "When a great and decisive work is to be done, God chooses men and women to do this work, and it will feel the loss if the talents of both are not combined."[25] Thus she reiterated that the participation of women in the work of the gospel is not merely an option to be allowed in exceptional circumstances, but is an essential element for the highest success in preaching the gospel. "Women can be the instruments of righteousness, rendering holy service," she wrote in 1879. "It was Mary that first preached a risen Jesus. . . . If there were twenty women where now there is one, who would make this holy mission their cherished work, we should see many more converted to the truth. The refining, softening influence of Christian women is *needed* in the great work of preaching the truth."[26]

She believed women to be indispensable in ministry, because they can minister in ways that men cannot. "The Lord has a work for women as well as for men. . . . They can do in families a work that men cannot do, a work that reaches the inner life. They can come close to the hearts of those whom men cannot reach. Their labor is *needed*."[27] Elsewhere she affirmed that

> There is a great work for women to do in the cause of present truth. Through the exercise of womanly tact and a wise use of their knowledge of Bible truth, *they can remove difficulties that our brethren cannot meet.* We *need* women workers to labor in connection with their husbands, and should encourage those who wish to engage in this line of missionary effort [emphasis added].[28]

To those who questioned the legitimacy of a woman preaching to congregations, Ellen White cited her own experience.

> When in my youth God opened the Scriptures to my mind, giving me light upon the truths of his work, I went forth to proclaim to others the precious news of salvation. My brother wrote to me, and said, "I beg of you do not disgrace the family. I will do anything for you if you will not go out as a preacher." "Disgrace the family!" I replied, "can it disgrace the family for me to preach Christ and him crucified! If you would give me all the gold your house could hold, I would not cease giving my testimony for God. I have respect unto the recompense of the reward. I will not keep silent, for when God imparts his light to me, he means that I shall diffuse it to others, according to my ability."[29]

Furthermore, Ellen White insisted that women who devote their full time to ministry should be paid just as male ministers are.

> Injustice has sometimes been done to women who labor just as devotedly as their husbands, and who are recognized by God as being necessary to the work of the ministry. The method of paying men laborers, and not paying their wives who share their labors with them is a plan not according to the Lord's order, and if carried out in our

conferences, is liable to discourage our sisters from qualifying themselves for the work they should engage in.[30]

Ellen White could have argued that as it is expected of every layperson to spread the gospel without pay, women should not object to these conditions. To the contrary, however, she urged the necessity of fair pay for ministering women. Asking women to do full-time ministerial work without pay, she calls "exaction," "partiality," "selfishness," and "robbery." "When self-denial is required because of a dearth of means, do not let a few hard-working women do all the sacrificing. Let all share in making the sacrifice."[31] She warned of the danger of discouraging women from devoting themselves to ministry as a vocation. She believed large numbers of women ("twenty . . . where now there is one") should be "preaching the truth,"[32] "qualifying themselves" for "the work they should engage in,"[33] and that to hinder them would be to hinder the work of God.

"Seventh-day Adventists are not in any way to belittle woman's work," she affirmed. "If a woman puts her housework in the hands of a faithful, prudent helper, and leaves her children in good care, while she engages in the work, the conference should have wisdom to understand the justice of her receiving wages."[34]

Finally, Ellen White asserted the legitimacy of paying women ministers from the tithe, which she elsewhere maintained is to be sacredly reserved for the support of the gospel ministry.[35] "The tithe should go to those who labor in word and doctrine, be they men or women,"[36] she wrote.

Many of the pertinent quotations mention "wives" of ministers.[37] Other references, however, apply the same concept to women not specified as minister's wives, and to widowed women, showing that Ellen White saw some form of ministry as an appropriate career choice for women.

> Some women are now teaching young women to work successfully as visitors and Bible readers.[38] Women who work in the cause of God should be given *wages proportionate to the time they give to the work.* . . . . As the devoted minister and his wife engage in the work, they should be paid wages proportionate to the *wages of two distinct workers,* that they may have means to use as they shall see fit in the cause of God. The Lord has *put His spirit upon them both.* If the husband should die, and leave his wife, *she is fitted to continue her work in the cause of God, and receive wages* for the labor she performs [emphasis added].[39]

Seven elements in Ellen White's call for women in ministry have been noted: (1) "There are women who should labor in the gospel ministry;" (2) women's work is "essential," and without it the cause will "suffer great loss;"[40] (3) women in ministry should receive just wages; (4) these wages may appropriately come from the tithe; (5) the call to ministry can in some cases take priority over housework and child care;[41] (6) some women should make ministry a lifelong vocation in which they earn their livelihood; and (7) conferences should not "discourage" women from "qualifying themselves" for ministerial work.[42] All these factors in her appeal justify the conclusion that she considered the call to promote and encourage the participation of women in ministry, not merely as an option, but as a divine mandate, the neglect of which results in diminished ministerial efficiency, fewer converts, and "great loss" to the cause, compared with the fruitfulness of the combined gifts of men and women in ministry. Next we will consider what roles Ellen White envisioned for women in ministry.

Role Descriptions for Women in Ministry

The purpose of this section is to examine the evidence regarding the scope of Ellen White's call to women in ministry. What specific roles did she envision? What place did she see for women in relation to men in ministry?

The most frequently mentioned vocations in which Ellen White called women to minister are those of house-to-house ministry to families,[43] giving Bible studies,[44] in either evangelistic or pastoral contexts,[45] teaching in various capacities,[46] and "canvassing."[47] Also mentioned are medicine (specifically obstetrics and gynecology),[48] chaplaincy for medical and other institutions,[49] personal counseling with women,[50] and temperance leadership (particularly in connection with the Women's Christian Temperance Union).[51]

Supporting Roles in Team Ministry

Many of Ellen White's statements regarding women in ministry are set in the context of a team ministry in which women employ their gifts largely but not exclusively in teaching, visiting, and counseling private individuals and small groups, especially families. She specifically says that women will be more successful in this area of ministry than will men.

The Lord has a work for women, as well as for men. They may take their places in His work . . . and He will work through them. If they are imbued with a sense of their duty, and labor under the influence of the Holy Spirit, they will have just the self-possession required for this time. The Saviour will reflect upon these self-sacrificing women the light of His countenance, and will give them *a power that exceeds that of men*. They can do in families *a work that men cannot do,* a work that reaches the inner life. *They can come close to the hearts of those whom men cannot reach.* Their labor is needed [emphasis added].[52]

These women are called "self-sacrificing" specifically in the sense that they most often carry supporting rather than leading responsibilities in their respective ministerial teams. Yet despite their relatively lesser public recognition (because they spend more of their time in private and small-group teaching, counseling, and visitation), it is precisely in this supporting role that they are promised "a power that exceeds that of men," to "do in families a work that men cannot do," and "come close to the hearts of those whom men cannot reach."[53]

Ellen White's references to women as teachers were not, however, limited to the private teaching of individuals, families, and small groups. She also mentioned Sabbath school teachers and superintendents, teachers of camp meeting Bible classes, and elementary school teachers, as well as those who teach from the pulpit.[54] During her ministry in Australia, she spoke approvingly of two Bible instructors, Sister R[obinson] and Sister W[ilson] who were "doing just as efficient work as the ministers." She reported that at "some meetings when the ministers are all called away, Sister W[ilson] takes the Bible and addresses the congregation."[55]

Women as Teachers

One of the objections sometimes raised against Ellen White's own ministry was that women were not to "teach" men (1 Tim 2:12). This her colleagues refuted by arguing that this "general rule with regard to women as public teachers" did not constitute a rigid or universal prohibition.[56] J. N. Andrews argued that "there are some exceptions to this general rule to be drawn even from Paul's writings," as well as "from other Scriptures." Then he cited Paul's women co-workers (Phil 4:3); Phoebe's position as deaconess (Rom 16:1); Priscilla's association with Paul (Rom 16:3) and her participation in "instructing Apollos" (Acts 18:26); Tryphena, Tryphosa, and Persis (Rom 16:12); Philip's daughters who prophesied (Acts 21:8-9); and others to prove that women were not absolutely excluded from teaching roles. He concluded that Rom 10:10, which requires public confession of the faith as integral to salvation, "must apply to women equally with men."[57]

Ellen White seldom spoke in her own defense on this point. She generally allowed her male colleagues to formulate such responses. For example, note her account of a meeting in Arbuckle, California, at which S. N. Haskell was called on to explain this issue. "Before I commenced in talking," Ellen White recalled,

> Elder Haskell had a bit of paper that was handed in[,] quoting certain texts prohibiting women speaking in public. He took the matter in a brief manner and very clearly expressed the meaning of the apostle's words. I understand that it was a Campbellite who wrote the objection and it had been well circulated before it reached the desk; but Elder Haskell made it plain before all the people.[58]

While Ellen White did not often refer to the Pauline passages on women as teachers, she did cite the work of Aquila and Priscilla in teaching Apollos as an example of "a thorough scholar and brilliant orator" being taught by two laypersons, one of whom was a woman.

> The educated orator received instruction from *them* with grateful surprise and joy. Through *their* teachings he obtained a clearer knowledge of the Scriptures. . . . Thus a thorough scholar and brilliant orator learned the way of the Lord more perfectly from the teachings of a Christian man *and woman* whose humble employment was that of tent making [emphasis added].[59]

Thus she implicitly rejected the traditional interpretation of 1 Tim 2:12. On the contrary, she urged A. G. Daniells, then General Conference president, to employ in public evangelism "many men and women who have ability to preach and teach the Word." She continued,

> Select women who will act an earnest part. The Lord will use intelligent women in the work of teaching. And let none feel that these women, who understand the Word and who have ability to teach, should not receive remuneration for their labors. They should be paid as verily as are their husbands. There is a great work for women to do in the cause of present truth. Through the exercise of womanly tact and a wise use of their knowledge of Bible truth, they can remove difficulties that our brethren cannot meet. We need women workers to labor in connection with their husbands, and should encourage those who wish to engage in this line of missionary work.[60]

While Ellen White specifically commended women who served in supporting ministerial roles, she also encouraged women with greater gifts

for public leadership to fully exercise those gifts. When Mrs. S.M.I.
Henry, national evangelist for the Women's Christian Temperance
Union, became a Seventh-day Adventist,[61] Ellen White encouraged her to
continue her public ministry.

> We believe fully in church organization, but in *nothing that is to
> prescribe the precise way in which we must work*; for *all minds are not
> reached by the same methods.* . . . *Each person has his own lamp to keep
> burning.* . . . You have many ways opened before you. Address the
> crowd whenever you can; hold every jot of influence you can by any
> association that can be made the means of introducing the leaven to the
> meal [emphasis added].[62]

Notice the emphasis on the freedom and responsibility of each individual
under God to find the ministry in which her gifts can be most fruitful,
and Ellen White's belief that no one should "prescribe the precise way in
which" another Christian "must work." It should also be noted, however,
that her counsel to S.M.I. Henry does not primarily concern participation
in the organized church, but in a parachurch women's organization.

"Women Who Should Be Engaged in the Ministry"

Three further statements deserve more detailed examination. They
refer respectively to ministry, to pastoring, and to women as
administrative leaders in the local church. The first of these, published in
1903, is ambiguous regarding the specific roles of women in ministry.

> The Lord calls upon those connected with our sanitariums,
> publishing houses, and schools to teach the youth to do evangelistic
> work. Our time and energy must not be so largely employed in
> establishing sanitariums, food stores, and restaurants that other lines of
> work will be neglected. *Young men and young women who should be
> engaged in the ministry, in Bible work, and in the canvassing work should
> not be bound down to mechanical employment.*
>
> The youth should be encouraged to attend our training schools for
> Christian workers, which should become more and more like the
> schools of the prophets. These institutions have been established by the
> Lord, and if they are conducted in harmony with His purpose, the
> youth sent to them will quickly be prepared to engage in various lines
> of missionary work. *Some will be trained to enter the field as missionary
> nurses, some as canvassers, and some as gospel ministers.*[63]

The ambiguity occurs in the final sentence of the first paragraph. "Young
men and young women who should be engaged in the ministry, in Bible

work, and in the canvassing work should not be bound down to mechanical employment." The reason for the ambiguity is that both "Bible work" and "canvassing" are referred to elsewhere as aspects of "ministry."[64] The fact that she enumerates them individually would seem to imply that she is distinguishing them as different vocations, hence the usage "the ministry" most likely refers here to the pulpit preaching and administrative office of ministry in contrast to the more individual and family-oriented ministry of the Bible worker and the literature-distributive ministry of the canvasser. Of Ellen White's many references to women "in ministry," the majority refer specifically to the ministry of evangelistic and pastoral visiting, giving Bible instruction and spiritual guidance in families—the calling here spoken of as "Bible work."[65]

Women as Pastors

At least two statements from Ellen White mention women in pastoral roles.[66] The central question, of course, is what did she mean by "pastoral"? Ellen White sometimes used pastoral terminology to denote the personal visitation aspects of a minister's work, as contrasted with public pulpit ministry.[67] In this vein she denounced ministers who "only preach," or worse yet, merely "sermonize," but "neglect personal labor" because they lack the "watchful, tender compassion of a shepherd. The flock of God have a right to expect to be visited by their pastor, to be instructed, advised, counseled, in their own homes."[68] Again, she says, "The pastor should visit from house to house among his flock, teaching, conversing, and praying with each family," as well as seeing that prospective members are "thoroughly instructed in the truth."[69] This is precisely the work Ellen White elsewhere recommends for women in team ministry—"visiting from family to family, opening the Scriptures to them."[70] It is in this pastoral work that they are promised "a power that exceeds that of men."[71]

"Women to Do Pastoral Labor"

The foregoing provides the necessary background for a consideration of two statements which indicate that the spiritual gift of pastoring is given to women as well as men.

The first of these occurs in *Testimonies*, 4:390.

If there is one work more important than another, it is that of getting our publications before the public, thus leading them to search the

Scriptures. Missionary work—introducing our publications into families, conversing, and praying with and for them—is a good work and one which will educate men and women to do pastoral labor.[72]

According to this paragraph, door-to-door "missionary work" literature evangelism has two particular benefits: (1) "It is good work" in itself; and (2) it is a useful preparation for larger responsibilities. It "will educate men and women to do pastoral labor." The same two themes also permeate the context of another mention of women as "pastors."

"Pastors to the Flock of God"

The themes that (1) literature evangelism is itself a form of pastoral ministry, and (2) that it also gives preparation for pastoral ministry within a congregation, are clearly evident in a citation from *Testimonies*, 6:322. The sentences are numbered for ease of reference.

[1] All who desire an opportunity for true ministry, and who will give themselves unreservedly to God, will find in the canvassing work opportunities to speak upon many things pertaining to the future, immortal life. [2] The experience thus gained will be of the greatest value to those who are fitting themselves for the ministry. [3] It is the accompaniment of the Holy Spirit of God that prepares workers, both men and women, to become pastors to the flock of God.[73]

Sentence 1 indicates that "the canvassing work" is "true ministry." Sentence 2 recommends this work to "those who are fitting themselves for *the* ministry," i.e., ministerial leadership of a church. Sentence 3 affirms that the Holy Spirit "prepares workers, both men and women, to become pastors to the flock of God." The deduction seems clear that the clause "prepares . . . to become pastors" in the third sentence stands in parallelism to "fitting . . . for the ministry" in the previous sentence.

This theme of preparation recurs several times in the immediate context. The chapter in which the quoted passage occurs bears the title, "The Canvasser a Gospel Worker," and opens with the declaration that "The intelligent, God-fearing, truth-loving canvasser should be respected; for he occupies a position equal to that of the gospel minister."[74] That is theme one: literature evangelism is ministry. One concern of this chapter is to elevate the importance of the work of the canvasser or colporteur[75] to an equality with other forms of ministry. However, the next sentence shows that Ellen White was not just promoting the canvassing work, she was promoting it specifically to "young ministers and those who are fitting for the ministry." That is theme two: literature evangelism as preparation for "the" regular ministry.

> Many of our *young ministers* and *those who are fitting for the ministry* would, if truly converted, do much good by working in the canvassing field. And by meeting the people and presenting to them our publications they would *gain an experience* which they cannot gain by simply preaching. As they went from house to house they could converse with the people, carrying with them the fragrance of Christ's life. In thus endeavoring to bless others they would themselves be blessed; they would *obtain an experience* in faith; their knowledge of the Scriptures would greatly increase; and they would be constantly *learning* how to win souls for Christ [emphasis added].

Three paragraphs later occurs the passage under consideration.

> The experience thus gained will be of the greatest value to those who are *fitting themselves for the ministry. It is the accompaniment of the Holy Spirit of God that prepares workers, both men and women, to become pastors to the flock of God* [emphasis added].[76]

The theme of preparation and growth in evangelistic effectiveness continues in the rest of the paragraph. Canvassers who are "fitting themselves for the ministry" will "learn," "be educated," "practice," "be purified," "develop," and "be gifted" with spiritual power.[77]

On the next page occurs another explanatory connection with the main sentence under consideration. "The *preaching* of the word is a means by which the Lord has ordained that His warning message shall be given to the world. In the Scriptures the faithful *teacher* is represented as a *shepherd* of the flock of God. He is to be respected and his work appreciated. . . . [T]he canvassing work is to be a part both of the medical missionary work and of the ministry" (emphasis added).[78]

Ellen White repeatedly applies to the literature ministry terms commonly associated with the ministry of preaching, to show that the true literature evangelist is a preacher. Similarly, she uses terms associated with teaching to reinforce her concept of the canvasser as a teacher. Thus the paragraph that groups the terms "preaching," "teacher," and "shepherd of the flock of God" constitutes a statement that not only the regular minister, but the canvasser also preaches and teaches, hence also deserves to be "respected" and "appreciated" as a "shepherd to the flock of God."

Finally, "shepherd of the flock of God" stands in direct parallel to the expression "pastors to the flock of God" on the previous page, showing that by "pastors," Ellen White includes all who teach and preach the gospel, including literature evangelists. Comparing these parallel statements suggests that the Holy Spirit "prepares workers, both men and women, to become pastors," i.e., "shepherds to the flock of God," but this shepherding role may take a variety of vocational forms.

On one hand, literature evangelists who truly minister to the individuals they visit are, through their literature and their presence, giving immediate pastoral care. On the other hand, the experience gained prepares the faithful canvasser to give pastoral care in other contexts as well.

Finally, the references to the "Holy Spirit," "gifts," "pastor," "teacher," and "shepherd," as well as the focal sentence "the Holy Spirit . . . prepares workers, both men and women, to become pastors to the flock of God,"[79] imply that the spiritual gift of pastor-teacher (Eph 4:11) is given to both men and women.

"Adapted to the Successful Management of a Church"

That Ellen White saw both women and men as potentially qualified for church leadership is shown by her statement that "it is not always men who are best adapted to the successful management of a church." The context is a scathing rebuke to a Brother Johnson who had "a disposition to dictate and control matters" in a certain local church, and who had only "sneers" for the work of women in the same church. "Jesus is ashamed of you," she wrote, and on the next page continued,

> You are not in sympathy with the great Head of the church. . . . This contemptible picking, faultfinding, seeking spot and stain, ridiculing, gainsaying, that you with some others have indulged in, has grieved the Spirit of God and separated you from God.
>
> *It is not always men who are best adapted to the successful management of a church. If faithful women* have more deep piety and true devotion than men, they could indeed by their prayers and their labors do more than men who are unconsecrated in heart and life [emphasis added].[80]

The words "It is not always men" point to the addressees' assumption that in any situation, the best leader for a church would always be a man. Ellen White asserts that there are times when the person best qualified to lead a church is a woman. The words "best adapted" point to personal talents and spiritual gifts, which, along with "deep piety and true devotion," constitute the qualifications for spiritual leadership. The primary determinant of fitness for church leadership is not gender, but character.[81]

Set Apart by Prayer and Laying on of Hands

One further citation remains to be carefully examined in its historical context. It comes from the decade that Ellen White spent pioneering in Australia, and appeared in the *Review and Herald,* 9 July 1895. It is the one statement where she explicitly recommends an ordination service for women.

The burden of the article in which this statement occurs is the noninvolvement of the majority of church members in the work of the church. "A few persons have been selected as spiritual burden-bearers, and the talent of other members has remained undeveloped." To remedy this, she urges ministers to involve the congregation both in "planning" and in "executing the plans that they have had a part in forming." She further urges "every individual who is considered a worthy member of the church" be given a definite part in the work of the church. Then occurs the paragraph about women.

> Women who are willing to consecrate some of their time to the service of the Lord should be *appointed* to visit the sick, look after the young, and minister to the necessities of the poor. *They should be set apart to this work by prayer and laying on of hands.* In some cases they will need to counsel with the church officers or the minister; but if they are devoted women, maintaining a vital connection with God, they will be a power for good in the church. This is another means of strengthening and building up the church. We need to branch out more in our methods of labor. Not a hand should be bound, not a soul discouraged, not a voice should be hushed; let *every* individual labor, privately or publicly, to help forward this grand work [emphasis supplied].[82]

A few observations may be made at this point. These are laywomen, who are "willing to consecrate some of their time," not their full time, to church work. Thus it is clear that this is not a career choice by which they will earn their livelihood, but a part-time volunteer ministry.[83] Regarding the terms "appointed" and "set apart . . . by prayer and laying on of hands," there can be no doubt that these were Ellen White's characteristic expressions for a ceremony of ordination.[84]

No extensive research has been done to discover the extent of the church's response to this appeal. Three instances are known, however. On 10 August 1895, about a month after Ellen White's article was published in the *Review* (but possibly in response to an earlier local circulation of the prepublication manuscript), the Ashfield Church in

Sydney, not far from where Ellen White was then working, held an ordination service for newly elected church officers. "Pastors Corliss and McCullagh of the Australian conference set apart the elder, deacons, [and] deaconesses by prayer and the laying on of hands."[85] Notice that identical ordination terminology is used for all three offices. Another record from the same church five years later (6 January 1900) again reports the ordination of two elders, one deacon, and two deaconesses. The officiating minister was W. C. White, whose diary of the same date corroborates the records of the Ashfield Church clerk.[86] A third example comes from February or March, 1916, when E. E. Andross, then president of the Pacific Union Conference, officiated at a women's ordination service and cited Ellen White's 1895 *Review and Herald* article as his authority.[87]

Both the internal evidence of Ellen White's 1895 article and the responses of those close to her at the time—the Ashfield Church; her son W. C. White; and E. E. Andross, who was a church administrator in California during Ellen White's Elmshaven years[88]—seem to confirm that Ellen White approved the formal ordination of laywomen to a role then associated with the office of deaconess in the local church. The work of a deaconess was not confined to ritual functions at the Lord's Supper and footwashing, but was rather seen as a work of practical ministry to persons in need. This is the apparent significance of Ellen White's job description, "to visit the sick, look after the young, and minister to the necessities of the poor."

This evidence shows, first, that Ellen White did not view ordination, as such, to be a gender-specific ordinance, but a ceremony of consecration that may rightly be conducted for both men and women. It includes "designation to an appointed office," "recognition of one's authority in that office," and a request for "God to bestow His blessing" upon the one ordained.[89]

Second, the association of ordination with the office of deaconess suggests a line for further investigation. In current usage, both the office of deacon and its feminine equivalent, deaconess, have become stereotyped as largely ceremonial offices, expanded slightly to include (for the men) physical upkeep of the church building and grounds, and (for the women) cooking and cleaning and serving at social functions. However, the New Testament word transliterated as deaconess is rightly translated "minister" (see Eph 3:7, where Paul uses the same root word for his own ministry), and there were women who filled this ministerial office (see Rom 16:1).[90]

Finally, note also that of the original seven who were elected to "serve tables" in Acts 6:2, two of them far superseded the terms of their ordination, becoming highly successful public speakers and evangelists. In view of Ellen White's endorsement of ordaining women as deaconesses, perhaps the significance of the New Testament precedent needs to be more fully explored, remembering that Ellen White's motivation for recommending this ritual was to stimulate the involvement and mobilization of the rank and file of church members by vividly impressing on them their divine calling to exercise outwardly the priesthood of every believer bestowed on them at their baptism.[91] If the church would even now act on the instruction given a century ago that women "should be set apart to this work by prayer and laying on of hands"—a ritual that connotes the delegation of church authority and a request for the bestowal of divine blessing[92]—the church should not be surprised if some of those "set apart" to minister to the "sick," the "young," and the "poor" would go on to evangelizing and planting churches in which the sick, the young, and the poor would become healthy, mature, and prosperous, and continue the expansion of the Kingdom.

Conclusions

Regarding Ellen White's concept of the ministerial responsibilities that might appropriately be exercised by women, five points may be noted.

1. The combined talents of both men and women are essential for the highest success in the work of the ministry. Therefore the ideal is team ministry, especially by husband-and-wife ministerial teams.

2. The list of roles open to women in gospel ministry embraces a wide range of job descriptions and vocational options, including preaching, teaching, pastoral care, evangelistic work, literature evangelism, Sabbath School leadership, chaplaincy, counseling, and church administration.

3. She believed that the spiritual gifts of pastoring and teaching (Eph 4:11) are given by the Holy Spirit to both men and women, and some women possess gifts and abilities for the "successful management" of churches.

4. Ellen White's most strongly worded recommendation regarding women in ministry was that self-sacrificing wives who join their husbands in team ministry should receive wages proportionate to the time they devote to ministry. The issue of fair pay for every ministerial wife who

chooses to devote herself to ministry rather than to some other profession was certainly a higher priority with Ellen White than ordination; yet her strong denunciations of paying only the male half of the ministerial team are still, with a few isolated exceptions, largely disregarded.[93]

5. Ellen White recommended the ordination of laywomen to a local ministry that would meet the needs of "the sick," "the young," and "the poor." Thus she showed her understanding that ordination is an ordinance of appointment and consecration that may rightly be conducted for both men and women. Her contemporaries understood this as a call for ordaining deaconesses on the same basis as deacons, but the practice was never widely accepted in the church.

Since she believed ordination is important for laywomen in a ministry to physical and emotional needs, would she also see some form of ordination as important for women who are laborers "in word and doctrine"? In any case, woman's place in ministry is secure. Even if "the hands of ordination have not been laid upon her, she is accomplishing a work that is in the line of ministry."[94]

Endnotes

1. Ellen G. White, "Words to Lay Members," *Review and Herald*, 25 August 1902, 7-8. For the context of this phrase, see p. 186.

2. See, e.g., James White, *A Word to the Little Flock* (Gotham, ME: James White, 1847), 13; James White, quoted in "Doings of the Battle Creek Conference, October 5 and 6, 1861," *Review and Herald*, 8 October 1861; both reproduced in *Witness of the Pioneers Concerning the Spirit of Prophecy: A Facsimile Reprint of Periodical and Pamphlet Articles Written by the Contemporaries of Ellen G. White* (Washington, DC: Ellen G. White Estate, 1961), 4, 26; see also, Arthur L. White, "The Position of 'The Bible and the Bible Only' and the Relationship of This to the Writings of Ellen G. White," Washington, DC: Ellen G. White Estate, 1971.

3. Eph 4:11-13; Joel 2:28-29; Rev 12:17, 19:10.

4. Ellen G. White, *Great Controversy*, vii.

5. *Seventh-day Adventist Church Manual* (Silver Spring, MD: General Conference of Seventh-day Adventists, 1990), 28.

6. Ibid.

7. Ellen G. White, *Colporteur Ministry*, 6, 101, 8.

8. Ellen G. White, *Counsels on Health*, 558, 557.

9. Ellen G. White, Manuscript 79, 1900, in *Evangelism*, 546.

10. Ibid., 557, 558.

11. Ellen G. White, *Messages to Young People*, 211.

12. Ellen G. White, *Loma Linda Messages*, 386.

13. Ellen G. White, "The Laborer is Worthy of His Hire," MS 43a, 1898, *Manuscript Releases*, 5:325.

14. Ellen G. White, *Manuscript Releases*, 5:325; also cited in *Evangelism*, 472.

15. White, *Manuscript Releases*, 5:325.

16. Ibid.

17. Ibid., 324.

18. Ibid., 323-327.

19. White, *Manuscript Releases*, 5:323-324.

20. For a historical example, one could hardly recall a more illustrious figure in the annals of Adventist women than that of Mary E. Walsh (1892-1997), evangelistic Bible instructor, author, and sometime pastor, who never married. "Mary Walsh, Pioneer Bible Worker, Pastor, Dies at 105," *Adventist Review*, 20 November 1997, 23.

21. Ellen G. White to A. G. Daniells, 27 October 1909 (Letter 142, 1909), *Manuscript Releases*, 17:37. The Scripture reference appears to be a conflation of Rom 16:3 and Phil 4:3, possibly with 2 Cor 1:11 in the background.

22. Ellen G. White, *Acts of the Apostles*, 554.

23. White, *Manuscript Releases*, 5:324.

24. Ibid, 325.

25. Ellen G. White, Letter 77, 1898, cited in *Evangelism*, 469; see also *Counsels on Health*, 544, 547.

26. Ellen G. White, *Review and Herald*, 2 January 1879, cited in *Evangelism*, 472; cf. *Desire of Ages*, 568.

27. Ellen G. White, *Review and Herald*, 26 August 1902, cited in *Welfare Ministry*, 145.

28. Ellen G. White, Letter 142, 1909, cited in *Evangelism*, 491.

29. Ellen G. White, "Looking for that Blessed Hope," *Signs of the Times*, 24 June 1889.

30. Ellen G. White, *Gospel Workers*, 1915 ed., 452-453, cited in *Evangelism*, 492-493.

31. Ellen G. White, Manuscript 47, 1898, excerpted in *Evangelism*, 492; see also *Manuscript Releases*, 5:323-327; 12:160-167; 17:36-37.

32. Ellen G. White, *Evangelism*, 471-472.

33. Ibid., 492.

34. Ibid., 492-493.

35. Ellen G. White, *Counsels on Stewardship*, 81, 101-103; *Testimonies*, 9:247-250.

36. Ellen G. White, Manuscript 149, 1899, cited in *Evangelism*, 492.

37. See, e.g. *Manuscript Releases*, 12:160-167.

38. "Bible readers" refers to persons who give "Bible readings," a question-and-answer form of Bible study.

39. Ellen G. White, "The Laborer is Worthy of His Hire," Manuscript 43a, 22 March 1898, *Manuscript Releases*, 5:323-324.

40. White, *Evangelism*, 493.

41. Similarly, in *Testimonies*, 8:229-230, she wrote that "young men and young women who should be engaged in the ministry, in Bible work, and in the canvassing work should not be bound down to mechanical employment."

42. Ibid., 492.

43. White, *Evangelism*, 459, 464, 470, 471, 478, 491.

44. White, *Evangelism*, 493, "carrying the truth into families;" see also ibid., 456, 469, 470, 475, 477. *Evangelism*, 491-493, speaks of women sharing with men in evangelistic work. Though roles are not specified, the context and SDA history imply the specific roles of visitation, Bible studies, other teaching roles, and pulpit preaching. See chapter by Michael Bernoi.

45. Ellen G. White, *Testimonies*, 2:322-323; 4:390; 8:229-230; *Evangelism*, 467-473, 491-493.

46. White, *Evangelism*, 469, 473-477. "Again and again the Lord has shown me that women teachers are just as greatly needed to do the work to which He has appointed them as are men." The context refers to house-to-house pastoral-evangelistic visiting and Bible teaching (E. G. White, "The Laborer is Worthy of His Hire," Manuscript 43a, 22 March 1898, *Manuscript Releases*, 5:325).

47. "Canvassing" denotes door-to-door sales of Christian books and periodicals, a vocation currently called "literature evangelism" (idem, 469-470; *Testimonies*, 2:322-323; *Testimonies*, 8:229-230).

48. "It is not in harmony with the instructions given at Sinai that gentlemen physicians should do the work of midwives. The Bible speaks of women at childbirth being attended by women, and thus it ought always to be. Women should be educated and trained to act skillfully as *midwives* and *physicians* to their sex. It is just as important that a line of study be given to educate women to deal with women's diseases, as it is that there should be gentlemen thoroughly trained to act as physicians and surgeons. And the wages of the woman should be proportionate to her services. She should be as much appreciated in her work as the gentleman physician is appreciated in his work" (idem, *Counsels on Health*, 365, emphasis added).

49. White, *Testimonies*, 8:143-144.

50. White, *Evangelism*, 460.

51. Ellen G. White, *Manuscript Releases*, 1:125.

52. Ellen G. White, "Words to Lay Members," *Review and Herald*, 20 August 1902, 7-8; this paragraph is quoted in idem, *Welfare Ministry*, 145.

53. A pronouncement Mrs. White made with reference to wages seems equally applicable to issues of rank and position: "As we bring ourselves into right relationship with God we shall have success wherever we go; and it is success that we want, not money [or rank or position, but]—living success, and God will give it to us because He knows all about our self-denial. He knows every sacrifice that we make. You may think that your self-denial does not make any difference, that you ought to have more consideration and so on. But it makes a great difference with the Lord. Over and over again I have been shown that when individuals begin to reach out after higher and still higher wages [or rank or position], something comes into their experience that places them where they stand no longer on vantage ground. But when they take the wage that carries on the face of it the fact that they are self-sacrificing, the Lord sees their self-denial and He gives them success and victory. This has been presented to me over and over again. The Lord that seeth in secret will reward openly for every sacrifice that His tried servants have been willing to make" (Ellen G. White, MS 12, 1913, quoted in *Selected Messages*, 2:179-180).

54. White, *Evangelism*, 469, 473-477; *Counsels on Sabbath School Work*, 90-96.

55. Ellen G. White, Letter 169, 1900, cited in *Evangelism*, 473; names supplied from idem, "The Laborer Is Worthy of His Hire," Manuscript 43a, 22 March 1898.

56. J. N. Andrews, "May Women Speak in Meetings?" *Review and Herald*, 2 January 1879.

57. Andrews, "May Women Speak in Meetings?" emphasis his; see also, Uriah Smith, "Let Your Women Keep Silence in the Churches," *Review and Herald*, 26 June 1866; James White, "Women in the Church," *Review and Herald*, 29 May 1979.

58. Ellen G. White to James White, from Oakland, CA, Letter 17a, 1 April 1880, *Manuscript Releases*, 10:70.

59. Ellen G. White, *Sketches from the Life of Paul*, 119, emphasis added.

60. Ellen G. White to A. G. Daniells, 27 October (Letter 142), 1909, *Manuscript Releases*, 17:35-36.

61. A. L. White, *Ellen G. White: The Australian Years* (Hagerstown, MD: Review and Herald, 1983), 346-348.

62. Ellen G. White to S.M.I. Henry, 24 March 1899 (Letter 54, 1899), quoted in *Review and Herald*, 9 May 1899, and excerpted in *Evangelism*, 473.

63. White, *Testimonies*, 8:229-230.

64. White, *Manuscript Releases*, 5:323; *Testimonies*, 6:323, quoted in *Colporteur Ministry*, 101.

65. See, e.g., MS 43a, 1898, *Manuscript Releases*, 5:325, 323-327.

66. White, *Testimonies*, 4:390; 6:322-323.

67. See White, *Testimonies*, 3:232-233; *Evangelism*, 350.

68. Ellen G. White, *Appeal and Suggestions to Conference Officers*, Pamphlet no. 2, 17.

69. Ellen G. White, *Gospel Workers* (1915), quoted in *Evangelism*, 350.

70. White, *Manuscript Releases*, 5:323; cf. 325-7.

71. Ellen G. White, *Welfare Ministry*, 145.

72. Ellen G. White, "Our Publications," in *Testimonies*, 4:390.

73. White, *Testimonies*, 6:322.

74. Ibid., 321.

75. The "evangelistic canvasser" (*Testimonies*, 6:325), or "colporteur" (ibid, 323), was a door-to-door seller of Christian books and periodicals, who not only sold them, but read and explained them to people, seeking to lead them to a personal and growing relationship with Christ.

76. Ibid., 321-322.

77. Ibid., 322.

78. Ibid., 323.

79. White, *Testimonies*, 6:322-323.

80. Ellen G. White to Brother Johnson, Letter 33, 1879, *Manuscript Releases*, 19:55-56.

81. See chapters by Richard M. Davidson and Peter M. Van Bemmelen in this book.

82. Ibid.

83. Ellen G. White, *Conflict and Courage*, 342; idem, *Acts of the Apostles*, 355.

84. See, e.g., White, *Acts of the Apostles*, 160-161; idem, "Separated Unto the Gospel," *Review and Herald*, 11 May 1911; idem, *Gospel Workers*, 15, 452; idem, *Manuscript Releases*, 5:29, 323; idem, *Testimonies*, 6:444; idem, *Manuscript Releases*, 2:32, 8:189; idem, *Messages to Young People*, 226; idem, *Testimonies to Ministers and Gospel Workers*, 188. See also chapters by Keith Mattingly and Denis Fortin in this book.

85. Minutes of the Ashfield SDA Church, Sydney, Australia, 10 August 1895, cited by Arthur N. Patrick, "The Ordination of Deaconesses," *Adventist Review*, 16 January 1996, 18-19.

86. Minutes of the Ashfield SDA Church, Sydney, Australia, 6 January 1900, and W. C. White Diary, 6 January 1900, cited by Patrick, "The Ordination of Deaconesses," 18-19.

87. Mrs. L. E. Cox to C. C. Crisler, 12 March 1916; reproduced in Roger W. Coon, "Ellen G. White's View of the Role of Women in the SDA Church." Shelf Document, E. G. White Estate, 1986. Mrs. Cox says, "I have been a Bible worker for a number of years and have recently been granted a ministerial license." She reports that she "was in a recent meeting where Elder A[n]dross set aside women by the laying on of hands. . . ." Crisler, in reply, calls the service "the ordination of women who give some time to missionary work." (C. C. Crisler to Mrs. L. E. Cox, 22 March and 16 June 1916, both reproduced in full in Coon, "Ellen G. White's View of the Role of Women in the SDA Church," Appendix H, pp. 24-25).

88. *SDA Encyclopedia*, 1995 ed., s.v. "Andross, Elmer Ellsworth."

89. White, *Acts of the Apostles*, 162; see also Keith Mattingly's chapter, "The Laying on of Hands."

90. See Robert Johnston's chapter in this book.

91. Ellen G. White, "Our Work," *Signs of the Times*, 25 August 1898, cited by Denis Fortin, "The Concept of Ordination in the Writings of Ellen G. White," chapter 6, above.

92. White, *Acts of the Apostles*, 162.

93. James A. Cress, "Selective Disobedience," *Ministry*, June 1998, 28-29.

94. White, *Manuscript Releases*, 5:323.

CHAPTER 11

NINETEENTH-CENTURY WOMEN IN ADVENTIST MINISTRY AGAINST THE BACKDROP OF THEIR TIMES

MICHAEL BERNOI

Introduction

Many opinions have been expressed on women in ministry and especially on their ordination to the gospel ministry. Authors on both sides of the issue have sought to prove their positions from Scripture and Ellen White. Articles, position papers, compilations, and even several books have been written, all seeking a greater understanding of women's role and function within the Adventist Church. Often, however, the historical context of the evidence cited for both Scripture and Ellen G. White's statements has been overlooked, or at best inadequately understood.

History, by its very definition, never unfolds in a vacuum. Any history is the story of a particular group, written for a particular purpose. Tragically, women are often left out of that story or relegated to a "back seat," even though they may have played important roles in the story. The history of this church and its people—especially the role women have played, first in Millerism and then in the early Seventh-day Adventist Church—becomes clearer when understood within the context and culture of its times. Ellen White herself noted that to understand and apply the *Testimonies*, "time and place must be considered."[1]

This chapter will provide a glimpse into the sociological/cultural climate of Ellen White's day, thus placing Ellen White's statements concerning women and their role and function in ministry in their appropirate context. Second, the article will survey the role of women in the Seventh-day Adventist Church, beginning with Millerism.

I trust the material which follows will be thought-provoking and stimulating. History can be a powerful teacher if we will but let it. We now turn our attention to Ellen White's world—nineteenth-century America.

Nineteenth-century America

Ellen Harmon was born in Maine in 1827 and died in California in 1915. Her life spanned the better part of the nineteenth century, a time when the ideal woman was a far cry from reality. The place of women in the ideal was different from her place in the real world, and especially in the world of the church.

Women in Their Place

During the nineteenth century, the United States underwent fundamental change. "Major shifts in the economy, both North and South, in the first half of the nineteenth century had a dramatic effect on women's lives." This was due in large part to the cotton revolution and the significant role women played in it. In rural New England, for example, young women flocked to the mill towns. "White single women constituted the overwhelming majority of the early textile work force. By 1831, women comprised nearly forty-thousand of the fifty-eight thousand workers in this industry."[2] In 1850 women represented 24 percent of the total workforce in America's number one industry—cotton. However, society still designated domesticity and the household as woman's domain and primary role.[3] The woman who deviated from this narrow role met with stern disapproval. But if she was young and single, then she might be encouraged to earn pay outside the home as a temporary measure, to tide her over until marriage. This was especially true for lower- and middle-class females who were expected to supplement, rather than drain, family income before they wed.

The vast majority of women, however, did not work outside the home. The factory system had not yet replaced the home industry, which allowed male and female workers greater control over their hours, working conditions, and type of trade or skills. In the early part of the century, America had still primarily an agriculturally driven economy. Work and home were integrated spheres for most households.

But for the women and men of the mill towns of New England, life was changing. It could be hard and strict. The waking hours of mill workers were controlled by their employers. Single employees were required to live in company boardinghouses with strict rules. Their doors closed at ten o'clock in the evening; all employees were to conduct themselves properly and observe the Puritan Sabbath.[4] Furthermore, when daylight hours lengthened, so did working hours; for many that meant starting the day at 5 a.m. and working until 7 p.m.

Many women wrote descriptions of their plight. For example, Catherine Clinton cites a verse composed by a factory girl: "Amidst the clashing noise and din/Of the ever-beating loom/Stood a fair young girl with throbbing brow/Working her way to the tomb."[5]

Most women escaped factory work to marry, teach, or perform domestic service.[6] By the mid 1840s, factory life had become so bad that women workers began to organize labor reform associations. In 1845, one woman ended her plea for justice in a local journal with a rousing indictment:

> Producers of all the luxuries and comforts of life, will you not wake up on this subject? Will you sit supinely down and let the drones in society fasten the yoke of tyranny, which is already fitted to your necks that you do not feel it but slightly—will you, I say, suffer them to rivet that yoke upon you, which has crushed and is crushing its million in the old world to earth; yea to starvation and death? Now is the time to answer this all important question. Shall we not hear the response from every hill and vale, "EQUAL RIGHTS, or death to the corporations?"[7]

Life was little better for the plantation mistress of the South—not to mention the plight of Black people! Men often left their wives alone to care for the estate while they tended to business in town, held a political office, or conducted military campaigns. The women of the home were left to manage the slaves, negotiate with overseers, and tend to merchants and creditors, as well as perform their daily round of chores.[8] They were trapped on the estate, subject to their "lord and master," for this is how the husband was viewed. A typical day for a woman—northern or southern—might include: growing herbs, blending medicines, planting corn, spinning cloth, knitting socks, sewing clothes, slaughtering animals, scouring copper cooking utensils, preserving vegetables, churning butter, dipping candles, weaving rugs, caring for the education of the children—moral, spiritual, and intellectual—and a myriad of other required household chores simply to exist in daily domestic life.[9]

No wonder Ellen White penned these words!

> In many a home the wife and mother has no time to read, to keep

herself well informed, no time to be a companion to her husband, no time to keep in touch with the developing minds of her children. There is not time or place for the precious Saviour to be a close, dear companion. Little by little she sinks into a mere household drudge, her strength and time and interest absorbed in the things that perish with the using. . . . Let the homemakers resolve to live on a wiser plan. Let it be your first aim to make a pleasant home. Be sure to provide the facilities that will enlighten labor and promote health.[10]

While life for a woman in the nineteenth century was often drudgery, she was constantly assailed by an ideal to which she could not live up. Whether they lived in the North or the South, women of the dominating culture of this period were caught up in the nineteenth century's social and ideological revolution—the cult of domesticity.[11] The cultural myth of the "model woman" bore little resemblance to any woman's daily life, yet it was thrust upon the women of the day by over one hundred magazines which addressed the quandaries and delights of ladies and mothers.[12] Nearly all the publications of the day claimed that a woman's chief contribution was in her role as wife and mother. Confinement to the domestic sphere was the chief goal and aim of godly women. As one antebellum author put it:

Whenever she . . . goes out of this sphere to mingle in any of the greater public movements of the day, she is deserting the station which God and nature have assigned to her. . . . Home is her appropriate and appointed sphere of action."[13]

The idea that woman's God-ordained place was in the home permeated every level of society in Ellen White's day. Well-informed, educated, and prominent women, like Sophia Peabody Hawthorne, wife of the great novelist Nathaniel Hawthorne (1804-1864), whose family called her a "liberal," believed this to be so.[14] In a letter to her mother, Sophia declared: "It is always a shock for me to have women mount the rostrum. Home, I think, is the greatest arena for women."[15]

Some might even think that Ellen White's counsel to women concerning "their place" was narrowing in a similar sense: "God has given the mother, in the education of her children, a responsibility paramount to everything else."[16] Speaking of the nineteenth century, Barbara Epstein points out that "child raising was difficult, but fortunately, women were assured, they had special abilities for it, largely due to their innate warmth and morality." In fact, the "female breast" was considered "the natural soil of Christianity."[17]

In the nineteenth century, Epstein notes, "the ideal woman accepted her class position gracefully." To corroborate this, she quotes sources from the times: "In polite life [her] manners are peculiarly engaging. To her superiors, she shows the utmost deference and respect; to her equals, the most modest complaisance and divinity; while every rank experiences her kindness and affability." Therefore, "abandoning any personal ambition, she accommodates herself to her husband's position in society."[18]

Whereas for the Puritans and authors of the late eighteenth-century ladies' books, motherhood was only *one* of woman's many tasks, nineteenth-century writers saw motherhood as the most important of a woman's responsibilities. This is borne out by women's guides and marriage manuals of the period. Whether written by men or women, these guides "stressed the importance of a woman's adoption of a subservient stance in relation to her husband."[19]

Nineteenth-century women did not have the right to vote, to sign contracts, or to hold title to their own property or earnings—even when it was theirs by inheritance or dowry.[20] Eleanor Flexner points out that "a working woman could be compelled to hand over every penny of her wages to a drunkard husband, even if she was left with nothing for her own subsistence or the maintenance of her children, and even if the husband was known to be making no provision for them."[21]

In the early-nineteenth century, women had no public voice. It would take the abolition movement and the compassion of women for the plight of the Negro slave, along with their own interests for liberation, to push them to learn to organize, hold public meetings, and conduct petition campaigns. As abolitionists they would win the public's ear. But this would be a long and tedious process with many setbacks.[22]

For example, in 1838, "the General Association of Congregational Ministers of Massachusetts denounced such activities and urged women to refrain from any public works save only leading souls to pastors for instruction."[23] These ministers, representing the largest denomination in Massachusetts, publicly denounced the "behavior" of Sarah and Angelina Grimke, two sisters in the reform movement, as "unwomanly and unchristian."

> We invite your attention to the dangers which at present seem to threaten the female character with widespread and permanent injury. The appropriate duties and influence of women are clearly stated in the New Testament. Those duties, and that influence are unobtrusive and

private but the sources of mighty power. When the mild, dependent, softening influence upon the sternness of man's opinions is fully exercised, society feels the effect of it in a thousand forms. *The power of a woman is her dependence, flowing from the consciousness of that weakness which God has given her for her protection.* . . .

But when she assumes the place and tone of man as a public reformer, . . . she yields the power which God has given her for her protection and her character becomes unnatural.[24]

Thus the central elements of the nineteenth-century ideology of femininity were that (1) women were to create the homes their husbands needed; (2) children required undivided motherly attention; (3) women were especially endowed to provide such care; (4) domesticity would shield women from the evils of the outside world; and (5) in the home women would find status and power, mediated through their families.[25]

The abolition and reform movements brought upheaval and change to America. They also served as vehicles by which women gained footholds in the public arena. Change in the social fabric also brought change to America's religious fabric.

Women in the Church

During the late-eighteenth century, church attendance fell to an all-time low. This may have happened in response to the United States' newly adopted Constitution, which clearly called for the separation of church and state, signaling a new era as well as a decline of the influence of many religious leaders.[26] At the same time other factors—including the popularity of deist philosophers such as Thomas Paine and William Godwin, a sense of freedom from America's oppressors, and a new age dawning with hope for the future—contributed to the decline of spiritual interest.[27]

With the nineteenth century came the evangelistic crusades of the Second Great Awakening. Commenting on the revivals that took place, Clinton notes: "With this spiritual dragnet stretched across the frontier to snag the sinful and world-weary, divines discovered that women, not men," were most concerned with their spiritual welfare and responded.[28] As an example, Clinton points out that "records of revivals in the burnt-over district of western New York reveal the disproportionate 'saving' of young women through grace: during a Baptist revival in Utica in 1838; when the population was only half female, 72 percent of the converts were women."[29]

Thus, more women than men participated in nineteenth-century

North American religious life. Epstein points out that "their increasing domination of church membership was itself a symptom of deeper changes in women's role in the family and in society, changes that also were reflected in the transformation of women's religious experience."[30]

Because religion was increasingly women's domain, they were now accorded essential roles within the realm of religion. For example, females began entering what was once exclusively the all-male domain of missionary work, even if that only meant support as a wife. Concurrent with this phenomenon, women also began stepping outside of their immediate domestic domain, by expanding their interests in a concentric fashion beyond the home in arenas such as teaching and moral reform.[31] By 1870, more than half of all primary and secondary school teachers in America were women.[32] Domestic feminists argued that teaching was a natural extension of woman's maternal role. Additionally, both evangelism and the temperance movement (which had its roots in religiously and morally inspired social reform) provided another opportunity for women to express old concerns, rooted in the relations between the sexes, in a new and more socially effective way.

George Knight, in *Millennial Fever*, writes of the opening for active participation of women in nineteenth-century ministry.

> Not only was the women's-rights movement getting a major boost from female participation in abolitionism, but restorationism and the Second Great Awakening were also giving them new opportunities. The Christian Connection, in particular, had a strong tradition of women preachers. And during the 1830s female participation in public religion received encouragement from the revivalism of Charles Finney, while the ministry of Phoebe Palmer was renewing the acceptability of women leading out in public worship in the Methodist tradition.[33]

Phoebe Palmer, the holiness preacher, met with great success as she championed the cause of Christ in the mid-1800s. Her success as an evangelist/preacher is described in an 1857 report:

> Revival broke out at evangelistic meetings led by Walter and Phoebe Palmer in Hamilton, Ontario, in Canada during October 1857. Attendances reached 6,000, and five to six hundred professed conversion including many civic leaders. . . .
>
> Walter Palmer, a Holiness Methodist physician, assisted his talented wife Phoebe, a firebrand preacher. Her preaching, teaching, half-a-dozen books, and editing of *The Guide to Holiness* left "an indelible impact on both Methodism and the wider Church."[34]

Out of the Woman's Crusade of 1873-74 came the most prominent women's organization of the day—the Woman's Christian Temperance Union (WCTU).[35] Of that reform movement, Ellen White wrote: "Light has been given me that there are those with most precious talents and capabilities in the W.C.T.U. . . . . Some of our best talent should be set at work for the W.C.T.U."[36] The battle against liquor was not the only one that the WCTU waged. Epstein describes:

> Frances Willard and other WCTU women consistently supported equal rights for women in every area of public life. In addition, Willard, at least, argued that women should be trained and educated and that occupation outside the home should be made available to them, so that they would not have to depend upon marriage for a livelihood. She also believed that men should become more involved in family life in general and parenting in particular and that husband and wife should treat one another as equals.[37]

Significantly, both Willard and the WCTU distanced themselves from feminism, mostly because of its strong political and controversial stances, such as its association with the woman's suffrage movement, those who advocated "free love," spiritualism, and doing away with "this vile system of marriage."[38]

Thus, during the nineteenth century, while the ideal was the domestic woman, women gained public position and prominence, first in the church, then in education, and finally in moral reform movements tied closely to the ideal of the family.

Adventist Women in Ministry

Adventist women began preaching before the Great Disappointment. They have continued proclaiming the Good News ever since. This section focuses on women evangelists in the Millerite movement, on historical developments that affected the role of women in the early Seventh-day Adventist Church (1863-1915), and closes with brief sketches of notable women in ministry.

Millerite Women Evangelists

A great religious movement, Millerism became part of the nineteenth-century fabric in the mid-1800s and rode the crest of the wave of the Second Great Awakening. This millennial movement, inaugurated by William Miller, proclaimed the premillennial return of Jesus in the 1840s.

Its preachers included talented women, willing to be used by God, as itinerant preachers and lecturers.

One of the women who responded to God's calling and turned Advent preacher was Lucy Maria Hersey, born in Worcester, Massachusetts, in 1824. Converted at an early age, she attended several Millerite meetings in 1842 and accepted Miller's exposition regarding the Second Coming. Shortly after that, she was so impressed that the Lord wanted her to proclaim the gospel that she quit her teaching post to preach the message.

Not long after this, she accompanied her father, Lewis Hersey, who had already written on Advent views in 1841, to Schenectady, New York. Considering that it might be offensive to ask a female to speak, a believer asked Lucy's "non-clergyman father to address a non-Adventist group on the evidence for his faith."[39] After several moments of awkward silence, as the father could find nothing to say, the host remarked, "Brother Hersey has a daughter here who talks when in some conference meetings in N.E. at home, and if there is no objection raised by any one present, we would like to hear from her."[40]

Lucy Hersey spoke with such effect that the people soon obtained the courthouse for her, so that "she could preach to the people." Reporters attending her meetings printed her lectures in the following day's paper. Her ministry was both fruitful and lengthy, "and included the conversion of several men who took up the preaching of the advent message."[41] Isaac Welcome pointed out that Lucy Hersey (later married to a preacher by the last name of Stoddard) had been "the humble instrument of gathering sheaves for the Kingdom of God." He went on: "Elder Jonas Wendall and many other ministers now proclaiming the gospel state that their conversion to the truth was through her preaching. This should encourage others, whom the Lord calls, not to refrain because they are females."[42]

Other women included among the Advent preachers were Olive Maria Rice and Sarah J. Paine Higgins, noted for being the "first female that preached in Massachusetts the Advent of Christ at hand," with great success in soul winning. Emily C. Clemons and Clorinda S. Minor not only preached but went on to edit a periodical especially for women, *The Advent Message to the Daughters of Zion*, which appeared in May of 1844.[43]

Abigail Mussey, who at first feared to be called a "preacher woman," did most of her preaching after the Disappointment. In her autobiography, which she wrote at age 54, she described her experience:

Preachers that oppose female laborers can shut up their houses, and refuse to give out their appointments; but they can't shut up the private houses, or school-houses, and they cannot hinder others from giving out appointments; so there is no danger of shut doors or the way being hedged up. . . . Doors opened, and I moved on, with sword in hand and the gospel armor on, with loving all and fearing none. I knew in whom I believed, in whom I trusted, and who had sent me out. My mission was from heaven, not from man. My faith stood not in the wisdom of men, but in the power of God.[44]

Lauretta Elysian Armstrong Fassett was another Advent woman preacher who "had to break through her own and her husband's prejudices against women preachers."[45] Like most women of her day, she had been taught never to speak in public, as it was forbidden by the apostle Paul. But being "prevailed upon by entreaty, she threw aside her prejudices, stifled her feelings, overcame her training, and made the attempt to please others, and satisfy herself if the Lord's will was in it." Her husband (O. R. Fasset, a physician) would later write in her biography:

The spirit of the Lord was with her; and there came to me, though as opposed as herself to women's taking the place as teacher or preacher in public, the scripture: "On my servants and on my handmaidens I will pour out in those days of my spirit; and they shall prophecy [sic]." (Acts 2:18.) This kept me from ever hindering, or placing the least thing in the way of her duty, fearing I might grieve the Holy Spirit, by which she was divinely aided in reaching the hearts of her hearers with the words of life as they fell from her devoted lips.[46]

This part of Adventist history and the society in which it was birthed are significant. Out of this context God formed the husband-and-wife team of James White and Ellen G. Harmon. The work of these women took place in spite of the cultural prejudices and the misconstrued idea that Scripture forbade women to speak in church or teach men.

Women in Early SDA Ministry

In the second half of the nineteenth century, several Adventist women were prominent in evangelism and leadership. By 1878, at least three women ministers had been licensed to preach.[47] These were followed by others—more than 31 women who were recognized by the church and licensed to preach between the years 1872 and 1915, the year of Ellen White's death.[48] Three women were elected as General Conference treasurer before the turn of the century: Adelia Patten Van

Horn (1871-1873), Fredricka House Sisley (1875-1876), and Minerva Jane Loughborough Chapman (1877-1883).

Women's influence did not stop there. In 1905, 20 out of 60 conference treasurer positions were held by women. In 1915, nearly two thirds of the 60 educational department leaders and more than 50 of the 60 Sabbath school department leaders were women.

Any survey of nineteenth-century Adventist women in ministry must begin with the most outstanding: Ellen White. In addition, certain historical developments affecting women in ministry must be considered.

Ellen G. White (1827-1915). From the age of 17 until her death, Ellen White wrote, preached, encouraged, and warned the church. Though called and ordained by God, Ellen had to face the social prejudices of the day, as well as the misunderstanding of Scripture concerning women's role in the public sphere and the church.

One of Ellen White's brothers provides an example of the current thinking concerning women preachers. In an 1889 sermon, Ellen referred to an incident that occurred "when in my youth," in which her brother had written, "I beg of you, do not disgrace the family. I will do anything for you if you will not go out as a preacher." Ellen wrote back, "Can it disgrace the family for me to preach Christ and Him crucified? If you would give me all the gold your house could hold, I would not cease giving my testimony for God."[49] This position is consistent with the stand she and others in the movement, turned church, held concerning the public preaching and teaching ministry of women—and not just in defense of her "special" role as a prophetic voice and leader in the young church.

Ellen White and the early Seventh-day Adventist Church appear to have "pushed the borders" of ministry in the eyes of the culture, by including women. This may be seen in a letter from Ellen White to her son Willie, written from Pleasanton, Kansas, 17 October 1870:

> Tuesday we left the camp-ground. In the depot we met two Methodist women—one had been brought up a Quaker, but had joined the Methodists. They seemed so glad to have had the privilege of hearing me speak on Sunday. They said that they had felt that women who had the cause of God at heart, could exert a great influence if they would give themselves to the work of preaching Jesus. Some they said were opposed and much prejudiced against women talking. They came to hear me and they prayed God would let His Spirit rest upon me, and said they, "Our expectations were more than realized. The impression upon the people was great."[50]

Ellen White's actions and convictions were clearly contrary to the traditional teaching and popular belief of her day. Yet she was willing to oppose tradition in order to follow both her convictions and her calling regarding public preaching and ministry—as a woman. She encouraged many other women to stand with her and to pursue a public gospel ministry. An entire chapter of this book deals with her writings on the topic. And Ellen White did not stand alone on these convictions. The early pioneers also encouraged women to follow their divine calling.

Defense of women in ministry. In 1858 James White spoke favorably in the *Review and Herald* on women's role in the church, basing his remarks on Joel 2:28-32. Notice a part of his defense: "Some have excluded females from a share in this work, because it says, 'your young men shall see visions.' They seem to forget that 'man' and 'men' in the Scriptures generally means both male and female. The infidel Paine would have been ashamed of a quibble involving such ignorance."[51]

In their 30 July 1861 issue, the editors of the *Review* published a lead article, "Women as Preachers and Lecturers," in which J. A. Mowatt affirmed, "Neither Paul nor any other apostle forbade women preaching, or lecturing. I affirm that such a command is nowhere in the Bible." Uriah Smith wrote the foreword:

> We consider the following a triumphant vindication of the right of the sisters to take part in the public worship of God. The writer applies the prophecy of Joel—"Your daughters shall prophecy," &c., to female preaching; but while it must embrace public speaking of some kind, this we think is but half of its meaning. We have nothing to say upon what the writer claims to have been done by certain females. That to which the attention of the reader is especially called is the argument by which he shows that they have a *right* to do this, or any amount besides in the same direction.

J. N. Andrews affirmed, in a 2 January 1879 article in the *Review and Herald*, that it was impossible to understand 1 Cor 14:31-36 as meaning that women could not speak in church. Quoting Rom 10:10, he indicated that "confession unto salvation" must be made by women as well as men. A few months later, James White pointed out in a *Review* article that Paul's admonition in 1 Cor 14:34-36 only applied to the errors in Corinth and was intended to establish order there. He reiterated his position that Joel's message that "sons and daughters" would prophesy indicated the participation of women in preaching.[52]

In 1880, Ellen White and Elder S. N. Haskell were traveling, doing evangelistic work in upstate New York. On that trip she wrote to her son Willie concerning the difficulties of travel in doing the work. She particularly commented on Haskell's defense of her right as a woman to preach and teach, in the face of Campbellites who held that Paul prohibited women in the pulpit in 1 Cor 14:34-35 and 1 Tim 2:11-12.

> I had in the evening, it was stated, the largest congregation that had ever assembled at Arbuckle. The house was full. Many came from five to ten and twelve miles. The Lord gave me special power in speaking. The congregation listened as if spell-bound. Not one left the house although I talked above one hour. Before I commenced in talking, Elder Haskell had a bit of paper that was handed (him) in quoting certain texts prohibiting women speaking in public. He took the matter in a brief manner and very clearly expressed the meaning of the apostle's words. I understand it was a Campbellite who wrote the objection and it had been well circulated before it reached the desk; but Elder Haskell made it plain before all the people. After I closed, he made some remarks in regard to their temperance organization. Not one left the house.[53]

What Elder Haskell said is not recorded. But that he affirmed Ellen White's right to the pulpit is clear. And he did so in the face of opposition consonant with the historical climate of the day.

Through the years others would continue to defend *the sisters* and their prominent roles in the work of God. In the 24 May 1892 *Review and Herald*, G. C. Tenney defended women who labored publicly in the gospel. Tenney sought to make a strong defense for the public labor of women by attempting to "get behind" Paul's words found in 1 Cor 14:34. Notice both his scholarship and his logic:

> There are three Greek words from which "to speak" is translated, *"ei-pon," "le-go," and "la-lé-o;"* they may be used interchangeably, though to the latter is given by Donnegan the following definitions: "To talk; to speak; to prate; to prattle; to babble; to chatter"; etc., and this is the world used in 1 Corinthians 14:34, where it is said women are not permitted to *speak* in the churches. None of these undignified terms are used in defining the other words, a fact which shows that the apostle was rebuking garrulity rather than prohibiting Christians from witnessing for the cause of Christ.

In referring to Phil 4:3—"help those women which labored with me in the gospel," Tenney continued:

> According to the views of some people, he should have written: "Stop those women, for I don't allow a woman to labor in the gospel"—a very

different thing from that which he did write. If anybody still remains in doubt about Paul's attitude, let him read Romans 16, especially noting verse 12: "Salute Tryphena and Tryphosa, who labour in the Lord."

And finally Tenney rested his case by stating: "A fundamental principle of the gospel is that 'God is no respecter of persons,' a principle that applies to men and women."[54]

What would cause these early pioneers to be so passionate in defense of "women preachers" as well as other leading women in our early church? The fact is, women were both highly effective "in the cause of God" and successful in spreading his last day message. The successful ministry of women led the General Conference to consider their ordination in 1881.

The 1881 ordination resolution. The effective ministry of women in the Adventist Church ultimately led to a resolution on the ordination of women at the General Conference session of 1881. This resolution reads:

Resolved, That females possessing the necessary qualifications to fill that position, may, with perfect propriety, be set apart by ordination to the work of the Christian ministry.

This was discussed . . . and referred to the General Conference Committee.[55]

This committee consisted of George Butler, Stephen Haskell, and Uriah Smith. These brethren seem to have been uncertain at the time as to whether or not women could be ordained "with perfect propriety."[56] There is no record of further discussion or implementation of the resolution voted. However, as Roger Coon points out, "the fact that this could be at least discussed on the floor of a G. C. Session indicates an open-mindedness on the part of the delegates toward the subject."[57] It also clearly demonstrates the open-mindedness toward women serving in the gospel ministry during this time period in the Adventist Church's history.

Since women were serving as gospel ministers, the issue seems not to have been one of qualification. Rather, the whole debate seems to have revolved around the question of "perfect propriety." It was a question of correctness!

If only Ellen White's 1895 landmark statement had come fourteen years sooner!

Women who are willing to consecrate some of their time to the service of the Lord should be appointed to visit the sick, look after the young, and minister to the necessities of the poor. They should be set apart to this work by prayer and laying on of hands [ordination].[58]

It would seem that even this clear instruction was not generally followed. Willie White, however, did participate in the ordination of deaconesses at the Ashfield church, in Sydney, on 6 January 1900.[59] The practice has not been followed in Adventism, to the extent that the 1976 edition of the *SDA Encyclopedia* can say, "Since in the New Testament there is no record of deaconesses having been ordained, they are not ordained in the SDA Church."[60]

Decline of SDA Women in Ministry. After Ellen White died, a dramatic decline in women's involvement in ministry and licensing to preach took place. By the 1940s they had all but disappeared from conference leadership.[61] Part of the reason for this decline was the requirement, voted in 1923, that every departmental leader should be a soul winner, with previous success in evangelism, and preferably ordained.[62]

Ordination or not, Adventist women took their place as pastor-evangelists and church administrators. Brief presentations of some of the most outstanding serve to illustrate their participation in ministry.

Sketches of Notable Women in Ministry

It would be impossible to present a full biography of all women in Adventist ministry in the late-nineteenth and early-twentieth centuries. Sketches of a few of the most notable must suffice.

Ellen Lane (-1889). Usually considered as the first woman to receive a ministerial license, Lane was licensed to preach by the Michigan Conference in 1868. Ten years later, she was granted another license at the 1878 session of the General Conference. She worked with her husband, was skilled in house-to-house visitation, and preached powerfully as well. After telling her story, Richard Schwarz comments: "Another Ellen [referring to Ellen White], remembering that the first preacher to tell of a risen Christ was a woman, expressed the view that 'the refining, softening influence of Christian women is needed in the great work of preaching the truth. . . . Zealous and continued diligence in our sisters . . . would astonish us with its results.'"[63]

Sarah A. Lindsey (1843-1912). With her husband John, Sarah pioneered the work in western New York and Pennsylvania. Her 1872 license permitted her to preach, hold evangelistic meetings, and lead out in church business and committee sessions. During a series of meetings in Pleasant Valley, New York, Sarah preached "twenty-three times on the second advent."[64] She and John shared the task of evangelists and church planters, not flock tenders, for that task was left to the lay people of the local church.

Minerva Jane Loughborough Chapman (1829-1923). This capable woman gave 26 years of service to the Review and Herald, as typesetter, secretary, and editor. In 1877, according to John Beach,

> With complete confidence and respect for her ability, she received appointment to the following positions: (1) treasurer of the General Conference, (2) editor of the *Youth's Instructor*, (3) secretary of the Publishing Association, and (4) treasurer of the Tract and Missionary Society. It is doubtful that anyone, male or female, can surpass—even equal—such a distinguished achievement.[65]

Margaret Caro (1848-1938). Ellen G. White met this dentist and Bible worker at the first campmeeting in Australia, and later had Dr. Caro extract her teeth and fit dentures. In an 1893 letter, Ellen White had the following comments:

> Sister Caro is a superior dentist. She has all the work she can do. She is a tall stately woman, but sociable and companionable. You would love her if you should see her. She does not hoard her means, she puts it into bags which wax not old. She handles an immense amount of money, and she uses the money to educate young men to become laborers for the Master. I am greatly attached to her. She holds her diploma as dentist and her credentials as minister. She speaks to the church when there is no minister, so you see that she is a very capable woman. Her husband is a physician and surgeon.[66]

Notable here is the reference to her ministerial credential. In later years, Margaret Caro worked in New Zealand, where her "strength of character, courage, and enthusiasm for God's work" were noted along with her "advocacy of health reform."[67]

Sarepta Myrenda Irish Henry (1839-1900). A prominent public speaker in the temperance and reform movements, her ministry was several times affirmed by Ellen White.[68] One of Henry's most famous speaking engagements occurred at Northwestern University, where she had been refused enrollment because of her gender. Now, because of her fame, the university decided to invite her to address a crowd of twelve hundred parents and teachers—many of whom were distinguished theologians and philanthropists. Beach relates that Oliver Willard, editor of the Chicago *Post*, recognized her speech as "one of the most beautiful pieces of word painting" he had ever heard.[69]

At the age of 57, Henry became convicted of Seventh-day Adventist teachings, and began advocating what she called "woman ministry," lecturing on the role of women in home and society from coast to coast. In 1898 she was issued a ministerial license as a vote of confidence in her women's ministries activities for the church. In 1899 she was invited to address the General Conference of Seventh-day Adventists in session. Her words were pointed:

> The gospel has never gone as it ought to have gone. . . . Our brethren have seemed to be crippled. There has seemed to be something not discernible upon the surface, which has hindered the progress of the gospel; and I want to tell you . . . that if everything was all right in the homes which are represented by this people, the gates of hell could not prevail against you."[70]

In a letter of encouragement to S.M.I. Henry, Ellen White urged:

> I have so longed for women who could be educators to help them arise from their discouragement, and to feel that they could do a work for the Lord. And this effort is bringing rays of sunshine into their lives, and is being reflected upon the hearts of others. God will bless you, and all who shall unite with you, in this grand work.
>
> If we can, my sister, we should speak often to our sisters, and lead them in the place of saying "Go." . . . We are learners that we may be teachers. This idea must be imprinted in the mind of every church member. . . .
>
> Teach our sisters that every day the question is to be, Lord, what wilt thou have me to do this day? . . .
>
> Speak the words that are given you of God, and the Lord will certainly work with you.[71]

Hetty Hurd Haskell (1857-1919). An indication of the esteem in which she was held is her obituary in the *Review and Herald*, written by Elder J. N. Loughborough and almost three columns long. Her career spanned over three decades and four continents; she worked in North America, England, South Africa, and Australia. Not only was she a trainer of Bible workers, she also gained a reputation as a powerful preacher. For a number of years both she and Ellen White were listed together in the *Yearbook* as ministers credentialed by the General Conference, Ellen White as ordained and Mrs. Haskell as licensed. Her marriage to Stephen N. Haskell in 1897 simply put two dedicated workers together in training others to work for God.[72]

Lulu Russell Wightman (unknown dates). Lulu Wightman, with the support of her husband John (who was gifted in graphic arts), ministered as a successful evangelist and lecturer. She received ministerial credentials in 1897, while he received his in 1903. That same year, S. M. Cobb wrote the conference president that she had "accomplished more in the last two years than any minister in the state."[73] Her name was considered for ordination in 1901, but the brethren felt "that a women could not be properly ordained—just now at least." Thus, her husband noted in a 1904 letter regarding her pay, they had "fixed her compensation as near the 'ordained rate' as possible."

After her husband was licensed to the full-time gospel ministry in 1903, they raised up several churches together. Mrs. Wightman's gospel ministry can be traced by reading the local newspapers of the day, which reported on her work and progress, wherever she held evangelistic meetings. In one year, 34 of 65 New York state's new members in the Seventh-day Adventist Church came in as a direct result of two licensed ministers and one Bible worker: Mr. and Mrs. Wightman and Mrs. D. D. Smith. Of these, 27 were credited to Lulu. The other 26 new members were won by ten other workers.[74] She later became a public lecturer on religious liberty. In 1910 the Wightmans parted company with the church.[75]

Lorena Florence Faith Plummer (1862-1945). Of all the women who labored in the gospel ministry while Ellen White was still alive, Flora Plummer was perhaps the most notable. Mrs. Plummer was elected secretary of the Iowa Conference in 1897. In 1900, when Clarence Santee was called to California, she became acting conference president.[76] From 1913 until her retirement in 1936, she headed the Sabbath School Department of the General Conference.

Anna Knight (1874-1972). This chapter would be remiss if it failed to notice Anna Knight's service to God. She overcame great obstacles, managing to attend Mount Vernon Academy, and then Battle Creek College. After her graduation as a missionary nurse in 1898, she returned to her home in Jasper County, Mississippi, where she raised up a school for Blacks and did temperance work. In view of her successful work, Anna was invited by Dr. J. H. Kellogg to be a delegate to the General Conference Session at Battle Creek in 1901.

Here God called her to India, where she served for six years. On her return Knight continued her work, first in her home state. In 1909 she was called to work for African Americans in Atlanta. In 1913 she became Associate Home Missionary secretary for the Southeastern Union Conference. After six years, she was asked to direct the Home Missionary department, which she did until her retirement in 1945.[77]

Many other examples could be given of faithful women who heeded the call of their Lord, in spite of the prevailing attitudes and prejudices of the nineteenth-century.[78] These women, whether single or part of a husband and wife team, were simply following in the footsteps of their Millerite predecessors, and those of one of their Church's beloved leaders—Mrs. Ellen White.

Conclusion

(1) When we read the history of women in ministry within the Seventh-day Adventist Church, (2) when we understand the context of the culture in which Ellen White lived, (3) when we carefully consider Ellen White's statements alongside the New Testament models of ministry, it is clear that Ellen White continually broadened the nature, functions, and roles of women in ministry at a time when women were discouraged from placing themselves in the public eye.

For Ellen White, the active involvement of women in ministry—in an increasingly complex world, and an ever-expanding gospel work—was not merely an option; it was mandatory.

> If men *and women* would act as the Lord's helping hand, doing deeds of love and kindness, uplifting the oppressed, rescuing those ready to perish, the glory of the Lord would be their reward. . . .
>
> Of those who act as his helping hand the Lord says, 'Ye shall be *priests* of the Lord; men shall call you *ministers* of our God [Isaiah 61:6]. . . . Shall we not try to crowd all the goodness and love and compassion we can into the lives, that these words may be said of us?[79]

In spite of difficulties, Adventist women of the nineteenth century responded to God's call and proclaimed the Good News. They were notable women of spirit; theirs is a legacy of courage, giftedness, and dedication.

Endnotes

1. Ellen G. White, *Selected Messages*, 1:27.

2. Catherine Clinton, *The Other Civil War* (New York: Hill and Wang, 1984), 21, 22.

3. Ibid.

4. Ibid., 24.

5. Ibid., 25.

6. Ibid.; Eleanor Flexner, *Century of Struggle: The Woman's Rights Movement in the United States* (Cambridge, MA: Belknap, 1959), 29: "Teaching was the first of the 'professions' open to women, but since they had no training and only the most rudimentary schooling, their prestige was low and they could not command salaries anything like those of men who were often college or university graduates."

7. Clinton, 27.

8. Ibid., 38.

9. Ibid., 38-39.

10. Ellen G. White, *Ministry of Healing*, 368, 369.

11. The prevailing attitude at Oberlin college, one of the first learning institutions to open its doors to all—regardless of race, color or gender—"was that women's high calling was to be the mothers of the race, and that they should stay within that special sphere in order that future generations should not suffer from the want of devoted and undistracted mother care. . . . Washing the men's clothes, caring for their rooms, serving them at table, listening to their orations, but themselves remaining respectfully silent in public assemblages, the Oberlin's 'co-eds' were being prepared for intelligent motherhood and a proper subservient wifehood" (Flexner, 30).

12. Clinton, 40; Flexner, 29. The most popular such publication of the day appears to have been *Godey's Lady's Book*, edited by Sarah Josepha Hale.

13. Clinton, 41.

14. Julian Hawthorne, *Nathaniel Hawthorne and His Wife* (Boston: Houghton and Mifflin, 1884), 1:61.

15. Ibid., 1:257.

16. Ellen G. White, *Welfare Ministry*, 158.

17. Barbara Leslie Epstein, *The Politics of Domesticity* (Middletown, CT: Wesleyan, 1981), 82.

18. Ibid., 74.

19. Ibid, 78.

20. Flexner, 8.

21. Ibid., 63.

22. Ibid., 41.

23. William L. O'Neill, *Everyone Was Brave: The Rise and Fall of Feminism in America* (Chicago: Quadrangle, 1969), 11.

24. Flexner, 46; emphasis supplied.

25. Epstein, 81.

26. Clinton, 42.

27. Ibid.

28. Ibid.

29. Ibid., 43.

30. Epstein, 65.

31. Clinton, 44; one such was Catherine Beecher, promoter of the academy movement, domesticity, and sister to author and prominent reformer Harriet Beecher Stowe.

32. Ibid., 46.

33. George R. Knight, *Millennial Fever and the End of the World* (Boise: Pacific Press, 1993), 119; see also Kit Watts, "Why Did Women Begin to Preach?" *Adventist Review*, 30 March 1995, 11-13.

34. C. Geoff Waugh, *Fire Fell: Revival Visitations* (Brisbane: Renewal, n.d.); condensed version can be found on the internet (www.pastornet.net.au/renewal/fire/2-1800.html).

35. Epstein, 90.

36. White, *Welfare Ministry*, 164.

37. Epstein, 147.

38. Epstein, 47; O'Neil, 27-28; see Alicia Worley's chapter on this topic.

39. Knight, 119.

40. Carole Ann Rayburn, "Women In Millerism, 1820-1870," term paper, Andrews University, 1979, Adventist Heritage Center, James White Library, 7.

41. Knight, 120.

42. Isaac Wellcome, *History of the Second Advent Message* (Boston: Advent Christian Publication Society, 1874), 156.

43. See Knight, 121; Rayburn, 15; Rayburn's paper contains the historical document.

44. Abigail Mussey, *Life Sketches and Experience* (Cambridge, MA: Dakin and Metcalf, 1865), 163-164.

45. Knight, 121.

46. O. R. Fassett, *The Biography of Mrs. L. E. Fassett, A Devoted Christian* (Boston: Advent Christian Publication Society, 1885), 26-27.

47. Josephine Benton, *Called by God: Stories of Seventh-day Adventist Women Ministers* (Smithsburg, MD: Blackberry Hill, 1990), 154.

48. Ibid., 229-233.

49. From a sermon Ellen White preached in Washington DC, on 26 January 1889 entitled, "Looking for that Blessed Hope," quoted in *Signs of the Times*, 24 June 1889, 2.

50. Ellen G. White to Willie White, letter W-16-1870, Ellen G. White Research Center, Andrews University (EGWRC).

51. James White, "Unity and Gifts of the Church," *Review and Herald*, 7 January 1858, 69.

52. James White, "Women in Church," *Review and Herald*, 29 May 1879, 172.

53. Ellen G. White to James White, letter W-17a-1880, EGWRC.

54. George Tenney, "Woman's Relation to the Cause of Christ," *Review and Herald*, 24 May 1892.

55. *Review and Herald*, 20 December 1881.

56. Bert Haloviak, "Longing For the Pastorate: Ministry in 19th Century Adventism," (EGWRC, DF 2097-a, January 1988), 18.

57. Roger Coon, "Ellen White's View on the Role of Women in the Church," EGWRC.

58. "The Duty of the Minister and the People," *Advent Review and Sabbath Herald*, 9 July 1895, 2.

59. Arthur Patrick, "The Ordination of Deaconesses," *Review and Herald*, 16 January 1986, 18-19.

60. *Seventh-day Adventist Encyclopedia*, s.v. "Deaconess."

61. "Women in Early Adventism," *Adventist Review*, 4 February 1988, 21.

62. "Actions of the Autumn Council," 9-17 October 1923.

63. Richard W. Schwarz, *Light Bearers to the Remnant* (Mountain View, CA: Pacific Press, 1979), 135.

64. Ibid.

65. John G. Beach, *Notable Women of Spirit: The Historical Role of Women in the Seventh-day Adventist Church* (Nashville: Southern Publishing, 1976), 23-24.

66. Ellen G. White to Jennie Inggs, Letter 33, 1893. Caro is listed in the *Seventh-day Adventist Yearbook* for 1894, as a ministerial "licentiate."

67. *Seventh-day Adventist Encyclopedia*, s.v. "Caro, Margaret."

68. White, *Evangelism*, 473.

69. Beach, 91.

70. Ibid., 92.

71. Ellen G. White to S.M.I. Henry, 25 March 1899.

72. See Benton, 154-156; *Seventh-day Adventist Encyclopedia*, s.v. "Haskell, Hetty (Hurd)."

73. Letter from Elder S. M. Cobb, Lockport, NY, to Elder A. E. Place, Rome, NY, August 6, 1897; quoted in Benton, 70.

74. Bert Haloviak, "The Adventist Heritage Calls for the Ordination of Women," *Spectrum* 16, no. 3 (1985): 53-56.

75. Benton, 67-84.

76. *Sabbath School Worker*, 1900, 122, 207.

77. Benton, 89-90; *Seventh-day Adventist Encyclopedia*, s.v. "Anna Knight"; Jannith L. Lewis, "Five Notable Women in the History of Oakwood College," *Adventist Heritage*, March 1996, 56.

78. See Schwarz, *Light Bearers to the Remnant*; Coon, "Ellen White's View on the Role of Women in the Church"; Benton, *Called to Serve*; Haloviak, "The Adventist Heritage Calls for the Ordination of Women"; Kit Watts, "Ellen White's Contemporaries: Significant Women in the Early Church," in *A Woman's Place*, ed. Rosa Taylor Banks (Hagerstown, MD: Review and Herald, 1992), 41-74.

79. "God's Helping Hand," *Review and Herald*, 15 October 1901, 1.

CHAPTER 12

SDA WOMEN IN MINISTRY 1970-1998

RANDAL R. WISBEY

A s one looks at the sweep of Seventh-day Adventist history, and
specifically at the church's recognition of the gifts and abilities
of women in ministry, one notices a multitude of defining
moments. As has been pointed out in earlier chapters, women played an
important role in the early days of the Advent movement. Great strides
to involve women in every area of ministry took place in early
Adventism.[1] In 1975, before the church ended its hundred-year practice
of issuing ministerial licenses to women, more than 65 women had held
this license and worked as treasurers, department directors, and pastors.[2]

In more recent years, however, the Seventh-day Adventist Church
has struggled in its attempts to fully recognize women as equal partners
in the mission and ministry of the church. As Elder Calvin Rock noted
in his opening remarks as chairman of the 5 July 1995, General
Conference business meeting in Utrecht, the church has often considered
the issue of ordaining women, and has, at times, come amazingly close to
doing so. Prior to beginning the debate on the request of the North
American Division to provide "each division the right to authorize the
ordination of individuals within its territory in harmony with established
policies," Elder Rock explained how the church, at the General
Conference session of 1881, had voted that women might, "with perfect
propriety, be set apart for ordination to the work of the Christian
ministry." The action was then referred to the General Conference
Committee. After that, as Elder Rock so eloquently explained, "Nothing
happened." Nearly 90 years later in 1968, leadership in Finland officially
requested that women be ordained to the gospel ministry.[3]

Since that seemingly simple request, the Seventh-day Adventist Church has been involved in a journey to recognize and celebrate the gifts of women in ministry. It is the task of this chapter to consider the recent history and current situation of women in SDA ministry.[4]

The 1970s: A Time of Study and Hope

Following the request of Finland and the Northern European Division for counsel on ordaining women in 1968, the General Conference officers appointed a committee to study ordination. However, before the *ad hoc* committee on the role of women in the church convened in 1973, a worldwide flurry of activity began to take place, making it imperative for the church to act. In 1972, the Potomac Conference, with the official involvement of the Columbia Union, ordained Josephine Benton as the first woman to serve as a local church elder. This action, along with requests from the Far Eastern Division for counsel about ordaining women, and a request from Germany to ordain Margarete Prange as an elder (rising from her success as a pastor), resulted in General Conference President Robert H. Pierson's calling of the Camp Mohaven Conference.

The Biblical Research Institute (BRI) of the General Conference had been studying the roles of women in the SDA Church since 1972. However, it was not until 1973 that 29 papers were discussed by a group of 27 Bible teachers and church leaders at Camp Mohaven in Ohio. At the conclusion of the conference, the *ad hoc* committee recommended that women be ordained as local church elders, that those with theological training be hired as "associates in pastoral care," and that a pilot program leading to the ordination of women in 1975 be implemented. However, the 1973 General Conference Annual Council, while voting to "receive" the Camp Mohaven report, also voted that "continued study be given to the theological soundness of the election of women to local church offices which require ordination," and that "in areas receptive to such action, there be continued recognition of the appropriateness of appointing women to pastoral evangelistic work."[5]

While many church members had great interest in the research papers presented at the conference, it was decided not to make them available to the church at large. In 1975 the BRI completed work on a set of 13 scholarly papers, based on the Camp Mohaven work. However, the papers were first released to Sligo Church in 1977 (to aid the church in its consideration of ordination for women elders). Not until 1984 were 100 copies made available to interested readers.[6] Gordon Hyde, BRI director, in reflecting on the theological issue of women in ministry, asked, "If God has called a woman, and her ministry is fruitful, why should the church withhold its standard act of recognition?"[7]

In 1974, the General Conference Annual Council once again called for further theological study and reflection on the issue. At that time, the body concluded that the "time is not ripe nor opportune; therefore, in the interest of the world unity of the church, no move [should] be made in the direction of ordaining women to the gospel ministry."[8]

At the 1975 General Conference Spring Meeting, advocates for women in ministry experienced both joy and pain as the body voted to approve women's ordination as deaconesses and as local church elders (if "the greatest discretion and caution be exercised"), and to encourage women to serve as Bible workers and assistant pastors. However, the church also voted that women would be granted only a missionary license or missionary credential, effectively ending one hundred years of granting ministerial licenses to women.[9]

The next several years saw church leadership continue to struggle with their understanding of the role women should play in serving their church. While Margarete Prange became the sole pastor of four churches in East Germany in 1976, the General Conference Annual Council of 1977 chose to utilize a new term, "Associates in Pastoral Care," to identify persons employed on pastoral staffs who were not in line for ordination.[10]

In 1979 the SDA Church, once more during a General Conference Annual Council, made two decisions that dramatically challenged the status quo: special internship monies for Bible Instructors and Associates in Pastoral Care were to be distributed, beginning in 1980, by the North American Division to encourage women in ministry; and changes in the North American Division Working Policy permitted unordained male pastors to baptize in their local church.[11] While the first decision was seen as necessary to more fully recognize what women were capable of doing in ministry, the second decision further exacerbated the already present feelings that men and women were not being treated equally.

Yet even amid these often agonizing deliberations and decisions, women continued to serve in the church. In 1979, the Potomac Conference assigned Josephine Benton to serve the Rockville SDA Church as sole pastor, a position she held until 1982.

The 1980s: Much Study, Little Hope

The 1980s saw a great deal of activity in the continuing debate on the role of women in the church. The journey saw moments of hope as well as devastating setbacks.

President Neal C. Wilson, in his keynote address at the 1980 General Conference Session, stated as his fifth priority that

> The church must find ways to organize and utilize the vast potential by our talented, consecrated women. . . . I am not only urging that women be represented in the administrative structure of the church, but also that we harness the energies and talents of all the women so as to better accomplish the task of finishing the work assigned by our Lord.[12]

The church seemed to be galvanized by Elder Wilson's words, as the following years showed. A significant number of women began graduate work at the SDA Theological Seminary at Andrews University. In 1982, Becky Lacy and Collette Crowell, both graduates of Walla Walla College, were the first women sponsored by their conferences to work on the Master of Divinity degree.

The year 1982 also saw the organization of the Association of Adventist Women. President Betty Howard was clear about its mission and message: to encourage Adventist women to achieve their full potential.

Though a "woman ministry" was begun in 1898 by S.M.I. Henry with the blessing of Ellen White and the leaders of the General Conference, the ministry faded with the death of Mrs. Henry. In 1983 a North American Division Women's Commission was organized by the Office of Human Relations. One woman from each union conference was selected to serve on the commission, designed to meet one day each year.[13]

Indeed, all three of these events: seminary sponsorship for women, a proactive women's association, and a commission to organize women's ministries throughout North America showed a strong commitment to carry out the mandate in Elder Wilson's challenge.

Yet there were additional ways in which the church was challenged in this spoken commitment. On 11 February 1984, the Potomac Conference Executive Committee authorized eight ordained local elders to perform baptisms in their respective churches. Of this number, three were women pastors who baptized 12 candidates over the next few weeks.[14] During the following months, conversations among Potomac Conference, North American Division, and General Conference leaders took place. Eventually, on 16 August the entire Potomac Conference

Executive Committee was summoned by the General Conference leaders. The five-hour session concluded with Potomac Conference agreeing to table a 16 May Potomac Conference Executive Committee action to license women pastors in the conference (until after the 1984 General Conference Annual Council). The leaders of Potomac Conference likewise agreed to have the women stop baptizing until the world church reached consensus. The General Conference leadership, at Potomac Conference's request, promised to renew a study of women's ordination.[15]

The General Conference appeared to take Potomac Conference's request seriously, and at the 1984 General Conference Annual Council reaffirmed the 1975 decision that women might be ordained as local elders. The Council also voted to extend the provision made for the North American Division to the world field as would be deemed helpful. In addition, it voted to call together a Commission on the Role of Women in the Church, to bring together representatives from each division to give continued study to women's ordination.

The Commission on the Role of Women in the Church first met 26-28 March 1985 in Washington, D.C. The 1985 General Conference session in New Orleans formally accepted the work of the commission, voting for "affirmative action" by requesting that leaders use their exec-utive influence to open to women all aspects of ministry in the church that do not require ordination. They also promised to reform the then-current practice of ordaining men who were not in full-time ministerial service.

At the time of the 1985 General Conference, Nancy Vyhmeister, associate professor of Biblical Studies at the Seventh-day Adventist Theological Seminary, Far East, made a presentation to the women's session regarding the work of Adventist women worldwide. She documented the variety of ministries in which women were involved throughout the world field. Of those serving as pastors or Bible instructors, most were located in the North American, Far Eastern, and Euro-Africa Divisions. Of the women she surveyed, 85 reported receiving pay for full-time activity in pastoral and soul-winning activities.[16]

Not long after that session, the 1985 General Conference Annual Council rejected the North American Division's recommendations that women pastors with seminary training be allowed to baptize and solemnize marriages in the same way as young men with the same qualifications had been doing since 1979. This, accompanied by a General Conference Annual Council statement that women might work as ministers but should not expect ordination, proved daunting to the North

American Division, as well as to many parts of Europe and Australia.

During the same council, the General Conference Women's Advisory Committee was established, with Betty Holbrook as coordinator. Elizabeth Sterndale, only two days later, was appointed to serve as Women's Advisory Representative for the North American Division.

In the fall of 1986, against the Annual Council decision of the previous year, the Southeastern California Conference voted to treat unordained men and women equally. The effect of the vote was that on 20 December, Pastor Margaret Hempe of the Loma Linda University Church (the denomination's largest congregation), at the request of the pastoral staff and church board, baptized two candidates.

At this time several important research studies were conducted by the Institute of Church Ministry at Andrews University. Roger Dudley, surveying pastors in North America, found that 46 percent believed it "appropriate for women who have demonstrated their calling to the ministry to be ordained as gospel ministers."[18] The study also found that education and age made a difference in the pastors' response: those with a bachelor's degree generally opposed ordination for women, while those with graduate education usually favored ordination, and those under 50 were more likely to favor ordination than those over 50.[19]

A second research study surveyed the views of religion teachers at the 11 senior colleges of the North American Division, at the 32 senior colleges or seminaries outside North America, and at the SDA Theological Seminary. When asked to respond to the statement, "It is appropriate for women to serve as local elders if elected by their congregations," 85 percent of the total said "yes" (compared with 93 percent of the North American respondents). With the statement, "It is appropriate for women who have demonstrated their calling to the ministry to be ordained as gospel ministers," 69 percent of the total agreed (compared with 83 percent of the North American respondents).[20] These studies continued to fuel the strong conviction, especially in North America, that the church was ready to use the ministerial gifts of women.

A third study, conducted in 1988 by the Institute of Church Ministry at Andrews University, reported 960 ordained women elders serving in the 3,036 Seventh-day Adventist churches in the North American Division alongside 14,495 male elders. Carole L. Kilcher and G. T. Ng, researchers, found that women elders existed in churches of every racial and cultural background, disproving the notion that women as elders were only a Caucasian phenomenon.[21]

General Conference President Neal Wilson, in an *Adventist Review* report on the 1988 Commission on the Role of Women in the Church (the second such international commission which he chaired), urged church members "to avoid further controversy and argument, . . . to abstain from circulating books, pamphlets, letters, and tapes that stir up the debate and often generate confusion." To church officials and members he stated: "It is time for us to be done with argument and discussion about this issue, time for us to utilize every resource, every talent, every ability, every gift. It is time for us to unite to finish the work and go home to live with our blessed Lord forever."[22]

In reality, this plea was largely ignored, as a number of organizations published materials that gathered a great deal of attention. Probably the most influential of the antiordination materials was Samuele Bacchiocchi's *Women in the Church*. Bacchiocchi—a professor in the religion department at Andrews University—was often thought to teach in the seminary, and his book was mistakenly seen as representing the views of the majority of seminary professors. In actuality, this was not the case, as is evidenced by the 22 seminary professors who took a formal stand in favor of women's ordination as elders in "A Statement of Support for the Ministry of Women as Local Elders at PMC," published in the spring of 1987 at Andrews University.

In January of 1988, the Adventist Women's Institute was organized in California, with Fay Blix serving at its head. The group's mission was to pursue for women full and equal participation in the church. Four months later, on the other side of the continent, Time for Equality in Adventist Ministry (TEAM) was founded in Maryland with the specific goal of working toward the ordination of candidates to the gospel ministry regardless of race, social class, or gender. Patricia Habada served as its first chair. Both groups began the task of informing Adventists of the need for women to serve the SDA Church as pastors.

The 1980s concluded with a variety of actions that continued to raise the level of awareness of women in ministry. In May of 1988, North American Division leaders, meeting in Loma Linda, California, unanimously voted their objection to the discrepancies in the treatment of men and women who had the same training and qualifications. A succession of local conferences echoed this sentiment. In the same month Potomac Conference voted to permit women to baptize and marry in a local church. In April 1989 the Ohio Conference endorsed Pastor Leslie Bumgardner for full ordination, and the commitment was echoed by the

Columbia Union Conference executive committee on 4 May 1989.[23] On
21 May 1989, the Southeastern California Conference constituents passed
a resolution mandating that local qualified pastors, regardless of gender,
be considered for ordination. On 7 June 1989, the Pacific Union
Conference voted a resolution urging the General Conference "to eliminate gender as a consideration for ordination to the gospel ministry."
Finally, the North American Division union conference presidents voted
unanimously to send an endorsement of women's ordination to the
Commission on the Role of Women, which would hold its meeting in
Cohutta Springs, Georgia.

This third Commission on the Role of Women in the Church, with
representatives from every world division, began its work on 12 July
1989. Rejecting the North American Division's endorsement, they voted
"No" for the ordination of women. However, they did vote to
recommend that divisions might authorize qualified women in ministry
to perform baptisms and marriages.

In September the *Adventist Review* published a report of an
international survey of Adventist women in leadership. Of 1,872 women
leaders identified, 875 responded to the survey. Seventy-four percent of
the women surveyed believed it was appropriate for women to serve as
associate pastors, and 65 percent believed that women pastors should be
ordained.[24]

In a series of tension-filled meetings, the 1989 General Conference
Annual Council listened to the concerns of the world on these issues.
One of the speeches that galvanized the gathering was by Elder Charles
Bradford, president of the North American Division. Near the end of a
grueling day, he spoke from his heart:

> The [Women's] Commission met in March of a year before and met
> again this summer. It has been on the minds, and, I say, on the lips of
> many for a number of years, almost, brother chairman, a decade. . . .
> Meanwhile, we're still discussing, *we are still discussing.*
>
> It is a terrible burden trying to lead the division in soulwinning
> when you are constantly discussing these all-consuming issues. . . . Here
> we are in 1989, facing the last decade in the 20th century, looking on
> the eve of the third millennium, *on the eve of the third millennium!*
> That's where we are! And we have discussed this matter and discussed
> it and people have taken sides and some have said, "I'm not going to
> lose! I will use every ruse I can, every political, every parliamentary
> motion and maneuver, I'll use it, so that I will not lose! I will have my
> way!" I would hope that in the church of the living God, we could

come to the place where it would not be a win-lose situation. . . .

Now my brothers and sisters, the time has come. We must put aside all our preferences. I said to the division brethren, Elder Wilson, you allowed me to say it in Cohutta [Springs]; I said to them: "Brethren, will this provision made for commissioned ministers damage your field?" You'll remember I said that. "Will it damage you? Will it bring you to ruin? If it will, we'll turn aside."

They said, "No, it won't."

I said, "Well then, if it will not damage you, then allow the church to roll on; let the church move on. And if we have made a horrible mistake, there is such a thing as the Spirit's ministry and He will bring us back. Because, as Ellen White says, we are captives of hope. He has us in His hands. We are the remnant people of God."

Oh, I want us to march on. I want to hear the Word of God ringing throughout the North American Division, ringing throughout the world. I want to see ministers on fire and the laymen going from door to door, and this continent stirred from stem to stern so that the brethren in other denominations will say, "You Adventists have filled this whole continent with your doctrine!" That's what I want to see happen.

But it will never happen as long as we're standing on this line and you're on that line. I think this is the time for us to get on God's line. Will you please, brethren, have mercy on us? For mercy is needed.[25]

In the end, the delegates voted the two recommendations: to deny ordination to women, on one hand, and to allow women pastors to baptize and to officiate at weddings, on the other. The council also encouraged each organizational entity to give study to the concerns "so as to achieve the spirit and purpose of this proposal." This challenge was carried to Indianapolis, Indiana, and the 1990 General Conference.

The 1990s: Baptism "Yes!" Ordination "No!"

Much was at stake at the 1990 General Conference, as this was the first time since 1881 that the world church would have the opportunity to vote for the ordination of women. Beginning Tuesday afternoon, 10 July , delegates began to debate the report and recommendations made by the Commission on the Role of Women in the Church as recommended by the 1989 Annual Council. Under the heading "Ordination of Women to the Gospel Ministry," the report stipulated that:

1. A decision to ordain women as pastors would not be welcomed or meet with approval in most of the world Church.

2. The provisions of the *Church Manual* and the *General Conference*

Working Policy, which allow only for ordination to the gospel ministry
on a worldwide basis, have strong support by the divisions.

The two-page recommendation ended with items from the 1989 Annual
Council decision:

> 1. While the Commission does not have a consensus as to whether
> or not the Scriptures and the writings of Ellen G. White explicitly
> advocate or deny the ordination of women to pastoral ministry, it
> concludes unanimously that these sources affirm a significant, wide-
> ranging, and continuing ministry for women which is being expressed
> and will be evidenced in the varied and expanding gifts according to the
> infilling of the Holy Spirit.
> 2. Further, in view of the widespread lack of support for the
> ordination of women to the gospel ministry in the world Church and
> in view of the possible risk of disunity, dissension, and diversion from
> the mission of the Church, we do not approve ordination of women to
> the gospel ministry.[26]

Debate was lively. Speakers lined up to speak for and against the
report. The next morning the debate continued with 45 delegates lined up
to speak. However, a motion to close debate easily passed, and the
delegates were asked to vote on the main motion. The final vote: 1,173
for the motion to deny ordination; 377 opposed.[27]

Thursday, 12 July debate on the role of women in the church centered on the Annual Council's recommendation that would give licensed
or commissioned ministers, including women, the privilege, along with
unordained male ministers, to baptize and to perform marriages. Once
again, Europeans and North Americans called for the body to accept women fully working alongside their male peers in ministry. Susan Sickler,
a laymember from the Columbia Union, challenged the body to consider
the young people of the church:

> I think that it is time that someone speaks for the most valuable
> resource this church has in our children. They are the ones who are
> going to suffer because of the decisions that we make in this room.
> Yesterday, when this body voted not to ordain women, a young pastor
> of a large college church was sitting near me. He put his head in his
> hands and said, "What am I going to do? When I get home young
> people are going to be lining up outside my door waiting to resign their
> membership in the Seventh-day Adventist church." When our young
> people feel that their church has a lower standard for treating all people
> with justice and equality than the secular society has, they tend to feel
> that the church has nothing to offer them and they leave.[28]

In the late afternoon the delegates finally voted. In a surprising turn from the experience of the day before, 776 voted in favor of allowing women to baptize and to perform weddings, while 496 remained opposed.[29]

While both sides left Indianapolis feeling that they had been heard, many agreed that once again a mixed signal had been sent to the church: women may do the work of ministry, just as their male colleagues do, yet the women cannot be fully recognized.

In the months following the 1990 General Conference, advocates for women in ministry began, once more, to move forward. On 19 September the North American Division established the Office of Women's Ministries, with Elizabeth Sterndale as director. On 4 October, by recommendation of General Conference President Robert Folkenberg, the General Conference established the Office of Women's Ministries, with Rose Otis as its director. This office became a General Conference Department in 1995. Its mandate is to foster the participation of all Adventist women in all types of ministry. Women's Ministries does not deal with the question of ordination because its concern is for the ministry of all women.

In order to survey the attitudes of Adventist women in ministry following the Indianapolis decision, TEAM published *Keeping Hope Alive* in 1993. Surveying 72 women pastors, chaplains, and religion teachers in the North American Division, the study found that nine out of ten women believed their call to ministry was valid whether or not the denomination recognized it with credentials of any kind. However, a majority did feel that the denomination's failure to fully recognize their call to ministry constituted a serious deafness to the Holy Spirit.[30]

During the years leading up to the 1995 General Conference, a great deal of information was once more disseminated regarding the subject of women in ministry. While in 1993 the Association of Adventist Women remembered the twentieth anniversary of Camp Mohaven and V. Norskov Olsen published his pro-ordination study *Myth and Truth: Church, Priesthood and Ordination*, 1994 saw the publication of retired seminary professor Raymond Holmes' *Tip of an Iceberg*. Holmes asserted that the uniqueness of the Adventist message would be threatened if the Bible were interpreted to allow women's ordination. His book was widely distributed around the world and endorsed by several influential Adventist leaders, many of whom understood it to be the official position of the church.[31]

In 1994, the Association of Adventist Women published the photos and stories of 90 women in ministry from the Baltic Union, Canada, Finland, Germany, Norway, Russia, Sweden, Switzerland, and the United States. The *Adventist Review* and *Ministry* published a series of articles dealing with ordination in which the editors took pro-ordination stands. In April of 1995 TEAM published *The Welcome Table: Setting a Place for Ordained Women*, in which 14 Adventist authors and scholars supported the ordination of women in ministry.

At the 1994 General Conference Annual Council, members listened once more to North America's plea to make ordination gender inclusive. Alfred McClure, president of the North American Division, asked the world church to honor a request voted by the North American Division Executive Committee. As he recounted the decisions that had led women not only to be trained for ministry but to do the work of ministry, he reminded the body of previous deliberations:

> I have come to the conclusion that the church crossed the theological bridge when we voted to recognize the ordination of women as local elders. For while admitting that there is clearly a distinction in function, it appears to be ecclesiological hairsplitting to say that we will recognize ordination of women on one hand and refuse it on the other hand, while calling them both scriptural positions.[32]

On 9 October the Annual Council voted overwhelmingly the following request:

> To request the Annual Council to refer the following action to the General Conference session for consideration: The General Conference vests in each division the right to authorize the ordination of individuals within its territory in harmony with established policies. In addition, where circumstances do not render it inadvisable, a division may authorize the ordination of qualified individuals without regard to gender. In divisions where the division executive committee take specific actions approving the ordination of women to the gospel ministry, women may be ordained to serve in those divisions.[33]

This vote signaled a difference; gone was the language of the 1989 request in which North America clearly enunciated to the world church its commitment to proactively recognize the equality of men and women in ministry.

In January 1995 Elder Folkenberg, writing in the *Adventist Review*, declared 1995 the "Year of the Adventist Woman." While he shied from the question of women's ordination, he enthusiastically declared:

> It's apparent that there's an energizing spirit emerging among the

women of the church. I see it as I travel. And I believe the Holy Spirit is using it as a means of augmenting effectiveness in carrying out the gospel commission. I see it as a fulfillment of Acts 2:17, 18. "In the last days, God says, I will pour out my Spirit on all people. . . . Even on my servants, both men and women, I will pour out my Spirit" (NIV). How exciting to be part of a movement in which partnership in mission is becoming a reality.[34]

As delegates to the 1995 General Conference prepared to make their way to Utrecht, Holland, there was a great deal of expectation. Meeting for only the second time outside of the United States, (the 1975 General Conference in Vienna, Austria, had been the first) the agenda, in the words of *Adventist Review* editor William G. Johnsson, "comes loaded with important items." When writing of "potentially divisive items," he reminded readers of one specifically: "The request for each division to decide who may be ordained without reference to gender. . . . Our unity will be tested as never before at this session."[35]

As one reviews the voluminous material produced at Utrecht, it is clear that Johnsson's words were prophetic. While many of the session's actions were integral to the life and governance of the church, none garnered as much attention as the debate on women's ordination. Even before the conference began, individuals representing a host of organizations and ideologies were on the street handing out pamphlets and materials either decrying or upholding the North American Division's request.

Wednesday afternoon, 5 July, delegates packed into the hall to listen to Elder McClure, North American Division president, make an eloquent plea for the world church to recognize that the concern for women's ordination was clearly linked to the mission of the church:

> Our sisters who stand with us in ministry deserve the same acknowledgment of their call that the church confers on their male colleagues. . . . You may rest assured that it is not driven by any kind of feminist agenda. Our motive is simple. God has given lavish spiritual gifts to the church, irrespective of gender. We need all those gifts to fulfill the gospel commission, and it violates no scriptural teaching that the rite of ordination be extended to anyone who meets these criteria. We are not asking the other divisions to join us where it may not be acceptable. We are simply asking that you grant to each division the same permission that was granted them by the General Conference at Annual Council on the matter of ordination of local elders. We believe that it is a responsible request.[36]

Following the presentation, Elder Charles Bradford, past president of the

North American Division, asked for permission to speak:

> I would simply say that the Holy Spirit, brothers and sisters, is the one
> who selects and chooses people for ministry. Ordination is not a right.
> Ordination is a ceremony, a selection ceremony, a recognition
> ceremony. God has already chosen as His minister the one who is
> ordained.[37]

Next, two presentations were made by SDA Theological Seminary professors, P. Gerard Damsteegt and Raoul Dederen. Damsteegt, Associate Professor of Church History, argued that the Bible is clear that women must never exercise "headship" or "authority" over men, and are, because of the authority that comes with the office of pastor, disqualified from seeking ordination. He challenged the idea of women speaking about their call to ministry: "Some will proclaim, 'I had a call from the Lord. The Lord told me to lead out in the church and take charge of the whole church.' Remember, not every call or gift comes from God. 'Test the spirits to see whether they are from God.'"[38]

Dederen, Professor Emeritus of Theology and former dean of the SDA Theological Seminary, in responding to his colleague, reminded the delegates that there is a vast difference, at times, between the literal statement and the spirit of the biblical passage:

> My brothers and sisters, tell me, have we followed the instruction? Can
> you assure me that we have never transgressed that specific statement,
> "I permit no woman to have authority over man or to teach?" Do we
> not have women in teaching capacities, even if only on the Sabbath
> school level?[39]

For a church that only the day before had recognized and honored two women pastors from China, Zhou Hui-Ying and Wu Lan-Ying (who had each raised up churches of more than 1,000 members; Mrs. Zhou had personally baptized more than 200 in Wuxi, China), this was especially poignant.

Following the two presentations, Elder Rock opened the floor for debate, and delegates swarmed to the "for" and "against" microphones. It was clear that not only was the issue perceived to be theological, but was very much an issue of culture as well.[40] Finally, after 5 p.m., a motion was made to cut off debate. After a short presentation and prayer by Elder Folkenberg, the vote was taken. Of the 2,145 ballots collected, 673 voted YES, while 1,481 voted NO.

The Aftermath of Utrecht

In the months following that decisive day in Utrecht, the Seventh-day Adventist Church has continued to move forward, in those countries where women serve as capable and effective pastors, in a spirit of hope and determination. In the August 1995 *Adventist Review*, Elder McClure pastorally reminded his congregation in North America that the church must look for ways to support and enlarge the ministry of women. He reminded readers that "the General Conference session decision did not in any way exclude women from ministry nor diminish their role or effectiveness."[41]

In a *Statement of Commitment to Women in Gospel Ministry*, written on 13 October 1995, the North American Division Union presidents reaffirmed their belief "in the biblical rightness of women's ordination." While applauding McClure's steps to establish a Presidential Commission on Women in Ministry, they pledged their support to authorize full equality of practice in ministry, enhance the Commissioning Service, increase the role of women in the church, and clarify the church's theology of ordination.[42]

A sidelight to the official discussion occurred when church members who had long benefitted from women pastors felt that what the church had not been able to do on a worldwide scope must be accomplished at the local church level. On 23 September 1995, Sligo Church in Takoma Park, Maryland, held a service billed in the printed program as an "Ordination to the Gospel Ministry" for three women serving in the Washington metropolitan area. Considerable confusion surrounded the use of that language, but Arthur R. Torres, senior pastor, attempted to clarify the issue in two documents. In an email news release on 25 August, Torres stressed the right of the congregation to ordain persons to full-time ministry in the local congregation in the very same way it had authority to ordain persons to part-time ministry as local elders. And in a general letter to members distributed at church on 9 September he wrote: "Thus, Sligo Church will not ordain anyone to the gospel ministry, as that phrase is understood by Seventh-day Adventists. We make no claim that this ordination is to the world church, or that it has any authority outside our local area." North American Division president Alfred McClure cited Torres' letter in published statements about the meaning of the Sligo service.[43]

The Sligo service, attended by approximately 1,100 people, celebrated the lives and ministry of Kendra Haloviak, a religion professor at Columbia Union College; Penny Shell, a chaplain at Shady Grove Adventist Hospital; and Norma Osborn, one of two women pastors at Sligo Church.

Since Sligo's ordination, similar services have taken place at the La Sierra University Church, the Loma Linda Victoria Church, the Garden Grove Church, and the Loma Linda University Church.

On 9 October 1997, the North American Division year-end meeting formally accepted the report of the President's Commission on Women in Ministry, which contained 13 recommendations aimed at affirming and encouraging women in ministry. These included the appointment of a woman as ministerial associate secretary (on this item the North American Division was asked to move with a sense of urgency) and the development of a professional association for women serving in pastoral ministry. Also recommended were the development of additional ways to aid communication, including an electronic linkage service to help seasoned women pastors to serve as mentors of women ministerial students and interns; the development of a newsletter, database, placement service, and speaker's bureau for women in ministry; and a recommendation to church magazines to publish more articles about women in ministry. The report also recommended that conferences promptly conduct commissioning services for eligible women and that the church be encouraged to hire increasing numbers of women pastors. In addition, the report also encouraged conferences to set realistic goals for gender diversity on boards, committees, and staffs. The development of a Resource Center for Women in Ministry was recommended, and the commitment to educate church members on the topic of women in ministry was affirmed.[44]

Facing the Future: Five Key Realities

In conclusion, it seems appropriate to ask, what have we learned as we have journeyed through nearly three decades of Seventh-day Adventist history? What does the recent history of women in ministry say to the members of a church that longs to be faithful to the word and work of Jesus in our world?

First, the 5 July 1995, vote in Utrecht did not, in any way, signal the end of the matter. In reality, ordination was just a portion of the motion voted down. Many delegates later remarked that while they were supportive of women being ordained, they could not in good conscience vote for a motion that gave permission for divisions in the church to act on their own. While divisions often implement church policy based on their specific needs, the issue of church unity became so dominant at Utrecht that many could not accept North America's request.

Second, it is not enough simply to read about women in ministry. Congregations that have been exposed to the ministry of women pastors react far differently than those who have never had that privilege. In a recent study of 20 Seventh-day Adventist congregations pastored by women ministers, Roger Dudley found that while 75 percent were initially favorable to having a woman pastor, support had grown to 87 percent during the pastor's tenure. As Dudley states, "familiarity tends to make a concept more favorable. The female pastors have won some members over."[45] If churches are to understand women in ministry, it will be necessary for them to be exposed to the capable and caring pastoral leadership of women.

Third, we must take seriously the historical path of Adventism, not only in recognizing women in ministry, but in preparing them for this ministry. For many, it is impossible to think of asking women to take the same steps of ministerial preparation, to assume the same roles of ministry, to produce the same quality of work as their male colleagues, and then to ordain them as local church elders, while withholding ordination to the gospel ministry. To many Seventh-day Adventists, it is morally reprehensible to hold back from women the one thing that formally recognizes their work within the church.

Fourth, it seems apparent that the forces of history continue to move forward. It is impossible not to recognize that many of the official stands we now celebrate when affirming the role of women in Seventh-day Adventist ministry were at one time unacceptable. We do not know the long-term effect that congregational ordinations will have on the church's stand on women's ordination. However, history reaffirms that had local churches and conferences recognizing the spiritual gifts of women, whether as ordained deaconesses, ordained elders, or as pastors who baptize and perform marriages, many of these ministries might still not be accepted within the church today.

Finally, for a denomination that looks to a woman as one of its founders and as a prophetic voice, it is imperative that we recognize that many members today long for the church to act with justice, with mercy, and with courage on behalf of its women: the very ones who make up the majority of our worldwide membership. In a time that decries hurtful relationships, many today see the church as promoting invisible barriers and walls that keep some from full participation. As a church that longs to pass its faith on to the next generation and is committed to creating a place where all people are appreciated and used by God, we must actively work to tear down these barriers and embrace the wide diversity of ministry gifts so beautifully demonstrated in the lives and work of all of our people, both women and men.

As one looks over these past three decades, it would be easy to become disillusioned with the process, the constant wavering, and the defeats that seemed to accompany the victories. It is possible to wonder if God can indeed speak his will to us when we, as a Seventh-day Adventist family, are so diverse and so often removed from each other's cares and hurts, so easily moved by emotion and arguments that have little grounding in the life of Jesus and in the word of Scripture. And yet, as we have been reminded by the voices in this chapter, we remain a people of hope and faith, waiting for God to continue to pour out his Spirit on whom he will.

Endnotes

1. Kit Watts, "The Rise and Fall of Adventist Women in Leadership," *Ministry*, April 1995, 6-10. It is widely recognized that women were most influential as decision makers in the Seventh-day Adventist Church between 1900 and 1915. In 1905, women held 20 out of 60 conference treasurer positions, and by 1915 more than 50 of the 60 Sabbath School department leaders were women.

2. Ibid., 8.

3. "Thirteenth Business Meeting," *Adventist Review*, 7 July 1995, 23.

4. The author is indebted to Kit Watts' excellent research: "An Outline of the History of Seventh-day Adventists and the Ordination of Women," in *The Welcome Table*, ed. Rebecca F. Brillhart and Patricia A. Habada (Langley Park, MD: TEAM, 1995), 334-358. Dr. Leona Running, Professor Emeritus, SDA Theological Seminary, provided a wealth of information regarding women in ministry in her growing collection, "Women in Church and Society," housed in the Adventist Heritage Center at Andrews University. Special thanks to Jim Ford, director of the Adventist Heritage Center, for help in locating resources.

5. General Conference Annual Council Minutes, 18 October 1973.

6. In 1995 the papers were republished and widely distributed. See General Conference of Seventh-day Adventists, *The Role of Women in the Church* (Boise, ID: Pacific Press, 1995).

7. "Response from Readers: The Ordination of Women," *Advent Review and Sabbath Herald*, 28 October 1976, 13.

8. General Conference Annual Council Minutes, 17 October 1974.

9. General Conference Spring Meeting Minutes, 3 April 1975.

10. General Conference Annual Council Minutes, 12-20 October 1977; this title was only used to identify women in ministry.

11. General Conference Annual Council Minutes, 9-17 October 1979.

12. Neal C. Wilson, "To Do the Right Thing at the Right Time," *Adventist Review*, 20 April 1980, 4.

13. Pat Benton, "We're Rediscovering Ourselves: An Interview with Elizabeth Sterndale," *Adventist Review*, March 1995, 25.

14. It should be noted that Margarete Prange had been conducting baptisms in her churches in East Germany before the decision that enabled Jan Daffern, Marsha Frost, and Frances Wiegand to perform baptisms in the North American Division.

15. Roy Branson and Diane Gainer, "Potomac Conference Yields: Baptisms by Women Halted," *Spectrum* 15 (October 1984): 2-4.

16. "Session Actions," *Adventist Review*, 11 July 1985, 20.

17. Nancy Vyhmeister, "Not Weary in Well Doing," *Ministry*, April 1986, 11-13.

18. Roger L. Dudley, "Pastoral Views on Women in Ministry," *Adventist Review*, 4 June 1987, 18.

19. Ibid., 19.

20. Roger L. Dudley, "Religion Teachers' Opinion of the Role of Women," *Ministry*, August 1987, 16.

21. Carole L. Kilcher and Gan Theow Ng, "Survey on the Status of Women Elders in the North American Division," Institute of Church Ministry, Andrews University, October 1988. For example, the research indicated that African-American churches select female elders as frequently as do Caucasian churches. Hispanic churches fell only one percentage point behind African American and Caucasian churches in the North American Division.

22. Neal Wilson, "Role of Women Commission Meet," *Adventist Review*, 12 May 1988, 7.

23. Pastor Bumgardner was not, however, ordained, as both the Columbia Union and Ohio Conference voted to delay implementing ordination until the General Conference approved the action.

24. Karen Flowers, "The Role of Women in the Church," *Adventist Review*, 28 September 1989, 15-18.

25. Charles Bradford, "Approaching the Third Millennium," *Spectrum* 20 (December 1989): 16-18.

26. Tenth Business Session, 55th General Conference Session, Indianapolis, Indiana, 11 July 1990.

27. Tenth Business Session, 55th General Conference Session, Indianapolis, Indiana, 11 July 1990.

28. "Speaking in Turn: Excerpts from Delegates' Speeches on the Ordination of Women," *Spectrum* 20 (August 1990): 35.

29. Tenth Business Session, 55th General Conference Session, Indianapolis, Indiana, 11 July 1990.

30. *Keeping Hope Alive: The Attitudes of Adventist Women in Ministry after the Indianapolis Decision*, (Langley, MD: TEAM, 1993), 5. In 1995 a similar survey was made; by this time the number had grown to 130.

31. It is interesting to compare the information disseminated in different parts of the worldwide church. While pastors and lay members in North America, through the pages of the *Adventist Review* and *Ministry*, had since 1985 been exposed to a great deal of information regarding both the positive and negative sides of the ordination issue, the materials produced for other parts of the world (such at *Ministerio Adventista*, the Spanish language version of *Ministry*), often highlighted only the negative side of the issue of women's ordination. Samuel Koranteng-Pipim's *Searching the Scriptures: Women's Ordination and the Call to Biblical Fidelity* (Berrien Springs: Adventists Affirm, 1995) was supplied to blocks of delegates who erroneously assumed the book was backed by the SDA Theological Seminary, where the author was a doctoral student.

32. Alfred C. McClure, "NAD's President Speaks on Women's Ordination," *Adventist Review*, February 1995, 15.

33. 1994 General Conference Annual Council Minutes, 9 October 1994.

34. Robert S. Folkenberg, "Affirming Women in Ministry," *Adventist Review*, January 1995, 12.

35. William G. Johnsson, "Will This Session Be a Watershed?" *Adventist Review*, 30 June 1995, 4.

36. "Thirteenth Business Meeting," *Adventist Review*, 7 July 1995, 24-25.

37. Ibid., 25.

38. Ibid., 26.

39. Ibid., 28.

40. One individual, speaking in opposition to the motion, asserted that a spirit of Babylon was behind the request (another speaker alluded to women seeking ordination as being similar to the angels who followed Lucifer). One gentlemen pointed out that no one can replace the call of the Christian mother to raise up God's servants. On the other hand, one

North American woman challenged the group to remember that there were countries where women cannot vote, while in other countries women have been elected to the highest office of their nation.

41. Alfred C. McClure, "After the Vote, Now What?" *Adventist Review*, August 1995, 5.

42. "A Statement of Commitment to Women in Gospel Ministry from the North American Division Union Presidents, 13 October 1995.

43. "McClure Reaffirms Division's Position," *Adventist Review*, 1 February 1996, 6.

44. 1997 North American Division Year-end Meeting Minutes. Also see Kermit Netteburg, "New Plan Encourages Women Pastors," *Adventist Review*, November 1997, 21.

45. Roger L. Dudley, "How Seventh-day Adventist Lay Members View Women Pastors," *Review of Religious Research* 38 (December 1996): 137.

PART FOUR: PERCEIVED IMPEDIMENTS TO WOMEN IN MINISTRY

After careful consideration, the committee agreed that the most serious obstacles to the acceptance of the ordination of women were four: the concept of the headship of all males over all females, Paul's demand that women be silent in church (1 Cor 14:34, 35), his instruction that women should not teach or "exercise authority" (1 Tim 2:12), and a quotation from Ellen White which appears to indicate that any who pursue women's rights are at odds with the third angel's message. Chapters 13 through 17 carefully examine these perceived impediments.

CHAPTER 13

Headship, Submission, and Equality in Scripture

RICHARD M. DAVIDSON

One of the basic issues in the discussion of the role of women in Scripture concerns the questions of headship, submission, and equality in male/female relationships. The answers to these questions are foundational to determining whether or not women should be ordained as elders and pastors in the church.

In the evangelical Christian community, the issue of headship/submission/equality lies at the heart of the fundamental differences between the two major proactive groups in the ordination debate.[1] The Council on Biblical Manhood and Womanhood,[2] representing those who oppose women's ordination, ultimately bases its biblical argument on the premise that the divine plan in creation affirmed equality of the sexes in spiritual status but included role distinctions involving the headship of man over woman. This ordinance of male headship is reaffirmed after the Fall in Genesis 3, and is binding both in the home and the church, throughout Scripture and still today. Those holding this position have been referred to as "patriarchalists," "hierarchalists," or (their preferred self-designation) "complementarians."

The second group, Christians for Biblical Equality,[3] representing evangelicals who support women's ordination, argue that the divine plan at Creation affirmed full equality of the sexes without any male headship or female submission. Genesis 3 is typically seen to provide a description of the perversion of the divine ideal, and this "curse" is removed by the gospel, both in the home and in the church. Those holding this view have been referred to as "Christian feminists" or (their preferred self-designation) "egalitarians."

These two positions on the question of headship/submission and equality have been widely represented within the Adventist Church as well. In this chapter, I will argue that both positions maintain important elements of biblical teaching that must be heeded and, at the same time, that both groups may have overlooked or misinterpreted aspects of the relevant biblical passages.

In our discussion, we will pay particular attention to the foundational opening chapters of Scripture, Genesis 1-3, which have been widely recognized as of seminal character and determinative for the biblical role of women. Then we will briefly trace the divine pattern of headship/submission/equality throughout the Old Testament and New Testament and draw implications for the issue of ordination of women to ministry.

In the Beginning[4]

Before the Fall (Genesis 1-2)

Gen 1:27 describes the Creation of humankind: "So God created man [humankind, *hā 'ādām*] in His image; in the image of God He created him; male and female He created them." It is crucial to note the equal pairing of male *and* female in parallel with *hā 'ādām* in this verse. There is no hint of ontological or functional superiority/inferiority or headship/submission between male and female. Both are "equally immediate to the Creator and His act."[5] Both are given the same dominion over the earth and other living creatures (vv. 26 and 28). Both share alike in the blessing and responsibility of procreation (vv. 29-30). In short, both participate equally in the image of God.

The narrative of Gen 2:4b-25 provides a more detailed account of the creation of man than the terse summary statement of Genesis 1. Over the centuries the preponderance of commentators on Genesis 2 have espoused the hierarchical interpretation, a view that has been reaffirmed in a number of modern scholarly studies.[6] The main elements of the narrative which purportedly prove a divinely-ordained hierarchical view of the sexes may be summarized as follows: (a) man is created first and woman last (2:7, 22), and the first is superior and the last is subordinate or inferior; (b) woman is formed for the sake of man—to be his "helpmate" or assistant, to cure man's loneliness (vv. 18-20); (c) woman comes out of man (vv. 21-22), which implies a derivative and subordinate position; (d) woman is created from man's rib (vv. 21-22), which indicates her dependence upon him for life; and (e) the man names the woman

(v. 23) which indicates his power and authority over her.

On these points Phyllis Trible asserts that "although such specifics continue to be cited as support for traditional interpretations of male superiority and female inferiority, not one of them is altogether accurate and most of them are simply not present in the story itself."[7] Let us look at each point in turn.

Man created first. It has been asserted that because man was created first and then woman, "by this the priority and superiority of the man, and the dependence of the woman upon the man, are established as an ordinance of divine creation."[8] A careful examination of the literary structure of Genesis 2 reveals that such a conclusion does not follow. Hebrew literature often makes use of an *inclusio* device or envelope construction in which the points of central concern to a unit are placed at the beginning and end of the unit.[9] This is the case in Genesis 2; the entire account is cast in the form of an *inclusio* or "ring construction,"[10] in which the creation of man at the beginning of the narrative and that of woman at the end correspond to each other in importance. The narrator underscores their equal importance by employing precisely the same number of words (in Hebrew) for the description of the creation of the man as for the creation of woman. As Trevor Dennis puts it, "the writer has counted his words and been careful to match the lengths of his descriptions exactly."[11] The movement in Genesis 2, if anything, is not from superior to inferior, but from incompleteness to completeness. Woman is created as the climax, the culmination of the story. She is the crowning work of Creation.[12]

Two subpoints of this first argument relate to Adam's priority in speaking and being spoken to in the narrative. It has been claimed that Adam's headship over his wife before the Fall is revealed in that God addresses Adam, and not Eve, and also in that Adam does the speaking in the narrative of Genesis 2, not Eve. However, these points fail to take into account the movement of the narrative from incompleteness to completeness and climax, as noted above. As part of the process of bringing Adam to realize his "hunger for wholeness,"[13] his need for a partner, God speaks to Adam, warning him not to eat of the forbidden tree. Such information was crucial for the human being to avoid transgression and to be a free moral agent with the power of choice. But the divine impartation of such knowledge to Adam before Eve was created does not thereby reveal the headship of Adam over his partner. Likewise, that only Adam speaks in Genesis 2 does not reveal his pre-Fall headship over Eve any more than only Eve speaking outside the Garden (Genesis 4) reveals Eve's headship over Adam after the Fall.[14]

Woman formed for sake of man. Genesis 2:18 records the Lord's deliberation: "It is not good that the man should be alone; I will make him *ʿēzer kᵉnegdô* (KJV—"a help meet for him"; RSV—"a helper fit for him"; NASB—"a helper suitable to him"). These words have often been taken to imply the inferiority or the subordinate status of woman. For example, John Calvin understood that woman was a "kind of appendage" and a "lesser helpmeet" for man.[15]

The word *ʿēzer* is usually translated as "help" or "helper" in English. This, however, is a misleading translation, because the English word "helper" tends to suggest an assistant, a subordinate, an inferior, whereas the Hebrew carries no such connotation. In fact, the Hebrew Bible most frequently employs *ʿēzer* to describe a superior helper—God himself as the "helper" of Israel.[16] This is a relational term, describing a beneficial relationship, but in itself does not specify position or rank, either superiority or inferiority.[17] The specific position intended must be gleaned from the immediate context, here the adjoining *kᵉnegdô*.

The word *neged* conveys the idea of "in front of" or "counterpart,"[18] and a literal translation of *kᵉnegdô* is thus "like his counterpart, corresponding to him."[19] Used with *ʿēzer*, this term indicates no less than equality: Eve is Adam's "benefactor/helper," one who in position is "corresponding to him," "his counterpart, his complement."[20] Eve is "a power equal to man";[21] she is Adam's "partner."[22]

Woman came out of man. It has been argued that since woman came out of man, since she was formed from man, she has a derivative existence, a dependent and subordinate status. That her existence was in some way "derived" from Adam cannot be denied. But derivation does not imply subordination. Adam also was "derived"—from the ground (v. 7), but certainly we are not to conclude that the ground was his superior. Again, woman is *not* Adam's rib. The raw material, not woman, was taken out of man, just as the raw material of man was "taken" (Gen 3:19, 23) out of the ground.[23] Samuel Terrien rightly points out that woman "is not simply molded of clay, as man was, but she is architecturally 'built' (2:33)." The verb *bnh*, "to build," used in the Creation account only with regard to the formation of Eve, "suggests an aesthetic intent and connotes also the idea of reliability and permanence."[24] As the man was asleep while God created woman, man had no active part in the creation of woman that might allow him to claim to be her superior or head.[25]

Woman created from man's rib. While this argument has been used to support the hierarchical view of the sexes, the very symbolism of the rib points rather to equality. The word ṣēlāᶜ can mean either "side" or "rib."[26] Since ṣēlāᶜ occurs in the plural in v. 21 and God is said to take "one of" them, the reference is probably to a rib from Adam's side. By "building" Eve from one of Adam's ribs, God appears to be indicating the "mutual relationship,"[27] the "singleness of life,"[28] the "inseparable unity"[29] in which man and woman are joined. The rib "means solidarity and equality."[30] As Ellen White puts it, "Eve was created from a rib taken from the side of Adam, signifying that she was not to control him as the head, nor to be trampled under his feet as an inferior, but to stand by his side as an equal, to be loved and protected by him."[31] This interpretation is further confirmed by the man's poetic exclamation when he sees the woman for the first time (v. 23): "This at last is bone of my bones and flesh of my flesh!" The phrase "bone of my bones and flesh of my flesh" indicates a person "as close as one's own body."[32] It denotes physical oneness and "a commonality of concern, loyalty and responsibility,"[33] but does not lead to the notion of woman's subordination or submission to man.

Man named woman. Some argue that in man's naming of woman (v. 23) is implied man's power, authority, and superiority over her. True, assigning names in Scripture often does signify authority over the one named.[34] But such is not the case in Gen 2:23. In the first place, the word "woman" (ʾiššāh) is not a personal name, but only a generic identification. This is verified in v. 24, which indicates that a man is to cleave to his ʾiššāh ("wife"), and further substantiated in Gen 3:20, which explicitly records the man's naming of Eve only after the Fall.

Moreover, Jacques Doukhan has shown that Gen 2:23 contains a pairing of "divine passives," indicating that the designation of "woman" comes *from* God, not man. Just as woman "was taken out of man" *by* God, with which the man had nothing to do, so she "shall be called woman" a designation originating in God and not man. Doukhan also indicates how the literary structure of the Genesis Creation story confirms this interpretation.[35] The wordplay in v. 23 between ʾîš (man) and ʾiššāh (wo-man) and the explanation of the woman being taken out of man are not given to buttress a hierarchical view of the sexes, but rather to underscore man's joyous recognition of "his second self."[36] In his ecstatic poetic utterance the man is not determining who the woman is, but delighting in what God has done, recognizing and welcoming woman as the equal counterpart to his sexuality.[37] After the Fall Adam *did* give his wife the name Eve, probably signifying his exercise of headship authority over her; such was not the case at Creation.

In light of the foregoing discussion, there is nothing in Genesis 2 to indicate a hierarchical view of the sexes. The man and woman before the Fall are presented as fully equal, with no hint of headship of one over the other or a hierarchical relationship between husband and wife.

After the Fall (Genesis 3)

When God comes to the Garden after Adam and Eve sinned, he initiates an encounter that constitutes nothing less than "a legal process," a "trial punishment by God."[38] God begins the legal proceedings with an interrogation of the "defendants," and the defensive and accusatory responses by Adam and Eve (vv. 9-14) indicate the rupture in husband-wife and divine-human relationships that has occurred as a result of sin. Following the legal interrogation and establishment of guilt, God pronounces the sentence in the form of curses (over the serpent and the ground, vv. 14, 17) and judgments (for the man and the woman, vv. 16-19).

The judgment pronounced upon the woman is of particular concern (v. 16):

(a) I will greatly multiply your pain [labor] in childbearing;
(b) in pain [labor] you shall bring forth your children;
(c) yet your desire shall be for your husband,
(d) and he shall rule over you.

The meaning of the last two enigmatic lines (v. 16c and d) of the divine sentence upon the woman is crucial for a proper understanding of the nature of God's design for sexual relationships throughout the rest of Scripture.

Five major views have been advanced in the history of scriptural interpretation. The first, and perhaps the most common, position maintains that the subordination of woman is a Creation ordinance, God's ideal from the beginning, but as a result of sin this original form of hierarchy between the sexes is distorted and corrupted and must be restored by the gospel.[39]

The second major interpretation also views subordination as a Creation ordinance but sees in Gen 3:16 not as a distortion but a reaffirmation of subordination as a blessing and a comfort to the woman in her difficulties as a mother. The meaning of v. 16*c-d* may be paraphrased: "You will have labor and difficulty in your motherhood, yet you will be eager for your husband and he will rule over you (in the sense of care for and help you and not in the sense of dominate and oppress you)."[40]

The third major view contends that the subordination of woman to man did not exist before the Fall, and the mention of such a subordination in Gen 3:16 is only a *description* of the evil consequences of sin—the usurpation of authority by the husband (to be removed by the gospel)—and not a permanent *prescription* of God's will for husband-wife relationships after sin.[41] Proponents of this position underscore the culturally-conditioned nature of this passage and vigorously deny that it represents a divinely ordained normative position for sexual relationships after the Fall.

A fourth major position concurs with the third view that the submission of wife to husband is part of the evil consequences of the Fall and did not exist as a Creation ordinance. But in the fourth view, Gen 3:16 is to be understood as *prescriptive* and not merely *descriptive*. It presents God's normative pattern for the relationship of husband and wife after the Fall.[42]

A final view agrees with the second that v. 16*c-d* is a blessing and not a curse, but differs in denying that subordination of woman to man is a Creation ordinance. This position also argues, in effect, that even in Genesis 3 no hierarchy or headship in the sexes is either prescribed or described.[43] In this view the word for "rule" (v. 16*d*) is often translated "to resemble" or "to be like," emphasizing the equality of husband and wife.[44] Another variation of this view argues that man "rules" or "predominates" only in the area of sexuality, i.e., "female reluctance is overcome by the passion they feel toward their men, and that allows them to accede to the males' sexual advances even though they realize that undesired pregnancies (with the accompanying risks) might be the consequence."[45]

These major positions are summarized in the following chart:

Man-Woman Relationships in the Beginning (Genesis 1-3): Major Views

Creation (Genesis 1-2)	Fall (Genesis 3)	Divine Judgments on Eve (Gen 3:16)
1. Hierarchical (Subordination of woman)	Perverted	Subordination Restored
2. Hierarchical (Subordination of woman)	Continues	Subordination Reaffirmed
3. Equality (With no subordination of woman)	Ruptured Relationship	Description of sinful consequences (to be removed by gospel), husband usurps authority
4. Equality (With no subordination of woman)	Ruptured Relationship	Permanent prescription of divine will for harmony after sin, husband "first-among-equals"
5. Equality (With no subordination of woman)	Continues	Blessing of equality (no headship or hierarchy)

In assessing the true intent of this passage, we must immediately call into question those interpretations which proceed from the assumption that a hierarchy of the sexes existed before the Fall (views 1 and 2). The analysis of Genesis 1-2 has shown that no such subordination or subjection of woman to man was present in the beginning.

Furthermore, view 3 (Gen 3:16 only descriptive, not prescriptive) appears to be unsatisfactory because it fails to take seriously the judgment/punishment context of the passage. As already noted, Gen 3:16 comes in a legal trial setting. God's pronouncement is therefore not merely a culturally-conditioned description; it is a divine sentence. Just as God destines the serpent to crawl on its belly (v. 14), just as God ordains that woman's childbirth is to involve her "going into labor" (*'iṣṣābôn*, v. 16), just as God curses the ground so that it will not produce crops spontaneously but require man's cultivation and "hard labor" (*'iṣṣābôn*, v. 17), just as humankind will inevitably return to dust in death

(v. 19)—so God pronounces the sentence upon Eve with regard to her future relationship with Adam. Just as none of the other judgments were removed or reversed at the Cross, but stay in force until the consummation of salvation history, so this judgment remains in force until the removal of sinful world conditions at the end of time. This is not to say that it is inappropriate for humankind to seek to roll back the judgments/curses and get back as much as possible to God's original plan—by advances in obstetrics to relieve unnecessary hard labor during delivery; by agricultural and technological advances to relieve unnecessary hard labor in farming, by scientific and medical advances to delay the process of death. In the same way it is not inappropriate to return as much as possible to God's original plan for total equality in marriage, while at the same time retaining the validity of the headship principle as necessary in a sinful world to preserve harmony in the home.

The divine origin and prescriptive nature of the judgment upon Eve is underscored by the Hebrew grammar of God's first words in the legal sentence: "I will greatly multiply." The use of the first-person singular "I" refers to the Lord Himself, who is pronouncing the judgment, while the emphatic Hebrew infinitive absolute construction implies "the absolute certainty of the action." Carol Meyers rightly concludes that the judgment upon Eve represents a "divine prescription" and not just a description, a divine "mandate" and "divine oracle."[46]

According to Gen 3:16c-d a change is instituted involving the subjection/submission of the wife to the husband. The force of the last line (v. 16d) is difficult to avoid: "he [your husband] shall rule over you." The word *māšal* in this form in v. 16d means "to rule" (and not "to be like") and definitely implies subjection.[47] Theodorus Vriezen correctly concludes that woman's position after the Fall is one of subjection to her husband: "this is considered as a just and permanent punishment in Gen iii."[48] Umberto Cassuto aptly paraphrases and amplifies the divine sentence: "measure for measure; you influenced your husband and caused him to do what you wished; henceforth, you and your female descendants will be subservient to your husbands."[49]

Ellen White clearly adopts this interpretation.

> In the creation God had made her [Eve] the equal of Adam. Had they remained obedient to God—in harmony with His great law of love—they would ever have been in harmony with each other; but sin had brought discord, and now *their union could be maintained and harmony preserved* only by submission on the part of the one or the other. Eve had been the first in

transgression; and she had fallen into temptation by separating from her companion, contrary to the divine direction. It was by her solicitation that Adam sinned, and she was now placed in subjection to her husband. Had the principles enjoined in the law of God been cherished by the fallen race, this sentence, though growing out of the results of sin, *would have proved a blessing to them*; but man's abuse of the supremacy thus given him has too often rendered the lot of woman very bitter and made her life a burden."[50]

The word *māšal* "rule" employed in v. 16 is not the same word used to describe humankind's rulership over the animals in Gen 1:26, 28, where the verb is *rādāh*, "to tread down, have dominion over."[51] A careful distinction is maintained between humankind's dominion over the animals and the husband's "rule" over his wife. Furthermore, although the verb *māšal* does consistently indicate submission, subjection, or dominion, "the idea of tyrannous exercise of power does not lie in the verb."[52] In fact, in many passages *māšal* is used in the sense of servant leadership, to "comfort, protect, care for, love."[53]

The semantic range of the verb *māšal* thus makes it possible to understand the divine sentence in v. 16 as involving not only punishment but blessing, just as the sentence pronounced upon the serpent and man included an implied blessing.[54] That the element of blessing is especially emphasized in this verse appears to be confirmed by recognizing the probable synonymous parallelism between v. 16c and v. 16d.[55] God pronounces that even though the woman would have difficult "labor" in childbirth—an ordeal that would seem naturally to discourage her from continuing to have relations with her husband—"yet," God assures her, "your desire shall be for your husband." The meaning of the Hebrew word *t'šûqāh*, "strong desire, yearning,"[56] which appears only three times in Scripture, is illuminated by its only other occurrence in a context of man-woman relationship, i.e., Cant 7:11 (Hebrew).[57] In this verse, the Shulamite bride joyfully exclaims, "I am my beloved's, and his *desire* [*t'šûqāh*] is for me." Along the lines of this usage of *t'šûqāh* in the Song of Songs to indicate a wholesome sexual desire, the term appears to be employed in Gen 3:16c to indicate a positive blessing accompanying the divine judgment. A divinely ordained sexual yearning of wife for husband will serve to sustain the union that has been threatened in the ruptured relations resulting from sin.

If Gen 3:16d is seen to be in close parallelism with v. 16c, the emphasis upon blessing as well as judgment seems to accrue also to man's relationship with his wife. The husband's "rule" over his wife, even though it grows out of the results of sin, may be regarded as a blessing in preserving the harmony and union of the relationship.[58] As is implied in the semantic range of *māšal*, and becomes explicit in the Song of Songs, this is not to be a "rule" of tyrannous power, but a servant leadership of protection, care, and love. In modern idiom, the husband is to lovingly "take care of" his wife.

We thus conclude that of the suggested interpretations for Gen 3:16 described above, view 4 is to be preferred, in that there is a normative divine sentence announcing a subjection/submission of wife to husband as a result of sin. This involves, however, not only a negative judgment but also (and especially) a positive blessing (as suggested in view 5) designed to lead back as much as possible to the original plan of harmony and union between equal partners.

Two final points must be underscored with regard to Genesis 3. First, although in Genesis 3 the husband is assigned the role of "first among equals"[59] to preserve harmony and union in the marriage partnership, this does not contradict or nullify the summary statement of Gen 2:24 regarding the nature of the relationship between husband and wife, clearly written to indicate its applicability to the post-Fall conditions. God's ideal for the nature of sexual relationship after the Fall is still the same as it was for Adam and Eve in the beginning—to "become one flesh." The divine judgment/blessing in Gen 3:16 is to facilitate the achievement of the original divine design within the context of a sinful world, and it is thus appropriate for marriage partners to seek to return as much as possible to total egalitarianism in the marriage relationship.

Second, the relationship of subjection/submission prescribed in v. 16 is *not* presented as applicable to man-woman relationships in general. Genesis 3 provides no basis for suggesting that the basic equality between male and female established in Creation was altered as a result of the Fall. The context of Gen 3:16 is specifically that of marriage: a *wife's* desire for her husband and the *husband's* "rule" over his wife. The text indicates a submission of wife to husband, not a general subordination of woman to man. The servant headship of the husband prescribed in this passage (v. 16 *d*) can no more be broadened to refer to men-women relationships in general than can the sexual desire of the wife (v. 16*c*) be broadened to mean the sexual desire of all women for all men. Any attempt to extend this prescription beyond the husband-wife relationship is not warranted by the text.

The Old Testament Pattern

Beyond Genesis 3, the divine pattern for man-woman relationships established in Eden remains God's consistent plan throughout the rest of the Old Testament. The submission of the wife to her husband's "headship among equals" in the home is assumed in precept and practice, but this does not bar women from positions of influence, leadership, and authority over men in the covenant community. We will briefly survey the Old Testament pattern of headship/submission/equality, first as it applies to husband-wife relationships in the home (physical family), and then as it affects men-women relationships in general in the covenant community of Israel.

Headship/Submission/Equality in Husband-Wife Relationships

Immediately after the record of divine judgment upon the first couple, Adam exercises his new "headship" role by naming his wife Eve (Gen 3:20). The headship of the husband is again demonstrated in the life of Abraham and Sarah (Gen 18:12), with Sarah referring to her husband as "my lord" (*adonî*). The husband's "headship" in the marriage is likewise indicated by the frequent use of *ba'al* ("lord"—both as a verb and a noun) to identify the husband.[60]

The attendant headship assigned to the man in the husband/wife relationship in Gen 3:16 seems clearly reaffirmed in the Mosaic legislation concerning unfaithful wives in Num 5:11-31. Verse 29 summarizes, "This is the law of jealousy, when a wife, under [the headship of] her husband, goes astray and defiles herself." Another law indicating the headship function of the husband is found in Num 30:3-16, where the husband has the right to revoke legal commitments (vows) of his wife.

There is little question that in ancient Israel (and throughout the ancient Near East) a patriarchal structuring of society was the norm, and the husband/father was the titular head of the ancient family. In marital/familial situations the husband/father assumed legal responsibility for the household. His leadership and legal headship are evidenced in such concerns as genealogy, family inheritance and ownership of property, contracting marriages for the children, initiating divorce, and overall responsibility in speaking for his family.

While recognizing the clear Old Testament evidence for the husband headship principle in marriage, we must hasten to underscore that such headship does not override the basic equality between the marriage partners, nor does it imply the husband's ownership, oppression, domination, or authoritative control over the wife.[61] Nor does the husband headship prevent husbands and wives from coming as close as possible to the original egalitarian design for marriage. This is revealed in the descriptions of the day-to-day relationships between Old Testament husbands and wives, in which the "ancient Israelite wife was loved and listened to by her husband, and treated by him as an equal."[62] "The ancient Israelite woman wielded power in the home at least equal to that exercised by the husband . . . ; she participated freely and as an equal in decisions involving the life of her husband or her family."[63] (See Jo Ann Davidson's chapter dealing with biblical women for a survey of recent narrative studies verifying these conclusions.)

The most extensive and penetrating Old Testament presentation of the divine ideal for husband-wife relationships in the post-Fall setting is in the Song of Songs.[64] In parallel with Gen 2:24, the lovers in the Song are presented as full equals in every way. Canticles "reflects an image of woman and female-male relations that is extremely positive and egalitarian."[65] The keynote "of the egalitarianism of mutual love"[66] is struck in Cant 2:16: "My beloved is mine and I am his." The Song of Songs begins and closes with the woman speaking; she carries the majority of the dialogue.[67] She initiates most of the meetings and is just as active in the lovemaking as the man. She is as eloquent about the beauty of her lover as he is about hers. The woman also is gainfully employed—as shepherdess and vineyard keeper. In short, throughout the Song she is "fully the equal of the man."[68] As in Gen 2, she is man's "partner . . . , 'the one opposite him.'"[69]

At the same time, in the Song of Songs voices repeatedly speak of post-Fall conditions which impinge upon the couple's relationship (see 1:6; 2:11; 2:15, 3:1-4; 5:6-8; 6:1; 8:6). The way of "woman and man in mutual harmony after the fall"[70] is likewise portrayed in imagery consonant with the divine norm given in Gen 3:16. Note in particular Cant 2:3:

> As an apple tree among the trees of the wood,
>   so is my beloved among young men.
> With great delight I sat in his shadow,
>   and his fruit was sweet to my taste.

Francis Landry has not failed to catch the intent of the imagery: "The apple-tree symbolizes the lover, the male sexual function in the poem; erect and delectable, it is a powerful erotic metaphor. It provides the nourishment and shelter, traditional male roles—the protective lover, man the provider."[71] Cant 8:5 seems to continue the apple-tree-protector motif:

> Who is that coming up from the wilderness leaning upon her beloved?
> Under the apple tree I awakened you . . .

The Song of Songs has recovered the true "lyrics" of the "symphony of love" for post-Fall sexual partners. In the garden of Canticles the divine plan for man's post-Fall role in the sexual relationship—*māšal,* "to protect, love, care for"—is restored from its accumulated perversions and abuses outside the Garden of Eden. That this *māšal* is the "rule" of love and not tyrannical power is made explicit in the Song by attributing to the man the "strong desire" (*tᵉšûqāh*) which is connected with the woman in Gen 3:16. As in the divine judgment God promises to the woman that still "Your desire (*tᵉšûqāh*) shall be for your husband," now in the Song the woman says, "I am my lover's and for me is his desire (*tᵉšûqāh*)." She thus joyfully acknowledges the mutuality of love that inheres in the ideal post-Fall relationship even as she is leaning upon, and resting under, the protecting shadow of her lover.

Headship/Submission/Equality of Men and Women in the Old Testament Covenant Community

While the patriarchal social structure is clearly present in Israel, including patriarchal "heads of the father's houses," and while such patriarchy is presented in a positive light,[72] it is significant to note that such patriarchy did not bar women from positions of influence, leadership, and even headship over men in the Israelite community (See chapter 9).

I note particularly the leadership role of Deborah the prophetess and judge (Judges 4-5). Deborah clearly exercised headship functions over men as the recognized political leader of the nation, the military leader of Israel on an equal footing with the male general Barak,[73] and a judge to whom men and women turned for legal counsel and divine instruction. There is no indication in the text that such female leadership over men in the covenant community was looked upon as unusual or was opposed to the divine will for women.

Special mention should also be made of the prophetess/musician Miriam, whose influence and leadership capabilities have been underscored by recent narrative analysis. The headship teaching role of

Huldah, even over the king (2 Kgs 22:14-20), is highly significant, especially in light of the availability of male teacher/prophets like Jeremiah at the time. No less significant are the numerous "wise women" of the Old Testament (Judg 5:28-30; 2 Sam 14; 2 Sam 20; etc.), a special class of women who exercise clear headship teaching functions over men.

In short, while the headship principle of Gen 3:16 clearly functions to regulate the Old Testament husband-wife relationship, this principle is not widened in the covenant community in such a way as to cause the rejection of women leaders on the basis of gender—even women leaders exercising headship over men.

The New Testament Pattern

It is beyond the scope of this chapter to examine the relatively low status of women in first-century Judaism and other Mediterranean cultures,[74] or to look at the New Testament elevation of women's status in radical ways in the Gospels, Acts, and Epistles.[75] The focus is specifically on the issue of headship/submission/equality in New Testament passages dealing with male/female relationships.

There is a clear distinction between counsel regarding husband-wife relationships and general men-women relationships in the church. Hence we can subdivide this section under the same twofold categorization as the Old Testament discussion.

Headship/Submission/Equality in Husband-wife Relationships

In considering the New Testament position on headship/submission/equality, we will look at the terms for headship and submission, and then briefly investigate the New Testament passages which contain these terms in the context of husband-wife relations.

Terminology. There has been much discussion regarding the meaning of "head" (*kephalē*) in its seven occurrences in a metaphorical sense,[76] with the debate polarizing into two camps. Some have vigorously argued that *kephalē* in first-century Greek often means "source" (as in the "head" of a river) and rarely or never "head" (as in superior rank),[77] while others have just as vigorously argued for the common meaning of "head" (as in superior rank) and rarely or never "source."[78] While the most responsible treatment of the evidence seems to favor the latter argument, still the best conclusion seems to be to recognize that both meanings appear in first-century secular Greek and are possible in New Testament usage, and thus the immediate context must be the final determiner of meaning.[79] Two occurrences of *kephalē* occur in a context of man-woman relationships: 1 Cor 11:3 and Eph 5:23.

The New Testament term used for "submit" in husband-wife relationships is *hypotassō*, a verb which appears in some form some 39 times in the New Testament (23 times in Pauline Epistles and 6 times in 1 Peter). The root verb (*tassō*) means "order, position, determine," and with the prepositional prefix *hypo* means, in the active voice, "place under, subordinate, subject, submit"; in the passive voice, "become subject [to someone or something]"; and in the middle voice, "[voluntarily] submit oneself, defer to, acquiesce, surrender one's rights or will."[80] Seven occurrences of *hypotassō*—all in the middle voice—occur in the context of man-woman relationships: 1 Cor 14:34; Eph 5:21, 24; Col 3:18; Tit 2:5; 1 Pet 3:1, 5.

Eph 5:21-33. This is the foundational New Testament passage dealing with husband-wife relations, and the only New Testament passage on this issue that contains both the word *kephalē* ("head") and *hypotassō* ("submit"). There is no question that the husband-wife relationship is in view and not men-women relationships in general. Ephesians 5 is part of a series of "Household Codes"[81] providing counsel for proper relationships between various members of domestic households: husbands and wives (Eph 5:22-33), children and parents (Eph 6:1-4), and servants and masters (Eph 6:5-9). Unmistakably in Ephesians 5 the counsel concerns the husband as the head of his own wife.

Although attempts have been made to translate *kephalē* as "source" (or a related concept), the pairing of *kephalē* with *hypotassō* ("submit") seems to indicate a ranking of relationship, and not the idea of origin or source. This parallels the similar usage of *kephalē* as "preeminence" or "superior rank" with reference to Christ in Eph 1:22 and Col 2:10.

The following points emerge clearly from this passage:

(1) The context of the Pauline counsel for husbands and wives (Eph 5:22-33) is one of "mutual submission," described in v. 21: "submitting to one another in the fear of God."[82]

(2) The word *hypotassō*, whether actually present in v. 22 or implied in v. 21 (manuscript evidence is divided here), occurs in the middle voice ("Wives, submit yourselves"), indicating that the wife's submission is a "voluntary yielding in love,"[83] not forced by the husband. There is no permission given for the husband to demand that his wife submit to his headship.

(3) The wife's submission is not a blind yielding of her individuality; she is to submit only "as to the Lord" (v. 22).

(4) The nature of the husband's headship is paralleled to that of Christ, who "loved the church and gave Himself for it" (v. 25). The husband's "headship" is thus a loving servant leadership. It means "head servant, or taking the lead in serving,"[84] not an authoritarian rule. It consists of the husband's loving his wife as his own body, nourishing and cherishing her, as Christ does the church (vv. 28-29).

(5) The emphasis in the headship/submission relationship seems underscored in the summary of v. 33: love (of the husband for his wife) and respect (of the wife for her husband).

(6) Though mutual submission is implied between husband and wife, yet this does not quite approach total role interchangeableness in the marriage relation. The term "head" is used only of the husband. As Witherington puts it, "There is a mutuality of submission, but this works itself out in different ways involving an ordering of relationships, and exhortations according to gender."[85]

(7) The respective roles of husband and wife are not defined by the social setting or the qualifications of the partners, but from the model of Christ and his church. Thus they transcend cultural circumstances.

(8) The ultimate ideal for husband-wife relations is still the partnership of equals that is set forth from the beginning in Gen 2:24: "the two shall become one flesh" (quoted in Eph 5:31).

Other _kephalē_ ("headship") passages. Aside from Eph 5:23, the only other New Testament passage utilizing _kephalē_ in the context of man-woman relationships is 1 Cor 11:3, part of a passage (vv. 3-16) thematically parallel to Eph 5:22-33. In chapter 15 of this book, Larry Richards has clearly shown how the context in 1 Corinthians 11 is one of wives submitting to the headship of their own husbands, and not the headship of men over women in general. Even though the Greek word _gynē_ can mean either "woman" or "wife," and the Greek word _anēr_ can likewise mean either "man" or "husband," Richards indicates how the context of 1 Corinthians 11 clearly favors the translation "husband" and "wife." Recognizing this context, the RSV and the NRSV correctly translate v. 3: "the head of a woman is her husband." The wearing of the head covering described in 1 Corinthians 11 was a sign of the wife's submission to her husband's headship, not to the headship of all men.[86] While this passage affirms the headship principle in the marital relation as in Ephesians, it also affirms the mutuality of the marriage partners

(v. 11; see chapter 15 for a more detailed discussion of this passage).

Other *hypotassō* ("submission") passages. Aside from Ephesians 5, four more New Testament passages utilize the verb *hypotassō* ("submit") in the context of man-woman relationships: 1 Cor 14:34; Col 3:18; Titus 2:5; and 1 Pet 3:1-7. A final passage utilizes the noun *hypotagē* ("submission") from the same verbal root: 1 Tim 2:12. We will look briefly at each in turn.

1 Cor 14:34 states: "Let the wives [*gynaikēs*] learn in silence, for they are not permitted to speak; but they are to submit themselves [*hypotassesthōsan*], as the law also says." Some have suggested that there is a contradiction between this instruction and 1 Cor 11:2-16, where Paul permitted women to speak in church by praying and prophesying. But such a suggestion fails to recognize that Paul here is meeting a particular situation in the Corinthian congregation. Paul is not addressing women in general in these verses, but certain Corinthian *wives*, since the same Greek word *gynē* can mean either "woman" or "wife," depending upon the context. This becomes obvious in light of v. 35, in which reference is made to the husbands of these women: "And if they want to learn something, let them ask their own husbands at home." Because of this contextual indicator, most commentators agree that this passage is speaking of wives and their relationship to their husbands, and not women-men relationships in general.[87]

A recognition of the husband-wife context provides the clue to understanding the exhortation for the wives to "submit themselves [middle voice of *hypotassō*], as the law also says" (v. 34). The law most probably refers here to the Old Testament, as it unquestionably does just a few verses earlier (v. 21). More specifically, it seems likely that Paul is alluding to Gen 3:16, the foundational Old Testament passage prescribing the submission of wives to the headship of their husbands. As Krister Stendahl points out, in 1 Cor 14:34 "it is still Gen 3:16 which is alluded to."[88]

We do not have enough information to be certain of the exact nature of the problem Paul was addressing; v. 35 suggests that the wives were asking questions of their husbands in the worship setting. Paul had just given instructions for prophesying in the church worship (vv. 22-29), and this involved the "testing" or evaluating of the prophetic messages (v. 29), when those not receiving a revelation were to keep silent. It seems that also during this time the wives were to be silent out of respect for their husbands. E. Earle Ellis explains:

I Cor. 14:34-35 represents the application, in a particular cultural context, of an order of the present creation concerning the conduct of a wife *vis-a-vis* her husband. It reflects a situation in which the husband is participating in the prophetic ministries of a Christian meeting. In this context the coparticipation of his wife, which may involve her publicly "testing" (*diakrinein*, 14:29) her husband's message, is considered to be a disgraceful (*aischron*) disregard of him, of accepted priorities, and of her own wifely role. For these reasons it is prohibited.[89]

Sharon Gritz gives a similar assessment: "The prohibition has nothing to do with ecclesiastical authority. Paul's concern here centers in maintaining the wife-husband relationship even when both spouses participate together in worship. Wives should exercise their gifts in a way that does not involve the violation of their husbands' headship."[90] In this context, Paul's call for the wives to "be silent" (*sigaō*) was a particular silence while their husbands' prophecies were being tested, and did not indicate total silence in the worship service any more than the other calls to silence (also *sigaō*) in particular circumstances in the same context (vv. 28-30).

The last three New Testament passages with occurrences of *hypotassō* are all part of "household codes" like Ephesians 5, and all undisputably refer to the submission of wives to their husbands and not women to men in general. The Colossian household code regarding husbands and wives covers basically the same ground as in Ephesians, in an abbreviated form. Col 3:18-19 reads: "Wives [*hai gynaikes*], submit yourselves [*hypotassesthe*] to [your own] husbands [*tois andrasin*], as is fitting in the Lord. Husbands [*hoi andres*], love [your] wives [*tais gynaikas*], and do not be bitter towards them." As in Ephesians 5, the counsel to husbands and wives is followed by counsel to children and parents (vv. 20-21).[91]

Titus 2:4-5 asks older women to "admonish the young women [*neas*] to be lovers of [their own] husbands [*philandrous*], to be lovers of [their own] children [*philoteknous*], to be discreet, chaste, managing well the home,[92] good, submitting themselves [*hypotassomenas*] to their own husbands [*tois idiois andrasin*], that the word of God may not be blasphemed." By adding the possessive pronominal adjective idios ("*one's own*"), this household code emphatically underscores that a wife is to submit to her *own* husband, and not to all husbands.

The household code concerning husbands and wives in 1 Pet 3:1-7 likewise utilizes the possessive pronoun *idios* ("one's own") to underscore that the wife's submission is restricted to her own husband. Verses 1, 5, and 6, which refer to submission, read: "Likewise, wives [*gynaikes*], submit yourselves [*hypotassomenai*] to your own husbands [*tois idiois andrasin*], that even if some do not obey the word, they, without a word, may be won by the conduct of their wives, . . . [vv. 2-4 describe appropriate adornment]. For in this manner, in former times, the holy women who trusted in God also adorned themselves, submitted themselves [*hypotassomenai*] to their own husbands [*tois idiois andrasin*], as Sarah listened to [*hypēkousen*] Abraham, calling him lord, whose daughters you are if you do good and are not afraid with any terror."

In brief, Peter gives basically the same "household code" counsel found in the Pauline materials, but specifically addresses wives whose husbands are unbelievers. The call to "chaste conduct" (v. 2), inward adornment of a "gentle and quiet spirit" (v.4), and submission to one's own husband (vv. 1, 5-6) is not just a culturally bound strategy for winning the unbelieving spouse; it is behavior "very precious in the sight of God" (v. 4) and an imitation of the Old Testament example of Sarah's submission to her believing husband Abraham (vv. 5-6). To the believing husbands, Peter gives counsel comparable to that of Paul: he urges the husband to "live considerately with" and "give honor to the wife, as to the weaker vessel,"[93] with whom he is equal partner, "joint heirs of the grace of life" (v. 7).

We turn now to 1 Tim 2:8-15, the final New Testament "submission" passage in a context of men-women relationships. Since this passage has already been examined in detail in chapter 16, we will address only whether the instruction in vv. 11-12 refers to men and women in general or specifically to husband-wife relationships, and to whom the "submission" (*hypotagē*) in v. 11 is to be made.

Already with Martin Luther, 1 Tim 2:11-12 was understood as referring to the husband-wife relationship and not to men and women in general.[94] A number of other commentators since then have contended for the marital reference in this passage.[95] In the same trajectory of understanding, the Williams version of the New Testament renders vv. 11-12 in this way: "A married woman must learn in quiet and perfect submission. I do not permit a married woman to practice teaching or domineering over a husband. She must keep quiet."[96]

More recently, several scholars have argued cogently that *gynē* and *anēr* in these verses should be translated as "wife" and "husband" respectively, and not simply "woman" and "man."[97] A number of lines of evidence strongly support this conclusion.

First, as Hugenberger demonstrates, everywhere else in the Pauline writings, and in fact throughout the whole New Testament, where *gynē* and *anēr* are found paired in close proximity, the reference is consistently to wife and husband and not women and men in general.[98]

Second, the movement from the plural in vv. 8-10 to the singular in vv. 11-12 seems to highlight the focus upon the wife and her husband, especially in these latter verses.[99]

Third, the reference to the married couple, Adam and Eve, in vv. 13-14, provides a marital context to the passage.

Fourth, the reference to childbirth in v. 15, and the shift back to the plural "they" (probably referring to both husband and wife as parents of the child, or perhaps broadening again to speak of wives in general as in vv. 9-10), certainly provides a marital context.

Fifth, the reference to "submission" (*hypotassō*) in a setting of man-woman relationships elsewhere in Paul always refers to the submission of the wife to her husband. Hugenberger rightly points out that "in the face of this established pattern of usage only the most compelling evidence should be allowed to overturn the presumption that *hypotagē* ("submission") in 1 Timothy 2 has to do with a requirement specifically for wives rather than women in general."[100]

Sixth, strong parallels with 1 Cor 14:34-36 (a passage dealing with husbands and wives, as discussed above) point to a similar context of husband-wife relationships in 1 Timothy 2. In particular, E. E. Ellis has noted striking verbal and conceptual similarities between the two passages: "to allow or permit" (*epitrepesthai*), "silence" (*sigaō, hēsychia*), "submission" (*hypotassesthai, hypotagē*), "learn" (*manthanō*), and the allusion to Genesis 2-3.[101]

Finally, the most determinative line of evidence supporting the "husband-wife" context of 1 Tim 2:8-15 is found in the extensive verbal, conceptual, and structural parallels between this passage and the household code of 1 Peter 3. Various scholars have recognized that the parallels between these two passages are so impressive that one passage must be dependent upon the other or both go back to a common tradition.[102] Hugenberger has set forth most comprehensively the extensive parallelism. In a chart displaying the two passages in parallel columns he highlights the detailed verbal correspondences, including the rare New Testament terms for "adornment," "quiet," and "braided" hair.[103]

Both passages have the same structural flow of logic and thought, moving from a discussion of wifely submission, to the specific counsel on her proper adornment, and then to an Old Testament paradigm for proper marital relationships (Adam-Eve, Abraham-Sarah). The only significant difference in order is that Paul puts the additional counsel to husbands first (1 Tim 2:8), while Peter puts it last (1 Pet 3:7). But even this counsel to husbands shows striking linkages between the two passages, since the shared warning of problems hindering prayer life occurs only rarely elsewhere in Scripture. Inasmuch as 1 Peter 3 is a "household code" unambiguously dealing with interrelationships of husbands and wives, it is difficult to escape the same conclusion for the corresponding Pauline passage in 1 Timothy 2.[104]

In light of the preceding lines of evidence, Paul here addresses the relationship of husbands and wives and not men and women in general. It would be in harmony with this conclusion to see the "submission" (*hypotagē*) called for on the part of the wife (v. 11) as submission to her husband, as in all the other *hypotassō* passages dealing with man-woman relations, although it must be recognized that the passage does not explicitly state to whom the wife is to submit.[105]

The thrust of Paul's counsel in this passage serves to safeguard the headship/submission principle in the marital relation between husband and wife. Paul "do[es] not permit a *wife* (*gynaiki*) to teach—that is, to boss her *husband* (*andros*); she must be *quiet* (*hesychia*)."[106] Hugenberger rightly concludes that "Paul's concern is to prohibit only the sort of teaching that would constitute a failure of the requisite wifely 'submission' to her husband."[107]

We must briefly note than in 1 Tim 2:13 Paul is not arguing for a creation headship of man over woman, as has often been assumed. Rather, he is correcting a false syncretistic theology in Ephesus, which claimed that *woman* was created first and *man* fell first, and therefore women were superior to men. Because of this false theology, wives were apparently domineering over their husbands in public church meetings.[108]

Conclusion. We have surveyed all of the New Testament passages employing the terms "head" (*kephalē*) and "submit" (*hypotassō*). Our conclusion is straightforward and unambiguous: the New Testament writers remain faithful to the Old Testament pattern established in the Garden of Eden. Just as in Genesis 3 the headship/submission principle was established for husband-wife relationships, so the New Testament passages affirm this ordering of roles. But just as the equal partnership was described in Gen 2:24 as the divine ideal for after the Fall as well as before, so the New Testament counsel calls husbands and wives to a loving partnership of mutual submission.

Perhaps the most crucial finding of this survey is that *all* of the New Testament passages regarding "headship" and "submission" between men and women are limited to the marriage relationship.

Headship/Submission/Equality of Men and Women in the Christian Church

A headship/submission principle is at work in the apostolic church. But it does not consist of male leaders in the headship role and women submitting to the male headship. Rather, according to the New Testament witness there is only one Head—Jesus Christ. He is the "husband" to the church, and all the church—both men and women, as His bride—are to submit to His headship. This is the clear teaching of Ephesians 5.

Neither is there any earthly priestly leader in the early church, no clergy functioning as a mediator between God and the people. The New Testament clearly presents the "priesthood of all believers" (1 Pet 2:5, 9; cf. Rom 12:1; Heb 13:15; Rev 1:6), in which all Christians are priests ministering for and representing God to the world. Within this priesthood of all believers, there are various spiritual gifts involving leadership functions (Rom 12:3-8; Eph 4:11-15; 1 Cor 12:1-11) that are distributed by the Spirit "to each individually as He will" (1 Cor 12:11), with no mention of any restrictions based upon gender.[109]

In the New Testament, the Magna Charta of true biblical equality is contained in Paul's emphatic declaration: "There is neither Jew nor Greek, there is neither slave nor free, there is neither male nor female: for you are all one in Christ Jesus" (Gal 3:28). This is not merely a statement on equal access to salvation (cf. Gal 2:11-15; Eph 2:14-15). Rather, it specifically singles out those three relationships in which God's original plan in Eden had been perverted by making one group unequal to another: (1) Jew-Gentile, (2) slave-free, and (3) male-female. By using the rare terms "male-female" (*arsen-thēly*) instead of "husband-wife" (*anēr-gynē*), Paul establishes a link with Gen 1:27 and thus shows how the Gospel calls us back to the divine ideal, which has no place for general subordination of females to males. At the same time, Paul's choice of terminology upholds the equality of men and women in the church, without changing the position of the husband as head of the family.[110]

Within the social restraints of his day, Paul and the early church (like Jesus[111]) did not act precipitously. The inequality of Gentiles was difficult to root out, even in Peter (Gal 2:11-14). Slavery was not immediately abolished in the church (Eph 6:5-9; Col 3:22; 1 Tim 6:1), and yet the principles of the gospel were set forth to begin to lead back to the Edenic ideal (as evidenced in Paul's revolutionary counsel to Philemon). While women may not have immediately received full and equal partnership with men in the ministry of the church, the evidence of women in leadership roles in the early church is sufficient to demonstrate that they were not barred from positions of influence, leadership, and even headship over men.

Examples of women in church leadership/headship roles have been ably presented in Robert Johnston's and Jo Ann Davidson's chapters (chaps. 3 and 9). Deacons included the woman Phoebe (Rom 16:1) and probably the women referred to in 1 Tim 3:11.[112] The evidence points toward Junia as a female apostle.[113] The women at Phillippi, including Euodia and Syntyche (Phil 4:2, 3), are described as the leaders of the local congregation.[114] The "elect lady" (2 John 1) may have been an ecclesiastical title; and the one bearing this title, to whom John addresses his second epistle, may have been a prominent woman church leader with a congregation under her care.[115] The woman Priscilla assumed an authoritative teaching role over men (Acts 18),[116] and women prophetesses carried out authoritative teaching roles in the early church.[117] Paul also mentions other women that ministered together with him as coworkers (*synergos*),[118] and his readers are instructed to "submit" (*hypotassō*) to such workers (see 1 Cor 16:16).

In short, there is ample New Testament evidence that nothing barred women in the earliest Christian churches from holding the highest offices of leadership, including authoritative teaching roles that constituted "headship" over men.

Conclusion and Implications

Along with the spate of books and articles representing the "egalitarian" and "hierarchical" positions on women's ordination, a growing body of literature in the evangelical scholarly community realizes that the Bible goes beyond *both* "egalitarian" and "hierarchical" models. These studies of man-woman relationships in the Old Testament and in the earliest churches are showing that throughout Scripture the headship/submission principle remains in effect in husband-wife relationships (in harmony with the view of the "hierarchialists" but contrary to the views of most "egalitarians"). At the same time, this headship/submission principle does not extend into the man-woman relationships in the covenant community, to bar women from positions of influence, leadership, and even headship over men (in harmony with the views of "egalitarians" but contrary to the views of "hierarchalists").

An example of this research is the work of Donald Bloesch, who sees Scripture consistently supporting the concerns of *both* "patriarchalism" ("hierarchalism") and "feminism" ("egalitarianism"). Bloesch states: "As the wife of her husband, the woman is obliged to serve and support him as a helpmate in the Lord. But as a sister in Christ, she has equal spiritual status with her husband."[119]

Ben Witherington similarly concludes that the New Testament continues biblical patriarchy ("headship") in the home, and at the same time affirms new roles for women in the church that do not preclude women's ordination to ministry. He writes:

> The question of women's ordination is not discussed or dismissed in the New Testament, but there is nothing in the material that rules out such a possibility. If the possibilities for women in the earliest churches, as evidenced in the New Testament, should be seen as models for church practice in subsequent generations, then it should be seen that women in the New Testament era already performed the tasks normally associated with ordained clergy in later times. These roles seem to be clearly supported by various New Testament authors.
>
> At the same time, note that there is no evidence in the New Testament material investigated in this study of any sort of radical repudiation of the traditional family structure. Headship comes to mean head servant, or taking the lead in serving, but this is not quite the same as some modern notions of an egalitarian marriage structure.[120]

One more example will be cited. Sharon Gritz, in her recent study of 1 Tim 2:9-15 in its larger religious and cultural context, concludes that this passage is dealing with husband-wife relations. She then draws the broader implications:

> This interpretation eliminates any contradiction between this passage and other biblical materials. It restates the teaching of 1 Cor. 14:34-36. It also permits the exercise of spiritual gifts by all women, both married and single. Thus, 1 Tim. 2:9-15 does not contradict Jesus' relation with and teachings about women nor Paul's relationship with women coworkers and his affirmation of their participation in the worship of the church (1 Cor. 11:2-16). All women do have the right to enter the ministry as God so calls and equips them. The New Testament

examples verify this. The normative principle underlying 1 Tim 2:9-15 is that marriage qualifies a married woman's ministry. A wife's commitment and obligations to her husband should shape her public ministry.[121]

Our conclusions coincide with these recent studies. We have found that the biblical witness is consistent with regard to the divine ideal for headship/submission/equality in man-woman relationships. Before the Fall there was full equality with no headship/submission in the relationship between Adam and Eve (Gen 2:24). But after the Fall, according to Gen 3:16, the husband was given a servant headship role to preserve the harmony of the home, while at the same time the model of equal partnership was still set forth as the ideal. This post-Fall prescription of husband headship and wife submission was limited to the husband-wife relationship. In the divine revelation throughout the rest of the Old Testament and New Testament witness, servant headship and voluntary submission on the part of husband and wife, respectively, are affirmed, but these are *never* broadened to the covenant community in such a way as to prohibit women from taking positions of leadership, including headship positions over men.

Endnotes

1. For a succinct overview of the recent debate over the ordination of women in evangelical churches, see Stanley J. Grenz, *Women in the Church: A Biblical Theology of Women in Ministry* (Downers Grove, IL: InterVarsity, 1995), 13-35.

2. This group was organized in Danvers, Massachusetts in December 1987 and published its manifesto on the relationship between the sexes (called the "Danvers Statement") in November 1988. A major collection of essays propagating this position is: John Piper and Wayne A. Grudem, eds. *Recovering Biblical Manhood and Womanhood: A Response to Evangelical Feminism* (Wheaton, IL: Crossway, 1991).

3. This group was organized in 1987 under the special impetus of its founder, Catherine Clark Kroeger, and received its formal nonprofit organization status in 1988. From the first CBE (Christians for Biblical Equality) conference in the summer of 1989 came the position document entitled "Statement on Men, Women and Biblical Equality." Representative publications include Catherine Kroeger and Richard Kroeger, *I Suffer Not a Woman: Rethinking 1 Timothy 2:11-15 in Light of Ancient Evidence* (Grand Rapids: Baker, 1992); and Rebecca Merrill Groothuis, *Good News for Women: A Biblical Picture of Gender Equality* (Grand Rapids: Baker, 1997).

4. The material in this section is a revision and adaption of parts of my two articles, "The Theology of Sexuality in the Beginning: Gen 1-2," *Andrews University Seminary Studies* 26 (1988): 5-24; and "The Theology of Sexuality in the Beginning: Gen 3," *Andrews University Seminary Studies* 26 (1988): 121-131.

5. Helmut Thielicke, *The Ethics of Sex* (New York: Harper & Row, 1964), 7.

6. See, for examples, Samuele Bacchiocchi, *Women in the Church: A Biblical Study on the Role of Women in the Church* (Berrien Springs, MI: Biblical Perspectives, 1987), 31, 71-79; Karl Barth, *Church Dogmatics*, 3/1 (Edinburgh: T & T Clark, 1960), 300; Barth, 3/2, 386-387; Stephen B. Clark, *Man and Woman in Christ: An Examination of the Roles of Men and Women in the Light of Scripture and the Social Sciences* (Ann Arbor, MI: Servant Books, 1980), 23-28; Jerry D. Colwell, "A Survey of Recent Interpretations of Women in the Church" (Master's thesis, Grand Rapids Baptist Seminary, 1984); Susan T. Foh, *Women and the Word of God: A Response to Biblical Feminism* (Phillipsburg, NJ: Presbyterian and Reformed, 1979), 61-62; S. H. Hooke, "Genesis," *Peake's Commentary on the Bible* (London: Thomas Nelson, 1962), 179; James B. Hurley, *Man and Woman in Biblical Perspective* (Grand Rapids: Zondervan, 1981), 206-214; Edmond Jacob, *Theology of the Old Testament* (New York: Harper, 1958), 156-157; Piper and Grudem, 99.

7. Phyllis Trible, *God and the Rhetoric of Sexuality* (Philadelphia: Fortress, 1978), 73.

8. C. F. Keil, *The First Book of Moses (Genesis)* (Grand Rapids: Eerdmans, 1949), 1:89.

9. For discussion of this construction, see especially the following: James Muilenburg, "Form Criticism and Beyond," *Journal of Biblical Literature* 88 (1969): 9-10; Mitchel Dahood, *Psalms*, Anchor Bible (New York: Doubleday, 1966), 1:5; Phyllis Trible, "Depatriarchalizing in Biblical Interpretation," *Journal of American Academy of Religion* 41 (1973): 36.

10. Muilenburg, 9.

11. Trevor Dennis, *Sarah Laughed: Women's Voices in the Old Testament* (Nashville: Abingdon, 1994), 13. Both Gen 2:7 and 2:21b-22 contain 16 Hebrew words describing the creation of man and woman, respectively.

12. Dennis notes: "Indeed, [her creation] represents the high point of the whole story of the Garden" (16).

13. This is the phrase coined by Sakae Kubo, *Theology and Ethics of Sex* (Washington, DC: Review and Herald, 1980), 19.

14. As we will see below, the interpretation of Genesis 2 set forth here does not contradict Paul's reference to this passage in 1 Tim 2:13.

15. John Calvin, *Commentary on Genesis* (Grand Rapids: Eerdmans, n.d.), 217-218.

16. Exod 18:4; Deut 33:7, 26; Ps 33:20; 70:5; 115:9, 10, 11.

17. R. David Freedman argues that the Hebrew word '*ēzer* etymologically derives from the merger of two Semitic roots, '*zr*, "to save, rescue" and *gzr* "to be strong," and in this passage has reference to the latter: woman is created, like the man, "a power (or strength) superior to the animals" ("Woman, A Power Equal to Man," *Biblical Archaeology Review*, Jan-Feb. 1983, 56-58).

18. Ludwig Kohler and Walter Baumgartner, *Lexicon in Veteris Testament Libros*, 2d ed. (Leiden: E. J. Brill, 1958; Grand Rapids: Eerdmans, 1951), 591; Samuel L. Terrien points out that the semantic range of *neged* includes connotations of "vigor, courage, efficiency,

adventurousness, and presence," and that "the verbal root *nagad*, 'to go ahead,' suggests achievement, pioneering, risk, and deliberate thrust into the unknown" (*Till the Heart Sings: A Biblical Theology of Manhood and Womanhood* [Philadelphia: Fortress, 1985], 11).

19. *The New Brown, Driver, and Briggs Hebrew and English Lexicon of the Old Testament* (Lafayette, IN: Associated Publishers and Authors, 1981), 617 (hereafter cited as BDB).

20. Gerhard von Rad, *Old Testament Theology*, trans. D.M.G. Stalker (New York: Harper & Row, 1962), 1:149.

21. Freedman, 56-58. Freedman notes that in later Mishnaic Hebrew *kᵉneged* clearly means "equal," and in light of various lines of Biblical philological evidence he forcefully argues that the phrase ʿ*ēzer kᵉnegdô* here should be translated "a power equal to him."

22. Ibid., 56; Gen 2:18, NEB. As we will see below, Paul's allusion to woman being created "for the man, and not man for the woman" (1 Cor 11:9) does not contradict the interpretation set forth here.

23. Trible, 101.

24. Samuel Terrien, "Toward a Biblical Theology of Womanhood," in *Male and Female: Christian Approaches to Sexuality*, ed. Ruth T. Barnhouse and Urban T. Holmes, III (New York: Seaburg, 1976), 18. Terrien also notes that "the use of the verb 'to build' for the woman implies an intellectual and aesthetic appreciation of her body, the equilibrium of her forms, and the volumes and proportions of her figure" (*Till the Heart Sings*, 12).

25. As we will see below, Paul's argument that "man is not from woman, but woman from man" (1 Cor 11:8) does not contradict the interpretation set forth here.

26. BDB, 854. Numerous theories have been propounded to explain the meaning of the rib in this story. For example, J. Boehmer suggests that the "rib" is a euphemism for the birth canal which the male lacks ("Die geschlechtliche Stellung des Weibes in Gen 2 und 3," *Monatschrift für Geschichte und Wissenschaft des Judentums* 79 [1939]: 292); Paul Humbert proposes that the mention of the "rib" explains the existence of the navel in Adam (*Etudes sur le récit du Paradis* [Neuchâtel: Secrétariat de l'Université, 1940], 57-58); and Gerhard von Rad finds the detail of the rib answering the question why ribs cover the upper but not lower part of the body (*Genesis: A Commentary*, trans. John H. Marks [London: SCM, 1972], 82). Such suggestions appear to miss the overall context of the passage, with its emphasis upon the *relationship* between man and woman.

27. Claus Westermann, *Genesis* (Neukirchen-Vluyn: Neukirchener Verlag, 1974), 230.

28. Raymond Collins, "The Bible and Sexuality," *Biblical Theology Bulletin* 7 (1977): 153. It may be that the Sumerian language retains the memory of the close relationship between "rib" and "life," for the Sumerian sign signifies both "life" and "rib." See Samuel N. Kramer, *History Begins at Sumer: Thirty-nine Firsts in Man's Recorded History* (Garden City, NY: Doubleday, 1959), 146. This is not to say, however, that the detail of the rib in Genesis 2 has its origin in Sumerian mythology. The story of Creation in Genesis 2 and the Sumerian myth in which the pun between "lady of the rib" and "lady who makes live" appears (James B. Pritchard, ed. *Ancient Near Eastern Texts Relating to the Old Testament*, 3d. ed. [Princeton, NJ: Princeton Univ. Press, 1969], 37-41) have virtually nothing in common.

29. Keil, 1:89.

30. Trible, "Depatriarchalizing," 37.

31. Ellen G. White, *Patriarchs and Prophets*, 46. Peter Lombard makes a similar remark: "Eve was not taken from the feet of Adam to be his slave, nor from his head to be his ruler, but from his side to be his beloved partner" (quoted in Stuart B. Babbage, *Christianity and Sex* [Chicago: InterVarsity, 1963], 10); a similar statement is attributed to other writers as well.

32. Collins, 153.

33. Walter Brueggemann, "Of the Same Flesh and Bone (Gen 2:23a)," *Catholic Biblical Quarterly* 32 (1970): 540.

34. For examples of the Oriental view of naming as the demonstration of one's exercise of a sovereign right over a person, see 2 Kgs 23:34; 24:17; Dan 1:7. Cf. *Interpreter's Dictionary of the Bible*, 3:502.

35. See Jacques Doukhan, *The Genesis Creation Story* (Berrien Springs, MI: Andrews Univ. Press, 1978), 46-47. For other lines of evidence disaffirming man's authoritative naming of woman in Gen 2:23, in contrast to his authoritative naming of the animals in Gen 2:19-20, see especially Trible, *God and the Rhetoric of Sexuality*, 99-100; and Gerhard Hasel, "Equality from the Start: Woman in the Creation Story," *Spectrum* 7, no. 2 (1975): 23-24.

36. White, 46.

37. See Barth, 3/2:291; Trible, *God and the Rhetoric of Sexuality*, 100.

38. Ibid., 96.

39. Calvin, for instance, sees woman's position before the Fall as "liberal and gentle subjection," but after the Fall she is "cast into servitude" (172). Keil similarly understands the original position of man-woman as rule/subordination rooted in mutual esteem and love, but he argues that after sin the woman has a "desire bordering on disease" and the husband exercises 'despotic rule' over his wife" (103). Hurley concurs with a pre-Fall hierarchy of the sexes and a post-Fall distortion, but argues that Gen 3:16 should be interpreted along the lines of the similarly worded statement of God to Cain in Gen 4:7 (218-219). Just as God warned Cain that sin's *desire* would be to *control* him, but he must *master* it, so woman's desire would be to control/manipulate man and the husband must master her desire. Cf. a similar position in Bacchiocchi, 79-84.

40. Clark, 35. Clark does not rule out view two as a possibility, but he more strongly favors view one. See also Ambrose, *De Paradiso* 350 (quoted in Clark, 677): "Servitude, therefore, of this sort is a gift of God. Wherefore, compliance with this servitude is to be reckoned among blessings."

41. Gilbert G. Bilezikian, *Beyond the Sex Roles: A Guide for the Study of Female Roles in the Bible* (Grand Rapids: Baker, 1985), 54-56; Collins, 19; Patricia Gundry, *Woman Be Free!* (Grand Rapids: Zondervan, 1977), 60-63; Mary Hayter, *The New Eve in Christ: The Use and Abuse of the Bible in the Debate about Women in the Church* (Grand Rapids: Eerdmans, 1987), 107, 113-114; Paul K. Jewett, *Man as Male and Female: A Study of Sexual Relationships from a Theological Point of View* (Grand Rapids: Eerdmans, 1975), 114;

William E. Phipps, *Genesis and Gender: Biblical Myths of Sexuality and Their Cultural Impact* (New York, 1989), 51-52; Elizabeth Schüssler-Fiorenza, "Interpreting Patriarchal Traditions," in *The Liberating Word: A Guide to Nonsexist Interpretation of the Bible*, ed. Letty M. Russell (Philadelphia: Westminster, 1976), 48-49; Leonard Swidler, *Biblical Affirmations of Women* (Philadelphia: Westminster, 1979), 80; Thielicke, 8; Trible, "Depatriarchalizing," 41.

42. See Francis Schaeffer, *Genesis in Space and Time: The Flow of Biblical History* (Downers Grove, IL: InterVarsity, 1975), 93-94; cf. Theodorus C. Vriezen, *An Outline of Old Testament Theology*, 2d rev. ed. and enl. (Oxford: Blackwell, 1970), 399.

43. John H. Otwell, *And Sarah Laughed: The Status of Women in the Old Testament* (Philadelphia: Westminster, 1977), 18.

44. Within this same general "feminist" perspective, Carol L. Meyers provides a drastic sociological reinterpretation in which the whole Genesis 3 story is derived from a Palestinian social condition requiring more intense agricultural work and increased childbirths. According to Meyers, the story does not concern the "Fall" at all; Gen 3:16 calls for woman to increase both (*agricultural*) labor (*ʿiṣṣābôn*) and *procreation*, while the man is also to increase his labor, in fact "predominate" (*māšal*) over the woman, i.e., do more agricultural work than she, because she has the responsibility of childbirths that he does not. This whole reinterpretation assumes the nonhistorical character of Genesis 3 and a much later hypothetical *Sitz im Leben* ("Gender Roles and Gen 3:16 Revisited," in *The Word of the Lord Shall Go Forth: Essays in Honor of David Noel Freedman in Celebration of His Sixtieth Birthday*, ed. Carol L. Meyers and M. O'Connor [Winona Lake, IN: Eisenbrauns, 1983], 337-354).

45. Carol Meyers, *Discovering Eve: Ancient Israelite Women in Context* (New York: Oxford Univ. Press, 1988), 117.

46. See the discussion in Meyers, 99; also 110-111.

47. See *Theological Wordbook of the Old Testament* (*TWOT*), 1:534. Recent attempts by some feminists to translate *māšal* as "to be like" or "to resemble" instead of "to rule" face insurmountable lexical/grammatical/contextual obstacles. It is true that (following BDB nomenclature) the root *mšl^I* in the *Niphʿal* does signify ("to be like, similar,") but in Gen 3:16 the root *mšl* is in the *Qal*. Both *mšl^II* ("to use a proverb") and *mšl^III* ("to rule") occur in the *Qal*, but the context of Gen 3:16 seems to clearly preclude the idea of "use a proverb" (*mšl^II*). That *mšl^III* "to rule" is intended in this passage is confirmed by the use of the accompanying preposition *bʿ*, the normal preposition following *mšl^III* (cf. BDB, 605), and other Hebrew words of ruling, governing, restraining (*mlk, rdh, šlt, śr*, etc.), and never used with *mšl^I* or *mšl^II*. Tempting as they may be, arguments based largely on the meaning of ancient Semitic cognates (where *māšal* does consistently mean "to resemble") cannot be allowed to override the biblical context, grammar, syntax, and usage. Suggestions of the the retrojection of the meaning "to rule" back into the Fall narrative by later redaction, under the influence of an Egyptian cognate, although appealing, unfortunately rest on speculation without textual support.

48. Vriezen, 399.

49. Umberto Cassuto, *A Commentary on the Book of Genesis*, (Jerusalem: Magnes, 1989), 1:165.

50. *Patriarchs and Prophets*, 59; emphasis supplied.

51. BDB, 921-922; *TWOT*, 2:833.

52. John Skinner, *Genesis*, International Critical Commentary (Edinburgh: T. & T. Clark, 1930), 53.

53. See, e.g., 2 Sam 23:3; Prov 17:2; Isa 40:10; 63:19; Zech 6:13. See Robert D. Culver, "Māshal III," *TWOT*, 1:534: "*Māshal* usually receives the translation 'to rule,' but the precise nature of the rule is as various as the real situations in which the action or state so designated occur." Specific examples follow to support this statement. Note, e.g., that the first usage of *māšal* in Scripture is in reference to the two great lights created by God (Gen 1:16)—they were to "dominate" (*Tanach*; New Jewish Version) the day and night.

54. Hurley has rightly pointed out how in each of the divine judgments in this chapter there is a blessing as well as a curse (216-219). In the curse upon the serpent appears a veiled blessing in the *Protoevangelion* (3:15): "the warfare between Satan and the woman's seed comes to its climax in the death of Christ" (Hurley, 217). For persuasive evidence in favor of this traditional interpretation, in contrast to the modern critical tendency to see here only an aetiological reference, see Walter C. Kaiser, *Toward an Old Testament Theology* (Grand Rapids: Zondervan, 1978), 35-37. Likewise, in the curse of the ground and the "toil" that is the punishment of Adam, there is at the same time a blessing in that God promises the ground will continue to yield its fruit and man will still be able to eat of it. Furthermore, the term *ba⁻bûr* employed in v. 17 probably means "for the sake of" (KJV) and not "because of" (RSV), inasmuch as the meaning of "because" is already expressed by *kî* earlier in the verse. The ground is cursed "for his [Adam's] sake"—that is, the curse is for Adam's benefit. Though it did result from Adam's sin, it also is to be regarded as "a discipline rendered needful by his sin, to place a check upon the indulgence of appetite and passion, to develop habits of self-control. It was a part of God's great plan for man's recovery from the ruin and degradation of sin" (White, *Patriarchs and Prophets*, 60).

55. Otwell cogently argues that the normal structure of Hebrew parallelism is followed here in that Gen 3:16*a* and *b* are in parallel and 3:16*c* and *d* are likewise in parallel. As the first two parallel members of this verse duplicate content with regard to childbearing, so "we may expect . . . that 'he shall rule over you' parallels 'your desire shall be for your husband'" (18). Otwell's argument is strengthened by the use of the conjunctive *waw* which serves to unite v. 16*a-b* with *c-d*, and is best translated by "yet" (RSV).

56. See BDB, 1003; *TWOT*, 2:913.

57. The only other occurrence of this word in the Hebrew Bible is Gen 4:7, which has no reference to a man-woman relationship. Despite the similarity of grammar and vocabulary, the latter verse must not be held up as a standard of interpretation for Gen 3:16, which involves a completely different context. Those who interpret Gen 3:16 by means of 4:7 generally hold to the hierarchy of the sexes as a creation ordinance, and therefore must find something *more* than subordination in 3:16. But it hardly seems justified to compare the experience of Eve with the picture of sin as a wild animal crouching in wait for his prey (Derek Kidner, *Genesis: An Introduction and Commentary* [Downers Grove, IL: InterVarsity, 1975], 75). For a discussion of the possible reasons for similar wording between the widely different contexts of Gen 3:16 and 4:7, see Cassuto, 1:212-213.

58. See Ellen White, *Patriarchs and Prophets*, 59.

59. Hasel, "Equality from the Start," 26. Note the parallel relationship of God the Father and Christ after the Incarnation (1 Cor 3:23; 11:3; 15:27-28).

60. As a verb: Gen 20:3: Deut 21:13; 22:22; 24:1; Isa 54:1, 5; 62:4-5; Jer 3:15; 31:32. As a noun, Gen 20:3; Exod 21:3, 22; Deut 22:24; 24:4; 2 Sam 11:26; Joel 1:8; Prov 12:4; 31:11, 23, 28; Esth 1:17, 20. The meaning of this word must not be pressed too far, however, for it often may simply denote polite respect.

61. Of course the Bible does depict occasions in which the husband usurps power and exploits his wife, treating her as inferior, as chattel, or even a nonperson, but these cases are not cited approvingly.

62. Roland de Vaux, *Ancient Israel: Its Life and Institutions* (Toronto: McGraw-Hill, 1961), 40.

63. Otwell, 111-112.

64. For evidence that the Song of Songs is a unified song of two lovers (Solomon and the Shulamite) who are bride and groom, and after the marriage ceremony (in the chiastic center of the book) become husband and wife, see Richard M. Davidson, "Theology of Sexuality in the Song of Songs: Return to Eden," *Andrews University Seminary Studies* 27 (1989): 1-19.

65. Swidler, 92.

66. Ibid. See also the discussion of the equality/mutuality theme in Phipps, 94-95. Phipps is probably correct in asserting that "Nowhere in ancient literature can such rapturous mutuality be paralleled" (94).

67. The count may vary, depending upon the interpretation of the sometimes ambiguous first-person statements. Donald Broadribb counts 207 poetic lines in the Song and attributes 118 of these to women ("Thoughts on the Song of Solomon," *AbrNahrain* 3 [1961-1962]: 18).

68. Trible, *God and the Rhetoric of Sexuality*, 161.

69. McCurley, 101.

70. Trible, "Depatriarchializing," 48.

71. Francis Landy, "The Song of Songs and the Garden of Eden," *Journal of Biblical Literature* 98 (1979): 526.

72. See Guenther Haas, "Patriarchy as an Evil That God Tolerated: Analysis and Implications for the Authority of Scripture," *Journal of Evangelical Theological Society* 38 (1995): 321-336. This is not to deny that the Old Testament does depict many incidents of gross inequalities for women perpetrated by men under the patriarchal system, but these situations were never the divine norm. They rather reflect perversion of the divine ideal set forth in Genesis 1-3. Note, e.g., the "texts of terror" concerning women as analyzed by Phyllis Trible, *Texts of Terror: Literary-Feminist Readings of Biblical Narratives* (Philadelphia: Fortress, 1984).

73. There is evidence that Deborah as a "judge" was in fact an elder of Israel. See Deuteronomy 1, which melds together Exodus 18 (the appointment of judges) and Numbers 11 (appointment of the 70 elders), with the implication that the two chapters are referring to the same office.

74. On this issue, see especially the syntheses by Ben Witherington, III, *Women in the Earliest Churches*, Society for New Testament Studies, Monograph Series (Cambridge: Cambridge Univ. Press, 1988), 5-23; Hurley, 58-78; Gregory E. Sterling, "Women in the Hellenistic and Roman Worlds (323 BCE–138 CE)," in *Essays on Women in Earliest Christianity*, ed. Carroll D. Osburn (Joplin, MO: College Press, 1993), 1:41-92; and Randall D. Chesnutt, "Jewish Women in the Greco-Roman Era," in *Essays on Women in Earliest Christianity*, 1:93-130.

75. On this issue, see the chapters by Jo Ann Davidson and Robert Johnston; cf. the surveys by Witherington, 128-182; Grenz, 71-80; and the excellent summary in Clarence Boomsma, *Male and Female, One in Christ: New Testament Teaching on Women in Office* (Grand Rapids: Baker, 1993), 21-26.

76. 1 Cor 11:3; Eph 1:22; 4:15; 5:23; Col 1:18; 2:10, 14.

77. See especially Berkeley and Alvera Mickelsen, "What Does *Kephalē* Mean in the New Testament?" in *Women, Authority and the Bible*, ed. Alvera Mickelsen (Downers Grove, IL: InterVarsity, 1986), 97-110; Gilbert G. Bilezikian, "A Critical Examination of Wayne Grudem's Treatment of *Kephalē* in Ancient Greek Texts," in *Beyond Sex Roles* (Grand Rapids: Baker, 1985), 215-252; Catherine Kroeger, "The Classical Concept of Head as 'Source,' in *Equal to Serve: Women and Men in the Church and Home*, ed. Gretchen G. Hull (Old Tappan, NJ: F. H. Revell, 1987), 267-283; and Gordon D. Fee, *The First Epistle to the Corinthians* (Grand Rapids: Eerdmans, 1987), 502-503. The impetus for this position seems to come from the study by S. Bedale, "The Meaning of *Kephalē* in the Pauline Epistles," *Journal of Theological Studies* 5 (1954): 211-215.

78. See Wayne Grudem, "Does *Kephalē* ('Head') Mean 'Source' or 'Authority Over' in Greek Literature? A Survey of 2,336 Examples," *Trinity Journal* 6, New Series (1985): 38-59; and idem, "The Meaning of *Kephalē* ('Head'): A Response to Recent Studies," Appendix 1 in Piper and Grudem, 425-468; Joseph A. Fitzmyer, "Another Look at *Kephalē* in 1 Corinthians 11:3," *New Testament Studies* 35/4 (1989): 503-511. Cf. Walter Bauer, *A Greek-English Lexicon of the New Testament and Other Early Christian Literature*, trans. and adapt. W. F. Arndt and F. W. Gingrich; 2d. ed., rev. F. W. Gingrich and F. W. Danker (Chicago: Univ. of Chicago Press, 1979), 431, where *kephalē* is seen "in the case of living beings, to denote superior rank."

79. See Kenneth V. Neller, "'Submission' in Eph 5:21-33," in *Essays on Women in Earliest Christianity*, 1: 251-260. See also Richard S. Cervin, "Does *kephalē* Mean 'Source' or 'Authority Over' in Greek Literature? A Rebuttal," *Trinity Journal*, New Series 10 (1989): 85-112. Cervin recognizes both the meaning "source" and "authority over" outside the New Testament (the latter only in the Septuagint and the *Shepherd of Hermas*), but suggests that in the Pauline usage, *kephalē* means neither "source" nor "authority over" but rather denotes "preeminence." I also avoid the use of the phrase "authority over" to describe headship and lean rather toward the denotation of "preeminence."

80. See Bauer, 855. Cf. James W. Thompson, "The Submission of Wives in 1 Peter," in *Essays on Women in Earliest Christianity*, 1: 382-385; Neller, 247-251.

81. For a succinct discussion of the New Testament "household tables" or *Haustafeln* in recent literature and in Ephesians 5, see Witherington, 42-61. Other New Testament "household codes" include Col 3:18-4:1; 1 Tim 2:8-15; 6:1-2; Titus 2:1-10; 1 Pet 2:18-3:7.

82. Scholars debate whether the phrase "submitting to one another" means that all parties in the discussions that follow (wives-husbands, children-parents, and slaves-masters) should have an attitude of submission to one another, or whether this means that in each of the relationships discussed, the one in inferior rank should submit to the one in superior rank. Regardless of what position is taken on this point, the context of Ephesians 5 indicates that the husband's role is one of a submissive servant leader (as we note below).

83. Bauer, 855.

84. Witherington, 220.

85. Ibid., 56.

86. See *Seventh-day Adventist Bible Commentary* 6:754, and numerous other commentators (some cited by Richards) who support this interpretation of 1 Cor 11:3.

87. See, for example, Carroll D. Osburn, "The Interpretation of 1 Cor. 14: 34-35," in *Essays on Women in Earliest Christianity*, 1:219-242; Sharon Gritz, *Paul, Women Teachers, and the Mother Goddess at Ephesus: A Study of 1 Timothy 2:9-15 in Light of the Religious and Cultural Milieu of the First Century* (Lanham, MD: University Press of America, 1991), 88-90; William Orr and James Walther, *I Corinthians: A New Translation* (Garden City, NY: Doubleday, 1976), 312; J. Massingbyrde Ford, "Biblical Material Relevant to the Ordination of Women," *Journal of Ecumenical Studies* 10 (1973): 681; E. Earle Ellis, "The Silenced Wives of Corinth (1 Cor. 14:34-35)," in *New Testament Textual Criticism: Its Significance for Exegesis*, ed. Eldon J. Epp and Gordon D. Fee (New York: Oxford Univ. Press, 1981), 218; Mary J. Evans, *Woman in the Bible: An Overview of All the Crucial Passages on Women's Roles* (Downers Grove, IL: InterVarsity, 1983), 100.

88. Krister Stendahl, *The Bible and the Role of Women: A Case Study in Hermeneutics*, trans. Emilie T. Sander (Philadelphia: Fortress, 1966), 29. See also the interpretation of *Seventh-day Adventist Bible Commentary*, 6:793: "The Scriptures teach that, on account of her part in the fall of man, woman has been assigned by God to a position of subordination to her husband (see Gen. 3:6, 16)."

89. Ellis, 218.

90. Gritz, 89.

91. See the helpful discussion of husband-wife relationships in the Colossian household code by Witherington, 47-54. The same basic points emerge from this passage as from Ephesians 5.

92. For a very helpful discussion showing that this is the meaning of the Greek and not that the wives should stay at home, see Stanley N. Helton, "Titus 2:5—Must Women Stay at Home?" in *Essays on Women in Earliest Christianity*, 1: 367-376.

93. There is no support for interpreting "the weaker vessel" in terms of intelligence or moral capabilities. The context of physical suffering and submission seems to indicate that what is intended here is the wife's physical weakness compared to her husband, or her submissive role relative to her husband's headship.

94. *Commentaries on 1 Corinthians 7, 1 Cor 15, Lectures on 1 Timothy, Luther's Works* 28, ed. H. C. Oswald (St. Louis, MO: Concordia, 1973), 276.

95. See bibliography in Gordon P. Hugenberger, "Women in Church Office: Hermeneutics or Exegesis? A Survey of Approaches to 1 Tim 2:8-15," *Journal of the Evangelical Theological Society* 35 (1992): 350-351.

96. Charles B. Williams, *The New Testament: A Translation in the Language of the People* (Chicago: Moody, 1937).

97. The most comprehensive presentation of evidence and critique of alternate views is Hugenberger, 350-360. See also B. W. Powers, "Women in the Church: The Application of 1 Tim 2:8-15," *Interchange* 17 (1975): 55-59; C. K. Barrett, *The Pastoral Epistles in the New English Bible* (Oxford: Clarendon, 1963), 55-56; Gritz, 125, 130-135; N. J. Hommes, "'Let Women Be Silent in Church': A Message Concerning the Worship Service and the Decorum to Be Observed by Women," *Calvin Theological Journal* 4 (1969): 13. Cf. M. Griffiths, *The Church and World Mission* (Grand Rapids: Zondervan, 1980), 196; R. Prohl, *Woman in the Church* (Grand Rapids: Zondervan, 1957), 80; F. Zerbst, *The Office of Woman in the Church* (St. Louis, MO: Concordia, 1955), 51.

98. Hugenberger, 353-354. In the Pauline writings, besides the "headship" and "submission" passages we have already looked at above, the following passages are in view: Rom 7:2-3; 1 Cor 7:2-4, 10-14, 16, 27, 29, 33-34, 39; 1 Tim 3:2, 3, 11-12; 5:9; Titus 1:6. In the rest of the New Testament, the only exceptions to this are where the terms occur in listings of individuals that stress the mixed nature of the group being described. Hugenberger concludes his lexical survey: "In summary, besides the use of *anēr* and *gynē* in lists (where the terms are generally found in the plural) there are no examples where *anēr* and *gynē* bear the meanings 'man' and 'woman' when the terms are found in close proximity" (354).

99. As we will argue from the parallel passage in 1 Peter 3 below, the context of the entire passage seems to be that of husbands and wives, but vv. 11-12, moving to the singular for both *gynē* and *anēr*, focus more directly on a wife's role vis-a-vis her husband.

100. Hugenberger, 355.

101. Ellis, 214.

102. E.g., E. G. Selwyn, *The First Epistle of St. Peter*, 2d ed. (London: Macmillan, 1946), 432-435; M. Dibelius and H. Conzelmann, *The Pastoral Epistles*, Hermeneia (Philadelphia: Fortress, 1972), 5. The interdependence and/or commonality of these two passages should not be surprising when it is remembered that according to available evidence both Paul and Peter wrote them about the same time (early A.D. 60s), Peter from Rome, and Paul just after having left Rome.

103. Hugenberger, 355-358.

104. This probably also implies that the setting of 1 Tim 2:8-15 is not primarily the church worship, but the home. See the careful argumentation by Powers, 55-59, and Hugenberger, 357-358.

105. Another alternative is that the submission is to the message of the gospel, as argued by Nancy Vyhmeister in chapter 16.

106. Translation of Hugenberger, 356. Italics and supplied Greek words his.

107. Ibid., 358. Hugenberger shows how this interpretation also indicates another parallel with 1 Peter 3. In both passages, the apostles are counseling the wives not to "teach" their husbands. Paul explicitly uses the words "teach" and "play the boss over" (1 Tim 2:12), while Peter (1 Pet 3:1) expresses the same warning with the synonymous phrase "without a word" (*aneu logou*), thus addressing "the very real danger of a wife vaunting herself over her husband with her superior knowledge" (ibid.).

108. For a careful analysis of the evidence for these conclusions, see Hommes, 5-22; Gritz, *passim*; and Nancy Vyhmeister's chapter in this book.

109. See the excellent discussion of spiritual gifts and equality in Grenz, 188-192. It should be noted that the qualifications for elder/bishop in 1 Tim 3:2 and Titus 1:6, are *not* gender exclusive, despite the claims of many hierarchalists. Both 1 Tim 3:1 and Titus 1:6 introduce the ones eligible for this office with the pronoun *tis* "anyone," not *anēr* "man." The phrase "husband of one wife"—literally "of-one-wife husband," with the word "one" (*mias*) put first in the phrase—is clearly emphasizing monogamy and not gender exclusiveness. This is confirmed a few verses later by 1 Tim 3:12, where the same phrase is used in the qualifications for a deacon, an office held by women in NT times (Rom 16:1).

110. For discussion of Gal 3:28, see Jan Faver Hailey, "'Neither Male and Female' (Gal. 3:28)," in *Essays on Women in Earliest Christianity*, 1:131-166; Grenz, 99-107; Witherington, 76-78; Boomsma, 31-41.

111. While Jesus treated women and Gentiles in a way that was revolutionary for His day (see Jo Ann Davidson's chapter on this), yet He did not ordain as one of His disciples either a Gentile or a woman. But this pattern was no more normative for the future roles of women in church leadership than for future roles of Gentiles.

112. See Barry L. Blackburn, "The Identity of the 'Women' in 1 Tim. 3:11," in *Essays on Women in Earliest Christianity*, 1: 302-319.

113. Along with Johnston's discussion, see also the evidence presented by Witherington, 114-115, and Grenz, 92-96.

114. See especially A. Boyd Luter, "Partnership in the Gospel: The Role of Women in the Church at Philippi," *Journal of the Evangelical Theological Society* 39 (1996): 411-420; and J. Paul Pollard, "Women in the Earlier Philippian Church (Acts 16:13-15; Phil 4:2-3) in Recent Scholarship," in *Essays on Women in Earliest Christianity*, 1:261-280.

115. See Grenz, 91-92. Another alternative is that the "elect lady" refers symbolically to the church; see Ellen White, *Acts of the Apostles*, 554.

116. See especially Wendell Willis, "Priscilla and Aquila—Co-Workers in Christ," in

Essays on Women in Earliest Christianity, 2:261-276.

117. See Gary Selby, "Women and Prophecy in the Corinthian Church," in *Essays on Women in Earliest Christianity*, 2:227-306.

118. See, e.g., the seven women mentioned in the list of Rom 16:1-16.

119. Donald G. Bloesch, *Is the Bible Sexist? Beyond Feminism and Patriarchalism* (Westchester, IL: Crossway, 1982), 55.

120. Witherington, 219-220.

121. Gritz, 158.

CHAPTER 14

EQUALITY, HEADSHIP, AND SUBMISSION IN THE WRITINGS OF ELLEN G. WHITE

PETER M. VAN BEMMELEN

Male and Female in Creation: Equal in All Things

Ellen White's views on the biblical teaching regarding the relationship between men and women naturally start with her understanding of that relationship in Creation. In a foundational chapter, "The Creation," she stresses that "man was not made to dwell in solitude; he was to be a social being." God provided Adam, created in his image, with an equal companion of the same nature. "Eve was created from a rib taken from the side of Adam, signifying that she was not to control him as the head, nor to be trampled under his feet as an inferior, but to stand by his side as an equal, to be loved and protected by him."[1] Clearly, neither of "the holy pair"[2] was to rule over the other; but "bone of his bone and flesh of his flesh, she was his second self, showing the close union and the affectionate attachment that should exist in this relation."[3]

Ellen White does not refer to Adam as the head of Eve in their sinless state, nor does she use words such as submission, subjection, or subordination to designate Eve's relation to Adam. On the contrary, she emphasizes their equality and companionship.

> When God created Eve, He designed that she should possess neither inferiority nor superiority to the man, but that in all things she should be his equal. The holy pair were to have no interest independent of each other; and yet each had an individuality in thinking and acting.[4]

The fact that the man and the woman "were to have no interest independent of each other" highlights God's intention for the close relationship between these two human beings. At the same time, each of them was a distinct individual with a personal relationship with God and a personal responsibility. "Endowed with high mental and spiritual gifts, Adam and Eve were made but 'little lower than the angels' (Hebrews 2:7), that they might not only discern the wonders of the visible universe, but comprehend moral responsibilities and obligations."[5]

Ellen White refers to Adam as "the father and representative of the whole human family,"[6] who under God "was to stand at the head of the earthly family, to maintain the principles of the heavenly family."[7] In view of the fact that Eve "was his second self,"[8] that "in all things she should be his equal," and that they "were to have no interest independent of each other,"[9] we may conclude that Eve fully shared in Adam's headship of God's earthly family. In a similar fashion, when we read that "Adam was crowned king in Eden, to him was given dominion over every living thing that God had created,"[10] it is evident that Eve equally exercised this dominion with him. "While they remained true to God, Adam and his companion were to bear rule over the earth. Unlimited control was given them over every living thing."[11]

In different words and in a variety of ways, Ellen White stresses not only the equality and the companionship of the first human pair, but also their dependence on God. "For all created beings there is the one great principle of life—dependence upon and co-operation with God."[12] Their acceptance or rejection of this great principle was to be tested by the prohibition to eat from the tree of the knowledge of good and evil. Without freedom of choice, "man would have been, not a free moral agent, but a mere automaton."[13]

The Fall and Its Consequences: A Changed Relationship

Unfortunately the first human couple, deceived by Satan, chose to disobey God's prohibition and go their own way. Ellen White highlights the real issue in an article, "The First Temptation":

> "Your eyes," said Satan, pointing to the tree, "shall be opened, and ye shall be as gods,"—independent. This had been the aim of Satan; this was why he fell from his high and holy estate. Now he sought to instill the same principle into the mind of Eve. He told her that God had forbidden her to eat of the fruit, in order to show his arbitrary authority, and to keep the holy pair in a state of dependence and subjection. He told her that in the violation of this commandment, advanced light would be hers, that she would be independent, untrammeled by the will of a superior. But Satan knew, as Eve did not, the result of disobedience, for he had tried it.[14]

Independence from God was the chimera that led first Eve, then Adam, into transgression. It was a fatal deception. The opposite of independence was the result. "From that time the race would be afflicted by Satan's temptations . . . ; anxiety and toil were to be their lot. They would be subject to disappointment, grief, and pain, and finally to death."[15] The relationship between the man and the woman was changed: "After Eve's sin, as she was first in transgression, the Lord told her that Adam should rule over her. She was to be in subjection to her husband, and this was a part of the curse."[16]

The reason for this change in the relationship between the woman and the man Ellen White clearly attributes to their sin.

> In the creation God had made her [Eve] the equal of Adam. Had they remained obedient to God—in harmony with His great law of love—they would ever have been in harmony with each other; but sin had brought discord, and now their union could be maintained and harmony preserved only by submission on the part of the one or the other. Eve had been the first in transgression; . . . and she was now placed in subjection to her husband.[17]

According to Ellen White, "this sentence, though growing out of the results of sin, would have proved a blessing" if "the principles enjoined in the law of God had been cherished by the fallen race," but unfortunately "man's abuse of the supremacy thus given him has too often rendered the lot of woman very bitter and made her life a burden."[18] The "supremacy" God gave to the man was to be used to protect and cherish the woman, not to oppress or abuse her.

The biblical teaching that God made the husband the head in the marriage relationship in the fallen condition of the human race is affirmed throughout Ellen White's writings. She often quotes Ephesians 5 on the relationship between husbands and wives. However, it is evident that she never understood this headship to mean that husbands could lord it over their wives or that it granted them the right to suppress the individuality of the women or to become their conscience.

In a manuscript entitled, "Relation of Husbands and Wives," she explains: "The Lord would have the wife render respect unto her husband, but always as it is fit in the Lord."[19] She illustrates this principle with the example of Abigail, the wife of the selfish, overbearing Nabal. Being informed of her husband's rude refusal to provide food for David and his men, "Abigail saw that something must be done to avert the result of Nabal's fault, and that she must take the responsibility of acting immediately without the counsel of her husband." She knew that it was useless to consult with him, for he would reject her plans and "remind her that he was the lord of his household, that she was his wife and therefore in subjection to him, and must do as he should dictate."[20] Ellen White concludes that from this history "we can see that there are circumstances under which it is proper for a woman to act promptly and independently, moving with decision in the way she knows to be the way of the Lord."[21]

As an example of a woman rightly refusing to obey a command of her husband, Ellen White refers to the experience of Queen Vashti. She comments on the command of King Ahasuerus recorded in Esth 1:10-11: "It was when the king was not himself, when his reason was dethroned by wine drinking that he sent for the queen, that those present at his feast, men besotted by wine, might gaze on her beauty." Then she approvingly notes Vashti's refusal: "She acted in harmony with a pure conscience. Vashti refused to obey the king's command, thinking that when he came to himself, he would commend her course of action." However, "the king had unwise advisors. They argued it would be a power given to woman that would be to her injury."[22] Evidently, Ellen White considered Vashti's refusal to be a legitimate exercise of her God-given moral responsibility and individuality. In her estimation, "The king should have honored the judgment of his wife; but both he and his counselors were under the influence of wine, and they were incapable of giving him counsel of the right order."[23]

The rule or headship bestowed on the husband after the Fall was never intended by God to lead to oppression of the wife or to interfere with her right and duty to make moral choices under God. Neither did it mean that women could never be used by God in a role of leadership. Of Deborah, Ellen White writes: "There was dwelling in Israel a woman illustrious for her piety, and through her the Lord chose to deliver his people. Her name was Deborah. She was known as a prophetess, and in the absence of the usual magistrates, the people had sought to her for counsel and justice."[24] The woman God chose was a married woman, "the wife of Lapidoth" (Judg 4:4). It seems that Lapidoth recognized that the Lord had the highest claims on the devotion and talents of his wife. In a more general way we are told by Ellen White that "in ancient times the Lord worked in a wonderful way through consecrated women who united in His work with men whom He had chosen to stand as His representatives. He used women to gain great and decisive victories."[25]

The Purpose of Redemption: Restoration

To Ellen White, "The central theme of the Bible, the theme about which every other in the whole book clusters, is the redemption plan, the restoration in the human soul of the image of God."[26] Elsewhere she writes,

> The true object of education is to restore the image of God in the soul.
> . . . Sin has marred and well-nigh obliterated the image of God in man.
> It was to restore this that the plan of salvation was devised, and a life of probation was granted to man. To bring him back to the perfection in which he was first created is the great object of life—the object that underlies every other.[27]

This restoration includes, for Ellen White, the restoration of God's original design in the relationship between man and woman. She states: "Like every other one of God's good gifts entrusted to the keeping of humanity, marriage has been perverted by sin; but it is the purpose of the gospel to restore its purity and beauty."[28] She attributes great significance to the fact that Christ performed the first miracle of His public ministry by changing water into wine at the marriage in Cana.[29]

> Christ knew all about the human family, and at the beginning of His public ministry He gave His decided sanction to the marriage He had sanctioned in Eden . . . . Christ came not to destroy this institution, but to restore it to its original sanctity and elevation. He came to restore the moral image of God in man, and He began His work by sanctioning the marriage relation. He who made the first holy pair, and who created for them a paradise, has put His seal upon the marriage institution, first celebrated in Eden, when the morning stars sang together, and all the sons of God shouted for joy.[30]

For Ellen White this restoration of marriage "to its original sanctity and elevation" certainly implies a restoration of the equality of husband and wife. "We have an earnest desire that woman shall fill the position which God originally designed, as her husband's equal."[31] However, she recognizes that Christ's work of restoration included men and women in every condition of life, whether married or single. "He paid a great price to redeem every son and daughter of Adam. He would lift man from the lowest degradation of sin up to purity again, and restore to him his moral image."[32]

In her deeply spiritual work on the life of Christ—*The Desire of Ages*—as well as in many other writings, Ellen White pays much attention to Christ's work for and through women. This is illustrated, for instance, in a chapter on Christ's encounter with the Samaritan woman at Jacob's well and the radical change wrought in her life as a result. With divine tact and wisdom he led her to the point where he could reveal himself to her as the Messiah. Ellen White comments, "She accepted the wonderful announcement from the lips of the divine Teacher. . . . She was ready to receive the noblest revelation; for she was interested in the Scriptures, and the Holy Spirit had been preparing her mind to receive more light." The effect was electrifying. "As soon as she had found the Saviour the Samaritan woman brought others to Him. She proved herself a more effective missionary than His own disciples."[33] In view of the many things Christ did for and through women, as recorded in the Gospels, Ellen White concludes that "He is woman's best friend today and is ready to aid her in all the relations of life."[34]

Like his Lord, Paul, according to Ellen White, taught the equality of all human beings. In a description of the apostle's presentation on Mars Hill to the scholars of Athens she states: "In that age of caste, when the rights of men were often unrecognized, Paul set forth the great truth of human brotherhood, declaring that God 'hath made of one blood all nations of men for to dwell on all the face of the earth' [Acts 17:26]." To this she adds that "in the sight of God all are on an equality, and to the Creator every human being owes supreme allegiance."[35]

Throughout her writings Ellen White often quotes from or alludes to the words of Paul in Gal 3:28 and Col 3:11. For instance, "Christ has made all one. In Him there is neither Jew nor Greek, bond nor free. The Bible declares that all human beings are to be respected as God's property. He loves men and women as the purchase of His own blood."[36] A remarkable paragraph in which she argues that all human beings "are of one family by creation, and all are one through redemption," and that "Christ came to demolish every wall of partition, to throw open every compartment of the temple [which would include the women's court], that every soul may have free access to God," is substantiated by words quoted from Gal 3:28 and Eph 2:13, "In Christ there is neither Jew nor Greek, bond nor free. All are brought nigh by His precious blood."[37]

While Ellen White clearly maintains that Christ, as well as Paul, the apostle of Christ, taught that all human beings, whether Jew or Greek, slave or free, male or female, were equal before God through the gospel, she also holds that neither Jesus nor Paul tried to overturn the established social order of their time. She states that while the government "under which Jesus lived was corrupt and oppressive," and "on every hand were crying abuses," nevertheless, "the Saviour attempted no civil reforms," neither did he "interfere with the authority or administration of those in power."[38] In another context she similarly observes that "He refused to interfere in temporal matters."[39] The reason for this refusal was not "because He was indifferent to the woes of men, but because the remedy did not lie in merely human and external measures. To be efficient, the cure must reach men individually, and must regenerate the heart."[40] Regarding Paul's attitude, we are told: "It was not the apostle's work to overturn arbitrarily or suddenly the established order of society. To attempt this would be to prevent the success of the gospel."[41] While Ellen White writes this regarding Paul's attitude toward the degrading system of slavery, the statement would apply to other issues of social injustice such as the inferior status of women. The conclusion seems justified that, according to Ellen White, the primary aim of the Lord Jesus and of his apostle was not social revolution but spiritual transformation. Where the principles of the gospel were wholeheartedly received, the image of God would be restored and radical changes in social relationships would follow.

The question naturally arises regarding how Ellen White's understanding of the biblical teaching on the equality of all human beings in God's sight relates to Paul's teaching concerning the relationship between husbands and wives. Throughout her writings, Ellen White frequently quotes from or alludes to Paul's words in Eph 5:22-33. She introduces one such quotation with the clear affirmation that:

> Paul the apostle, writing to the Ephesian Christians, declares that the Lord has constituted the husband the head of the wife, to be her protector, the house-band, binding the members of the family together, even as Christ is the head of the church and the Saviour of the mystical body.[42]

The headship which God entrusted to the husband was designed by God, as Ellen White understands Paul's teaching, to be after the pattern revealed in Christ's relation to the Church. "The husband is to be as a Saviour in his family."[43] By contrast, "it was not the design of God that the husband should have control, as head of the house, when he himself does not submit to Christ. He must be under the rule of Christ that he may represent the relation of Christ to the church."[44] Ellen White stresses how the headship of the husband and the submission of the wife are qualified by another passage from Paul's letters, Col 3:18:

> The question is often asked, "Shall a wife have no will of her own?" The

Bible plainly states that the husband is the head of the family. "Wives, submit yourselves unto your own husbands." If this injunction ended here, we might say that the position of the wife is not an enviable one; it is a very hard and trying position in very many cases, and it would be better were there fewer marriages. Many husbands stop at the words, "Wives, submit yourselves," but we will read the conclusion of the same injunction, which is, "As it is fit in the Lord."[45]

To this exposition Ellen White adds incisive comments on the limits placed by God on the submission of a wife to her husband:

God requires that the wife shall keep the fear and glory of God ever before her. Entire submission is to be made only to the Lord Jesus Christ, who has purchased her as His own child by the infinite price of His life. God has given her a conscience, which she cannot violate with impunity. Her individuality cannot be merged into that of her husband, for she is the purchase of Christ. It is a mistake to imagine that with blind devotion she is to do exactly as her husband says in all things, when she knows that in so doing, injury would be worked for her body and her spirit, which have been ransomed from the slavery of Satan. There is one who stands higher than the husband to the wife; it is her Redeemer, and her submission to her husband is to be rendered as God has directed—"as it is fit in the Lord."[46]

Ellen White apparently saw no conflict in Paul's teaching between the headship of the husband and the equality and unity of male and female in Christ Jesus. Both were taught by Paul; both are reiterated and affirmed by Ellen White. Although she quotes or alludes to Gal 3:28 a number of times, she makes no explicit comment in regard to the phrase "there is neither male nor female." But that the gospel makes us all one and equal in Christ is clearly her understanding of that text: "Christ has made all one. In Him there is neither Jew nor Greek, bond nor free. The Bible declares that all human beings are to be respected as God's property."[47] That, for Ellen White, this has significant implications for the role of women in marriage and family, as well as in the church, which we explore next.

Women in Marriage and Family: Equality and Companionship

How does Ellen White apply the principles of Scripture in regard to the position and the role of women in the modern world? She is firm in her conviction that "the Bible has been addressed to everyone,—to every class of society, to those of every clime and age. The duty of every intelligent person is to search the Scriptures."⁴⁸ If we could ask her, in the light of her understanding of Scripture, what the position of woman should be, she would give the answer she gave a century ago: "Woman should fill the position which God originally designed for her, as her husband's equal."⁴⁹ Although she is certainly aware of the fact that many women and men are single, either because they never married, or are divorced or widowed, Ellen White presents marriage and the family relationship as the basic one intended by God for the human race. It should, therefore, come as no surprise that much of what she has to say about the role of women is found in the context of that relationship. However, this emphasis in her writings does not diminish but rather enhances the importance of the principle of equality for all Christian relationships.

A high estimate of the role of women pervades Ellen White's writings: "No work can equal that of the Christian mother."⁵⁰ Ellen White flatly rejects the idea that a mother's work should be regarded as domestic drudgery. On the contrary, the wife and mother "should feel that she is her husband's equal" and that her work "in the education of her children is in every respect as elevated and ennobling as any part of duty he may be called to fill, even if it is to be the chief magistrate of the nation."⁵¹

While Ellen White recognizes that "the husband and father is the head of the household,"⁵² she lays great stress on the fact that he is to honor his wife as an equal. She rebuked one dictatorial husband: "You . . . have not been willing that your wife's judgment should have the weight it should in your family. . . . You have not made her your equal."⁵³ A young man considering marriage should face the question: "Is his wife to be his helper, his companion, his equal, or will he pursue toward her such a course that she cannot have an eye single to the glory of God?"⁵⁴ God's design for the wife "is to stand by the side of the husband as his equal, sharing all the responsibilities of life, rendering due respect to him who has selected her for his lifelong companion,"⁵⁵ and of course the husband is to respect his wife! Equality and companionship are key concepts for Ellen White in connection with the marriage relationship.

> Woman, if she wisely improves her time and her faculties, relying upon God for wisdom and strength, may stand on an equality with her husband as adviser, counselor, companion, and co-worker, and yet lose none of her womanly grace or modesty.⁵⁶

Of special interest is how Ellen White perceives the issue of individuality and independence in the marriage relationship. Of Adam

and Eve she writes: "The holy pair were to have no interest independent
of each other; and yet each had an individuality in thinking and acting."[57]
Ellen White repeatedly stresses the importance of the individuality of
each marriage partner. "Neither the husband nor the wife should merge
his or her individuality in that of the other. Each has a personal relation
to God. Of Him each is to ask, 'What is right?' 'What is wrong?' 'How
may I best fulfill life's purpose?'"[58] Similarly, she emphasizes that "woman
should have a staunch, noble independence of character, reliable and true
as steel." Such a woman, "who has good sense, who is connected with
God," will have "a just appreciation and accurate conception of her
position as a wife and mother," who stands "by the side of her husband
as his safe counselor, her influence keeping him to the right, to honesty
and purity and godliness."[59] Such "staunch, noble independence" is the
opposite of the independence which Satan offered to Adam and Eve, for
it is an independence rooted in submission to God in Jesus Christ, not an
independence apart from God.

Headship, Submission, and Equality in the Church

Ellen White is convinced that the essence of Christ's work is to
redeem men and women from the bondage of sin, to restore in them the
image of God, to break down all the barriers erected by human pride and
prejudice, and to unite all who believe in him in one body, the church,
of which he is the Head. The only headship in the church is the headship
of Christ. She emphatically denies that Christ ever entrusted the headship
to Peter or to any other of his disciples.

> Instead of appointing one to be their head, Christ said to the disciples,
> "Be not ye called Rabbi;" "neither be ye called masters; for one is your
> Master, even Christ." Matt. 23:8, 10. "The head of every man is Christ."
> God, who put all things under the Saviour's feet, "gave Him to be the
> head over all things to the church, which is His body, the fulness of
> Him that filleth all in all." 1 Cor. 11:3; Eph 1:22, 23. The church is built
> upon Christ as its foundation; it is to obey Christ as its head. It is not
> to depend upon man, or be controlled by man.[60]

Never does Ellen White quote biblical "headship" language in reference
to the human leadership of the church; neither is there any evidence in
her writings that she referred to ordained ministers in terms of headship.
While she upholds the biblical teaching of the husband as the head of the
wife, if he truly follows Christ as his example, she says nothing of a
comparable male headship in the church, except that Christ is the Head

of the church. We must, therefore, question any argument which claims that women should be excluded from the ordained ministry on the basis of a so-called headship principle.

Similarly, while Ellen White endorses Paul's injunction in Col 3:18: "Wives, submit yourselves unto your own husbands," with emphasis on the added qualification "as it is fit in the Lord," she never extrapolates from this that in the church all women should be submissive to an all-male leadership. What Ellen White does stress is that all true Christians, both men and women, will submit themselves to Christ as Lord and Head of the church. "Meekness and humility will characterize all who are obedient to the law of God, all who will wear the yoke of Christ with submission. . . . In learning Christ's meekness and lowliness, we shall submit the entire being to His control."[61] As a human being, Christ submitted himself completely to the will of his Father. He expects the same of all his followers. "Christ taught that all true goodness and greatness of character, all peace and joy in the soul, must come through perfect and entire submission to the Father's will, which is the highest law of duty."[62]

The only other submission that is binding upon all Christians, both men and women, is submission to the judgment of the united church. Ellen White expresses her concern that "Many do not realize the sacredness of the church relation, and are loath to submit to restraint and discipline"; they "exalt their own judgment above that of the united church," and do not care whether "they encourage a spirit of opposition to its voice."[63] While giving up their individuality is not required, "God would have His people disciplined and brought into harmony of action." To achieve this ideal, the "carnal heart must be subdued and transformed." As a basis for her statements, Ellen White quotes 1 Pet 5:5; Phil 2:1-5; and Eph 5:21.[64]

Clearly, of a submission in the church on the basis of race, nationality, wealth, education, or gender Ellen White—like the Bible—knows nothing. On the contrary, in a significant article entitled "No Caste in Christ," she stresses the equality of all believers. "In Christ we are one. . . . Calvary forever puts an end to man-made separations between class and race. . . . All who are found worthy to be counted as the members of the family of God in heaven, will recognize one another as sons and daughters of God."[65] She further states:

> The secret of unity is found in the equality of believers in Christ. The reason for all division, discord, and difference is found in separation

from Christ. Christ is the center to which all should be attracted; for the nearer we approach the center, the closer we shall come together in feeling, in sympathy, in love, growing into the character and image of Jesus. With God there is no respect of persons.[66]

More than a hundred times the words of Jesus in Matt 23:8, "all ye are brethren," are quoted in the published writings of Ellen White. Although some late-twentieth-century reader might consider this an expression of male chauvinism, Ellen White certainly did not think so. She interpreted these words as including men and women, brothers and sisters in Christ. She wrote, "'All ye are brethren' will be the sentiment of every child of faith. When the followers of Christ are one with Him, there will be no first and last, no less respected or less important ones. . . . All will be equally one with Christ."[67]

This equality of all Christ's followers should be manifested in mutual respect and love among believers and in a recognition of the talents which God has bestowed on all, both men and women. Ellen White recognized that the primary role of many women will be that of wife and mother, which was in her estimate of supreme importance. But she also saw the talent of women being used by God in the church and in evangelism. This topic is treated at length in the chapters by Jerry Moon and Denis Fortin.

Conclusion

According to Ellen White, Christ came to restore that which was lost. He came to restore the image of God in men and women. He came to restore the original equality and companionship in the marriage relationship. But beyond that, Christ brought into existence his church, that through it he might reveal to the world the spirit and the principles of his kingdom. In the church all believers are equal in Christ. There is to be no first and last, no higher and lower, no male headship and female submission. The only Head is Christ, the only submission the entire submission of every believer to Christ, and within the bounds of conscience to the judgment of the united church.

We can say with assurance that Ellen White desired women to stand as equals, side by side with men in the cause of Christ. But she also recognized that equality in Christ can only be realized in the Spirit of Christ, never in the spirit of this world. True equality and true independence can only be found in entire submission to Christ as the Head of the church and as Lord of the individuality of each woman and man.

Endnotes

1. Ellen G. White, *Patriarchs and Prophets*, 46.

2. The expression "holy pair" to designate the first two human beings occurs more than a hundred times in the published writings of Ellen G. White.

3. White, *Patriarchs and Prophets*, 46.

4. Ellen G. White, *Testimonies for the Church*, 3:484.

5. Ellen G. White, *Education*, 17, 20.

6. White, *Patriarchs and Prophets*, 48.

7. Ellen G. White, *Counsels to Teachers, Parents, and Students*, 33.

8. White, *Patriarchs and Prophets*, 46.

9. White, *Testimonies for the Church*, 3:484.

10. Ellen G. White, "Redemption, No. 1," *Second Advent Review and Sabbath Herald*, 24 February 1874.

11. White, *Patriarchs and Prophets*, 50.

12. White, *Testimonies for the Church*, 6:236.

13. White, *Patriarchs and Prophets*, 49.

14. Ellen G. White, "The First Temptation," *Youth's Instructor*, July 1897.

15. White, *Patriarchs and Prophets*, 59.

16. White, *Testimonies for the Church*, 3:484.

17. White, *Patriarchs and Prophets*, 58.

18. Ibid., 59; cf. White, *Testimonies for the Church*, 3:484.

19. *Manuscript Releases*, 21:214.

20. Ibid., 21:213.

21. Ibid., 21:214.

22. Francis D. Nichol, ed. *Seventh-day Adventist Bible Commentary* (Washington, DC: Review and Herald, 1953-1957), 3:1139.

23. *Manuscript 39*, 1910.

24. "Defeat of Sisera." *Signs of the Times*, 16 June 1881.

25. Ellen G. White, *Medical Ministry*, 60. See chapter by Jo Ann Davidson.

26. White, *Education*, 125.

27. White, *Patriarchs and Prophets*, 595.

28. "The Mutual Obligations of Husband and Wife." *Review and Herald* 10 December 1908.

29. "The Marriage at Cana," (2SP 98-115); "At the Marriage Feast," (*Desire of Ages*, 144-153); "Marriage, and Christ's First Miracle" (*MS* 16, 1899, 1-11; *Manuscript Releases* 10: 197-203); "The Marriage in Cana of Galilee" (*Signs of the Times*, 30 August and 6 September 1899).

30. White, *Manuscript Releases*, 10:198, 203.

31. White, *Testimonies for the Church*, 3:565.

32. *Signs of the Times*, 9 August 1887.

33. Ellen G. White, *The Desire of Ages*, 190, 195.

34. Ellen G. White, *Adventist Home*, 204.

35. White, *Acts of the Apostles*, 238; cf. 20.

36. "This Do, and Thou Shalt Live," *Review and Herald*, 17 October 1899.

37. Ellen G. White, "Grace and Faith the Gifts of God," *Review and Herald*, 24 December 1908.

38. White, *Desire of Ages*, 509.

39. White, *Testimonies for the Church*, 9:218.

40. White, *Desire of Ages*, 509.

41. White, *Acts of the Apostles*, 459.

42. Ellen G. White, *Thoughts from the Mount of Blessing*, 64.

43. *Manuscript Releases*, 21:216.

44. Ibid., 21:215.

45. White, *Adventist Home*, 115-116.

46. Ibid., 116.

47. "This Do, and Thou Shalt Live," *Review and Herald*, 17 October 1899.

48. "The Bible to be Understood by All," *Signs of the Times*, 20 August 1894.

49. Ellen G. White, *Christian Temperance and Bible Hygiene* , 77; White, *Fundamentals of Christian Education*, 141; White, *Adventist Home*, 231.

50. "The Mother's Work," *Review and Herald*, 1 July 1877.

51. "The Importance of Early Training," *Review and Herald*, 1 June 1877; *Adventist Home*, 231.

52. Ellen G. White, *The Ministry of Healing*, 390; *Adventist Home*, 211.

53. White, *Testimonies for the Church*, 4:255.

54. *Manuscript Releases*, 8:429.

55. *Manuscript Releases*, 21:214.

56. Ellen G. White, *Evangelism*, 467.

57. White, *Testimonies for the Church*, 3:484.

58. White, *The Ministry of Healing*, 361.

59. *Manuscript Releases*, 10:71.

60. White, *The Desire of Ages* 414; cf. White, *Acts of the Apostles* 194-195.

61. "Take My Yoke Upon You," *Signs of the Times*, 22 July 1897.

62. "Christ's Followers the Light of the World," *Signs of the Times*, 1 January 1880.

63. "Unity of the Church," *Review and Herald*, 19 February 1880; *Testimonies for the Church*, 4:17.

64. *Testimonies for the Church* 3:360-361; cf. 5:107-108.

65. "No Caste in Christ," *Review and Herald*, 22 December 1891; *Selected Messages* 1:258, 259.

66. Ibid; *Selected Messages* 1:259.

67. *SDA Bible Commentary*, 5:1097.

CHAPTER 15

HOW DOES A WOMAN PROPHESY AND KEEP SILENCE AT THE SAME TIME? (1 CORINTHIANS 11 AND 14)

W. LARRY RICHARDS

Paul's statements in 1 Cor 11:2-16 and 14:33-35 delineating guidelines and requirements for women in public worship continue to be a source of controversy. Some scholars have gone so far as to suggest that Paul contradicts himself by approving women's participation in worship in 1 Corinthians 11 (praying and prophesying with the head veiled) while ordering them to keep silence in 1 Corinthians 14.

There do, in fact, seem to be two views on the role of women in the writings of Paul: one view is that of *subordination*; and the other, that of *equality*.[1] The natural question is: Are these two views in conflict? The question needs to be answered from the perspective of the first-century Christians as well as that of modern-day Christians.

Since the 1960s, many New Testament scholars have attempted to resolve the apparent discrepancies in Paul's reasoning. Possibly because of a heightened sensitivity to the concerns of women, a wide variety of solutions have been proposed[2], including the view that either 1 Cor 11:2-16 or 1 Cor 14:34-35, or both, are interpolations—that is, not genuine Pauline statements.[3] In this paper, both passages are considered to be authored by Paul.

In acknowledging the existence of views that *appear* to be different, students of the New Testament have generally taken one of two major positions. The first position, the traditional interpretation, holds that although there may be some tension, *there is no conflict* between the passages, either for the first century or for any later period. The second, more recent interpretation holds that *there is conflict* in the New Testament passages. First-century Christians may or may not have

313

recognized a conflict, but many Christians living in our time see a conflict and, therefore, look for a solution.

The traditional interpretation holds that the early Christian church adopted from Judaism the concept of women's subordination within society, while at the same time setting forth a new doctrine of its own, that is, that "in Christ" all persons are equal.[4] Thus the two separate arenas, the *social* (which requires subordination) and the *religious* (which espouses equality), are seen as not being in conflict.

A more recent interpretation is that of Krister Stendahl in his book *The Bible and the Role of Women: A Case Study in Hermeneutics*,[5] published in 1966, which differed from the traditional view by contending that the two arenas (the *social* and the *religious*) actually are in conflict. Stendahl argued that the theological position that emerges within Christianity, stated in its clearest terms in Gal 3:28, creates a tension with the New Testament passages which point to the subordination of women.[6] Believing this conflict to be resolvable, Stendahl asked: "Does the New Testament contain elements, glimpses which point beyond and even 'against' the prevailing view and practice of the New Testament church?"[7] He then answered in the affirmative. His argument is summarized in this comment, "It is our contention that all three of these pairs [Jew and Greek, slave and free, male and female] have the same potential for implementation in the life and structure of the church, and that we cannot dispose of the third by confining it to the realm *coram Deo* [before God]."[8]

In this chapter I shall examine the two passages separately, show that they are not in contradiction, and then give conclusions regarding their meaning for the church today.

1 Corinthians 11:2-17

In this passage Paul tackles the problem of Corinthian women attending worship services dressed in an unconventional manner[9]—that is, with their heads uncovered.[10] Some 2,000 years later his concern may appear to be a little peculiar and perhaps even illogical. For example, have you ever wondered why, on the one hand, it is considered a sign of *reverence* among most Christians for a man to remove his hat or cap when prayer is being offered, while, on the other hand, within Judaism (from which Christianity sprang), that very same action is considered a sign of irreverence?[11] When I take students to visit the Western Wall in Old Jerusalem on a Friday evening, where devout Jews are welcoming the beginning of the Sabbath, I remind them in advance that the men, not the women, must have their heads covered before entering the area near the Wall—which is just the opposite of what most of them are accustomed to!

The important point is that we must first understand Paul's counsels in their original setting, not in ours. Any attempt to understand this passage requires that we first know what was going on in Corinth in the early-to-mid-50s A.D.[12] What was the situation that opened the door for this alteration of the tradition regarding proper head attire for women in public worship?

The Setting at Corinth

It is not possible to provide a full picture of the background to this letter,[13] but a correct interpretation requires an understanding of what caused Paul to write his counsels, not only for our two passages (1 Corinthians 11 and 14), but for the entire letter.[14] This background information centers around the false apostles who brought to Corinth their heretical teachings. The heresy that was introduced was based on the belief that "knowledge" was the basis of salvation, not God's grace and love centered in the Cross. The heresy called gnosticism was not fully developed until the second century A.D. Scholars today refer to the gnostic thinking of the first century as "incipient gnosticism" or "proto-gnosticism," but for the sake of brevity and simplicity, we shall simply refer to the Corinthian heresy as gnosticism, with the understanding that the name is to a degree anachronistic.

While not all scholars accept that Paul's opponents in Corinth were gnostics,[15] scholars who have reservations continue to be puzzled by the two Corinthian letters that describe developments readily understood in the context of gnosticism.[16] When the two letters are studied together, the evidence, in my opinion, is overwhelming.[17] In any case, for this paper, the reader should understand that the terms "gnostic" and "gnosticism" refer to a developing system of heresy, not one that was already mature.

The "knowledge" (the Greek word is *gnōsis* from which we get "gnosticism") that brought the gnostics their salvation was the view that a gnostic was part of the divine, a person who was spiritual from all eternity. Furthermore, everything connected with the material world (the opposite of the spirit world) was considered evil.

The implications of this concept of "spiritual versus physical" are important for understanding both passages considered in this paper. Gnostics believed the following:

1. The creation of male and female, a wholesome and natural

feature of a good God's Creation, according to the Genesis record (1:27, 31),[18] was, for the gnostics, the byproduct of an inferior development within the cosmos.

2. The physical being, therefore, was of no value; and further, the physical nature actually hindered the gnostic in realizing his/her true spiritual (immortal) identity.

3. Gender distinctions should be ignored, because male and female belong to the world of "fallenness."

4. The gnostic female was no different from the gnostic male—both had the same divine spark.

In most Christian gnostic systems, the God of the Old Testament was actually the evil god responsible for the existence of everything evil. And one key reason he was "evil" was that he created matter—the material world, including human beings (Gen 1:27). For the gnostic, the plan of Creation in Genesis was flawed not only because it involved the creation of matter, but also because it was designed to produce more physical life (matter) through the union of male and female (Gen 1:28).

This gnostic understanding of reality (i.e., only the spirit/spiritual aspects are important) influenced some women within the Corinthian congregation to challenge conventional worship customs. According to the gnostics, a woman who wore a veil or kept her hair long was acknowledging a theological distinction gnostics wished to deny;[19] they therefore found it easy to cast aside traditions which they believed fostered "uninformed" positions about male and female. For them, the respect that was shown for angels (v. 10) by following conventional practices was pure nonsense. Not only did gnostic women and men consider themselves equal or superior to angels, but the "gnostic Christians" in Corinth behaved in such an audacious manner that Paul asked them if they thought they were stronger than the Lord (1 Cor 10:22).

Precisely how fully developed the gnostic thinking was at Corinth is not clear, but the problems in the Corinthian church reflect, at least in part, the gnostic attitudes referred to above. It is important to realize, therefore, that the subject of this passage is a concern over proper behavior in public worship insofar as the behavior misrepresented a basic Christian understanding of Creation and redemption. Paul is not in any sense of the word addressing the issues of male-female relationships as they are so often applied in our day, especially not to argue the pros and cons of women's ordination.

In Paul's time, among the Greeks and Romans, both men and

women remained bareheaded in public prayer. In Judaism and early Christianity, it was customary for women to veil their heads in the public worship setting.[20] This was done out of respect for the angels who were present at worship assemblies (v. 10). It was this established tradition that some women were tossing aside. An important part of the setting of Corinth is the "covering" or "veil." This has been interpreted in different ways: (a) The covering is simply the natural covering—a woman's hair; (b) Two coverings are involved: a woman's hair and a veil; one of which Paul requires;[21] and (c) Wearing a hat would today meet Paul's requirement.

Three Possible Lines of Interpretation

Before looking at Paul's six-point response to the bold and innovative worship practice introduced in Corinth,[22] we first mention the three major ways 1 Cor 11:2-16 has been interpreted,

1. The instruction is to be taken literally and is mandatory for all ages and cultures. This view holds that Paul's counsel is not temporary or merely cultural in nature. Because Paul has referred to the order of creation in vv. 7-9, his advice is not to be restricted to his time. Thus, in every age, women should cover their heads in public worship to show their proper position vis-à-vis men.

2. The instruction contains principles for all ages and cultures. This view holds that wearing the veil in itself is no longer required for modern times. On the other hand, the principle in the passage requires wives to always show respect for their husbands by submitting to their authority, just as man submits to Christ's authority.

3. The instruction is related to Paul's culture and only partially deals with principles. This view holds that Paul's counsel reflects social views of that time that are cultural in nature, and, therefore, with one key exception, apply only to the church at Corinth. Other passages from the New Testament speak to the principles of marriage relationships. The principle to be taken from this passage (the "one key exception") is found in vv. 11-12, where Paul emphasizes equality and mutual dependence between men and women who are "in the Lord." This emphasis coincides with Paul's counsels in 1 Corinthians 7, where everything he says about a woman, he also says about a man.[23]

Paul's Six-point Argument (vv. 2-16)

Paul makes six points in his case against the new and unacceptable practice in Corinth. Each is related to propriety in light of tradition, customs, respect, nature, and common sense. The veil itself was not the main issue for Paul. The statement that was being made by *not wearing* the veil was important for Paul because this action symbolized the false theology about the nature of humankind and the place of the Cross.

1. The importance of tradition (vv. 2 and 16). Paul begins and ends his case against the new practice with an appeal to the traditions of all the churches. The first reference is in the expression "holding to the teachings" (v. 2). Paul uses a word that is a technical term for something that is handed on from one to another (usually translated as "tradition"). The thing handed on may be bad (see Matt 15:2-6), even contrary to the will of God (see Mark 7:8), or it may be entirely good, as in this passage.[24] In his concluding appeal to the Corinthians on this subject, Paul wrote, "We have no other practice—nor do the churches of God" (v. 16). As in the previous section, Paul wanted everything to be done to the glory of God (10:31).

2. The importance of hierarchy (vv. 3 and 7-9). Verse 3 and vv. 7-9 can be combined, because in both places Paul deals with the place of hierarchy. "The head of every man (*anēr*) is Christ, the head of a woman is her husband (*anēr*),[25] and the head of Christ is God" (v. 3). Some New Testament scholars have argued that the word "head" (*kephalē*) should be understood as "source" (as in "source of the river").[26] Using this meaning, Robin Scroggs arrives at the following translation of v. 3:[27]

> I want you to know that
> every man's source is Christ,
> the source of woman is man, [i.e., woman came from Adam's rib]
> the source of Christ is God.

As attractive as the meaning of "source" for the Greek word *kephalē* is, we must, in the final analysis, rely on the passages written by Paul himself for a definition of *kephalē*. Elsewhere in Paul's writings, he uses the term in the sense of authority, not source (see Eph 1:21-22; 5:22-23; and Col 1:18); that is probably what he intends here.[28]

Paul gives a sequence of rank: a head and a subject who acknowledges the superiority of that head. He wants to show that violation of accepted social practices by a woman who wished to defy the distinctions of gender are unacceptable for a Christian.[29] At this point, then, Paul takes up the issue of veiling the head in public worship.

Given the setting at Corinth, it is clear that because Paul wished to emphasize the order of authority and administration in the divine arrangement of things (man is under Christ's authority, Christ is under God's authority, so the woman is under her husband's authority), the Corinthian woman should not be trying to show her authority by having her head uncovered, particularly when the "show of authority" represented a heretical stance.

It is important to notice that in the context of 1 Corinthians 11, the wife (*gunē*) is under the authority of her own husband (*anēr*). No mention is made of her subordination to any other man. Paul never, here or elsewhere, widens the wife's subordination to her husband within the family circle to a general subordination of women to men's authority, in the church or in society.[30]

It is also crucial that we keep in mind that Paul is making this argument, *not to put woman down, but to counter the gnostic position.* In fact, one could argue from a logical point of view, that since the creation of the woman is the final act of Creation, her creation is the crown and climax of all Creation.[31]

3. The matter of honor (vv. 4-6). When Paul writes that "every man who prays or prophesies with his head covered[32] dishonors his head" (v. 4), he uses the word "head" in two ways. The first use of "head" in this verse refers to man's physical head; the second use probably refers to his spiritual Head (Christ). When a man prayed or prophesied with his head (his own physical head) covered, he displayed dishonor toward Christ (his spiritual Head).

At the same time, Paul states that a woman who prays or prophesies[33] in public worship with her head uncovered (either with short hair or without a veil), dishonors her head,[34] so much so that it is the same as having her head shaved (v. 5). And since it is shameful for a woman to have her head shaved, she should have her head properly covered (either with long hair or with a veil, v. 6). When a woman appeared in a public service with her head uncovered (either by having her hair cut short or not wearing a veil), she was sending a message that said one of three things; (1) She was a person of loose morals and sexual promiscuity; (2) She had been publicly disgraced because of some shameful act; or (3) She was openly flaunting her independence (in this case, to support a heretical interpretation of human existence). The information we have about the conditions in Corinth at the time Paul was writing his letters strongly points to the third option. The total picture, however, is important for understanding the significance attached to the tradition.

4. "Because of the angels" (v. 10). This reason has been the center of all sorts of debate. The debate has revolved around two parts of the verse. First, who are the angels? Second, what does "a sign of authority on her head" mean? We look at the question of the identity of the angels first.

Some have argued that Paul believed the veil would protect women from evil angels (such as those referred to in Gen 6:2, 4, whom some interpreters believe to have cohabited with women). A far better understanding of this text would be that these are *holy* angels, who themselves veil their faces in the presence of God (see Isa 6:2). Furthermore, since the discovery of the Dead Sea Scrolls at Qumran we have specific information about the very conservative Essenes, a Jewish group who went out into the wilderness to "prepare the way for the Lord." We now know that worshipers at Qumran believed holy angels attended their services, and that respect for them was vital, so much so that persons with a physical defect of any kind could not attend the sacred assembly.[35] Another reason for believing that the "angels" referred to here are holy angels is that other New Testament passages indicate that angels are interested in the Christian's salvation (see 1 Tim 5:21 and especially 1 Pet 1:10).

The second question about the meaning of "the sign of authority on her head" is more difficult. In the Greek, the text reads literally, "therefore, a woman ought to have authority on her head, because of the angels." In no way does it speak of woman "under authority." The question is: How does the woman have "authority" on her head by the wearing of a veil[36] (or by keeping her hair long)? This is particularly important if the phrase "because of the angels" refers to having respect for holy angels.

Elsewhere in 1 Corinthians, the Greek word for authority, *exousia,* means the right or freedom to act (see 7:37; 8:9; 9:4, 5, 6, 12, 18; see also Rom 9:21; Rev 22:14). This is, no doubt, the meaning of the word here.[37] How does this usage affect this verse? The most natural meaning would be that a woman has "authority," that is, the freedom to act or to worship, simply by following proper decorum and conventional practices. If she brazenly refuses to follow the accepted custom, which in itself shows respect for angels, she forfeits the very authority she is attempting to claim for herself! Paul's conclusion is that women did have authority to worship by having the proper head covering, and did not have authority by the maverick action of the Corinthian women of casting the custom aside. As we have noted, "tradition" was not important for gnostic-thinking worshipers.

5. Equality and mutuality of man and woman (vv. 11-12). In Paul's six-point argument against the thinking and practice going on in Corinth, two verses without question address the gender issue in terms that transcend time and culture, vv. 11 and 12. "In the Lord, however, *woman is not independent* of man, *nor is man independent* of woman. For as woman came from man, so also man is born of woman. But everything comes from God." Man and woman are equal and mutually dependent. The key phrase for Paul is "in the Lord" (v. 11). Here Paul finds the solution of all problems and presents a corrective for any who would take his argument to support a woman's inequality with man. Thus, even as Paul attacks the theology of the gnostics, he still maintains the overarching principle within Christianity of equality "in Christ."

6. Appeal to common sense (vv. 13-15). Just before Paul completes the discussion by making his second appeal to tradition, he adds one final argument. This time he appeals to the Corinthians to maintain gender distinctions on the basis of one's ordinary understanding of what is natural and in harmony with common sense. "Judge for your-selves," Paul says; "Is it proper?" he asks. The Corinthians should recognize that women are not to pray with their heads uncovered as men do. Why? It is obvious that men with short hair are distinguished from women with long hair. Surely you would agree, Paul writes, that a man who has long hair is disgraced, and a woman with long hair has it to her glory (vv. 14-15).

Wanting the Corinthians to be conscious of how their actions would appear to others as "proper," Paul reenforces his argument with an appeal to nature itself: nature teaches us what is proper and what is improper! One's native sense of propriety, apart from custom, should settle the question (this same word is used in Rom 2:14). [38]

The Clinching Argument (v. 16)

Using a word that is found only here in the New Testament, Paul concludes that if any one wants to be "contentious"—that is, fond of strife—such a person, in today's language, is out of luck: "No other church does it this way, and neither will we at Corinth!" Paul thus ends a discussion that may not have been persuasive to all of his readers. In fact, he ends on a note that might not sit well with those who would consider the argument "Everybody does it this way" to be flawed logic. Paul would have, no doubt, as an intelligent and educated person, agreed with such a response. But for him, doing what he considered to be best for the Christian community might not always depend on pure logic.

Apart from the strength or weakness of any one of the six arguments Paul has made, and apart from the cultural setting of ancient Corinth, there are some helpful lessons and principles that we can glean from these verses.

1. Men and women are equal human beings (v. 12). In the Christian community, each Christian should treat everyone with mutual respect.

2. As equal human beings, men and women are still distinct sexes with special functions and positions.

3. The gender subordination discussed in this passage is specifically that of wives to their husbands, not of all women to all men.

4. As individuals and in corporate worship, Christians should relate to one another with a unity that allows for subordination to church leaders, without respect to gender or to the notion of superiority.

5. God is a God of order; worship therefore must also be peaceful and orderly (see comments on 1 Corinthians 14).

1 Corinthians 14:33-35

In the second passage, 1 Cor 14:33-35, Paul stated that women should keep silence in public worship and be subordinate. The two issues will be considered in turn.

> For God is not a God of confusion but of peace. As in all the churches of the saints, the *women should keep silence in the churches*. For they are not permitted to speak, but *should be subordinate*, as even the law says. If there is anything they desire to know, let them ask their husbands at home. For it is shameful for a woman to speak in church.

Those who think that Paul did not write these words find it easy to dismiss them as a later development of the text. They do not consider this as a sinister process, but a transcription of the way later church leaders attempted to apply Scripture to their own context.[39]

Keep Silence

Before examining Paul's words in this passage, we mention two major positions of those who accept Pauline authorship on the meaning of the passage.

1. Paul said it: Women are to keep silence in church. According to this understanding, women are barred from all church leadership and from public speaking in churches.[40] One might conclude: "Paul said it, I believe it, and there is nothing more to say!" Interestingly, persons inclined to draw their conclusions based on this particular rationale are not always consistent in their applications. For example, Paul enjoins (1) women to keep silence, (2) women to wear a veil in public worship, and (3) slaves to remain in subjection. Few of those who interpret this text as banning women from the rostrum insist that women in church must be veiled. Fewer still advocate the subjection of slaves.

2. Paul said it, but context is crucial for understanding the prohibition. As Paul did indeed make the statements, this passage is authentic. However, taking the context into consideration, the prohibition is not absolute.[41]

Women are told to keep silence, but "silence" with regard to what? The context seems to favor the view that because the tongues experience was leading to confusion, the involvement of women, especially gnostic women who might be exerting their newfound rights in a manner out of line with the traditional roles of women in public, was further contributing to the disorder. Coupled with this possibility, if the synagogue model (having the men and women separated during public services) was followed in Corinth, any verbal exchanges between husbands on one side of the room and wives on the other obviously would have been disrupting.

In this study we cannot look at all the verses that cover the larger context as we did for 1 Corinthians 11, but we do need to draw attention to four pivotal points about 1 Corinthians 14 itself.

1. This chapter is the concluding chapter on a major topic—the meaning of spirituality—which began with 1 Cor 12:1. One cannot separate the three chapters in the interpretation.[42]

2. Paul's primary concern in 1 Corinthians 14 is to clarify a serious misunderstanding regarding a *pneumatikos* ("spiritual person"). The Corinthians were claiming that their use of tongues was proof of their spirituality. Paul has attacked this understanding earlier in the letter, particularly in 1 Corinthians 2, 3, and 12. Coupled with his concern about their bold claims, Paul has stressed concern for others as the indispensable characteristic of a Christian. In chapter 14 he stresses the importance of doing everything in public worship for the edification ("building up") of the congregation. The word for "building up" (verb or noun) is used seven times in this chapter (vv. 3, 4 [two times], 5, 12, 17,

and 26); each time the concept is used to oppose the exercise of tongues in public worship. Edification of the church members ("building up") is of primary concern for Paul, not only in this chapter, but throughout the letter (1 Cor 3:9; 8:1, 10; and 10:23).

3. Verses 33-35 are related to a critical *secondary* concern, that all things be done in order; for God is a God of order, not a God of confusion (see vv. 33, 40).

4. It is natural to question why the other two commands to "keep silence" have not drawn the same attention as the one regarding women in v. 34. When the other commands to "keep silence" are added to the command for women to "keep silence," we can see Paul's real objective. The Greek word is exactly the same in all three instances.

In the first passage, 14:28, Paul wrote: "But if there is no one to interpret, let *each of them keep silence* in church and speak to himself and to God." In the second passage, 14:30, Paul wrote: "If a revelation is made to another sitting by, *let the first keep silence*." The remarkable fact is that in both of these passages, the one told to keep "silence" is masculine in gender. And even if one wished to argue that the use of the masculine gender in these verses is "gender inclusive," the point is not affected: *Men* are still being asked to keep silence! This observation alone shows that Paul has not singled out women to keep silence.

Given the orientation of the gnostic women in Corinth who were already defying traditional worship practices, as we noted in relation to 1 Corinthians 11, it is quite a simple matter to understand that these were women expressing themselves in a manner Paul considered excessive. This was even more objectionable in view of the overall confusion that the "tongues" experience was already causing.

When we look at the total picture and keep in mind the other verses in which Paul called for "silence," it becomes obvious that the command for women to "keep silence" does not, contradict his instructions in 1 Corinthians 11. Women may indeed participate in public worship by praying and prophesying (as long as their heads are covered), and yet they, along with the men, are to keep silence in those instances when order is best preserved by the silence.

Be Subordinate

Paul's words immediately following the ones about keeping silence are that women "should be subordinate" (v. 34b, RSV). This passage and others which speak of the subordination of women are often taken out of context. In the first place, the specific context is one of subordination of wives to their own husbands, not to men in general. A further confirmation of the husband-wife relationship is the mention of a "law" which commands submission. This is apparently a reference to Gen 3:16, where submission is a result of the Fall.

The concept of "subordination," frequently attached to women, needs to be studied in light of Paul's own understanding and usage. And as we have attempted to establish, his understanding may not fully coincide with ours. A study of the word for "subordination" gives us a striking insight into Paul's thought. In the following section, all English words translated from the Greek root, *hupotassō*, "to subordinate," are italicized, showing the variety of nuances of the term.

Submission is the correct thing for all Christians to do. Christians whose minds are set on spiritual matters *submit* to God's law, as Paul notes in Rom 8:7: "For the mind that is set on the flesh is hostile to God; it does not *submit* to God's law, indeed it cannot." Further, everyone, men and women, should *submit* to the governing powers, as is clear in Rom 13:1, 5: "Let every person *be subject* to the governing authorities. For there is no authority except from God, and those that exist have been instituted by God." "Therefore one must be *subject*, not only to avoid God's wrath but also for the sake of conscience" (see also Titus 3:1 and 1 Pet 2:13, where similar instruction is given, using the same Greek word). In the conclusion of his letter to the Corinthian church, Paul urges them to *be subject* to the household of Stephanas, his associates in ministry (1 Cor 16:16). Finally, Paul admonishes the Ephesians: "*Be subject* to one another out of reverence for Christ" (Eph 5:21).

Frequently, the general injunction to mutual submission (Eph 5:21; see also Col 3:18 and Titus 2:5) is forgotten as the submission or subordination of wives in Eph 5:24 is emphasized. This unbalanced treatment produces a seriously distorted view of the fundamental intention in *hupotassō*. "Submission" or "subordination" for Paul is something all Christians should be willing to do!

Perhaps one of the passages on slavery will help us to understand the dynamics of "submission": "Bid slaves to *be submissive* to their masters and to give satisfaction in every respect; they are not to be refractory" (Titus 2:9). This passage alone bears out the need to understand Paul's larger concern. Attitude, as the crux of his theology of submission, allows for social changes, but changes that are made in a nonrebellious frame of mind. That is, at the right time, slaves might not have to "submit" in the manner in which it was understood in the mid-50s A.D. The church has already made this shift in application of Paul's teaching on "subordination." The extension of the logic is obvious. Regardless of the time in which we live, all Christians should always have a "submissive" disposition. Grace can operate in such a setting.

Even the prophetic spirit is to submit: "And the spirits of prophets are *subject* to prophets" (1 Cor 14:32). Not only is submission to God and others; the individual practices submission or self-discipline.

The Lord himself set the example for Christians. Clearly, one of the most important passages on "submission" in all of the New Testament is the amazing theological point about the relationship of the Son with the Father in 1 Cor 15:24-28. Here Paul points out that at the end of the great controversy, Christ will *subject* himself to the Father for all eternity. What an extraordinary statement to a church group who wanted to exalt themselves! "For God has put all things in *subjection* under his feet." But when it says, "All things are put in *subjection* under him," it is plain that he is excepted who put all things under him. When all things are subjected to him, then the Son himself *will subject himself* to him who put all things under him, that God may be everything to every one (1 Cor 15:27-28).[43] In Paul's discussion of the resurrection in 1 Corinthians 15, the Incarnation is not an event that occurred at a moment in time; rather, our Lord will voluntarily *subject* himself for all eternity! Matchless love! Incomprehensible in any sense of the word. No wonder we will spend all eternity trying to grasp the full significance of our redemption.

When one reflects on this majestic demonstration of love, it becomes difficult to understand how we humans, the objects of this indescribable love, could be so embroiled over our own importance. Submission should surely be something every Christian is willing to do for the benefit of others. To cite Paul's words as a support for insisting on the subjection of someone else, be that woman, slave, or whoever, is to totally miss the message Paul wishes to convey in the verb *hupotassō*. The subjection demonstrated by heaven was completely unselfish: "Christ emptied himself" (for our benefit, Phil 2:6-7). "Christ *subjected himself*" (for our benefit, 1 Cor 15:24-28). In both statements Paul is using heaven's example to counter self-promotion among the church members, male and female. The word clearly refers to an attitude regarding one's own submission, not to what one should be insisting on for the other person.

Conclusions

Paul taught both social subordination and religious equality. That is evidenced most clearly in 1 Corinthians 11, where both positions are given. Even though it may not be a very attractive conclusion, the fact is that Paul did not call for the changes that we have looked for in modern times. Women *and* slaves were to show submission as long as they remained in their respective relationships.

In the first century, therefore, the equality "in Christ" and the subordination of slaves and women in society did not create a tension for Paul or his readers. The concepts (subordination and equality) existed side by side without any sense of contradiction. We must acknowledge this, regardless of how "unfair" it might seem to us some two thousand years later. We do not do justice to the text by trying to find in it something that does not exist, simply because we believe it should have been included in Scripture.

Furthermore, exegetes in our time must keep in mind that the text does not always directly address our *specific* needs. Our questions are often different from their questions, and it is important that we do not try to force the biblical passages to address questions they were never intended to answer. Paul, while arguing that women and slaves "in Christ" are equal, was already making a case for changing the status of Gentiles; they also are to be considered equal "in Christ."

In answer to our initial question: "How does a woman prophesy and keep silence at the same time?" we reply: Obviously, she cannot! Paul's admonition for women to keep silence in 1 Corinthians 14 must be understood in the context of the bold claim made by Paul's opponents, namely, that a gnostic woman was no different from a gnostic man. In order to counter this misunderstanding of the gender distinctions delineated in the creation of male and female (Genesis 1 and 2), Paul objected to the brazen behavior of women in public worship, not because he wanted them to keep silence in public worship, but because he wished to oppose behavior that was making a heretical theological statement. Under ordinary circumstances, a woman could both pray and prophesy in public worship (1 Cor 11:5). We saw, however, that even in the circumstances of 1 Corinthians 11 women were to abide by conventional practices by keeping their heads covered (either with a veil or with their "naturally" long hair). Women were not, even in this passage, permitted to ignore the gender distinctions of God's Creation.

Once we locate Paul's comments in 1 Corinthians 11 and 14 within the historical setting of first-century Corinth, and capture as far as possible the problems Paul was facing, we are able to much better make an application of his principles to our own time. As Ellen White noted, "The Bible was given for practical purposes."[44]

Endnotes

1. The passages which point to *subordination* include: for married women, Col 3:19; Eph 5:22-24; and Titus 2:4-5; for women in public worship, 1 Tim 2:11-15, and the two passages under consideration in this paper. The passages which refer to *equality* between men and women include Gal 3:28; and 1 Cor 11:11-12. See chapter 16, where Nancy Vyhmeister deals with the passage from 1 Timothy.

2. E. Kähler, *Die Frau in den paulinischen Briefen, unter besonderer Berücksichtigung des Begriffes der Unterordnung* (Zürich: Gotthelf, 1960), 45-46; M. Hooker, "Authority on her Head: an Examination of 1 Cor. xi:10," *New Testament Studies* 10 (1964): 410-416; two essays by R. Scroggs, "Paul: Chauvinist or Liberationist?" *Christian Century* 89 (1972): 307-309 and "Paul and Eschatological Woman: Revisited," *Journal of the American Academy of Religion* 40 (1972): 532-537; and in the same journal, E. H. Pagels, "Paul and Women: A Response to Recent Discussion," *Journal of the American Academy of Religion* 40 (1972): 538-549. C. K. Barrett, in his 1969 commentary on 1 Corinthians, offered strong support for new direction toward women (*A Commentary on the First Epistle to the Corinthians* [New York: Harper and Row, 1969], 153-187, 246-258, and 330-333). See also the entries in the next footnote; these reflect this new interest in Paul's writings and the feminist movement in the USA.

3. An ongoing debate has occurred on the subject. In the article that got the current debate started, William O. Walker, Jr., argued that 1 Cor 11:2-16 is an interpolation ("1 Corinthians and Paul's Views Regarding Women," *Journal of Biblical Literature* 94 [1975]: 94-110). Walker wrote, "My conclusion, then, is that 1 Cor 11:2-16 is an interpolation, that it consists of three originally separate and distinct pericopae, each dealing with a somewhat different though related topic, and that none of the pericopae is authentically Pauline" (109). In a brief comment in the Hermeneia commentary series, Hans Conzelmann stated that "the section is accordingly to be regarded as an interpolation" (*1 Corinthians* [Philadelphia: Fortress, 1975], 246). The Catholic scholar J. Murphy-O'Connor effectively defended Pauline authorship, specifically with regard to Walker's article, in "The Non-Pauline Character of 1 Corinthians 11:2-16?" *Journal of Biblical Literature* 95 (1976): 615-621. While applauding Walker for his undertaking, J. Murphy-O'Connor stated: "None of Walker's argument, therefore, stands up to close analysis, and in consequence the hypothesis that 1 Cor 11:2-16 is a post-Pauline interpolation must be rejected" (621). Lamar Cope offered a modification of Walker's thesis in "1 Cor 11:2-16: One Step Further," *Journal of Biblical Literature* 97 (1978): 435-436. In his article "On Attitudes toward Women in Paul and Paulinist Literature: 1 Cor 11:3-6 and Its Context" (*Catholic Biblical Quarterly* 42 [1980]: 196-215), G. W. Trompf argued that during the time Paul's letters were being circulated as a corpus, "they not only suffered from apparent excisions . . . but *received adjuncts as well*" (212, italics added). Murphy-O'Connor made his second response, again

persuasively, in "Sex and Logic in 1 Corinthians 11:2-16," *Catholic Biblical Quarterly* 42 (1980): 482-500. Another Catholic scholar, J. P. Meier, also made a good case for Pauline authorship, contra Walker, in his article "On the Veiling of Hermeneutics (1 Cor. 11:2-16)," (*Catholic Biblical Quarterly* 40 [1978]: 212-222). In his commentary on 1 Corinthians, Gordon D. Fee referred to the "alleged non-Pauline character" as "a counsel of despair" (*The First Epistle to the Corinthians* [Grand Rapids: Eerdmans, 1987], 492, footnote 3). Of the two passages, the stronger arguments for an interpolation are for 1 Cor 14:33b-35.

4. Madeline Boucher has argued that Judaism also held a view of equality for women, stated in language much like that of Gal 3:28. She acknowledges, however, that the parallels in the rabbinic literature entail dating problems (*Catholic Biblical Quarterly* 31 [1969]: 50-58).

5. Philadelphia: Fortress.

6. Ibid., 32.

7. Ibid., 34.

8. Ibid.; the expression *coram Deo* here is the same as "in Christ."

9. The expression "heads uncovered" has been the subject of many discussions. The basic issue is simply this: Were the women at Corinth out-of-line by attending public worship without a "veil" on their heads, or were they out-of-line by cutting their hair short as men did? (See footnote 36.) Either possibility is in harmony with the point Paul wants to make: Women are not men.

10. The problem at Corinth involved both men and women, and as Murphy-O'Connor wrote in his 1980 *Catholic Biblical Quarterly* article: 'The titles given to 1 Cor 11.2-26 in the major commentaries and translations attest the widespread conviction that the point at issue concerned women alone. Acceptance of this consensus inevitably colors the exegesis of the passage, to the point where some commentators refuse to take seriously the reference to men. . . . The problem, therefore, involved both sexes" (ibid., 483). And while I agree with this observation, it was primarily the actions of gnostic women, supported by some of the men, that revealed the nature of the Corinthian heresy.

11. J. W. Roberts discusses the history of head covering among the Jews, beginning with the Old Testament and continuing into the fourth century A.D., when the *tallith* or prayer cloth came into practice for male Jews ("The Veils in 1 Cor. 11:2-16," *Restoration Quarterly* 3 [1959]: 183).

12. Paul tells us about his opponents, the "super apostles," in several references in 2 Cor 11:5 and 12:11; it is clear that these are adversaries, for he even calls them "false apostles" and "deceitful workmen" (2 Cor 11:13, RSV).

13. See W. Larry Richards, "Introduction," *1 Corinthians*, Bible Amplifier Series (Boise, ID: Pacific Press, 1997).

14. Ellen G. White indicates that *before we can appreciate the text for our day*, we must first of all understand the text as far as possible as the original audience understood it. This means that we need to *enter into the thoughts and feelings of the original audience*. This involvement with the text opens the door for an understanding that brings vividness and

beauty as well as a valid application for us who live centuries later (*Mount of Blessings*, 1).

15. Schmithals, Jewett, Goppelt, Rudolph, among others, hold that gnosticism was the problem in Corinth.

16. One example: In 1 Corinthians 5, Paul is appalled that the church members have tolerated the behavior of a man who is living with his stepmother, an immorality that is not even condoned by the pagan world. Gnosticism accounts for this brazen defiance of social morality, both Christian and pagan.

17. The proof of this observation lies outside the range of this essay, however, to a large degree, this picture is provided in the Bible Amplifier series volume on 1 Corinthians, referred to above.

18. A number of scholars have held that Paul had Genesis 1 and 2 in mind in this section of his letter. We mention here a few of the important ones. A recent study by L. Ann Jervis, "'But I want you to know . . . ': Paul's Midrashic Intertextual Response to the Corinthian Worshipers (1 Cor 11:2-16)," *Journal of Biblical Literature* 112 (1993): 231-246. Jervis argues in her article that Paul has Genesis 1 in mind, and that he is writing to counter a misunderstanding of the Genesis record by the pneumatics in Corinth. For earlier studies, see also: E. E. Ellis, "Traditions in 1 Corinthians," *New Testament Studies* 32 (1986): 493; and Walter Vogels, "'It is not Good that the '*Mensch*' Should Be Alone; I will Make Him/Her a Helper Fit for Him/Her' (Gen. 2:18)," *Eglise et Théologie* 9 (1978): 9-35.

19. "Gnostic Christianity also seems to have shared some of the same insights with Paul, but in general there is one crucial difference between them. Both agree in eliminating value judgments of man over against woman. The gnostics seem to have wanted to go further, however, to obliterate all distinctions between the sexes. Paul is, as we shall see, passionate in keeping the reality of the distinctions; he just will not suffer any value judgment to be drawn on the basis of the distinctions" (Robin Scroggs, "Paul and the Eschatological Woman," *Journal of the American Academy of Religion* 40 [1972]: 285).

20. "Dress is in a great degree conventional. A custom which would be proper in our country, would be indecorous in another. The principle insisted upon in this paragraph is that women should conform in matters of dress to all those usages which public sentiment of the community in which they live demands. The veil of all Eastern countries was, and to a great extent still is, the symbol of modesty and subjection. For a woman, therefore, in Corinth to discard the veil, was to renounce her claim to modesty, and to refuse to recognize her subordination to her husband. It is on the assumption of this significance in the use of the veil that the apostle's whole argument in this paragraph is founded" (Charles Hodge, *An Exposition of the First Epistle to the Corinthians* [Grand Rapids: Eerdmans, 1965], 204-205). These comments, however, do not rule out the possibility that Paul may have been dealing with women who cut their hair short in the manner of men.

21. This position is taken by F. W. Grosheide, *First Corinthians*, New International Commentary on the New Testament (Grand Rapids: Eerdmans, 1955).

22. Other aberrant practices introduced by the gnostic elements in the church would include the slogan, "Jesus be cursed," in 12:3; a totally new interpretation of the Lord's

Supper, referred to in both chaps. 10 and 11; the view that sexual immorality was insignificant in chaps. 5 and 6; and the use of "tongues" as proof of spiritual superiority in chap. 14.

23. In 1 Corinthians 7 identical instruction is given to both men and women on the following: sexual intercourse, not ruling the other, rules for sexual abstinence, divorce, mixed marriages, the dissolution of mixed marriages, anxiety for the unmarried or married (vis-à-vis the Lord or the partner, respectively). Often the headings given by editors for the various sections of this letter obscure the fact that Paul repeatedly states in 1 Corinthians 7 that the same liberties for men are also liberties for women, and the same restrictions he mentions for women apply equally for the man.

24. The term is also used positively in 1 Cor 11:23 and 15:3.

25. The Greek word for "man" (*anēr*) means both "man" and "husband."

26. For example, Scroggs, "Paul and the Eschatological Woman"; he credits the idea to S. Bedale ("The Meaning of *kefalē* in the Pauline Epistles," *Journal of Theological Studies* 5 [1954]: 211-215). See also Robin Scroggs, "Paul and the Eschatological Woman: Revisited." Gilbert Bilezikian wrote, "Numerous instances have been found, however, where 'head' denotes a function of origination, provider or servanthood such as a 'person or thing from which something else is derived or obtained'" ("Hierarchist and Egalitarian Inculturations," *Journal of the Evangelical Theological Society* 30 [1987]: 423).

27. Scroggs, "Paul and the Eschatological Woman," 291; bracketed words added.

28. A thorough study of the use of *kephalē* was made by Joseph A. Fitzmyer, "Another Look at *kephalē* in 1 Corinthians 11:3," *New Testament Studies* 35 (1989): 503-511. Fitzmyer makes a strong case for the meaning "head" instead of "source" (see esp. 510). See also A. C. Perriman, "The Head of a Woman: The Meaning of *kephalē* in 1 Cor. 11:3," *Journal of Theological Studies* 45 (1994): 602-622. We should observe, however, a point that is not obvious in an English translation: Where Paul writes that the "husband" is head, he does not use the definite article ("head," not, "*the* head"). What does this mean? Simply this: Man is not *the* absolute head or the *only* head of the wife.

29. The problem Paul was facing in Corinth was similar to the one he dealt with in his letter to Timothy—gnosticism (a libertine form of gnosticism in Corinth, and an ascetic form in Ephesus); both called for similar counsel.

30. Ben Witherington, III, *Women in the Earliest Churches*, Society for New Testament Studies, Monograph Series (Cambridge: Cambridge Univ. Press, 1988), 219-220; Sharon Gritz, *Paul, Women Teachers, and the Mother Goddess at Ephesus: A Study of 1 Timothy 2:9-15 in Light of the Religious and Cultural Milieu of the First Century* (Lanham, MD: University Press of America, 1991), 158.

31. A number of well-reasoned essays on Genesis 1 and 2 have made this very point. I mention three: Thomas R. W. Longstaff, "The Ordination of Women: A Biblical Perspective," *Anglican Theological Review* 5 (1975): 316-327. Thomas makes two significant points about the creation of "man in our image": (1) Sexuality was not an essential component of the image of God (318); and (2) Both male and female received the blessing to "be fruitful and multiply" and "have dominion over . . ." (319). To "have dominion"

is a key expression that belongs also to the female! I would highly recommend the article by Walter Vogels, "It is not Good that the *'Mensch'* Should Be Alone." Vogels is quite helpful in his coverage of the hermeneutical aspects. See also Bilezikian, who wrote, "The Genesis creation account does not present even a hint of any hierarchical relation between Adam and Eve" (422). See also chapter 13 of this book, on headship, by Richard Davidson.

32. The Greek is elliptical; that is, it reads, literally: "having down from [his] head."

33. We know also from Acts 2:18 and 21:9 that women did prophesy.

34. It has been argued that Paul is concerned only with the way a woman wore her hair, rather than with the wearing of a veil, which is not mentioned in this clause. See for example, James B. Hurley, "Did Paul Require Veils or the Silence of Women? A Consideration of 1 Cor. 11:2-16 and 1 Cor. 14:33b-36," *Westminster Theological Journal* 35 (1973): 199-220. On the other hand, it seems from the following verses that the word "veil" (*kalumma*) is understood. The context has "unveiled" (*akatakaluptō*) in apposition and follows with *katakaluptetai* ("veils herself," v. 6) and *katakaluptesthō* ("let her veil herself"). It should be pointed out, however, that the word "veil" could also be "cover." The manuscript evidence gives two different readings in this verse: One refers to "her head"—which probably refers to her husband, and the other has "her own head"—which probably refers to her own physical head. The latter is the best reading and would include the idea that any dishonor done to her husband would also bring dishonor to herself (see Num 5:18, which Hurley uses to make his point).

35. One of the documents from Qumran Cave 1 has this statement, translated by H. Neil Richardson: "No man afflicted with the following may hold an office in the midst of the congregation: anyone afflicted in his flesh, crippled in feet or hands, lame or blind, deaf, dumb, or having any defect; one afflicted in his flesh (which may be) clearly seen or a staggering old man may not continue to hold a position in the midst of the congregation. These may not go in to appear in the midst of the congregation . . . because holy angels are in their congregation" ("Some Notes on 1QSA," *Journal of Biblical Literature* 76 [1957]: 120).

36. "The logical meaning from its connection is that conduct of women in appearing without the veil and thus seeming to disregard the respect due their husbands would shock the angels viewed perhaps as present at the meetings in question" (Roberts, 193).

37. This meaning agrees with the other biblical uses of the term. For examples: "have power over the water" (Rev 11:6) and "over fire" (Rev 14:18; 20:6). A few manuscripts read *kalumma* ("veil") instead of *exousia*. Another few have "shade" or "covering," while the Ethiopic reads, "head should be veiled."

38. All the available evidence points out that during this time, civilized men did not wear their hair long. In fact, it seems clear from all extant references, that men did not embellish in any way their hair as did women, with any kind of paraphernalia associated with hair, including wigs. Robert M. Johnston has personally viewed the lifelike busts of emperors and other officials in the Uffizi of Florence, as well as in the Vatican Museum and the Campidoglio in Rome which bear out this view of hair styles. Robertson and Plummer state in their commentary that "in the catacombs the men are represented with short hair" (*The First Epistle of St Paul to the Corinthians*, International Critical Commentary [Edinburgh: T. & T. Clark, 1914], 236).

39. Murphy-O'Connor wrote his third article in 1986 on the subject of interpolations, "Interpolations in 1 Corinthians," *Catholic Biblical Quarterly* 48 (1986): 81-94. In this article, he allows that the arguments for 1 Corinthians 14:33-35 being an interpolation merit consideration. In my opinion, the most persuasive argument that has been made for treating 1 Corinthians 14:33-35 as an addition, one that came later in the first century by Pauline practitioners, was made by Robert W. Allison in his article, "Let Women be Silent in the Churches (1 Cor. 14.33b-36): What Did Paul Really Say, and What Did It Mean?" *Journal of the Study of the New Testament* 32 (1988) 27-60. However, I hold to Pauline authorship.

40. There are many supporters of this position, and we mention an influential one, Grosheide's commentary on 1 Corinthians (ibid., 341).

41. David W. Odell-Scott believes that Paul authored these verses, but concludes that vv. 33b-35 represent the position of the Corinthians, not of Paul, and that Paul counters their position by his words in v. 36 ("Let the Women Speak in Church: An Egalitarian Interpretation of 1 Cor 14:33b-36," *Biblical Theological Bulletin* 13 [1983]: 90-93).

42. See my discussion in *1 Corinthians*, Bible Amplifier Series (Boise: Pacific Press, 1997).

43. I have translated the italicized verb in the middle voice rather than the passive in v. 28 (Christ subjected himself). The Greek allows this, and the passage thus agrees with the theology of Philippians 2, where Christ emptied himself.

44. White, *Selected Messages*, 1:20.

CHAPTER 16

PROPER CHURCH BEHAVIOR IN
1 TIMOTHY 2:8-15

NANCY JEAN VYHMEISTER

Introduction

Paul's instructions to Timothy in 1 Tim 2:8-15 have been discussed repeatedly. Each point of view on women in ministry has approached the passage in its own way. My purpose in this chapter is to present an interpretation of the passage that maintains the integrity and authority of Scripture while taking into consideration the context of the passage.

The hermeneutical principles followed in this study are those normally subscribed to by Adventist scholars; however, two deserve restating. The first maintains the unity of Scripture; that is to say, the message of Scripture is one. Correctly interpreted, the Bible message does not tell us in one place to do one thing and in another to do the opposite.[1] To understand difficult texts, we must study the whole message of Scripture, with the clearer passages assisting us in understanding those that are not so clear.[2] Thus, one must interpret 1 Tim 2:8-15 in the light of the rest of Scripture.

The second principle affirms that a text must be understood within its contexts.[3] Thus a study of our passage must take into consideration the different contexts of these verses. If these are considered to be "concentric circles," the outermost is that of the whole Bible; next follows that of the New Testament. The innermost is that of the epistle itself.[4] While respecting the first two contexts, discussed elsewhere in this book, this article focuses on the specific context of the epistles to Timothy.

The Context of the Passage

Within the epistle itself, a contextual study includes an inquiry into the purpose of 1 Timothy, called the "authorial intentionality" by Gordon Fee.[5] In addition, attention must be paid to the situation within the church, as well as the religious situation in Ephesus.

The Purpose of 1 Timothy

Paul partially lays out his purpose for writing the epistle in 1 Tim 1:3 and 3:14-15. These instructions should help Timothy and the congregations in Ephesus to "know how one ought to behave in the household of God, which is the church of the living God." The full impact of Paul's intention, however, is derived from the study of the whole epistle.

In the epistles to Timothy, Paul is clearly concerned with teaching. The Greek *didaskō* and its family appear 20 times. Paul speaks of his own teaching ministry (1 Tim 2:7; 2 Tim 1:11), of Timothy's teaching (1 Tim 4:11, 13, 16; 6:2; 2 Tim 4:2), and of the teaching of the church leaders (1 Tim 3:2; 5:17; 2 Tim 2:2, 24).

His major concern, however, has to do with false teachings and teachers. According to 1 Tim 1:3, Paul had left Timothy in Ephesus precisely to contain the teachers of false doctrines. These teachers occupied "themselves with myths and endless genealogies," promoting "speculations rather than the divine training that is in faith." By swerving from the truth, they had "wandered away into vain discussion," "without understanding either what they [were] saying or the things about which they [made] assertions" (1 Tim 1:4-7). One could safely affirm that Paul's purpose in writing 1 Timothy was to give instructions on how Timothy could deal with false teachings and teachers.[6]

The Church Setting

The situation in the church at Ephesus, or better in the Christian congregations at Ephesus, left much to be desired. Already in Acts 20:30-31 (which narrates events that occurred around A.D. 58), Paul had warned the Ephesian elders: "I know that after my departure fierce wolves will come in among you, not sparing the flock; and from among your own selves will arise men speaking perverse things, to draw away the disciples after them." The first letter to Timothy (written perhaps around A.D. 64) shows that his prediction had already come true, only a few years after it was made. Perhaps the reason for the later warning to the church of Ephesus in Revelation (probably penned in the last decade of the first century), "You have abandoned the love you had at first" (Rev 2:4), is related to the infiltration of these false teachings.

Neither the Ephesian heresy nor its leaders are designated by name. The character of the false teaching must be deduced from the text. The false teaching does "not agree with the sound words of our Lord Jesus Christ" (1 Tim 6:3). Its propagators, Paul contends, are "puffed up with conceit" and know nothing, but have "a morbid craving for controversy and for disputes about words, which produce envy, dissension, slander, base suspicions, and wrangling among men who are depraved in mind and bereft of the truth" (1 Tim 6:3-5). Among other things, these teachers "forbid marriage and enjoin abstinence from foods which God created to be received with thanksgiving" (1 Tim 4:3).

Paul warns Timothy about the origin of the false teaching: "deceitful spirits and doctrines of demons." The advice concludes: "Have nothing to do with godless and silly myths" (1 Tim 4:1-7). The first epistle closes with a poignant appeal: "Guard what has been entrusted to you. Avoid the godless chatter and contradictions of what is falsely called knowledge, for by professing it some have missed the mark as regards the faith" (1 Tim 6:20-21).

Second Timothy, Paul's last letter (written somewhere around A.D. 66), uses even stronger language; evidently the false teachers are still disturbing the church. The aged apostle warns Timothy: "Avoid such godless chatter, for it will lead people into more and more ungodliness, and their talk will eat its way like gangrene" (2 Tim 2:16, 17). Only a few verses later, he cautions: "Have nothing to do with stupid, senseless controversies; you know that they breed quarrels" (2 Tim 2:23). The final warning concerns people who "will not endure sound teaching, but having itching ears . . . will accumulate for themselves teachers to suit their own likings, and will turn away from listening to the truth and wander into myths" (2 Tim 4:3, 4).

The women of the church are not exempt from the activities of the false teachers. They are seduced by the false teachers, "who make their way into households and capture weak women, burdened with sins and swayed by various impulses, who will listen to anybody and can never arrive at a knowledge of the truth" (2 Tim 3:6, 7). Not only are women carried away by the false teachers, some of them "learn to be idlers, gadding about from house to house, and not only idlers but gossips and busybodies, saying what they should not" (1 Tim 5:13), evidently spreading false teaching. The "silly" myths of 1 Tim 4:7 are literally myths "characteristic of old women" or "old wives' fables" (KJV).

To summarize: The teaching is godless, has to do with myths and genealogies, involves and promotes speculation, contains elements of asceticism (such as forbidding marriage), and has a negative effect on believers, causing useless discussion and ultimate departure from truth. Women are somehow especially vulnerable to these false teachings.

Religious Background of Ephesus

Three systems stood out in the Ephesian socioreligious setting in the second half of the first century A.D. The first was the pagan worship of the mother goddess—in Ephesus, Artemis or Diana. The second was Judaism, while the third was incipient gnosticism.

Artemis of Ephesus. In Acts 19:23-41 Luke records the "stir" of the silversmiths and the populace of Ephesus in support of Artemis, "whom all Asia and the world worship." Artemis of Ephesus was called a virgin, not because she was indeed a virgin, but because she had not submitted to a husband: "No bonds tied Artemis to any male she would have to acknowledge as master."[7] Her worship required a multitude of priests and priestesses as well as other attendants. Each year the month of Artemision was dedicated especially to the goddess, with cultic rituals as well as athletic, dramatic, and musical contests. The city thrived on the Artemis cult; its inhabitants could not remain untouched by the Great Mother cult. Women were especially attracted to her worship because she was perceived as "chaste, beautiful, and intelligent," meeting the needs of the female worshippers.[8] The ultimate power in the cult was assumed by a high priestess; thus the Artemision and its cult made Ephesus "the bastion and bulwark of women's rights."[9]

As part of the Ephesian cultural context, tales and fables must be considered. Many of the most popular Greek myths were placed in Asia Minor; undoubtedly these were told and retold. The fable genre also developed in Asia Minor, with Aesop entertaining Croesus of Lydia with his tales of animals displaying human characteristics. Ephesus figures prominently in ancient novels, such as Xenophon's *Ephesian Tale* (4th century B.C.), on which Shakespeare based his *Romeo and Juliet*. Horace (65-8 B.C.) noted that old women who retold myths and stories were remarkably able to shape their material according to their own situation.[10] Classical authors noted that while the stories were mostly retold for entertainment—by mothers and caregivers of children—they also contained theological ingredients which served to shape religious opinion.[11]

On the western coast of Asia Minor there was a tradition of dominant women. Among the tales known in the area were those of the Amazons, women warriors who dominated the males.[12] Strabo (ca. 64 B.C.-ca. A.D. 23) affirms that these stories circulated in Asia Minor in his days, not necessarily as legend but as history.[13] For example, Artemisia of Halicarnassus had fought alongside Xerxes—as commander of five ships and Xerxes' advisor—at the naval Battle of Salamis, leaving the Greeks to bear the humiliation of having been bested by a woman.[14] In the tradition of Hercules and Omphale, Hercules was forced to be subject to the Lydian queen and to ply the shuttle and distaff. His acceptance of servitude to a woman brought purification.[15] In an early-second-century-A.D. hymn to Isis, often identified with Artemis, it is declared that the goddess vests women with power equal to that of men.[16]

Judaism. While first-century Judaism was in no way monolithic, the religious privileges of women were mostly limited to the home; at the temple in Jerusalem females were restricted to the women's court. While Ben Azzai said that "a man must give his daughter a knowledge of *Torah*," Rabbi Eliezer ben Hyrcanus affirmed that teaching Torah to a daughter was tantamount to teaching her lasciviousness (Mishnah *Sotah* 3:4). Another ruling stipulated that "a woman may not be a teacher of scribes" (Mishnah *Qidd.* 4:13). Toward the end of the first century A.D., Josephus could affirm that "the woman, says the law, is in all things inferior to the man."[17]

Philo of Alexandria (ca. 20 B.C.-ca A.D. 50) brings into Judaism Hellenistic notions about Eve, who is associated with wisdom and life. Philo has female figures such as Sarah, Rebecca, and Zipporah bringing divine enlightenment to their husbands and Eve directing "massed light" toward Adam's mind to "disperse the mist."[18]

The *Apocalypse of Adam*, a pseudepigraphical work that contains gnostic theology and may date from the first century A.D., takes up this theme, affirming that Eve taught Adam "a word of knowledge of the eternal God."[19] Thus, some strands of first-century Judaism constitute a bridge to gnosticism.

Gnosticism. Gnosticism flourished in the Mediterranean world from the second to the fifth century. The Nag Hammadi (Egypt) manuscripts are from the fourth century but contain earlier materials. There is evidence, indeed, that gnostic ideas began to circulate already in the first century. Paul admonished Timothy to "avoid the godless chatter and contradictions of what is falsely called knowledge [*gnōsis*]" (1 Tim 6:2).

If the dissident views reflected in the Pastoral Epistles are reflections of later gnostic ideas, two aspects of gnostic theology appear to be relevant to Paul's letter to Timothy: Eve's part in the Creation of Adam and the denigration of femaleness.

A sampling of gnostic statements on Eve's part in creation shows the tendency to exalt Eve. Adam addresses Eve: "You are the one who has given me life."[20] Eve is said to have "sent her breath into Adam, who had no soul."[21] Eve (*Zoē*) is the one who teaches Adam "about all the things which are in the eighth heaven"; she uncovers "the veil which was upon his mind."[22] Finally Eve declares herself the "mother of my father and the sister of my husband, . . . to whom I gave birth."[23]

Gnostic writings of Nag Hammadi repeatedly show a negative assessment of femaleness. In the *Gospel of the Egyptians* (early second century), Jesus announces: "I came to destroy the works of the female." He then points out that death will prevail as long as women bear children, to which Salome responds: "Then I have done well in bearing no children."[24] According to the *Gospel of Thomas* (ca. A.D. 140), Peter wanted to send Mary away, "because women are not worthy of life." Jesus then offered to make her into a male, "because every woman who will make herself male shall enter into the kingdom of heaven."[25] Female-ness is seen as a defect; salvation comes through masculinity, or even better, through the elimination of all sexuality.[26] Another of the gnostic writings called upon believers to "flee from the bondage of femininity and to choose for themselves the salvation of masculinity."[27]

Epiphanius (ca. 315-403) tells of a gnostic group, hated by the church of Ephesus and who disturb Pergamum (Rev 2:6, 15), whom he calls successors to the Nicolaitans. These rejected marriage and were opposed to childbearing, practicing coitus interruptus and going so far as to abort the fetus of a pregnant woman.[28]

To a certain degree, these three main religious currents interacted and fed upon each other. From this mixed environment came the women in the Ephesian congregations. Those from pagan backgrounds would need to learn that the excesses of Artemis worship, along with its ascetic or sensual practices, were inappropriate for Christian women. On the other hand, those from a Jewish background would need encouragement "to study, learn, and serve in the Christian community."[29]

The Content of the Passage

Although some see 1 Timothy 2 as giving general instruction for women, the passage is more often considered as instructions regarding public worship.[30] The chapter opens with an exhortation to prayer, especially for those in positions of authority, who would be able to provide for Christians a calm and peaceable life (vv. 1-4). In v. 8, Paul begins specific instructions for public prayer. Men are to pray, in the Jewish fashion, lifting their hands; their attitude is to be without anger or quarreling, undoubtedly referring to the underlying tensions in the Ephesian church.

Women in Prayer (vv. 9-10)

> I desire then that in every place the men should pray, lifting holy hands without anger or quarreling; also that women should adorn themselves modestly and sensibly in seemly apparel, not with braided hair or gold or pearls or costly attire but by good deeds, as befits women who profess religion. (RSV)

Just as Paul gives specific instructions to the men regarding their posture and attitude in prayer, he speaks to the women, introducing his comments with the word "likewise."[31] The women who prayed in the congregation were to have made themselves attractive (*kosmeō*) inwardly, with becoming or honorable conduct, in respect or modesty and reasonableness or good judgment. Outwardly they were to "adorn" themselves with good works, rather than extravagant hair styles, elegant clothing, gold, and pearls. Thus beautified, Christian women would be prepared to proclaim (*epaggellomai*) godliness appropriately (vv. 9-10).

To arrive at this expanded translation, two words are important. The first meaning of *kosmeō* is to "put in order," "to prepare"; a second meaning is "to adorn," "to decorate." By using "adorn," translators move the emphasis from the internal preparation of the honorable conduct with respect and good judgment to an accent on externals—braids, expensive clothing, gold, and pearls. The text emphasizes the first while not excluding the second. The basic meaning of *epaggellomai* is to "promise" or "announce" something (RSV so translates all New Testament occurrences except here and 1 Tim 6:21, where it uses "profess"). While the word is used to mean "profess" in extrabiblical literature, there appears to be no reason to prefer this translation. The demeanor—inward and outward—described by Paul made the Ephesian Christian women worthy "proclaimers" of the gospel.

Women in Learning (v. 11)

Let a woman learn in silence with all submissiveness. (RSV)

Having described a Christian woman, Paul now points out how she may become such a person: "Let her learn!" The word employed (*manthanō*) encompasses both formal instruction and practical learning. Here Paul departs from Jewish tradition, following rather Jesus' lead in allowing Mary and other women to learn from him (Luke 8:1-3; 10:39-42).

This learning should take place in *hēsychia*, peace/harmony/quietness and *hypotagē*, submission. The root meaning of the word *hēsychia* is rest, peacefulness. The same word appears in v. 2, where the governors and kings allow Christians to lead a *peaceful* life. Just as the men are admonished (v. 8) to pray "without anger or quarreling," the women are to be allowed to learn without being subjected to the dissensions and wranglings that exist among Ephesian Christians.

The women are to "submit," but the text does not say to whom. Some have suggested the authority figure to whom women must submit: their husbands, any male, or the presiding elder. While Paul does admonish wives to be subject to their husbands (Eph 5:22; Col 3:18), and many scholars suggest that in vv. 11 and 12 the shift from the plural "women" to the singular "woman" indicates that Paul is here talking about the husband-wife relation,[32] the text itself seems to be discussing attitudes in worship rather than the marriage relationship. The Bible does not elsewhere teach that all women are subject to all males. Submission to the teaching elder in 1 Tim 3:2 does not fit the text. A natural understanding of the verse would be that the women are to submit to the gospel, to the teaching of Jesus, not to an unnamed person. Theirs is to be a receptive attitude. J. Keir Howard calls it "submission to Christ in a quiet and gentle demeanor, . . . rather than the domineering attitude which some were showing, . . . calling into question the authoritative teaching of the church leaders."[33] Evidently Paul considers it important for women to learn, in an atmosphere of peace and tranquility, with an inner attitude of submission to the teaching, not in disputes and public debates. Thus they will be protected from the false teachers and from the temptation to become themselves false teachers.

In urging that women should learn quietly, Paul is both maintaining Jewish tradition and departing from it. To learn in silence was, according to Simon son of Rabban Gamaliel, the best way, since indulging in too many words brings about sin (Mishnah *Aboth* 17). On the other hand, the rabbis denied religious instruction to women (Mishnah *Sotah* 3:4; *Qiddushin* 4:13). Here Paul seems to be keeping the good of Judaism and introducing the better of the gospel teaching (cf. Luke 10: 39-42).

In the words of Gloria Redekop, Paul's urging was that

> women should make themselves attractive in honorable inner and outer demeanour with reverence and good mental judgment, not with anything braided and gold or with pearls or costly clothing, but women, by means of good works, should do what is necessary in order to proclaim a religion with conviction. Let a woman learn in (an atmosphere of) peace, harmony and reverence with all submission.[34]

Women in Teaching, Authority, and Quietness (v. 12)

I permit no woman to teach or to have authority over men; she is to keep silent. (RSV)

Verse 12 is at the heart of the controversy over women in ministry. As usually translated, this verse seems to forbid women to teach, to have authority over men, or even to speak out in church. This translation does not fit with what is said elsewhere about the work of women. Paul tells Titus that women should teach and train the younger women (2:3, 4); Priscilla and her husband Aquila "expounded" to Apollos the "way of God," teaching him what he did not yet know (Acts 18:26). Paul's recognition of his female coworkers (Rom 16:3, 6, 12) suggests that they did not keep silent. Even the "proclaiming" women in 1 Tim 2:10 may suggest that a blanket order for silence is not in view here.

The attempts to explain these difficulties have been many and diverse. Some commentators have dismissed the problem by proposing that this verse is not of Pauline origin. Others have called it entirely cultural, and thus ignored it. A recent approach has attempted to translate the verse: "I do not permit a woman to represent herself as originator of man."[35] None of these approaches may be considered entirely satisfactory, some because they take a low view of Scripture, others because of their contorted analyses.

A literal translation of the verse shows the difficult syntax: "But to teach for a woman I am not permitting (or do not permit) nor to *authentein* a man, but to be at rest." While recognizing these difficulties, we may attempt to elucidate some points.

(1) Here the verb *didaskō* is in the present infinitive, which means

"to teach" or "to continue teaching," showing lineal or continuous action. This verb usually appears with a modifier or a direct object, which may be either the person(s) taught or the content of the teaching. Of the 13 times this verb form appears in the New Testament, three are accompanied by a place, showing where the teaching took place; twice the verb appears with a direct object, showing who was taught; two show the content of the teaching; and three times show both the persons taught and the content of the teaching. This and two other instances have no modifiers at all (Luke 6:6; Acts 1:1). The verb itself is thus totally neutral, giving no clues regarding meaning.

(2) "I am not permitting" or " I do not permit" is the same verb that appears in 1 Cor 14:34 in the passive ("women are not permitted"). It is translated from a present tense, which normally indicates action taking place at the time of speaking or writing. There is not within the verb itself or in the tense in which it appears any indication of timelessness. Thus, without any violence to the text, Paul could be saying that he was currently not permitting women to teach, because of any number of reasons, or even that he was not permitting women to teach until such a time as they had learned sufficiently.

(3) The word *oude*, "nor," usually introduces two parallel elements, something like the English "neither . . . nor." However, the word order here is not usual, thus leading some to subordinate the next infinitive, *authentein*, to the first one, *didaskein*. This would make possible the translation: "I do not permit a woman to teach in a way that usurps the authority of man." However, this would not be a natural translation; it is better to understand that Paul here prohibits two parallel activities: teaching and *authentein*.

(4) The present infinitive *authentein* is the only instance of the verb *authenteō* in the New Testament; thus we have no help from other passages. Further, the infinitive form is not found "in the whole of extant Greek literature outside of later repetitions of 1 Tim. 2:12";[36] thus we have no illumination of the syntactic problem of the text. The etymology of the word is also obscure: it may come from *auto-thentes*, "the self involved in killing," or from *autos-hentes*, "achieving or realizing an action on oneself or by one's initiative."[37] Andrew Perriman thus points out that the word is more related to "authorship" than "authority."[38] A well-accepted etymological dictionary gives the noun form as "a responsible author, especially the author responsible for a murder."[39]

To elucidate the meaning of the term, L. E. Wilshire studied all the uses of the verb in the *Thesaurus Lingua Graece* (*TLG*) database, which covers some ten centuries of Greek writings. His conclusion is that the traditional translation of 1 Tim 2:12, the neutral "to have or exercise authority," comes from a later period.[40]

While it is difficult to trace the meaning of the word through time, it appears that in the first century A.D., *authenteō* had a negative connotation and related to "instigating or perpetrating a crime" or "the active wielding of influence (with respect to a person) or the initiation of an action."[41] Wilshire notes that while "authors, roughly contemporaneous with Paul . . . used the word almost exclusively with the meaning of 'to murder/murderer' or 'to perpetrate a crime/perpetrator of a crime,'" others "did use it with the meaning 'authority.'"[42] Wilshire asserts that "the preponderant number of citations from this compilation [*TLG*] have to do with self-willed violence, criminal action, or murder or with the person who does these actions."[43] Perriman admits the meaning "instigating or perpetrating a crime" but prefers to translate *authentein* as an "active wielding of influence or the initiation of an action."[44]

As the centuries pass, the meaning of the word appears to shift. Christian writers use it almost exclusively to refer to authority.[45] On the other hand, secular writers use the verb with two meanings: murder and exercise authority.[46] By the fifth century the lexicographer Hesychius defines *authentein* as "to execute authority," a synonym of *exousiazein*; and the related noun *authentēs* as (1) "one who executes authority," (2) "one who does things with his own hand," or (3) a "murderer."[47]

To summarize, then, the meaning of *authentein* in this verse would not refer primarily to occupying a position of authority. It might, however, refer to taking independent action, assuming responsibility, or even, according to Wilshire, "instigating violence." This last possibility would be in opposition to the peace or harmony and good judgment for which Paul called. Perhaps the situation at Ephesus was similar to that in the churches to which James wrote concerning the "fightings among" them (Jas 4:1).[48] Perriman points out that

> in v. 12 Paul is thinking specifically of what Eve did to Adam; and Eve did not *have* authority, but *in her action became* responsible for—became the cause of—Adam's transgression. In the light of these associations the connotation of "perpetrating a crime" is fully appropriate. In the overlapping of the two contexts—that of the scriptural "type" and that of the current circumstances at Ephesus—*authentein* refers both to what Eve once did and to what women now should not do.[49]

(5) *Hēsychia*, usually translated as "silence" in this passage, is the same word that appears in vv. 2 and 11. Its root meaning is "rest," "harmony," "quietness." There is no reason to choose a secondary meaning, not attested in the New Testament, when the primary meaning is logical.

It is, therefore, safe to say that Paul does not want women to teach at this time, certainly not until they have learned in quietness, submitting to the teaching of the gospel. Neither does he want them to take upon themselves the responsibility for violence or independent action of any kind. They should not emulate Eve, who in the next verse is presented as responsible for the fall of the human race.[50]

Adam and Eve (vv. 13-14)

> For Adam was formed first, then Eve; and Adam was not deceived, but the woman was deceived and became a transgressor.

In vv. 13 and 14, which clearly form a unit, Paul goes back to the Creation story to make his point:

> For Adam was created first,
>   then Eve;
> And Adam was not deceived,
>   but the woman fell into transgression through deceit.

These verses are often interpreted as Paul's reasons for forbidding women to teach: They are constitutionally not suited to the task because of their susceptibility to deception.[51] This interpretation would be in keeping with Jewish tradition as given in Sirach 25:24: "Woman is the origin of sin, and it is through her that we all die." A similar concept is enunciated by Philo: "The woman, being imperfect and deprived 'by nature,' made the beginning of sinning; but man, as being the more excellent and perfect nature, was the first to set the example of blushing and being ashamed, and indeed of every good feeling and action."[52] This teaching, however, does not agree with what Paul says elsewhere. In Rom 5:12-14 Adam is the one who sins and brings death to the human race.

On the other hand, these verses may be taken as an example of what happens when false teaching is propounded and accepted. Verse 13 is introduced by the conjunction "for," *gar*, which may introduce the reason for what has been said (as explained above) or an example of what has just been said.[53] In the second sense the meaning might be something like, "For consider what happened when Eve was deceived."[54] Thus we would have a close parallel to 2 Cor 11:3: "But I am afraid that as the serpent deceived Eve by his cunning, your thoughts will be led astray from a sincere and pure devotion to Christ." Philip Payne concludes: "Paul points to the example of Eve's deception which led to the fall as a warning to the church in Ephesus lest deception of women, there, too, lead to their fall."[55] Alan Padgett calls Eve a "cautionary type" here and in 2 Cor 11:2-3. Adam, he continues, stands for the men, "formed first" in a spiritual sense.[56] To make these verses the basis for teaching woman's culpability for the sin of the human race or a permanently heightened susceptibility to sin is to stretch their meaning. Only when one presupposes a "subordinate, helping role envisaged for them in creation," as does Douglas Moo, is it possible to read into these verses a lasting injunction of subordination.[57]

In v. 14, the Greek uses two different verbs for "deceived." The first, used for Adam, is *apataō*, "cheat," "mislead." The second, used for Eve, is *exapataō*, "lead away from [something good]"; its added preposition makes it emphatic—"completely led astray."[58] Other references to the activities of the false teachers (1 Tim 1:6, 9; 4:1; 5:15) suggest that here the same "leading astray" is in view.[59]

Paul here repeats what the biblical record clearly states: Adam was created first (Gen 2:7, 18, 21), and Eve was deceived by the serpent (Gen 3:13). In 1 Cor 11:8 Paul noted that woman was made from man. If there had been no doubt about whose creation came first, the assertion of v. 13 would not have been necessary. As noted in the section on the religious context of Ephesus, the idea that Eve was somehow prior to Adam and responsible for his enlightenment was current by the mid-first century. Paul wanted the record set straight. Eve was not created first, nor was she to be thanked for leading Adam into sin. Yet she was led completely astray. Ephesian women were in danger of the same fate.

Women Saved through Bearing Children (v. 15).

> Yet woman will be saved through bearing children, if she continues in faith and love and holiness, with modesty. (RSV)

Verse 15 presents serious difficulties, in vocabulary, syntax, and meaning—David Scholer calls it "notoriously difficult."[60] A literal translation, showing that the first phrase belongs with v. 14, would read: "But [the woman, v. 14] will be saved through *teknogonia*. When they remain in faith and love and sanctification with good judgment."

Vocabulary. The verb *sōzō*, here translated "will be saved," may mean to "heal," to "be well," or—in its eschatological sense—"to be saved." Scholars do not agree on the meaning intended here. For example, S. Jebb has posited that the woman would be "saved" from falling into the "error of usurping authority."[61] However, in Paul the verb *sōzō* is normally used "almost exclusively in reference to the saving activity of God. . . . There is thus no escaping the conclusion that the text is referring to the eternal salvation of women in its fullest New Testament sense."[62]

The preposition translated "through" can have many meanings. Stanley Porter notes several: (1) "by means of"; (2) "during the time of," possible but eliminated by translating "saved" as referring to final salvation; (3) "in spite of," which is not usual; and (4) "in the experience of," in an attempt to deal with the passage theologically. Of these, he finds that only the first is probable.[63] On the other hand, Kroeger and Kroeger point to the proper meaning as "throughout," or "within an attendant circumstance." The translation would then be, "she shall be saved within the child-bearing function."[64]

The word *teknogonia* appears only here in the New Testament. Literally it refers to childbirth, as is seen in the nonbiblical usage; however, Christian authors have attempted to broaden its meaning to include raising children as well as bearing them.[65] Perhaps it is best to leave the word to its normal, straightforward meaning.

Syntax. As already noted, the first phrase of v. 15 is the conclusion of v. 14 and one may assume that the subject of the sentence is the "woman" who was led astray. If this woman was Eve, who is the woman in v. 15? The first part of v. 15 is in the singular—she will be saved; the second is in the plural—when they remain. Who are "they"? Women in general? The women's children? Men and women? Husband and wife? Possibly the best interpretation is to take the plural as a broadening of the one representative woman in previous verses.

Between the singular result clause and the plural conditional phrase of the same sentence, the Nestlé-Aland Greek text places a period (full stop). While recognizing that punctuation was not part of the original text, one cannot but see that the syntactic difficulties of the verse confused the scholars. The fact that the next verse opens with the phrase, "Faithful is the word," followed by a period, does not simplify the interpretation. Does this phrase go with the statement about the women? Or does it apply to the desiring of spiritual leadership (1 Tim 3:1)?

Meaning. If understood literally, this verse would say that a childless woman could have no hope of salvation. For this reason, several interpretations have been suggested. In fact, Porter affirms that "what the text seems to be saying . . . is apparently formulated more on the basis of ideology than critical exegesis."[66] Some have attempted to do away with the difficulties by denying Pauline authorship. Others have suggested that "what Paul intends is that woman's salvation is to be found in her being a model, godly woman, known for her good works."[67] Yet others have referred this passage to *the* birth—Jesus born of Mary—through which salvation comes to all.[68] Some have interpreted it as meaning that godly women would be kept safe through childbirth, which in the first century was a major killer of women.

The meaning of v. 15 must be derived from the text and its context. Even Moo, who finds v. 12 a normative prohibition of women's teaching, is willing to admit that the advice of v. 15 "was clearly needed as an antidote to the false teachers, who counseled abstention from marriage (1 Tim 4:3) and generally, it seems, sought to denigrate those virtues and activities which Paul regarded as fitting for Christian women."[69] Evidently in this epistle Paul is fighting a heresy that promotes myths and genealogies (1 Tim 1:3, 4) and forbids marriage (1 Tim 4:3). Instead of gossiping (5:13), thus giving opportunity for slander (6:1), women should occupy their proper domestic role, not listening to the false teachers who taught that salvation was to be reached by asceticism and abstention from marital relations. David Kimberly suggests

> that 1 Tim 2:15 is expressed in response to erroneous gnostic teaching in Ephesus to the effect that childbearing was an occasion for condemnation of Christian women. The sense of the text is that women will be saved in childbearing, not condemned, as long as they continue in faith. Paul's intent is to restore this womanly vocation to its rightful place in contrast to the manner in which it was depreciated in gnostic circles.[70]

According to van der Jagt, "childbirth was associated with negative elements" in much of the ancient world. In Judaism, where purity was so important for salvation, childbirth rendered the woman impure, cut off from the temple community. In gnostic thinking, sexuality and procreation hindered salvation. Van der Jagt concludes: "1 Tim 2:15 contains a rehabilitation of the woman, of womanhood and of motherhood." While to us the message may sound reactionary, "the audience to whom the author addressed himself must also have heard a revolutionary message in the same words."[71] Kroeger and Kroeger find this passage a refutation of false doctrines, "an affirmation of the spiritual wholeness of woman-hood and a manifesto of women's God-given right to bear children."[72]

Conclusion

To summarize, the primary intention of 1 Tim 2:8-15 is not to spec-ify the relationship that should exist between men and women. Rather it contains advice directed to a specific situation in Ephesus. Within instruc-tions on worship, Paul encourages women to live godly lives, to learn quietly, to avoid being deceived by the false teachers as Eve had been de-ceived by the serpent, and to bear and raise children, all the time remain-ing firm in a reasonable faith bathed in love. In the words of van der Jagt:

> Women can have a good life and hope for eternal salvation without getting involved in power struggles. They can reach the same spiritual heights as men without renouncing their womanhood. What sounds so negative in the ears of many now would have sounded positive in the ears of those who heard the message in a different world from ours.[73]

The concern of this passage is not at all about women serving in the ministry or as local church elders, much less about ordination, since these were not issues in the congregations of Ephesus. While the sparseness of information and the complex construction of the passage make it difficult for modern readers to know precisely what Paul had in mind, it is clear that he was addressing some current concern that Timothy and the Christians in Ephesus would have readily understood. Furthermore, to take as eternally normative the limited prohibition of women's teaching (v. 12)—when in other passages Paul clearly approves female participation in teaching, praying, and prophesying—does violence to the hermen-eutical principle of the unity of Scripture. Likewise, to determine from v. 13 that priority in creation gives males the right to rule over women goes beyond sound biblical interpretation. The question of whether women can be ordained to the gospel ministry must be answered on other grounds than the interpretation of 1 Tim 2:8-15.

Endnotes

1. See Gerhard Hasel, *Biblical Interpretation Today* (Washington, DC: Biblical Research Institute, 1985), 101-103.

2. Grant R. Osborne, "Hermeneutics and Women in the Church," *Journal of the Evangelical Theological Society* 20 (1977): 338.

3. Hasel, 106-108.

4. Sharon Hodgin Gritz, *Paul, Women Teachers, and the Mother Goddess at Ephesus* (Lanham, NY: University Press of America, 1991), 3.

5. Gordon D. Fee, "Women in Ministry: The Meaning of 1 Timothy 2:8-15 in Light of the Purpose of Timothy," *Journal of the Christian Brethren Research Fellowship*, no. 123 (November 1990): 11.

6. See Thomas C. Geer, Jr., "Admonitions to Women in 1 Tim. 2:8-15," in *Essays on Women in Earliest Christianity*, ed. Carroll D. Osburn (Joplin, MO: College Press, 1993), 1:284-288.

7. Gritz, 39.

8. Ibid., 41-42.

9. Markus Barth, *Ephesians*, Anchor Bible (Garden City, NY: Doubleday, 1974), 2:661; this conclusion, notwithstanding claims to the contrary made by S. M. Baugh, "A Foreign World: Ephesus in the First Century," in *Women in the Church: A Fresh Analysis of 1 Timothy 2:9-15*, ed. Andreas J. Köstenberger, Thomas R. Schreiner, and H. Scott Baldwin (Grand Rapids: Baker, 1995), 13-63.

10. Horace *Satires* 2.6.77-78.

11. Cicero *On the Nature of the Gods* 3.5.12-13; Strabo *Geography* 1.2.8.

12. Diodorus of Sicily 3.52.4-54.7.

13. Strabo *Geography* 11.5.3.

14. Herodotus 7.99; 8.101-103; Philostratus *The Life of Apollonius of Tyana* 4. 21.

15. Richard Clark Kroeger and Catherine Clark Kroeger, *I Suffer Not a Woman* (Grand Rapids: Baker, 1992), 194-195.

16. "Invocation of Isis," papyrus 1380, *Oxyrhynchus Papyri* (London: Egypt Exploration Fund, 1915), 11: 214-216.

17. Josephus *Against Apion* 2.199.

18. Philo *On the Cherubim* 9-14, 61.

19. *Apocalypse of Adam* 1.3.

20. *Hypostasis of the Archons* 2.4.89.14-17.

21. *On the Origin of the World* 115.

22. Ibid., 104; *Apocryphon of John* 67-71.

23. *Thunder, Perfect Mind* 6.2.13.30-32.

24. See Clement of Alexandria *Miscellanies* 3.45.

25. *Gospel of Thomas* 114.

26. *Dialogue of the Saviour* 90-95; *Gospel of Thomas* 27.

27. *Zostrianos* 8.1.131.

28. Epiphanius *Panarion* 26.3-5.

29. Gritz, 43.

30. For example, supporting a general admonition: Martin Dibelius and Hans Conzelmann, *The Pastoral Epistles*, Hermeneia (Philadelphia: Fortress, 1972), 44. Supporting a worship setting: Thomas Schreiner, "An Interpretation of 1 Timothy 2:9-15: A Dialogue with Scholarship," in *Women in the Church: A Fresh Analysis of 1 Timothy 2:9-15*, 113; Gritz, 182; Thomas Oden, *First and Second Timothy and Titus*, Interpretation (Louisville: John Knox, 1989), 91-93.

31. Some authors, such as Richard Davidson in chap. 13, indicate that "women" should here be translated "wives." The Greek allows both translations, but I have chosen to use the more general word. On this scholarly discussion, see Geer, 289.

32. Gritz, 125; see also Gordon P. Hugenberger, "Women in Church Office: Hermeneutics or Exegesis? A Survey of Approaches to 1 Tim 2:8-15," *Journal of the Evangelical Theological Society* 35 (1992): 341-360. After surveying the different approaches to the text, Hugenberger concludes that Paul here prohibits a wife from teaching or having authority over her own husband. See also Richard Davidson's chapter in this book.

33. J. Keir Howard, "Neither Male nor Female: An Examination of the Status of Women in the New Testament," *Evangelical Quarterly* 55 (1983): 40.

34. Gloria Neufeld Redekop, "Let the Women Learn: 1 Timothy 2:8-15 Reconsidered," *Studies in Religion/Sciences religieuses* 19 (1990): 238, 240.

35. Kroeger and Kroeger, 103.

36. Leland Wilshire, "1 Tim. 2:12 Revisited: A Reply to Paul W. Barnett and Timothy J. Harris," *Evangelical Quarterly* 65 (1993): 48.

37. Ibid.

38. Andrew C. Perriman, "What Eve Did, What Women Shouldn't Do: The Meaning of *Authenteō* in 1 Timothy 2:12," *Tyndale Bulletin* 44 (Jan 1993): 137.

39. *Dictionnaire étymologique de la langue grecque: Histoire des mots* (Paris: Klincksieck, 1968), s.v. *"authenteō."*

40. Leland Wilshire, "The *TLG* Computer and Further Reference to *Authenteō* in 1 Timothy 2:12," *NewTestament Studies* 34 (1988): 120-134; idem., "1 Timothy 2:12 Revisited," 44. Interestingly, after studying the same database, H. Scott Baldwin concludes the opposite, that "to have authority" is the normal first-century meaning of the verb; his study, however, pays far more attention to the usage of the word in later centuries (especially by the Church Fathers) than to its use before Paul (H. Scott Baldwin, "A Difficult Word: *Authenteō* in 1 Timothy 2:12," and "Appendix 2: *Authenteō* in Ancient Greek Literature," in *Women in the Church: A Fresh Analysis of 1 Timothy 2:9-15*, 65-80, 269-306).47.

41. Perriman, 138.

42. Wilshire, "*TLG*," 130.

43. Wilshire, "1 Timothy 2:12 Revisited," 47.

44. Perriman, 138.

45. Wilshire, "*TLG*," 125.

46. Ibid., 127.

47. Ibid., 125.

48. Wilshire, "1 Tim. 2:12 Revisited," 48.

49. Perriman, 148.

50. Some scholars, holding that this verse is parallel to 1 Cor 11:1-6; 14:34-35: 1 Pet 3:1-6, take this verse to refer to the relation between *husband* and *wife*, rather than between men and women. Thus, 1 Tim 2:11, 12 would command wives not to teach their own husbands or take over their husband's authority "in the worship setting" (Gritz, 131; see also 125, 130). Davidson takes this position in chap. 13.

51. Douglas J. Moo, "1 Timothy 2:11-15: Meaning and Significance," *Trinity Journal* 1 (1980): 70.

52. Philo (Bohl, 1885), IV, 306; as cited in Stanley Glen, *Pastoral Problems in First Corinthians* (Philadelphia: Westminster, 1964), 135-136.

53. A. T. Robertson, *A Grammar of the New Testament Greek*, 1189-1191.

54. Philip B. Payne, "Libertarian Women in Ephesus: A Response to Douglas J. Moo's Article '1 Timothy 2:11-15: Meaning and Significance,'" *Trinity Journal* 2 (1981): 176-177.

55. Ibid., 177.

56. Alan Padgett, "Wealthy Women at Ephesus: 1 Timothy 2:8-15 in Social Context," *Interpretation* 41 (1987): 26.

57. Moo, 68; see also chap. 13 of this book.

58. Redekop, 243.

59. Timothy J. Harris, "Why Did Paul Mention Eve's Deception? A Critique of P. W. Barnett's Interpretation of 1 Timothy 2," *Evangelical Quarterly* 62 (1990): 348.

60. David M. Scholer, "Feminist Hermeneutics and Evangelical Biblical Interpretation," *Journal of the Evangelical Theological Society* 30 (1987): 417.

61. S. Jebb, "Suggested Interpretation of 1 Ti 2:15," *Expository Times* 18 (1970): 220-221.

62. David R. Kimberley, "1 Tim 2:15: A Possible Understanding of a Difficult Text," *Journal of the Evangelical Theological Society* 35 (1992): 481-482.

63. Stanley E. Porter, "What Does it Mean to Be 'Saved by Childbirth'" (1 Timothy 2:15)?" *Journal for the Study of the New Testament* 49 (1993): 96-98.

64. Kroeger and Kroeger, 176.

65. Ibid., 96.

66. Porter, 87.

67. Gordon Fee, *1 and 2 Timothy*, Good News Commentary (San Francisco: Harper, 1984), 38.

68. Payne, 180.

69. Moo, 72.

70. Kimberley, 486.

71. Krijn A. van der Jagt, "Women Are Saved through Bearing Children," *Bible Translator* 39 (1988): 207.

72. Kroeger and Kroeger, 176.

73. Van der Jagt, 208.

CHAPTER 17

ELLEN WHITE AND WOMEN'S RIGHTS

ALICIA A. WORLEY

> Those who feel called out to join the movement in favor of woman's rights and the so-called dress reform might as well sever all connection with the third angel's message. The spirit which attends the one cannot be in harmony with the other. The Scriptures are plain upon the relations and rights of men and women. Spiritualists have, to quite an extent, adopted this singular mode of dress. Seventh-day Adventists, who believe in the restoration of the gifts, are often branded as spiritualists. Let them adopt this costume, and their influence is dead.
> Ellen G. White, *Testimonies for the Church*, 1:421.

Introduction

Questions about women's rights and equality have long stirred up conflict in the United States and around the world. In the Seventh-day Adventist Church, these issues have most recently been taken up in the debate over women's ordination to gospel ministry. While some argue that withholding this privilege from women is an unjust denial of their rights, others warn that seeking such equality is a denial of a divinely ordained hierarchy of the sexes.

Ellen White's writings are significant to this discussion in light of her status as an inspired prophet to the church. How did she view women's rights? Did she see women's rights and the nineteenth-century women's rights movement as one and the same? Her statement quoted above, one of the few on women's rights, is one of the most direct, yet it is potentially ambiguous and misunderstood. In the debate over women's ordination it has used as evidence against ordaining women pastors.

The purpose of this study is to examine carefully this statement to gain a better knowledge of how Ellen White understood the rights of women. By so doing, we might be better able to project how she would advise today's church in its struggle over the issue of women's ordination. To accomplish this purpose, we will seek to answer three questions: Why did Ellen White speak against the movement in favor of women's rights and dress reform? What did she mean by saying "the Scriptures are plain upon the relations and rights of men and women"? What principles in this statement can guide our response to the issue of women's ordination? To understand White's position on women's rights, we will first look at the background of the statement. This will be followed by a consideration of the issues underlying the reasons for not joining the women's movement and by an analysis of the principles that emerge from these reasons. Finally, we will consider how these principles might be applied to the issue of women's ordination.[1]

The Statement in Context

This statement was first published in 1864 as one of several testimonies collected in a small volume entitled *Testimony No. 10*. The 13-page testimony containing this statement, entitled "The Cause in the East," warned against false excitement in worship, false doctrines, reckless attitudes, and the American costume. Our quotation is located in the discussion of this "so-called dress reform," so designated by Ellen White to distinguish it from the true dress reform she had seen in vision.[2]

Slight editorial changes occurred—mostly in the 1880s—between Ellen White's statement in the original and that published in *Testimonies to the Church*, 1:421.[3] White wrote, "the relations and rights of *women* and men," while the editors corrected to "of *men* and women" (italics added), probably to conform to common usage. If Ellen White was intentionally referring to women first, why might she have wished to emphasize women's rights over men's? Perhaps she believed women's rights were more endangered. Support for this possibility is suggested by her writing far more about the need for women to protect their personal boundaries, to develop themselves, to be sensitive to their call to service, and to see their coequal roles in the home than about men's needs in these areas.

Another change is perhaps more significant. The original wording was "Those who feel called out to join *the Woman's Rights Movement*," but this was replaced with "Those who feel called out to join the *movement in favor of woman's rights*" (italics added). The modification communicates a subtle but significant change in focus from the specific movement called the Woman's Rights Movement to the larger context of anyone favoring women's rights. Thus the specificity that *may* have been intended is removed in favor of a more general application.

The Social Context

Much of the nineteenth century was a time of social upheaval, a time when various groups were fighting for reform in areas as diverse as education, health, temperance, suffrage, and abolition. As society strained under pressure for reform, traditional views were challenged, even fundamental institutions such as marriage, family, and the church. The women's movement arose in response to the plight of women.

Women were not accorded what the twentieth century considers basic human rights. Politically, women were virtual nonentities. Their contributions were confined largely to the domestic realm. They could not secure employment in the occupation of their choice, and higher education was practically closed to them. In addition, they were not only denied the right to vote; they were, socially and individually, perceived as being under the jurisdiction of men. Once married, a woman lost all claim to any property she had previously owned; it was transferred to her husband. She had legal claims neither to her own body nor to her children in the event of divorce.

Even in the religious arena, women were limited. Most churches did not ordain women and either prohibited or frowned upon women speaking in public. Because a large sector of society perceived the church as responsible for the denigration of women, many elements in the women's movement became hostile to it. For example, powerful crusader Elizabeth Gage called the church "the bulwark of women's slavery."[4] For her, no entity was more offensive than organized religion. Thus freedom from religious orthodoxy became crucial to feminist leadership.[5]

In some cases, the bondage of women was not directly imposed by others, but came from their own cultural expectations, values, and choices. One such case was that of health and dress. Many recognized the unhealthfulness of women's clothing, with restrictive corsets and street-sweeping skirts, but women inflicted these upon themselves in the name of fashion. Women's rights leaders decried the enslavement of women to fashion, and some designed a costume that was not only more healthful, but included trousers which served to emphasize that women were "equal with" men. This outfit came to be known as the American Costume and was the "so-called dress reform" which Ellen White condemned. White was not alone in this condemnation; by the standards of society the costume was considered distracting and immodest. It expressed the extremist values and goals of the women's movement and was rejected by society at large, and eventually by the women's movement.[6]

Keeping this background in mind, we will now look at the quotation itself to identify the apparent reasons for White's position and the issues these reasons raise.

Reasons and Issues

Those who feel called out to join the movement in favor of woman's rights and the so-called dress reform might as well sever all connection with the third angel's message.

Ellen White left no doubt that her readers were not to join the women's rights movement—a Christian could not belong to both movements because they were incompatible. Three apparent reasons for this incompatibility emerge from this quotation: (1) The *spirit* of the women's rights movement and so-called dress reform contrasted with that of the third angel's message; (2) The *Scriptures* are plain about the *rights* and relations of men and women; and (3) The *influence* of Seventh-day Adventists would be compromised if they were identified with spiritualists and the American costume.

The Issue of Spirit

The spirit which attends the one cannot be in harmony with the other.

The spirit of the women's rights movement was questionable. Because the women's movement was a collective movement in which people accumulated and used power to accomplish their goals,[7] conflict and controversy abounded. Laws were frequently broken. The movement became so controversial that it brought upon itself the attacks of society at large. To be on either side of the debate was dangerous. To espouse this movement was to enter into controversy; to oppose it was to join those who were frequently "violent, loud, and often scurrilous."[8] As incredible as it may seem today, women who were not a part of the women's movement organized to *oppose* those fighting for the right to vote.

The non-Christian spirit attending the women's movement was in even greater contrast to the spirit on which the third angel's message was founded. Ellen White's statement was written only 20 years after the Great Disappointment. Those who had "accepted the truth" believed Christ would return as soon as they had completed their God-given mission, and all their energies were to be put forth in this task. There was no time to become involved in reform issues gripping a society so soon to face the end of the world.[9] The Adventist contribution to the women's rights movement was to be in their modeling of Christian principles in their churches and homes while pursuing their mission. Women were to represent the truth by being chaste, modest, blameless, sober, temperate, charitable, patient, truthful, courteous, obedient, self-sacrificing, and in all things above reproach.[10] Furthermore, the truth "should be presented in a manner which will make it attractive to the intelligent mind," and should be allowed to "stand on its own merits." Much of the rights movement did neither. The truth would elevate, refine, and sanctify the judgment. Those espousing the truth should have refined manners, shun oddities and eccentricities, and be in such harmony of spirit that they are "one."[11] The spirit of the women's movement was in total opposition to that of the third angel's message.

Ellen White was concerned about the spirit of God's people. In the paragraph immediately following the statement under study, she said: "With the so-called dress reform there goes a spirit of levity and boldness just in keeping with the dress. Modesty and reserve seem to depart from many as they adopt that style of dress." But even more revealing is her description, in the same article, of the spirit of fanaticism that plagued God's work in the East. She described it with adjectives such as noisy, rough, careless, excitable, overbearing, accusative, reckless, disorderly, trifling, restless, independent, quarrelsome, self-deceived, and emotional.[12] These words appropriately characterized the spirit of the movement favoring women's rights and the American costume. The wrong spirit also led to extremism, so prevalent in the early stages of the movement for women's rights. Leaders and followers alike took positions they later regretted or abandoned, as in the areas of marriage and the American costume. How could Adventists choose to identify with a movement that embodied the very spirit God was calling His people to renounce? It is not surprising that Ellen White spoke against such a spirit, refrained from associating with the secular reform movements of her time, and discouraged Adventists from becoming involved in these movements.

The Issue of Scripture and Rights

The Scriptures are plain upon the relations and rights of men and women.

Ellen White's second reason for avoiding involvement in the women's rights movement drew her readers' attention to the Bible as the criterion for determining the rights of men and women. Ellen White did not discuss rights systematically or point to specific chapters and verses where the Bible teaches about them. But because she did not, this sentence has provided opportunity for conflicting interpretations.

The concept of rights is a complex one. According to the dictionary, the word "right" "refers to a legally, morally, or traditionally just claim." To say that people have rights is to say they have "something, such as a power or possession to which [they have] an established claim."[13] "Rights" are usually thought of in an interpersonal context and carry the concept of "obligation." Rights may be protected fairly or unfairly by written or unwritten laws. The women's rights movement not only challenged the laws of society and government, but also the very foundation of society's understanding of human rights.

If we are to understand this sentence, we must know what Ellen White believed the Bible plainly taught about the rights of men and women. To accomplish this goal, a CD-ROM search of all her statements that included the word "rights"[14] was conducted; this uncovered more than 400 statements from books, letters, and manuscripts. The rationale for this method of research is that Ellen White's writings reflect what she believed the Bible said, and that biblical principles guided her advice. It further assumes that a fundamental harmony exists *within* her writings, so that representative statements reveal her position clearly enough to draw conclusions. Finally, we assume that her applications of these principles were not only appropriate for her time, but can speak to us today.

Basic Human Rights

The majority of Ellen White's statements on rights refer to basic rights. She believed that all human rights are God-given and the legitimate inheritance of every human being, male or female. The desire for rights is innate, reflecting an "inborn principle which nothing can eradicate."[15] Her list of fundamental human rights included the inalienable rights of life, liberty, pursuit of happiness, conscience, individuality, and independent thought.[16] Ellen White's belief in fair remuneration reflects her more general belief that the rights of others should be respected in social practice. For example, she spoke against wage imbalances between physicians and ministers, and argued that ministers, wives of ministers, women, and nurses were all to receive fair pay.[17] She felt so strongly that minister's wives should be recompensed for their work that she used some of her own tithe for this purpose.[18] General rights also carry with them an obligation to protect the social rights of others,[19] by engaging in acts of kindness and mercy even toward enemies;[20] ministering to the needs of the poor and suffering;[21] abstaining from theft, calumny, and slander against others;[22] and refraining from controlling another individual's thinking or behavior.[23] Christians are called to a higher standard than that of society.[24]

According to Ellen White, rights originate with God as the Creator of human beings. In response, everything we are—soul, body, spirit, mind, and talents—belongs to Him.[25] The guarantee for human rights is found in obedience to God's law and the gospel.[26] Obedience to the law is synonymous with having a "sacred regard for the rights of others, and should never be interpreted as contradicting human rights nor their exercise.[27] Indeed, one indication of false religion is the teaching that encourages adherents to be "careless of human needs, sufferings, and rights."[28] An absence of rights is evidence of Satan's work to bring humans into slavery.[29]

Ellen White sometimes referred "rights" to a person's obligation to him/herself, particularly in relationship to God.[30] But she also pointed to a biblical basis for rights in the context of interpersonal relationships. Because human beings live in community, identifying and protecting the boundaries of basic individual human rights becomes not only more complicated but also more essential. The "group"—whether it be government, church, or family—is responsible for guaranteeing the rights of those within its jurisdiction. The "leaders" of the group are responsible for carrying out those guarantees, and the "members" of the group are to maintain loyalty to the group while cooperating with the leaders to conserve the rights of one another.

Rights in Roles and Relationships

Interpersonal rights are an implementation of basic human rights in social contexts. In most cases, interpersonal rights relate to roles and responsibilities rather than sex or gender. Examples of such relationships discussed by Ellen White include government and citizen, church leadership and member, parent and child, and husband and wife.

Government and citizen. Governments are responsible for upholding order and protecting citizens. If these goals are to be achieved, however, citizens must submit to governmental authority. Therefore, laws—and obedience to them—guide the identification of the rights and responsibilities of governments and their citizens. This arrangement works well when God's laws, which "were designed to promote social equality," and thus order, form the basis of government laws.[31] When God's law "guards the rights, the individuality, of every human being," it "restrains the superior from oppression, and the subordinate from disobedience."[32] Ellen White stated that a government's neglect of God's plan leads to oppression, which in turn arouses "the passions of the poorer class. . . . [This creates] a feeling of desperation which would tend to demoralize society and open the door to crimes of every description."[33] The inequality, oppression, and lawlessness that characterized the women's rights movement of the nineteenth century illustrate the truth of this principle.

Church leadership and members. The church, as the bride of Christ, is to be an example of God's love and attention to the just treatment of every one of his children.[34] Church leaders are God's "government" for the community of believers. They have an obligation to nurture members through the "discipline which guards the rights of all and increases the sense of mutual dependence."[35] In general counsel and personal letters, Ellen White asserted the need for servant leaders who would "guard the interests of others as jealously as they would guard their own,[36] and for members who would cooperate by respecting and protecting one another's rights. Ellen White affirmed that there are

> certain rights that belong to every individual, in doing God's service. No man has any more right to take these rights from us than to take life itself. God has given us freedom to think, and it is our privilege and duty always to be a doer of the Word, and to follow our impressions of duty. We are only human beings, and one human being has no jurisdiction over the conscience of any other human being.[37]

Ellen White found it necessary to speak against leaders who mismanaged their power. "God never designed that one man's mind and judgment should be a controlling power," that anyone "should rule and plan and devise without the careful and prayerful consideration of the whole body, in order that all may move in a sound, thorough, harmonious manner." Because we are "individually the workmanship of God," we cannot be owned by another human being.[38] Noting the "high-handed power" among church leaders, she warned that "lording it over God's heritage will create such a disgust of man's jurisdiction that a state of insubordination will result."[39] Such a situation in secular society had contributed to the large number of participants in the women's rights movement who turned against religious institutions because of their repression of women's human rights. Ellen White warned one Adventist leader who was exhibiting an oppressive attitude to "the faithful sisters" in his church: "The feelings you cherish . . . are more satanic than divine. . . . It is not always the men who are best adapted to the successful management of a church."[40]

Parent and child. Ellen White presented the family relation as God-ordained.[41] Persons first learn to respect personal rights and to learn "submission, self-denial, and a regard for others' happiness" in the home.[42] God desires family members to respect individual rights in love and humble submission so the world can see the gospel in action. "Under the hallowed influence of such a home, the principle of brotherhood laid down in the word of God is more widely recognized and obeyed."[43]

Parents, as leaders of the home, "should acknowledge and respect" the rights of their children.[44] Children should receive not only physical care from their parents, but education and training that address their social and spiritual needs as well.[45] Whereas Ellen White held both fathers and mothers as responsible for this nurture, she wrote at great length about a mother's obligations. "Nothing can have a greater claim upon the mother than her children have."[46] To a woman who wished to leave her family and embark on a missionary career, Ellen White counseled, "Jesus does not lead you to forsake your family for this or for any other cause. God has made you a trustee, a steward, in your home. . . . Your husband has rights; your children have rights; and these must not be ignored by you."[47] What a contrast to the women's rights movement!

Lest we misunderstand, two other statements bring balance. First, Ellen White gave similar counsel to fathers: "Parents are fearfully neglectful of their home duties. They do not meet the Bible standard. But to those who forsake their homes, their companions, and children, God will not entrust the work of saving souls, for they have proved unfaithful to their holy vows . . . [and] sacred responsibilities."[48] Second, Ellen White encouraged women to actively participate in ministry when God called them to do so, and noted that formal ministry might take precedence over home duties. In one instance, she urged that a woman who turned over her household and children to a "faithful, prudent helper," to engage in formal ministry, should be paid for her labors.[49]

Husband and wife. The relationship of husband and wife carries with it special rights and obligations. For instance, marriage gives husband and wife exclusive rights to each other. Commenting on the story of Hagar, Ellen White upheld the sacredness of marriage, stating that "the rights and happiness of this relation are to be carefully guarded, even at a great sacrifice." As Abraham's true wife, Sarah had a right "no other person was entitled to share."[50] Mutual rights included the protection of health and body by both husband and wife. Ellen White spoke strongly against the sexual abuse prevalent within marriage,[51] an issue also given prominence in the women's rights movement.

In family governance, Ellen White appealed to the biblical concept of the husband's headship,[52] which directs the husband to protect his wife's individual rights, never ignoring her "will, . . . aspirations, . . . freedom of mind or judgment." In response, the wife is to offer her husband cheerfulness, kindness, and devotion, "assimilating her taste to that of her husband as far as it is possible to do without losing her individuality."[53]

Unfortunately, the marriage relationship does not always reflect the ideal. Although Ellen White admonished husband and wife to respect one another's rights,[54] she wrote much more about the need to protect women's rights. One of these was individuality. White stated, "In order to be a good wife, it is not necessary that woman's nature should be utterly merged in that of her husband. Every individual has a life distinct from all others, an experience differing essentially from theirs. It is not the design of our Creator that our individuality should be lost in another's."[55]

Whereas Ellen White urged confidence in the principles of Scripture to identify the true rights of men and women, many of the leaders of the women's movement took radical, unbiblical positions. Most obvious was their view of marriage. It was common to equate the nuclear family with bondage or "conjugal slavery."[56] "Free love" (a term with many meanings, all of them outside the standards of biblical morality) was a major tenet of many who wished to see women free from the abuse of husbands in the context of marriage.[57] Women's rights advocates compared marriage to slavery and to prostitution, portraying women as being forced to make a choice between degradation in marriage, destitution, or prostitution. In fact, some touted prostitution as better than marriage.[58] While Ellen White spoke to the need for women to be accountable to God above their husbands, she upheld the biblical principles of love and respect in the marriage relationship. Although she condemned the atrocities of male brutishness and the indulgence of animal passions at the expense of woman's health and freedom to control her body, she upheld the institution of marriage as basic to humanity and ordained by God. Her counsels presented a balanced response to the need for reform addressed by the women's rights movement.

Violation of Rights

Ellen White addressed numerous situations that involved the violation or denial of rights. In so doing, she reflected the tension we experience to this day—the tension between speaking out against rights violations and submitting to injustices with the humility of Christ. In her own experience, we find an example of response to a violation by the publishing houses of her rights as an author.[59] Ellen White refused, under God's direction, a contract offered by the publishing house; she did so to "speak out against that which was wrong." She said, "I was shown that schemes would be made to deprive men of their rights; but such plans were not after Christ's order. . . . My guide said, 'I have warned you. Speak my word fearlessly, whether men will hear, or whether they will forbear.'"[60]

Ellen White places a limit, however, on the extent to which Christians are to "fight for their rights." Those abused are to allow the denial of their rights in a spirit of humble submission. Here, her counsels regarding the Christian's response to the violation of rights contrast sharply with the values and practices of the movement for women's rights. She challenges Christians to follow Jesus' example by patiently bearing the violation of their rights.[61] Even the corporate church is to reflect the humility and love of Christ by keeping church matters within that community, and "if a Christian is abused, he is to take it patiently; if defrauded, he is not to appeal to courts of justice. Rather let him suffer loss and wrong."[62] Mrs. White advised that we may even need to extend forbearance to the state by waiving some of our rights to prevent "bitterness [and] unnecessary prejudice that would cut us off from influencing those for whom we labor."[63] Such advice based on Scripture would be unacceptable to those caught up in the movement for women's rights.

With comforting words for the oppressed and warnings for the oppressor, Ellen White assured her readers that justice would eventually be achieved. She admonished: "You can never exclude God from any matter in which the rights of His people are involved; . . . no man can wound your rights without smiting [God's] hand; you can wound no man's rights without smiting it. That hand holds the sword of justice. Beware how you deal with men."[64] Therefore Christians need not contend for their rights because "God will deal with the one who violates these rights. . . . An account is kept of all these matters, and for all the Lord declares that He will avenge."[65]

The Issue of Spiritualism

> *Spiritualists have, to quite an extent, adopted this singular mode of dress. Seventh-day Adventists, who believe in the restoration of the gifts, are often branded as spiritualists. Let them adopt this costume, and their influence is dead.*[66]

At first glance, it might seem difficult to connect spiritualism with the women's movement, but commonalities existed between them that extended far beyond dress reform. Although today we think of spiritualism as communication with the spirits of the dead, the nineteenth-century spiritualists were identified with a wide variety of reforms that ranged from abolitionism to vegetarianism to "free love." In fact, spiritualists were more involved in the reforms of their time than any other religious group. One study of 51 leaders who supported abolition found only one who openly opposed spiritualism and only one other who was not interested in it.[67] Spiritualists even entered the political arena by running a woman for president in 1872. Among her supporters was former Adventist minister Moses Hull, a spiritualist who himself was in a "free-love" relationship.[68] Indeed, spiritualism was a "magnet for social and political radicals throughout the nineteenth century."[69]

In her book *Radical Spirits*, Ann Braude studies the relationship between spiritualism and the women's rights movement. Both had roots in 1848 in New York.[70] Spiritualists "recognized the equality of woman"[71] and strongly identified themselves with the full range of women's rights, including self-ownership in legal and social relations.[72] Spiritualism also contributed considerably to the spread of the women's movement through the publication of newspapers, books, and lectures.[73]

According to Braude, "spiritualism's greatest contribution to the crusade for women's rights lay in the role of spirit medium."[74] "Mediums often lectured on women's rights while in a trance."[75] Mediumship circumvented the ecclesiastical structure that excluded women from religious leadership. By communicating directly with spirits, female mediums bypassed the need for education, ordination, or organizational recognition, which was securely monopolized by male religious leadership.[76]

The American costume was closely identified with spiritualism, prompting Ellen White to fear that "the people would place [Adventists wearing the costume] on a level with spiritists and would refuse to listen to them."[77] But spiritualism's connection with the supernatural through mediums appears to have caused the greatest concern. Adventist belief in the "restoration of the gifts" (specifically, the spirit of prophecy) appeared similar enough to spiritualism's use of women as mediums that White saw an urgent need to avoid identification with this movement.

White's hesitancy to accept the role to which God called her is somewhat mirrored by the experience of a medium: "'If it will make me better, purer, or more useful, I will welcome it. . . . [But] I fear I am an unworthy servant, unfitted for so high a calling.'"[78] Spiritualism was defended as "true" in that women—in their ignorance, innocence, and youth—were able to communicate their messages as well as men, who were qualified for leadership by wisdom, education, and experience. The close parallel between Ellen White's limited education, prophetic gift, penchant for reform, and dramatic role in the Adventist movement obviously made it imperative that the distinction from mediums remain clear. To join the women's rights movement or promote the American costume would make an apparent connection between spiritualism and Adventism appear all the more obvious.

Ellen White's wise advice to avoid any association with spiritualism was soon validated. After exerting significant force on religious thinking and various women's reform movements in the 1850s and early 1960s, spiritualism fell into disrepute and scandal in the 1870s. Spiritualists continued to fight for the radical reforms of the 1850s even after many women's rights leaders distanced themselves from spiritualism because its ideas of "free love" were not helping the cause. Thereafter women's rights leaders more narrowly focused on suffrage, which was achieved by the Nineteenth Amendment in 1920.

Emerging Principles and Their Application

The issues discussed above help to explain why Ellen White was opposed to Adventists joining the women's-rights movement. Three principles emerge from an understanding of her statement that are relevant for applying its meaning to the issue of women's rights in our context. These embody the issues discussed above: (1) the principle of *spirit*, (2) the principle of *Scripture*, and (3) the principle of *influence*.

1. Christians should reflect a godly spirit in attitude and behavior. The principle of spirit means that Christians should not only avoid anything that distracts from their obligation to God, but should seek to be in harmony with the mission and spirit of the gospel and the third angel's message. Where the rights of men and women are equal and should be protected by the church but are not, individuals are called to a spirit of submission and cheerful acceptance of the denial of their God-given rights knowing that He will avenge. Christians should avoid extremes, appeal from principle rather than passion, and model Christlike behavior rather than cowardice, lawlessness, or abusive power.

How does the principle of spirit apply to the women's ordination issue? Because today's ordination issue is not associated with secular, political, religious, or social reform movements such as those in the nineteenth century, this principle does not relate as it did when Ellen White wrote. However, it calls all members in the church to embody Christ's spirit in response to the challenge, even when speaking out for rights they believe are being compromised or violated. Leaders are expected to nurture a godly spirit by protecting and maintaining the rights of all members within their appropriate spheres.

2. The Scriptures should be used to identify women's rights. The principle of the authority of Scripture is found throughout the writings of Ellen White. Guidelines for all decisions and practices should come from Scripture, where God's principles are clearly revealed. The Scriptures should guide Christians' attempts to discern the spirit underlying advice, behaviors, or movements, as well as legitimate rights and appropriate responses to their violation. The Bible should guide Christians to balanced responses promoting common sense rather than extremes. Ellen White urged that even her own words be judged by the teachings of the Bible.

In her counsels, Ellen White made it clear that women, as human beings with inalienable God-given rights, should be granted rights in marriage, home, workplace, society, and God's service. She believed that the Scriptures support a woman's right to hear and respond to God's call to ministry, without shirking her responsibilities as a mother to do so. Biblical principles may be more radical than culture accepts, unlike current practice, and incorrectly interpreted because of experience, culture, or desires—but God, ever calling his people toward a higher ideal, can be trusted to reveal the true meaning of Scripture and its application in his time and his way.

Ellen White points out that the Bible presents God as just, demanding that humans not only respect, but protect, the rights of others. While Christians should not seek to force others to respect their rights, they can be sure that God takes note of violations, and that justice will one day be meted out. Furthermore, the church has a collective responsibility to protect the rights of its members. Ellen White had strong warnings for those leaders in the church who failed to do so. The biblical principle of humility and submission of each individual Christian does not eliminate the church's responsibility to make sure that all its dealings are just.

Where there is no direct biblical prohibition or the issue is not directly addressed, the church also has an obligation to find principles that relate to women's rights. The church should not seek a decision based on political or social agendas, even though reforms in government and society may reflect biblical principles, as was the case in many of the nineteenth-century reforms. To be an effective influence for good in the world, it should practice reforms using God's methods. Reforms should reflect balance, not extremes; reason, not fanaticism; humble submission, not passionate demanding; and an appeal to God, not to state or society for implementation.

How does the principle of Scripture apply to the women's ordination issue? Because Ellen White makes it clear that women have a right to accept a call from God to ministry, and all persons should receive equal remuneration and recognition for equal work performed, it seems likely she would support women's ordination. If today's church finds that women have a right to receive church recognition of their call to ministry, the principle of Scripture would encourage making bold and radical advances to establish and protect that right, unless doing so would limit or destroy the church's influence in spreading the gospel.

3. Nothing should be allowed to compromise Adventists' influence for spreading the gospel. The Adventist movement has at its heart the spreading of the gospel, and particularly the third angel's message. Ellen White repeatedly urged a balanced approach to evangelism, one that would draw people to the message. As long as we are in harmony with God's law, we are to adapt in any way possible in order to communicate truth rather than compromise it. Anything that impedes the spread of the message should be discarded if to do so does not ignore or violate God's commands. Even in the case of fighting for personal rights, Ellen White urged Christians to follow their Savior's example of humble submission wherever possible in order to avoid conflict that would hurt evangelistic efforts.

Ellen White illustrated the principle of influence in her response to the dress-reform issue. She had been given a vision from God regarding the necessity and manner of dress reform, which she then wrote and spoke about. When fanaticism and extremism surrounding this reform became problematic, she went so far as to say that it was better to suffer with unhealthful dress than to impede the spread of the message. When she once was criticized for not properly following the dress reform she herself advocated, she explained: "When I visit a place to speak to the people where the subject is new and prejudice exists, I think it best to be careful and not close the ears of the people by wearing a dress which would be objectionable to them." She continued, "But after bringing the subject before them and fully explaining my position, I then appear before them in the reform dress, illustrative of my teachings."[79]

How should we apply this principle to the women's ordination issue? At the heart of the principle of influence is the goal of reaching the world for Christ. If we agree that the Bible does not clearly prohibit the ordination of women to gospel ministry, and biblical principles support a woman's call, we must consider how the decision to ordain women would impact evangelism. Would women's ordination be looked upon by the society as legitimate, just, and reasonable? For example, to deny women the right to vote today would bring an outcry from many societies, but to grant suffrage was unthinkable 100 years ago. A correct application of this principle requires an awareness of societal expectations, which vary in different parts of the world. In some places, to allow women to function in ministry without the full privileges associated with their labors is seen as inconsistent and unfair in the eyes of government and society. This position presents a negative influence on those whom Adventists would reach with the gospel message. At the same time, in certain places ordaining women, or even allowing them to pastor, would be so radically countercultural as to compromise a positive influence for the gospel.

To suggest that ordination is not necessary in places where society values equality for men and women in the workplace is a denial of the principle of influence. In such a place, ordaining women is more likely to have a positive influence on the spread of the message—particularly when one considers the following questions: Would women's ordination help to reach people that might otherwise be difficult to reach? Would it provide more workers in the field?

Summary and Conclusion

Ellen White was clear about avoiding participation in or identification with the movement in favor of women's rights, but was she against the reforms they promoted? Even a casual reading of her writings shows her to be a strong, even radical advocate of reform, as judged by the standards of her time. Her counsels on diet, dress, medical care, education, wages and labor, public speaking, mutual responsibilities in marriage, and ministry roles for women are some of the areas in which she sharply departed from the norms of her day. She believed that women's rights were to be protected and maintained because women were human beings. She showed how women in their roles as mothers and members of society impact its future development, and urged women to develop themselves so they could be good models to their children and companions to their husbands.[80] She even addressed specific needs, stating that it was as essential for women to study medicine as it was for men.[81]

In these reforms, Ellen White advocated and even superseded many of the changes called for in the movement for women's rights. In many cases, even the language used was similar to that of the movement's leaders, such as saying women were "slaves of fashion" and decrying the male brutishness in the marital relation. Perhaps the original words of the quotation do a better job of illustrating this point: The women's rights movement as a movement, not the favoring of women's rights, was the problem. Because Ellen White had more to say about the protection of a woman's individuality, opportunities for personal growth, and service to God, her concern reflected a time and society in which women's rights were not well established or protected.

Why was Ellen White against involvement in the women's rights movement? It was not compatible with the purpose and mission of Adventists. The Adventist mission was religious rather than political, and Adventists were to avoid any identification or connection with those operating under a spirit from any other source than God. The Bible was to be their standard and source of guidance, and the women's movement contained many elements and methods that were antibiblical. Furthermore, the women's movement was controversial enough that to be allied with it would have seriously impeded the mission of the Adventist Church.

When taken together, Ellen White's counsels present a balanced approach. For example, in the area of dress reform, she turned to Scripture and common sense to support the importance of dress reform for health and usefulness. She condemned the wearing of the American costume as a violation of the Deuteronomic command prohibiting cross-dressing of the sexes, but also pointed out that the costume repulsed society. She was practical. She designed and promoted a reform dress that corrected the obvious problems of the fashions of the time, without eliciting the negative fallout that plagued the American costume.

Ellen White's position regarding the rights movement is even more clearly understood when we look at how she related to other reform movements of her time. For example, she spoke out against association with trade unions, even though they helped oppressed workers, with whom she sympathized. She warned that joining trade unions and secret societies would detract from the mission of taking the final message to the world and would endanger one's God-given right to answer to Christ alone.[82] While she spoke out against slavery, she advised that "as far as possible, everything that would stir up the race prejudice of the white people should be avoided. There is danger of closing the door so that our white laborers will not be able to work in some places in the south."[83]

On the other hand, she encouraged women to support the temperance movement, a reform movement that involved large numbers of women and did not carry the same stigma as the women's rights movement. Even then, however, she urged participants to keep their involvement in perspective with their primary mission, share the Adventist message with their fellow workers, and be aware that the time might come to disassociate from it.[84] As for the issue of women's right to vote, Ellen White apparently had little to say and saw herself as unprepared to deal with this issue.[85] She wrote to her husband James about a conversation with a Mrs. Graves who wanted her to get involved in women's suffrage, saying, "[Mrs. Graves] had been dwelling upon these things and her mind was ripe upon them, while my work was of another character."[86]

In the end, the woman's movement was secular, driven by political activities, and continually searching for ways to capture the support of public opinion. The focus of Ellen White was spiritual, driven by holy living and reform that advanced personal and corporate holiness. She wanted a religious, not political, reform movement.

God desires to bring about change in our lives and in our church. Too often the church has followed, rather than initiated, change in regards to human rights. As human beings, women have the right to minister, to hear and respond to the call of God in their lives. Those who work for the church are entitled to equal respect, recognition, and pay for equal work rendered.

Endnotes

1. The author wishes to thank Donna Worley for reading this paper and providing valuable comments and suggestions.

2. The testimony, "The Cause in the East," part of the *Testimony No. 10* collection, was later included in Ellen G. White, *Testimonies for the Church*, 1:409-422.

3. For the most part these revisions date from the 1880s.

4. Matilda J. Gage, *Woman, Church, and State: The Original Exposé of Male Collaboration against the Female Sex* (Watertown, MA: Persephone, 1980; reprint), xxvii.

5. Blanche G. Hersh, *The Slavery of Sex: Feminist-Abolitionists in America* (Urbana, IL: Univ. of Illinois Press, 1978), ix.

6. See appendix to *Testimonies*, 1:717-718, 1948 edition.

7. Ellen C. DuBois, *Feminism and Suffrage: The Emergence of an Independent Women's Movement in America, 1848-1869* (Ithaca: Cornell Univ. Press, 1978), 18.

8. Eugene A. Hecker, *A Short History of Women's Rights from the Days of Augustus to the Present Time: With Special Reference to England and the United States* (Westport, CT: Greenwood, 197; reprint of 1914 edition), 166.

9. For statements written before 1864, see Ellen G. White, "The Third Angel's Message," in *Early Writings*, 254-258, 258-261, and 277-282 and White, *Testimonies*, 1:77, 353.

10. White, *Testimonies*, 1: 409-420.

11. Ibid., 1: 414-420.

12. Ibid., 1: 409-420.

13. *The American Heritage College Dictionary* (1993), s.v. "Rights."

14. White's use of the word "relations" in this sense is similar to her usage of the word "rights," as will become evident in the discussion of specific rights and obligations within the context of relationships. In this paper, however, the term "rights" is used.

15. Ellen G. White, *The Great Controversy*, 295.

16. Ibid. See also Ellen G. White, *Mind, Character, and Personality*, 2:708; Ellen G. White, *Seventh-day Adventist Bible Commentary*, 1:1091.

17. Information here was taken primarily from *Governing Principles in the Remuneration of SDA Workers*, in White Estate Document File 243. This collection contains many of Ellen G. White's statements on the issue of wages. Exemplary statements may be found in *Testimonies*, 5:564, and *Counsels on Health*, 303.

18. Ellen G. White, Letter 137, 1898, *Manuscript Releases*, 5:29.

19. Ellen G. White, *Gospel Workers*, 123.

20. White, *Seventh-day Adventist Bible Commentary*, 1:1106.

21. Ellen G. White, *Christ's Object Lessons*, 382.

22. Ellen G. White, *Patriarchs and Prophets*, 311.

23. Ellen G. White, *Testimonies to Ministers*, 360-361.

24. For example, see Ellen G. White, *Testimonies to Southern Africa*, 1890; and Ellen G. White, *Health*, 1865.

25. Ellen G. White, Letter 92, 1895, *Manuscript Releases*, 19:213.

26. Ellen G. White, *Education*, 76.

27. White, *Testimonies*, 3:346.

28. Ibid., 3:286.

29. White, *Testimonies to Ministers*, 361; Ellen G. White, Letter 80a, 1895, *Manuscript Releases*, 4:7.

30. For example, Ellen White affirmed: "One of the very highest applications of these principles is found in the recognition of man's right to himself, to the control of his own labor" (*Testimonies*, 7:180). She further admonished: "You belong to God, soul, body, and spirit. Your mind belongs to God, and your talents belong to Him also. No one has a right to control another's mind, and judge for another, prescribing what is his duty. There are certain rights that belong to every individual, in doing God's service. No man has any more right to take these rights from us than to take life itself. God has given us freedom to think, and it is our privilege and duty always to be a doer of the Word, and to follow our impressions of duty. We are only human beings, and one human being has no jurisdiction over the conscience of any other human being" (Letter 92, 1895, *Manuscript Releases*, 19:213).

31. White, *Patriarchs and Prophets*, 534.

32. White, *Education*, 77.

33. White, *Patriarchs and Prophets*, 534.

34. Ellen G. White, *The Ministry of Healing*, 489.

35. Ellen G. White, Letter 92, 1895, *Selected Messages*, 3:16.

36. Ellen G. White, Letter 76, 1895, *The Ellen G. White 1888 Materials*, 1373.

37. Ellen G. White, Letter 92, 1895, *Manuscript Releases*, 19:213.

38. Ibid.

39. Ellen G. White, Letter 55, 1895, *The Publishing Ministry*, 127.

40. White, Letter 33, 1879, *Manuscript Releases*, 19:55-56.

41. Ellen G. White, "God's Word the Parent's Guide," *Signs of the Times*, 24 November 1881.

42. Ellen G. White, *Fundamentals of Christian Education*, 67.

43. Ellen G. White, Letter 272, 1903, *The Adventist Home*, 31.

44. White, Letter 47a, 1902, *The Adventist Home*, 306.

45. White, *Fundamentals of Christian Education*, 67. For examples of children's rights, see White, *Ministry of Healing*, 383-385, and "Child-Training," *Signs of the Times*, 23 April 1902.

46. Ellen G. White, "The Mother's Work," *Review and Herald*, 15 September 1891.

47. Ellen G. White, Letter 28, 1890, *Testimonies on Sexual Behavior*, 42-43.

48. Ibid.

49. White, *Gospel Workers*, 542-543; see also chapters by Jerry Moon and Mike Bernoi.

50. White, *Patriarchs and Prophets*, 147.

51. See, for example, Ellen G. White, "Christianity in the Marriage Relation," *Review and Herald*, 26 September 1899.

52. See Ellen G. White, Letter 34, 1890, *Testimonies*, 1:307.

53. Ellen G. White, Letter 3, 1886, *Manuscript Releases*, 18:314.

54. Further examples may be found in White, *Testimonies*, 2:93-94; and White, *Manuscript Releases*, 16:304.

55. Ellen G. White, "The Mother's Duty—Christ her Strength," *The Health Reformer*, 1 August 1877.

56. E. B. Clark, "The Politics of God and the Woman's Vote: Religion in the American Suffrage Movement, 1848-1895" (Ph.D. dissertation, Princeton University, 1989), 196.

57. Ibid., 176.

58. Ann Braude, *Radical Spirits: Spiritualism and Women's Rights in Nineteenth-Century America* (Boston, MA: Beacon, 1989), 121-123; see also Barbara Goldsmith, *Other Powers: The Age of Suffrage, Spiritualism, and the Scandalous Victoria Woodhull* (New York: Alfred Knopf, 1998), xiii-xiv, 48-49.

59. In 1886 White wrote letters to G. I. Butler and A. R. Henry defending her right to claim the royalties on her books ("Testimonies on Fair Dealing and Book Royalties," *Ellen G. White Pamphlets*, vol. 3, no. 102, 15-18). In 1895 she wrote regarding the failure of the publishing house to use appropriately the royalties for her book, *Great Controversy* (see Letter 15, 1895, *Publishing Ministry*, 207).

60. Ellen G. White, Letter T 76, written in 1895 to A. O. Tait, published in *The Ellen G. White 1888 Materials*, 1373.

61. White, *Early Writings*, 156.

62. *Manuscript Releases*, 5:410.

63. Ellen G. White, "A Study of Principles—No. 1", *Review and Herald*, 9 March 1911; see also White, *Selected Messages*, 3:299.

64. Ellen G. White, Letter 5, 1879, *Our High Calling*, 225.

65. Ellen G. White, MS 196, 1898, *Selected Messages*, 3:300.

66. White, *Testimonies*, 1:421.

67. Hersh, 148.

68. Braude, 171, 123; White, *Testimony No. 10* contains a 12-page message to Hull (*Testimonies*, 1:426-437).

69. Braude, 57.

70. Ibid., 3.

71. Elizabeth C. Stanton, Susan B. Anthony, and Matilda J. Gage, eds., *History of Woman Suffrage* (Rochester, NY: Fowler and Wells, 1881-1902), 3:530.

72. Braude, 77.

73. Ibid., 80.

74. Ibid., 82.

75. Ibid., 79.

76. Ibid., 84.

77. White, *Testimonies*, 1:421, immediately following the statement under study.

78. Braude, 83.

79. White, *Testimonies*, 1:465.

80. White, *Evangelism*, 467

81. White, *Medical Ministry*, 61.

82. Ellen G. White, Letter 114, 1903, *Mind, Character, and Personality*, 1:28.

83. White, *Testimonies*, 9:214.

84. See, for example, White's letter to Mrs. S.M.I. Henry, 24 March 1899, *Manuscript Releases*, 5:439-440.

85. Letter 40a, 1874, *Manuscript Releases*, 10:69.

86. Ibid. In other references to women's voting, White spoke of the need for women to first concern themselves with their tasks, stating that women's slavery to fashion and failure to develop themselves rendered them unprepared "to take a prominent position in political matters" (*Testimonies*, 3:565). Interestingly, in another place White spoke to "Christian men and *women*" asking how they could tolerate the intemperance allowed by the laws of the land and stating that "in our favored land, every voter has some voice in determining what laws shall control the nation" (*Gospel Workers*, 387; italics supplied). Certainly it can be said that White did not view the issue itself as morally wrong.

PART FIVE: OTHER CONSIDERATIONS

The Bible must remain the basis for a decision to ordain or not to ordain women to ministry. However, in the late 1990s other factors contribute to the discussion, especially in North America. Many view the action of allowing women to pastor and yet denying them the recognition of ordination as gross injustice; this topic is considered in chapter 18. White slaveholders used the Bible to sustain their subjugation of their Black brothers and sisters; chapter 19 explores the similarity between those arguments and the ones used to exclude women from the ordained ministry. In the late 1990s the Seventh-day Adventist Church is culturally, racially, and socially diverse; each member is part of a culture and thus views issues—even the Bible—differently. Therefore, we must remember that we are not culture-free in our own interpretation and must commit ourselves to study differing positions and prayerfully seek the Spirit's direction to resolve the issue of women in ministry (chap. 20).

CHAPTER 18

THE DISTANCE AND THE DIFFERENCE: REFLECTIONS ON ISSUES OF SLAVERY AND WOMEN'S ORDINATION IN ADVENTISM

WALTER B. T. DOUGLAS

Introduction

In this chapter our interest will focus on the way the Bible was used by the nineteenth-century American slaveholding society to legitimize and sanction slavery as a divinely established institution. We will also examine and critique the theological, cultural, and social arguments that the defenders of slavery used to bolster their position. Using what I call the "historical sense" (that is, the sense by which we perceive the past and, traveling away from ourselves into that past, gain perspective on the present), I will show how in some curious ways, the logic, arguments, and judgments of the proslavery movement anticipated the approach and methodology of some who now oppose women's ordination.

From this examination we will, I believe, gain a sense of the distance and the difference in the attitude of the Seventh-day Adventist Church in dealing with two complex and perplexing issues. Historically, discussions about how God speaks to his church in a particular time and place have been a matter of deep concern and thoughtful reflection for the faithful. Understandably, within the community of the faithful that we call church, there have always been those who believe with deep and unshakable conviction that the Word of God comes to us without being influenced by contemporary culture. Furthermore, they believe with deep passion in the inspiration of Scripture—that is to say, the process by which God chose to reveal Himself—namely, by speaking to and through the biblical authors. With equally firm conviction others within the same community of faith, who also believe in a high view of Scripture, argue for the importance of the cultural and historical backgrounds and influences in which the Word of God was communicated and understood. For them the reality of the cultural gap between the ancient world, in which God communicated with the biblical authors, and the modern or postmodern world, in which his Word is now received and obeyed, is critical to the church's life and mission.

> No word of God is spoken in a cultural vacuum. Every word of God was spoken in a cultural context. So you see, it is this cultural chasm between the biblical world and the modern world that determines the task of Biblical exposition and lays down our two major obligations: (a) faithfulness to the ancient text, and (b) sensitivity to the modern context. And it is within this combination of faithfulness and sensitivity that the preacher of integrity is to be found.[1]

Illustrative of this difference in approaches to understanding and interpreting the Scripture are the slavery debates of the nineteenth century and those surrounding women's ordination in the twentieth. Slavery was a hotly debated issue in which even Adventist pioneers were active participants. Some Christians in nineteenth-century America, particularly those in the South, defended slavery on the grounds that it was a divinely ordained institution because Paul admonished: "Slaves, obey your masters" (Eph 6:5-9).[2] John R. Stott, renowned evangelical scholar and preacher, expresses this sentiment:

John Knox is specific about the cultural aspect of Paul's writings on slavery:

> As to slavery, he looked upon it as a permanent institution. How could we expect anything else? But in his remarks about the relations of slaves to masters and about the obligations of each class to the other he obviously takes as humane a view as we could wish, given his tolerance of the institution itself. To assume that he would have been equally tolerant of it in our world, so different from his that he could not even have imagined it, is to be ignorant beyond belief. Yet we know that such ignorance abounded during the struggles against slavery a century ago.[3]

In our own church of the 1860s and 1870s, the slavery issue was surrounded by controversy.[4] This was a matter of deep concern for Ellen White, who spoke decisively against those who were prepared to capitulate to Southern prejudices against blacks in their defense of slavery as a positive good. For instance, she rebuked a fellow church member for his proslavery opinions and cautioned him that if he did not repudiate those ideas he could be disfellowshipped.[5]

Like the slavery issue in Ellen White's day, the issue of women's ordination is today debated in our church. The Bible was and is the source of authority and legitimation for both positions, pro and con, on the slavery issue as well as the issue of women's ordination. Both sides seem to take a high view of Scripture. The biblical text is inspired, unlike any other text, unique in its origin, nature, and authority. This conviction lies at the heart of this chapter.

Arguments for Slave Holding

Christian slaveholders in nineteenth-century America advanced two sets of arguments in favor of slavery. The first was biblical; the second had to do with cultural and economic necessities.

Biblical Arguments

The first argument came from Paul's letter to Onesimus regarding the runaway slave Philemon.

> I Paul, ambassador as I am of Christ Jesus, and now a prisoner, appeal to you about my child, whose father I have become in this prison. I mean Onesimus, once so little use to you, and to me. I am sending him back to you, and in doing so I am sending a part of myself. I should have liked to keep him with me, to look after me as you would wish, here in prison for the Gospel. But I would rather do nothing without your consent, so that your kindness may be a matter not of compulsion, but of your own free will. For perhaps this is why you lost him for a time, that you might have him back for good, no longer as a slave, but as more than a slave—as a dear brother, very dear indeed to me and how much dearer to you both as man and as Christian. If, then, you count me partner in the faith, welcome him as you would welcome me. (Philemon 9-17, RSV)

Paul was fully aware of his Greco-Roman culture. He knew that Onesimus' running away from his master was a rupture of the social codes within the household of Philemon. Despite this, Paul could accept that rupture as yielding some fundamental truth about living in the family of God—when one becomes a member of the family of God, one is no longer a slave, one has become a beloved brother or sister. Clearly, Paul was not speaking of the brother/sister in a biological sense. Instead, he used the word to emphasize the *shared status* found in the church by virtue of baptism.

The fundamental reality Paul brings out is that this runaway slave who has become a Christian now stands on a par with both Paul and

Philemon, his former master. Onesimus is their peer in the family of God. Paul insists that this reality of shared status is critical to the continuing mission of the church. It is indeed a mark of the church. Just as Philemon is Paul's brother, beloved by God, so is Onesimus.

This genuine and thoroughly moving letter was a thorn in the flesh for nineteenth-century American slaveholders. It created a moral and theological dilemma, because it was inconceivable for any slaveholder to think of his slave as a "brother" or as "part of himself." The moral and theological dilemma could be framed in the form of a question: How could slave owners preach the lofty ideals of the Christian faith—justice, equality, love, compassion, grace—and yet be slave owners? How could they preach the biblical doctrine of God's fatherhood and sovereignty, yet exploit and treat God's creation as nonpersons?

Many leading Southern theologians could not rest content with this irreconcilable contradiction. They had to find a method of interpretation of Paul's message and other scriptural passages to justify their particular social, economic, and intellectual construction of reality.

In an astounding policy statement, the proslavery theologians agreed that

> the Bible says nothing to condemn slavery as sinful, and some of us maintain that the Bible in fact commands slavery. Rooted in Noah's cursing of Ham—Canaan's descendants, slavery has been and should be practiced by God's people.[6]

The biblical support for slavery as a divinely established institution received fairly wide support in the slaveholding societies of the South. The advocates made what they considered to be an impressive and clear case for their beliefs by relying on several Old Testament texts. Among their favorite passages was Gen 9:18-28, particularly vv. 24-27:

> When Noah awoke from his wine and knew what his youngest son had done to him, he said "Cursed be Canaan; a slave of slaves shall he be to his brothers." He also said "Blessed by the Lord my God be Shem, and let Canaan be his slave. God enlarge Japheth, and let him dwell in the tents of Shem and let Canaan be his slave."

These proslavery advocates also used Lev 25:44-46:

> As for your male and female slaves whom you may have, you may buy male and female slaves from among the nations that are round about you. You may also buy from the strangers who sojourn with you, and their families that are with you, who have been born in your land; and

they may be your property. You may bequeath them to your sons after you, to inherit as a possession for ever, you may make slaves of them, but over your brethren the people of Israel you shall not rule, one over another, with harshness.

Using these biblical passages, the defenders of slavery maintained with rigor that God, through his servant Moses, not only sanctioned slavery but encouraged the slave trade unto the third and fourth generation. From these and other Old Testament passages the advocates of slavery and their sympathizers had the unshakeable conviction that the Bible does not condemn, but instead encourages and supports, slavery. They took the fundamental position that "you either believe the Bible and support slavery or throw out the Bible as God's authoritative Word."[7]

James Henry Thornwell, Thornton Stringfellow, Thomas Dew, and others employed literalistic interpretations of the Old Testament and New Testament passages in their defense of slavery and vigorously argued that in the social construction of the world in which the Bible was received, "Blacks" (in their universe of discourse slaves equaled Blacks) must forever serve Whites. According to Stringfellow, "May it not be said in truth, that God decreed this institution before it existed."[8] Indeed, "the first appearance of slavery in the Bible is the wonderful prediction of the patriarch Noah in Gen 9:18-28."[9]

Charles Hodge, the renowned Princeton professor, defender of slavery and provider of biblical and theological arguments for the proslavery position, wrote:

The obedience which slaves owe their masters, children their parents, wives their husbands, people their rulers, is always made to rest on the divine will as its ultimate foundation. It is part of the source which we owe to God. . . . In appealing, therefore, to the Bible in support of the doctrine here advanced, we are not, on the one hand, appealing to an arbitrary standard, mere statute book, but we are appealing to the infinite intelligence of a personal God, whose will, because of his infinite excellence is necessarily the ultimate ground and rule of all moral obligations.[10]

The same fundamentalist conviction gained increasingly widespread acceptance among slaveholding societies through the influence and writings of Stringfellow. He taught that God "ingrafted hereditary slavery upon the constitution of government."[11] And since women and children are the subservient parts of government, this law applied equally to them.

Stringfellow indicated that God gave the Hebrews written permission to buy, hold, and sell men and women and children in perpetual servitude. He then queried, why should we not do so as well?[12]

The challenge to relinquish claims of power and domination over others was met with an array of biblical passages, this time from the New Testament. The defenders of slavery argued that the hierarchical arrangement reflected in the household codes and domestic rules in Paul's day was still as normative for the master-slave and husband-wife relationships in their day.

Marshaling all of the key Pauline texts to bolster their position, they were clear that Paul's view of the cultural and biblical context was exactly their own. So they quoted Eph 6:5-8:

> Slaves be obedient to those who are your masters, with fear and trembling, and singleness of heart, as to Christ, not in the way of eyeservice, as men pleasers, but as servants of Christ, doing the will of God from the heart, rendering service with a good will as to the Lord and not unto men, knowing that whatever good anyone does, he will receive the same again from the Lord, whether he is a slave or free.

As already noted, they referenced Paul's letter to Onesimus as a testimony of the apostle's support for the fugitive slave law. With this view of the apostle's teachings, the proslavery theologians and biblical scholars frequently cited the following texts:

> Slaves obey in everything those who are your earthly masters, not with eyeservice, as men pleasers, but in singleness of heart, fearing the Lord. (Col 3:22)
> Masters treat your slaves justly and fairly, knowing that you also have a Master in heaven. (Col 4:1)
> Bid slaves to be submissive to their masters and to give satisfaction in every respect; they are not to be refractory. (Titus 2:9)

These selected portions of Paul's writings were pivotal in the defense of slavery. Slaveholders and their sympathizers maintained that in the Greco-Roman world the male head of the household exercised authority over wives, children, and slaves. For them any social order had to be grounded in divine sanction. From this perspective they developed their understanding of Christian morality, salvation, and human sinfulness. This particular view of Christian life and behavior was profoundly influential in shaping the slaveholders' worldview. It provided the *raison d'être* for the pervasive teaching: God created the color line in the races and evidently meant for it to remain. The defenders of slavery made it a necessary good written into the constitution of God's law and the structures of his creation. And they insisted the Bible told them so.

Turning to the life and ministry of Jesus, the slaveholders found support for their belief and practice by emphasizing Jesus' silence on the topic. J. H. Hammond wrote:

> It is vain to look to Christ or any of his apostles to justify such blasphemous perversions of the word of God. Although slavery in its most revolting form was everywhere visible among men, no visionary notions of piety or philanthropy ever tempted them to gainsay the Law, even to mitigate the severity of the existing system. On the contrary, regarding slavery as an *established*, as well as an *inevitable condition of human society*, they never hinted at such a thing as its termination on earth, any more than "the poor may cease out of the land," which God affirms to Moses shall never be. . . .
>
> It is impossible therefore to suggest that slavery is contrary to the will of God. It is equally absurd to say that American slavery differs in form or principle from that of the chosen people. We accept the Bible terms and definition of our slavery and its precepts as the guide of our conduct.[13]

Along the same thought, Thomas Dew stated that:

> When we turn to the New Testament we find not one single passage at all calculated to disturb the conscience of an honest slaveholder. No one can read it without seeing and admiring that the meek and humble Savior of the world in no instance meddled with the established institution of mankind: he came to save the fallen world, and not to excite the black passions of men.[14]

Interestingly, with regards to Jesus' attitude toward women and their role in society, the slaveholders and their supporting theologians were also quite clear, as shown in Albert Bledsoe's writing:

> If our women are to be emancipated from subjection to the law which God has imposed upon them, if they are to quit the retirement of domestic life, where they preside in stillness over the character and destiny of society; if they are to come forth in the liberty of men to be our agents, our public lecturers, our committee men, our rulers, if in studied insults to the authority of God, we are to renounce in the marriage contract all claims to obedience, we shall soon have a country . . . from which all order and virtue would speedily be banished. There is no form of human excellence before which we bow with profounder deference than that which appears in a delicate woman, adorned with

the inward graces and devoted to the peculiar duties of her sex; and there is no deformity of human character from which we turn with deeper loathing than from a woman forgetful of her nature and clamorous for the vocation and rights of men.[15]

Arguments from Cultural and Economic Necessity

The abolitionists, especially those from the North, spread their message for the dismantling of slavery. Fiery speeches against the leading proslavery theologians continued to find their mark in the South. More and more slaves were accepting Christianity and creating a moral dilemma for the slaveholders. To counter these developments, the proslavery advocates raised to a new level the significance of the cultural, social, and economic issues in the debate. Slavery, they insisted, fostered a superior culture. It provided both the economic and cultural basis for the development and nurturing of men of great intellect. Great scholars, writers, and statesmen developed because slavery created the condition for wealth, leisure, and the cultivation of talents.

Thornhill, Stringfellow, and Dew, using Thomas Carlyle to support their views, concluded that the black person was born to be a servant and useful in God's creation only as a servant. Remembering the social, cultural, and intellectual greatness of ancient Greece and Rome, these theologians and their colleagues contended that slavery was sanctioned and legitimized by the classical societies of those two civilizations. Aristotle, in discussing "proper household science,"[16] had defended slavery on the grounds that from the hour of their birth some are marked for subjection and others for rule. The ancient philosopher Plato had developed the philosophical view that society was ordered so that some of its citizens would be rulers of gold, guardians of silver, and workers of bronze. With these views, the defenders of slavery in the South reinforced their cultural arguments. They rationalized their actions by stating that the South was only following the examples set by the greatly respected societies of Greece and Rome.

This construction of society was reflected in the slaveholders' interpretation of the hierarchical male-female and master-slave relation-ship of dominance. According to Elizabeth Fox-Genovese, slaveholders considered themselves to be adhering to Christian principles when affirming the legitimacy of their authority over the slaves.[17] In addition, they held that

the first of those Christian principles was that God ordained power of men over women and the attendant duty of Christian women to submit to the authority of the fathers and husbands. . . . This superordination/ subordination by gender constituted the formulation of God's ordination of hierarchy in social relations.[18]

Thus, the cultural and economic arguments of the slavers were integral to their construction of reality and their structures of consciousness. Indeed, these arguments were raised to a level of divinely inspired teaching.

Abolitionist Arguments against Slavery

In responding to the biblical and theological claims of the slavers for justifying slavery as a divinely sanctioned institution, the abolitionists held firmly to the inspiration and authority of Scripture. They made a compelling case for the high moral ground on which all biblical interpretation must stand. They challenged the hermeneutical methods and theological interpretations of the proslavery advocates and accused them of mishandling the Word of God. The Christian faith, argued abolitionists Albert Barnes and George Bourne, two of the most influential thinkers and writers on the issue of slavery, condemns human sinfulness and structures of oppression. In a penetrating criticism of their opponents, Bourne wrote, "Yet multitudes of pro-slavery Christians contend, that these oppressive violations which overthrow and destroy ancient Israel are evidence that God sanctions the most oppressive practice in the world."[19]

In a systematic fashion, the leading abolitionist theologians and biblical interpreters, such as Barnes, Bourne, Wayland, and Weld, sought to dismantle the hierarchical structures of their opponents. Pointing specifically to Gen 9:25 ("Cursed be Canaan, a slave of slaves shall he be to his brothers"), Bourne and Weld called attention to the mishandling of the text by Stringfellow and Hodge. The curse of Canaan, they maintained, does not refer to the African race. There is no scriptural support for the slaveholders' claim that God specifically singled out the "Negroes" to be "hewers of wood and drawers of water." The prediction of Genesis 9 was fulfilled in the Canaanites who became slaves of Israel after the conquest of Canaan. In fact, the distinction between Egyptian slavery and the slavery in America must be recognized.[20]

They contended that God never sanctioned slavery as a part of his divine creation. This evil institution was wholly inconsistent with the nature and character of God and the teaching of Christianity. Barnes stated:

The consideration seems to be conclusive proof that Christianity was not designed to extend and perpetuate slavery, but that the spirit of the Christian religion is against it: and that the fair application of the Church's religion would remove it from the world, because it is an evil, and is displeasing to God.[21]

Francis Wayland, president of Brown University, pointed out that the Christian faith had ever been the greatest enemy of slavery. One who took the Scripture seriously and believed with conviction that there is an irreconcilable contradiction between Christian faith and the oppression or enslavement of God's creation would inevitably seek to work for the removal of that evil. Wayland insisted that "the Christian religion not only forbids slavery, but . . . provides the only method in which, after it has been once established, it may be abolished with entire safety and benefit to both parties."[22]

With regard to the slavers' argument from Jesus' silence on the issue of slavery, the abolitionists made the following point:

As we have no account whatever of any public preaching of Christ and the apostles against forgery, arson, piracy, counterfeiting, and twenty other heinous ancient as well as modern crimes, we are to presume from this supposed approving silence and acquiescence of theirs that the whole of those crimes are morally approbated and licensed in the New Testament, by the special example of Christ and the Apostles, so that we have no moral right whatever to disturb others in the commission of them.[23]

The abolitionists could not accept that because Jesus did not attack slavery as evil he approved it as a legitimate practice or institution. The argument from silence, they insisted, was a misrepresentation of the mind and the teachings of Jesus and the apostles. For them the formation of faith and the use of Scripture which deprived people of their freedom or encouraged the perpetuation of oppression were harmful to the Christian community, scandalized the gospel, and invalidated the relationship between confession and conduct.[24]

Indeed, the abolitionists claimed that the Christian faith made it possible for all women and men to experience freedom from injustice through Jesus Christ their Lord.[25] They pointed to the number of slaves that were embracing Christianity and insisted that it was sinful to enslave fellow Christians. Recalling Paul's warmhearted letter to Philemon to receive Onesimus not as a slave but as a brother, the abolitionists emphasized the principles of *shared status* and inclusive wholeness within the Christian community. Barnes wrote:

> The principles laid down in the epistle to Philemon . . . would lead
> to the universal abolition of slavery. If all those who are now slaves
> were to become Christian, and their masters were to treat them, not as
> slaves but as brethren, the period would not be far distant when slavery
> would cease.[26]

The Christian faith, as it was preached in the conservative South by
the antislavery preachers and theologians, emphasized the worth and
dignity of the individual and found its force in the biblical doctrines of
Creation and freedom in Christ. And even as the proslavery preachers
used religion to work on the psychological and ideological transformation
of the will of the slaves to make them more subservient ("slaves, obey
your masters, for this is right"), the abolitionists argued that the
transforming power of the gospel of Christ could change their will to
experience freedom.

We know from the literature on slave religion that many slaves
embraced the Christian faith and seem to have had a special devotion to
the biblical stories of Abraham, Joseph, and Moses, as well as the
teachings of Jesus and the prophets about justice, mercy, and the reign of
God. They knew that their oppression was contrary to God's justice and
compassion for all his creation. With great interest these slaves listened to
the preaching of the abolitionists and adopted much of their messages to
their own experience. Often these were put in song and dance, an
enduring legacy to American religious life and thought.

Ellen White and Slavery: A Profile in Courage

Those who oppose women's ordination often quote Ellen White to
bolster their position. Therefore her views on slavery, an issue equally
perplexing to the church in her time as women's ordination is today,
should prove instructive.

Among Adventists some embraced abolitionist views and were
strong advocates for the dismantling of the institution of slavery.
However, others were ambivalent or even supportive of the practices of
the slaveholders in the South. As the problem became more complex, the
need for theological and religious solution became acute. Beyond dispute,
one of the clearest and strongest voices to speak out against slavery was
Ellen White's. She minced no words in calling attention to the disgrace
such a system brought to the nation. She was bold, fearless and prophetic

in her denunciations, even challenging a president of the United States, as well as other political and civic leaders, to take their courage in both hands and work for the abolition of slavery. In one of her testimonies, Ellen White showed great courage and strength of character by declaring:

> The people of this nation have exalted themselves to heaven, and have looked down upon monarchical government, and triumphed in their boasted liberty, while the institution of slavery that was a thousand times worse than the tyranny exercised by monarchical governments, was suffered to exist and was cherished. In this land of light a system is cherished which allows portions of the human family to enslave another portion, degrading millions of human beings to the level of the brute creation. The equal of this sin is not to be found in heathen lands.[27]

In 1862 Ellen White denounced the nation for allowing slavery, an "ugly spectacle of humanity," to persist. She said, "God is punishing this nation for the high crime of slavery. He has the destiny of the nation in His hands. He will punish the South for the sin of slavery and the North for so long suffering its overreaching influence."[28]

On the issue of slavery, essentially a matter of subordination, submission, and denial of shared status, Ellen White held positions which brought her into conflict with many of her contemporaries. In a stunning testimony against Southern prejudices, especially some Adventists who cherished and even defended such prejudices, she wrote:

> I call upon every Church in our land to look well to your own souls. . . . God makes no distinction between the North and the South. Whatever may be your prejudices, your wonderful prejudices, do not lose sight of this fact, that unless you put on Christ, and his Spirit dwells in you, you are slaves to sin and Satan.[29]

She further stated: "All heaven beholds with indignation human beings, the workmanship of God, reduced by their fellow men to the lowest depths of degradation and placed on a level of the brute creation. Professed followers of that dear Saviour whose compassion was ever moved at the sight of human woe, heartily engage in this enormous and grievous sin, and deal in slaves and souls of men."[30]

Some fundamental principles to be drawn from Ellen White's firm and courageous stand against slavery could aid our understanding in dealing with the perplexing issue of women's ordination today. Rather than taking a rigid or even arrogant attitude in interpreting her theological ideas that speak to the well-being and mission of the faith community, we need to be guided by the Spirit to the principles that undergirded and buttressed her teachings and her convictions. In other words, I am challenging my church to share the convictions and embrace the principles that moved Ellen White to forcefully critique and reject slavery as a necessary evil, contrary to God's purpose for His creation.

If we follow her example, we will be better prepared, I believe, to move confidently and creatively into the future as far as women's ordination is concerned. Ellen White's convictions on slavery and racial attitudes are clearly written, and she is clearly right. They reflect her inspired vision of a *shared status* within the church. They uphold the lofty biblical principles of justice, compassion, humility, love, and mutuality. To think of Ellen White otherwise is beyond belief. Much later than emancipation she unambiguously expressed her disappointment over an action taken by the General Conference regarding segregated churches:

> At the General Conference of 1889, resolutions were presented with reference to the color line. Such action is not called for. Let no man take the place of God, but stand aside in awe, and let God work upon human hearts, both white and black, in His own way. He will adjust all these perplexing questions. We need not prescribe a definite plan of working. Leave an opportunity for God to do something. We should be careful not to strengthen prejudices that ought to have died just as soon as Christ redeemed the soul from the bondage to sin.[31]

Some may argue that in this powerful and clear statement Ellen White was addressing the issue of racial segregation, and not the issue of slavery. But we must remind ourselves that American racial thought was initially shaped by slavery and that Ellen White was an active participant in the slavery debate within the church. She always handled the situation with a sense of balance, flexibility, sensitivity, faithfulness, courage, compassion, and contextual appropriateness.

Ellen White was always concerned about principle and context when she wrote on the issue of slavery and racial attitudes. Over and over again she reminded us that time, place, and condition may determine that what is suitable in one place may not be appropriate or desirable elsewhere. But we must not hesitate to do what is best in the interest of God's mission. Some of our ideas and efforts will work in one place, but may prove ineffective elsewhere. We have to trust that what is good will succeed. Ellen White wrote: "The light that the Lord has given me at different times has been that the Southern field, where the greatest share of the population of the colored race is, cannot be worked after the same methods as other fields."[32]

Should not this same courage, flexibility, faithfulness, and strength of character be demonstrated in the church today as we deal with the issue of women's ordination?

Conclusion

Some opponents of women's ordination argue that if the church should move in the direction of ordaining women, such an action would constitute a departure from biblical authority and a misrepresentation of the pure Word of God. These authors insist that the church is in danger of abandoning its adherence to Scripture.[33] On this matter Ray Holmes notes:

> The Seventh-day Adventist church continues to face the crucial issue of whether or not to ordain women in ministry. It is crucial because what the church finally decides will reveal a great deal about the nature of its commitment to biblical authority and its approach to the interpretation of Scripture.[34]

In his widely-read book *Women in the Church*, Samuele Bacchiocchi argues against women's ordination on the basis of headship and subordination. He concludes that women cannot serve as pastors "not because they are less capable than men of piety, zeal, learning, leadership, or aptitudes required to serve as a pastor, but simply because [pastoral] roles are preserved in Scripture as being those of a spiritual father and not a spiritual mother." In a manner similar to that of some proslavery theologians, Bacchiocchi maintains that "to blur or eliminate the role distinctions God assigned to men and women in the home and in the church, means not only to act contrary to His creational design, but also to accelerate the breakdown of the family and church structure."[35]

Many proslavery theologians argued that the slaves' position of submission to their masters was a law God had imposed on them, and therefore to tamper with it would be a serious violation of the divine design. Similarly, to ordain a woman as a pastor/elder would be a grievous violation of the divine design.[36]

Like many proslavery theologians, some contemporary Adventists argue that the exclusion of women from the ordained ministry could be part of God's divine plan, written in the structure of his Creation. Holmes queries, "Could it be that women's exclusion from the Old Testament priesthood and from the New Testament roles of apostle and elder/pastor stems not from mere sociological or cultural factors, but rather from God's divine arrangement established at Creation?"[37] This was the position of several proslavery advocates in regard to slavery.[38] Stringfellow was clear in his belief that God revealed to Paul the doctrine of slavery as part of the divine plan.[39] Like some contemporary Adventists who oppose ordination, the proslavery theologians were unequivocal in their claim of biblical authority for their position.

Curiously, many of the contemporary Adventists who oppose ordination as having no biblical foundation and theological support from E. G. White, also oppose slavery as having no biblical or theological foundation. For instance, one writes:

> One cannot deny that in New Testament time (just as in our day) there were oppressive structures that often treated women and some races as inferior. For this reason, some try to compare the headship issue to slavery, which was also current in Bible times. But the headship principle is different from slavery in two major ways: (1) The headship principle was a creation ordinance, the headship principle is morally right and therefore morally binding on all God's people, irrespective of the place and time in which they live; but slavery, as a post-fall distortion of God's will for humanity, is morally offensive and cannot be justified under biblical Christianity. The book of Philemon shows this.[40]

Interestingly, the slavers saw and interpreted Paul's letter to Philemon in a vastly different light. Using the principle of scriptural authority, proslavery theologians, led by Hopkins and Armstrong, noted that "Paul sent back a fugitive slave, . . . to his Christian master again, and assigned as his reason for so doing that master's right to the services of his slave."[41] John Henry Hopkins pointed out the reason why Paul sent Philemon back to his master: "St. Paul was inspired, and knew the will of the Lord Jesus Christ, and was only intent on obeying it. And who are we, that in our modern wisdom presume to set aside the Word of God?"[42] Stringfellow insisted that the "one general principle, ordained of God, applicable alike in all countries and at all stages of the Church's future history," was "As the Lord has called everyone, so let him walk."[43]

There could be no doubt at all that as far as the proslavery theologians were concerned, Paul's letter to Philemon was a clear endorsement of the divine will for slavery. And they believed that anyone who taught that godliness or the Bible abolished slavery would be sharply rebuked by this text.

As one reads the literature of contemporary Adventists who oppose women's ordination as contrary to the Word of God, yet argue that the same Word of God explicitly condemns slavery on biblical and moral grounds, one is forced to ask the hermeneutical question: How could they embrace and use a liberating hermeneutic as far as slavery is concerned, while preaching and theologizing against women's ordination through the use of a literalist hermeneutic? When one compares the proslavery argument with the writings of the opponents of women's ordination, the picture presented in the table on the next page emerges.[44]

As John R. Stott commented, the cultural chasm between the biblical world and the modern world determines the task of biblical exposition and lays down our two major obligations: (a) faithfulness to the ancient text, and (b) sensitivity to the modern context. And it is within this combination of faithfulness and sensitivity that the preacher *of integrity* is to be found.

Just as the church today believes and preaches with integrity that slavery or any form of human bondage is contrary to the will of God and the teachings of the apostles, the same church should teach with equal fervor that God chooses whomsoever he will to proclaim his Word and lead his people. If the ordination of men is a necessary condition for full opportunities in pastoral leadership and administration in the church, then justice, integrity, consistency, and the biblical principle of *shared status* within the body of Christ should move the church to embrace the ordination of women. The women who are called to ministry are already empowered by the Holy Spirit. A recognition of such empowerment and affirmation by the official church speaks directly to the existential issue of what it truly means for all to be equal in the sight of God. Indeed, the difficult quest for women's ordination is integral to all discussions about equality. God has modeled for us in Jesus Christ the relationship that should exist among his people. He, the Head and Founder of his church, governs with patience, mercy, love, and grace. He invites members of his Body to reflect on and demonstrate those principles with humility in the pursuance of his mission and our service in the world.

Proslavery

1. Slavers argued that their position was based on a high view of Scripture. The fundamental issue was biblical authority and faithfulness to that authority.
2. Divine Creation ordinance. In Gen 9:24-27, Noah decrees Negro slavery in the new creation after the Flood.
3. Old Testament precedent: Abraham's slaves, Israel's laws favoring slavery
4. Jesus' New Testament precedent: reversed polygamy and divorce, but did not mention slavery. 1 Tim 6:1-6, slavery doctrine based on Jesus' own words. Luke 17 uses slaver-master analogy.
5. Apostles' New Testament precedent: approved of slavery, but not of its abuses (Eph 6:5-9; Col 3:22-25; 1 Tim 6:1-2; Titus 2:9-10; 1 Pet 2:18-19). Gal 3:28 only abolishes spiritual distinctions, not slavery. Paul's example: sent back fugitive slave.
6. Divine blessing in slavery. Slavery is a merciful institution which provides for gospel influence for slaves.
7. Slippery-slope argument: If slavery is abolished, soon all divine social laws will be in question.

Antiordination

1. Antiordination advocates insist their position is based on a high view of Scripture. The core issue is fidelity to Scripture.
2. Divine Creation ordinance in Gen 1 and 2: Man is head over woman.
3. Old Testament precedent: Male priesthood represented by Israel's male leaders.
4. Jesus' New Testament precedent: never ordained women but chose 12 male disciples.
5. Apostles' New Testament precedent: women should not be in authority over men (1 Tim 2:11-14, 3:1-2; Titus 1:5-6; 1 Cor 11:14-17, 14:34). Gal 3:28 only abolishes spiritual distinctions, not male authority over women. Paul's example: "I permit no woman to teach or have authority over a man" (1 Tim 2:12).
6. Blessing of male headship in the church.
7. Slippery-slope argument: If the church allows ordination of women, it will soon allow homosexuality.

Endnotes

1. John R. Stott, "A Call to Faithfulness: Biblical Preaching in the Modern World," unpublished lecture delivered at the 1996 Conference on Expository Preaching, Calvin Theological Seminary, 22 February 1996.

2. New Testament scholars refer to the complete household codes or domestic duties in Col 3:18-4:1; Eph 5:21-6:9; 1 Pet 2:18-3:7 as *Haustafeln*, codes or duties dealing principally with master-slave, husband-wife, or parent-child relationships.

3. John Knox, "Paul and the 'Liberals,'" *Religion and Life* 49 (1980): 419.

4. Joseph Bates, Joshua V. Himes, Charles Fitch, George Star, John Byington, and J. P. Kellogg were all abolitionists who spoke out against those in the church who supported slavery as a divinely established institution. See Keith Lockhart and Malcolm Bull, *Seeking a Sanctuary: Seventh-day Adventism and the American Dream* (San Francisco: Harper and Row, 1989), 193-194.

5. Ellen G. White, *Testimonies for the Church*, 1:359-360.

6. According to Willard M. Swarthley, this policy statement reflects the thinking and position of the leading proslavery theologians and their sympathizers, including John Henry Hopkins, Albert Taylor Bledsoe, Thornton Stringfellow, Charles Hodge, George Armstrong, and Governor Hammond of Virginia. See Swarthley, *Case Issues in Biblical Interpretation: Slavery, Sabbath, War, and Women* (Scottdale: Herald, 1983), 31-32.

7. John Henry Hopkins, *A Scriptural, Ecclesiastical and Historical View of Slavery from the Days of the Patriarch Abraham to the Nineteenth Century* (New York: W. I. Pooley, 1864), 16-17.

8. Thornton Stringfellow, *Cotton Is King and Pro-Slavery Arguments: Comprising the Writings of Hammond, Harper, Christy, Stringfellow, Hodge, Bledsoe, and Cartwright on This Important Subject*, ed. E. N. Elliott (Augusta, GA: Pritchard, Abbott, and Loomis, 1860), 463.

9. Ibid., 463ff.

10. Charles Hodge, "The Fugitive Slave Law," in *Cotton Is King*, 809ff.

11. Stringfellow, in *Cotton Is King*, 474.

12. Ibid., 474-479.

13. J. H. Hammond, "Letters on Slavery," *The Pro-Slavery Argument* (Charleston: Walker Richards, 1862), 107-108.

14. Thomas Dew, "Professor Dew on Slavery," in *The Pro-Slavery Argument*, 452.

15. Albert T. Bledsoe, "The Argument from the Scripture," in *Cotton Is King*, 379-380.

16. Hope Felder, *Stony the Road We Trod* (Minneapolis: Fortress, 1991), 209.

17. Elizabeth Fox-Genovese, "The Divine Sanction of Social Order," *Journal of the American Academy of Religion* 55 (1987): 211.

18. Ibid., 219.

19. George Bourne, *A Condensed Anti-Slavery Bible Argument: By a Citizen of Virginia* (New York: S. W. Benedict, 1845), 51.

20. Albert Barnes, *An Inquiry into the Scriptural Views of Slavery* (Philadelphia: Parry and McMillan, 1855), 84, 86.

21. Ibid., 375.

22. Francis Wayland, *The Elements of Moral Science on the Subject of Slavery* (Boston: Gould, Kendall, and Lincoln, 1836), 396.

23. Bourne, 70-71.

24. Ibid.

25. Barnes, 375.

26. Barnes, 330.

27. White, *Testimonies*, 1:258-259.

28. Ibid., 264.

29. Ellen G. White, *The Southern Work*, 9-10.

30. Ellen G. White, *Early Writings*, 275.

31. White, *The Southern Work*, 15.

32. Ibid., 98.

33. Three of the leading spokespersons in the Adventist church on the issue of women's ordination and their opposition to it based on their reading of Scripture are Samuele Bacchiocchi, *Women in the Church: A Biblical Study on the Role of Women in the Church* (Berrien Springs, MI: Biblical Perspective, 1987); C. Raymond Holmes, *The Tip of an Iceberg: Biblical Authority, Biblical Interpretation, and the Ordination of Women in Ministry* (Berrien Springs, MI: Pointer Publication, 1994); and Samuel Koranteng-Pipim, *Searching the Scriptures: Women's Ordination and the Call to Biblical Fidelity* (Berrien Springs, MI: Adventist Affirm, 1995). 120.

34. Holmes, 12.

35. Bacchiocchi, 209.

36. Ibid.

37. Ibid., 121.

38. Stringfellow, 474.

39. Ibid., 484-489.

40. See Samuel Koranteng-Pipim, "Saved by Grace and Living by Race: The Religion Called Racism," *Journal of the Adventist Theological Society* 5 (Autumn 1994): 37-78.

41. George D. Armstrong, *The Christian Doctrine of Slavery* (New York: C. Scribner, 1857), 33.

42. Hopkins, *A Scriptural, Ecclesiastical View of Slavery*, 164.

43. Stringfellow, 481-482.

44. I am indebted to Dr. Richard Davidson for his insightful comments on this issue.

CHAPTER 19

THE ORDINATION OF WOMEN IN LIGHT OF THE CHARACTER OF GOD

ROGER L. DUDLEY

In earlier chapters in this book we have seen that women served in various areas of ministry in New Testament times and that those few texts which might, at first glance, seem to prohibit such service are actually dealing with other problems and do not address the subject of ministry directly. We have also seen that women served in both leadership and ministerial positions in the early history of the Seventh-day Adventist denomination and have continued to serve—although in relatively few numbers—up to the present time. In other words, the Adventist Church has never barred women from any form of ministry, including the pastorate.

Given this state of affairs, the questions arise: Is it proper to ordain those women who have demonstrated their calling to ministry? If so, on what basis? Is it possible to find a biblical rationale for ordaining women ministers? Is the move to ordain women only the result of cultural pressure, or are there deeper theological considerations?

The ordination of women is a controversial and emotional topic, and I have no desire to raise the temperature. I do not wish to be dogmatic or suggest in any way that those who might disagree with me are not sincere Christians or able Bible students. I do not believe that either my Christian understanding or my conscience is superior to those of people who take a different view. I also write as a North American, and I freely confess my ignorance of societal conditions in many other parts of the world. I acknowledge that, like everyone else, I am influenced in my understanding of any issue by my culture and background.

Still, I would invite you to consider the arguments that I will present. If after a fair hearing you are not convinced, we can go our ways as friends. But I do represent the thinking of many Bible-loving Adventists who live in a society where men and women are equal under the law, in business, in education, and in other social enterprises.

In this chapter, then, we will explore the questions I have raised by consulting the Bible, the writings of Ellen White, and our God-given reasoning abilities on the overarching theme of the character of God. We start by recognizing the rather awkward position in which Adventists find themselves.

The Adventist Dilemma

Many Christian denominations have wrestled with the issue of the ordination of women; and, in a good proportion of the cases, their theologians have, like Adventists, attempted to find support for their positions, pro or con, from the Scriptures. Their task, while formidable enough, is not nearly as difficult and complex as that faced by Adventists. This is because in most Christian bodies *serving* in the pastoral office and *being ordained* to that office are one and the same thing.

For example, when Paul Jewett set out to define ordination, he noted that there is an office of ministry and "ordination is the way one is inducted into that office. One is set apart for and enters upon the Christian ministry by way of ordination." Again, "There is a consensus that ordination is [ordinarily] necessary if one is to function as a minister in Christ's church with the authority of one divinely called to the task" (brackets in original).[1] Thus in these denominations the question is: May women serve in pastoral ministry? If the Bible allows this, they can be ordained; if it does not, they cannot.

But Adventists cannot take this approach without serious difficulty, because this is not how ordination is employed among us. In Adventism ordination has been and is today an affirmation of ministry accomplished rather than the entry into it. Adventist policy typically requires a candidate to serve in pastoral ministry for a number of years (at least four) and demonstrate his calling by certain marks of success (e.g., number of converts) before the ceremony of ordination takes place. During this trial period the unordained minister may preach, win converts, baptize, solemnize marriages, celebrate communion, and administer churches.[2] This is true of both men and women pastors[3] except that at the conclusion of this probationary stage, men who have been successful are rewarded with ordination; women are not.

Given the Adventist understanding of ministry, then, I will not attempt to argue that women may serve in the pastoral office but will accept it as a given. That they may and do so serve has been shown in other chapters of this book, and that decision has been reaffirmed by recent Annual Councils and world sessions. Of course, I realize that some believe the church to be in error in allowing this and that previous actions should be rescinded and new policies adopted that would prohibit women from serving in the pastoral office. That is an important issue but not the burden of this chapter. Here we consider: If the church does permit women to serve as pastors, are there Bible reasons why they should not be ordained at the close of their probationary period?

We are led, therefore, to studying ordination directly. But here we run into another problem. The ordination of women is not mentioned in Scripture. The reason we do not find the problem addressed in the New Testament is the same reason we do not find other modern church dilemmas discussed—it was not a concern of the period, and no one ever raised the issue. In fact, while the qualifications for ministry are listed in the New Testament, a discussion of ordination in general is absent.

Confronted by the lack of direct scriptural evidence on the subject, both proponents and opponents of the ordination of women have reverted to using texts that deal with the service and functions of women. But since pastoral service and ordination are two different things (at least in Adventism), we cannot settle the ordination question with these texts.

Does this mean that there is no way to make the Bible relevant to this problem? I believe that the Bible does provide guidance in this matter, as it does for every modern concern. But it does not do so directly. Rather, it is necessary to discover the great themes of Scripture, which had local application in the first century, and prayerfully, under the guidance of the Spirit, seek to apply them to the conundrums we face today. While the Bible contains many timeless themes and principles, I would like to explore what I consider perhaps the major theme of Scripture and one that best illuminates the question of the ordination of women—the character of God.

The Great Controversy and the Character of God

Seventh-day Adventists believe that "all humanity is now involved in a great controversy between Christ and Satan regarding the character of God."[4] The whole tragedy of sin began when Lucifer in heaven questioned the fairness of God's character.

> From the beginning it has been Satan's studied plan to . . . misrepresent the character of God, to lead men to cherish a false conception of Him. The Creator has been presented to their minds as clothed with the attributes of the prince of evil himself,—as arbitrary, severe, and unforgiving,—that He might be feared, shunned, and even hated by men.[5]

The controversy was transferred to this earth when Lucifer, speaking through the serpent, insinuated that God was not fair in withholding superior knowledge from Eve (Gen 3:1-5). These assaults on God's character could undermine the stability of the universe by destroying trust in Him. Therefore, in his master strategy for the recovery from sin it has been necessary for God to deal with the character issue. "The plan of redemption had a yet broader and deeper purpose than the salvation of man. It was . . . to vindicate the character of God before the universe."[6]

The conflict over the character of God becomes especially intense as the end nears and Satan intensifies his efforts. Rev 18:1 predicts a final manifestation of God's glory (character) as an important factor in the climax of the great controversy. Ellen White wrote: "Those who wait for the Bridegroom's coming are to say to the people, 'Behold your God.' The last rays of merciful light, the last message of mercy to be given to the world, is a revelation of His character of love."[7]

Furthermore, the outcome is sure. The whole universe will come to see that God's character is just, loving, and fair. For, "when the great controversy shall be ended, . . . the plan of redemption having been completed, the character of God is revealed to all created intelligences."[8]

God's Justice and Fairness

No wonder, then, that a major purpose of the Bible is to reveal God. The Scriptures are his self-disclosure. While the most defining feature of his character is love (1 John 4:7-21), he also reveals himself as a God of justice and fairness. Indeed, these characteristics are inseparable, for if God was not just and fair, he could hardly be loving.

The Bible states that "the LORD is a God of justice" (Isa 30:18).[9] The Hebrew word *mishpat* has rich connotations. Stephen Mott points out the following:

> Justice is founded in the being of God, for whom it is a chief attribute. As such, God is the sure defender of the poor and the oppressed (Jer. 9:23-24; Ps. 10:17-18). . . . Since the justice of God is characterized by special regard for the poor and the weak, a corresponding quality is

demanded of God's people (Deut 10:18-19). When they properly carry out justice, they are the agents of the divine will (Isa 59:15-16). . . . The focus is on the oppressed with particular attention given to specific groups, such as the poor, widows, the fatherless, slaves, resident aliens, wage earners, and those with physical infirmities (Job 29:12-17; Ps 146:7-9; Mal 3:5). . . . Justice is a deliverance, rectifying the gross social inequities of the disadvantaged (Ps 76:9). It puts an end to the conditions that produce the injustice (Ps 10:18).[10]

Synonyms given are "equity," "fairness," and "impartiality." All these nuances appear in texts like Ps 99:4: "The King is mighty, he loves justice—you have established equity; in Jacob you have done what is just and right." Isaiah is inspired to lament: "Judgment is turned away backwards, and justice standeth afar off: for truth is fallen in the street and equity cannot enter" (Isa 59:14 KJV).

This theme was especially strong among the Old Testament prophets. Amos, for example, denounced Israel because they had oppressed the innocent and taken advantage of the powerless. God would not accept their worship; He despised their religious ceremonies. "But let justice roll on like a river, righteousness like a never-failing stream!" (5:24) was the formula Amos announced for renewing the covenant relationship. Likewise, Isaiah, Jeremiah, Hosea, and Micah showed strong concern for just treatment for the marginalized of society.

The purpose of the Proverbs was to aid the reader in "doing what is right and just and fair" (1:3). The wise counsel is: "If the king judges the poor with fairness, his throne will always be secure" (29:14).

The New Testament continues the theme. Matthew quoted Isa 42:1-4 as being fulfilled in and constituting the very essence of the ministry of Jesus:

Here is my servant whom I have chosen,
the one I love, in whom is my delight;
I will put my Spirit on him,
and he will proclaim justice to the nations.
He will not quarrel or cry out;
no one will hear his voice in the streets.
A bruised reed he will not break,
and a smoldering reed he will not snuff out,
till he leads justice to victory. (Matt 12:18-20)

Later, Jesus reproved the religious leaders because in their meticulousness in tithing the practically worthless, they had "neglected the more important matters of the law—justice, mercy, and faithfulness" (Matt 23:23).

Justice and fairness were important in the early church too. The occasion for the appointing of the "seven . . . known to be full of the Spirit and wisdom" (Acts 6:3) was an allegation that the Greek-speaking widows were being neglected in the daily distribution of assistance. Ellen White commented: "Any inequality would have been contrary to the spirit of the gospel."[11] After describing the apostles' solution, she continued: "The same principles of piety and justice that were to guide the rulers among God's people in the time of Moses and of David, were also to be followed by those given the oversight of the newly organized church of God in the gospel dispensation."[12]

A major theme of the New Testament is the struggle of the early church to grasp the truth that God would not have them discriminate between Jew and Gentile in the body of Christ. After the Spirit led him to the home of Cornelius, Peter saw the light and exclaimed: "I now realize how true it is that God does not show favoritism" (Acts 10:34). The Greek word *prosōpolēmptēs* appears only once in this form in the Bible[13] and means literally "acceptor of faces." The KJV has "God is no respecter of persons," and the NRSV renders it "God shows no partiality."

Satan claimed "that God was not just in imposing laws upon the angels; that . . . He was seeking merely the exaltation of Himself. It was therefore necessary to demonstrate before the inhabitants of heaven, and of all the worlds, that God's government is just, His law perfect."[14] Thus the whole Bible should be read as a testimony to the love, justice, and fairness of the character of God. Each individual story, vision, or letter of instruction is only an application of that theme as it is worked out in the particular cultural context in which it is given. In seeking to understand any portion of Scripture we must always ask: What is this particular passage revealing about the character of God?

Reflectors of God's Character

The Holy Scriptures reveal the justice and fairness of our God. But lest we misunderstand this revelation, God sent his only Son. "Anyone who has seen me has seen the Father," Jesus declared (John 14:9). In a study of his ministry we gain insight into how God regards every human diversity.

Christ recognized no distinction of nationality or rank or creed. . . .

[He] came to break down every wall of partition. . . . The life of Christ established a religion in which there is no caste, a religion by which Jew and Gentile, free and bond, are linked in a common brotherhood, equal before God.[15]

In listing a few examples of the walls Christ came to demolish, Ellen White did not specify gender. Yet her phrases "every wall" and "no caste" suggest that the application of the principle goes far beyond her examples to encompass every characteristic which would divide the body of Christ.

Before Jesus ascended back to heaven, he commissioned his followers to do the same work he had done: "As the Father has sent me, I am sending you" (John 20:21). "It is the work of the Christian in this life to represent Christ to the world, in life and character unfolding the blessed Jesus."[16]

The purpose which God seeks to accomplish through His people today is the same that He desired to accomplish through Israel. . . . By beholding the goodness, the mercy, the justice, and the love of God revealed in the church, the world is to have a representation of His character.[17]

This purpose is reflected in Adventist Fundamental Belief 13: Unity in the Body of Christ. It reads, in part:

The church is one body with many members, called from every nation, kindred, tongue, and people. In Christ we are a new creation; distinctions of race, culture, learning, and nationality, and differences between high and low, rich and poor, male and female, must not be divisive among us.[18]

The New Testament church evidently had some problems with discrimination, as James found it necessary to address the situation. Some were inclined to curry favor of the rich and ignore the poor. To these James wrote: "As believers in our glorious Lord Jesus Christ, don't show favoritism. . . . Have you not discriminated among yourselves and become judges with evil thoughts? If you show favoritism, you sin" (Jas 2:1, 4, 9).

Adventists have frequently used verse 10—"Whoever keeps the whole law and yet stumbles at just one point is guilty of breaking it all"—to show that those who do not observe the seventh-day Sabbath are not keeping God's commandments. This may be an appropriate application, but it is interesting to note that in its context this passage referred to demonstrating favoritism based on social differences.

Ellen White also stressed this message. "Those who are connected with God will not only shun all injustice, but will manifest his mercy and goodness toward all with whom they have to do. The Lord will sanction no respect of person."[19] The major theme in all this is that as Christians we represent the character of God. "When one who professes to serve God wrongs or injures a brother [or sister], he misrepresents the character of God to that brother [or sister].[20]

But What Is Justice?

Probably no one will object to what I have written above. All thoughtful people favor justice, fairness, and equity. The difficulty comes when we try to decide what constitutes justice. Is it the same in all times, places, and circumstances? Or does it vary with the situation? We would probably agree that there is an absolute standard of fairness and justice. But if our purpose as Christians is to reveal the character of God, I would like to suggest that the actions of his people must be perceived as just and fair by the community in which those actions occur.

This is analogous to the recommendations of child psychologists who tell us that discipline of a child will not be effective unless the child perceives the discipline as fair and deserved. It also corresponds to the reason why God did not immediately destroy Lucifer upon the onset of sin. God permitted rebellion to work its course so that the watching universe might be convinced that His way is loving and just.[21]

A helpful text at this point is Titus 2:10: "Shewing all good fidelity; that they may adorn the doctrine of God our Saviour in all things" (KJV). The NIV reads: "So that in every way they will make the teaching about God our Savior attractive." Or "they may be an ornament to the doctrine of God our Savior" (NRSV). This passage is intriguing because it was addressed to slaves, telling them to be faithful, respectful, and honest to their masters. We would think that justice and fairness would call for the abolition of slavery, and the impact of the gospel did eventually lead to that position.[22] But that was not Paul's message in the social context of that time. If he had called for the slaves to rise up and claim their freedom, Christianity would have been scandalized as an anarchist cult. Thus, the Christian God would not appear attractive to the Roman world. This suggests that we as Christians have a part to play in the vindication of the character of God. To put it somewhat bluntly, our job is "to make God look good" to the world who does not know him and who may have a distorted view of his character because of Satan's misrepresentations.

Now if the revelation of the character of our God as loving, just, and fair is a major theme of the Scriptures, an important subtheme of the New Testament is "adorning" the doctrine of God. Inspired writers showed concern for what the pagan world would think about this new Christian religion and the God it revealed. For example, believers were urged to "shine like the stars in the universe" before "a crooked and depraved generation" (Phil 2:15). They should "live such good lives among the pagans" that the latter might be led to "glorify God" (1 Pet 2:12). It would be an embarrassment to the cause to have church members going to law against one another "in front of unbelievers" (1 Cor 6:1-6). If a meeting featured a chaotic speaking in tongues, unbelievers were likely to conclude: "You are out of your mind" (1 Cor 14:23).

This same subtheme may offer a reason for texts such as 1 Cor 14:34 and 1 Tim 2:12, which call for order and submission on the part of women. That is, Paul had a concern that something that was happening among the members might bring disgrace upon the church and, by extension, upon the God whom the church represented. While these passages have been discussed in previous chapters, we might pause here to note this connection. It has been said that those against the ordination of women read the Bible literally, while those for it interpret it in the light of principles. This is not accurate. Neither view takes a literal approach, for the texts do not even hint at the subject of ordination. A literal reading would cause us to forbid women to teach or even speak in church. Only the most radical fringe would take that position.

Actually, both groups adopt a similar methodology. They decide what principle is behind these particular applications, and then they apply that principle, in a way that makes sense to them, to a modern problem—in this case the ordination of women. The difference is in the theme that is discovered—in the *content* of the interpretation—and not in the *method*. Opponents find the overarching theme in these and similar passages to be male headship and decide that females cannot be ordained because God desires them to be submissive to males. Although I do not agree with this interpretation, even if they *are* right, that would be no reason for excluding women from the ordained ministry—unless, of course, one believes that ordination places the minister *over* other members in some way different from the position of the unordained minister.

On the other hand, proponents of ordination have generally seen these passages as additional examples of the counsel to make the teachings about God attractive. Whatever the problems in Corinth and Ephesus, they were giving Christianity and its Author a bad name. They were making God look bad. While the local situation may be different, the message is timeless: we are God's representatives; our actions impact on what the world thinks of him.

Then do these New Testament passages often used by opponents of ordination for women really have nothing to do with the subject? Not directly, but if we look at them in light of our major theme of the vindication of the character of God, we may find an application. If ordaining women will reveal God as unjust, unfair, and arbitrary, then we ought not to do it. But if such a step will present his character as fair, just, and loving, then, by all means, we should move ahead. The question is always before us: How will our actions influence the watching world's opinion of the God we serve? Let's examine this thought a bit further.

A Just God and the Ordination of Women

The revelation of God's character and our understanding of that character are progressive. What is deemed permissible at one time may eventually come to be understood as not in God's ideal plan for His children. For example, polygamy, though not in God's original design, was permitted in the Old Testament. By New Testament times "the overseer must be above reproach, the husband of but one wife" (1 Tim 3:2). Today, in many areas of the world field, having multiple spouses would be cause for disfellowshipping. The standard did not change, but God's children have come to a better understanding of that standard as his character has been gradually unfolded to them.

As has been noted above, the same is true of human slavery. Though New Testament writers did not call for its abolition, Paul laid out a long-range plan for gospel transformation when he wrote: "There is neither Jew nor Greek, slave nor free, male nor female, for you are all one in Christ Jesus" (Gal 3:28). Here he set down the principle that the gospel, in its own time, transforms all human relationships.

Much of the New Testament period was devoted to breaking down the barriers between Jew and Gentile. In this struggle God's character was enhanced. Other barriers, such as slavery and gender were to tumble later, though Paul did admonish Christian slave owners to "provide your slaves with what is right and fair" (Col 4:1).

To our modern minds the right and fair course would have been to free those slaves. But Christianity proclaimed its message within its social context then and still does. The time for such a bold advance of justice was not yet, for such concepts of equity were not generally recognized. Still, in the just and fair character of God resided the seeds of the destruction of slavery. Someday Christians would come to see that they could not hold fellow humans in bondage and still be true to the gospel. They would lead out in championing the liberation of all peoples—a future perhaps hinted at by Paul in Philemon 13-14.[23]

When centuries later the time was ripe for this new revelation of Christian fairness and justice, God had prepared a prophet with his message: "Exact and impartial justice is to be shown to the Negro race," Ellen White wrote. "The religion of the Bible recognizes no caste or color. It ignores rank, wealth, worldly honor."[24]

The word "caste" is significant here. "A caste system is a social arrangement in which access to power and socioeconomic benefits are fixed, typically from birth, according to certain ascribed characteristics of the individual."[25] We are familiar with the caste system of Hinduism, and, certainly, racial distinctions comprised the caste system which Ellen White condemned. But, by this definition, gender might also constitute a caste system. If the privileges of a particular society were restricted to those who were born with characteristics over which they had no control—and gender is certainly one of those—then a caste system would exist. While it is beyond the scope of this chapter to document the fact, it is generally acknowledged that throughout much of human history women were placed in a position subservient to men simply because they were born female. How would a just God regard a gender caste system?

> No distinction on account of nationality, race, or caste, is recognized by God. He is the maker of all mankind. All men [generic term] are of one family by creation, and all are one through redemption. Christ came to demolish every wall of partition, to throw open every compartment of the temple, that every soul may have free access to God.[26]

To the ancient query: "What does the LORD require of you?" the prophet replied: "To act justly and to love mercy and to walk humbly with your God" (Mic 6:8). What does it mean to "act justly" in our human relationships? For one thing, that we do not show partiality in our treatment of individuals. We do not make decisions that limit or advance the potentialities of people on the basis of external characteristics over which they have no control. Of necessity some persons must be leaders and others followers. But these distinctions are to be based on abilities, on character, on spiritual calling. If they are determined by race, parentage, social class, or gender so that some humans have no chance at opportunities simply because they had the misfortune to be born Black, poor, or female, then justice is not served. Worse yet, if this discrimination is practiced within the Christian community, God's character is besmirched.

The Adventist Church in most parts of the world has come to see that it is not justice to bar Blacks from membership in "White" congregations or from attendance at "White" schools—though it once did those things. The church has slowly had its eyes opened to the truth that fairness and equity call for the opening of top leadership positions in the denomination to the variety of ethnic peoples who constitute its membership. The church, at least in some parts of the world, has even accepted the revelation that it is justice to pay equal wages to men and women who both perform the same tasks—though it needed a little legal pressure in coming to this understanding. Now what about equal treatment for men and women who have both been called to the sacred task of gospel ministry?

Please remember that in this chapter we are not discussing whether or not women can serve in the pastoral ministry. The Adventist Church has always accepted the concept of women as pastors and has reaffirmed this most recently in actions taken by the 1996 General Conference Annual Council meeting in Costa Rica. At this session the Council voted to amend policy GC B 17, "Human Relations," by adding language that strengthened the equal treatment of women. Notice the italicized language which indicates the changes:

> B 17 10 Official Position—*The world church supports nondiscrimination in employment practices and policies and upholds the principle that both men and women, without regard to race and color, shall* be given full and equal opportunity within the church to develop the knowledge and skills needed *for* the building up *of the church. Positions of service and responsibility (except those requiring ordination to the gospel ministry)** on all levels of church activity *shall* be open *to all* on the basis *of the individual's qualifications.*
>
> 2. The appointment of *individuals to serve as Bible instructors or chaplains, or in departmental or pastoral responsibilities,* shall not be limited by race or color. *Neither shall these positions be limited by gender (except those requiring ordination to the gospel ministry).**[27]

Thus the world Seventh-day Adventist Church has taken a stand that rejects any system or philosophy that discriminates against anyone on the basis of race, color, or gender. Certainly, the doctrine of God has been adorned; the teaching about God has been made more attractive. Many thoughtful people will have a higher regard for both the Adventist Church and the God whom it represents.

Since pastors are ordained after the trial period, some may feel that the phrase in parentheses, *except those requiring ordination to the gospel ministry*, bars women from serving in the pastoral office. This interpretation would be incorrect as it would contradict the rest of the action. Rather it refers to the fact that church policy states that the occupant of a few offices (such as conference president) must be an ordained minister. Since the church has not ordained any women, these positions obviously could not be filled by them. If, however, there were ordained women ministers, they would be eligible for such positions, since the restriction is based on ordination, not gender. There are very few positions in Adventism with such a requirement.

To make it even clearer, the * at the end of the exception phrase refers to a footnote which reads:

> *The exception clause and any other statement above shall not be used to reinterpret the action already taken by the world church authorizing the ordination of women as local church elders in divisions in which the division executive committees have given their approval.*[28]

Without question the world Adventist Church has come a long, long way in recognizing gender equality. Given this position, the query of this chapter is: Why wouldn't justice and fairness lead to the next step and permit ordination for those women who have demonstrated their call to pastoral ministry? On what basis would we remove all discrimination in allowing people to serve as pastors but discriminate in how we acknowledge or affirm that service? Certainly, not on any command of Scripture. And certainly not by any logical reasoning process.

But, the objection is heard, couldn't men and women be equal and still have different functions in God's work? Of course, but ordination, at least as practiced in the Adventist Church, is not a function. If a man enters the Adventist ministry, is assigned to pastor a church, is successful, and is finally ordained, his functions change little or not at all. As we have earlier noted, the unordained male minister, with permission from his conference, may essentially perform all the functions of ministry.[29] What changes? He achieves a new status of respect (the title "elder"), a recognition on the part of the body of believers that he has passed the "qualifying test"—his "board examinations," if you please. Ordination refers not primarily to *functions* performed but to *status* accorded.

With the woman pastor the situation is different. We permit her to serve like the male pastor but will not accord her the same status and affirmation. A woman and a man both serve as pastors. Both have the same seminary training. Both perform the same duties equally well. Both carry the same responsibilities. Both give proof of their calling by winning souls. But he is rewarded with the official recognition of ordination. She is bypassed for this perceived honor and for advancement solely because she is female. Is this really fair?

This simple sense of fairness is not limited to Western mentality, the academically educated, or social liberals. All people, whatever their cultural conditioning, have an innate sense of fairness. We see it even in little children. We know that to arbitrarily treat some people better than others solely on the basis of ethnicity, economic status, or gender is wrong. We instinctively sense that God wouldn't behave that way.

Recently I was listening to a sermon by Charles D. Brooks on the *Breath of Life* television program. The subject was hell. "What would you think of a judge," Brooks asked, "who said to the accused standing before him: 'You have been found guilty of stealing a candy bar. Therefore, I sentence you to life imprisonment without opportunity for parole'? You would say that the punishment didn't fit the crime. The judge was completely unfair."

Moving to make the application, Brooks continued. "Then what about a man who lived a sinful life for 70 years, and for punishment God caused him to burn in hell for 70 billion years?" Considering such an action, we all, the preacher stated, would exclaim: "It wouldn't be right; it wouldn't be fair; it wouldn't be just."

As Adventists, we would all agree. Even though there are a few Bible texts which, if interpreted in isolation, might suggest an ever-burning hellfire, one good argument against that doctrine is that it does not square with the character of a loving and just God. Therefore, we reject that interpretation in the light of other biblical evidence and construct a theology of hell that will allow us to see God as both fair and merciful.

The parallel is clear. While there are a few texts that taken out of context might be employed to discriminate against women in ministry, we reject that interpretation as being unworthy of the character of God. Rather we use the body of Scripture, which sheds light on God's fairness and loving acceptance, to develop a theology of women that accords with that character.

But the objection might be raised that as Christians we should humbly accept our position and not fight for our rights. We should do the Lord's work and not be concerned with status. Notice, I have never talked about "rights." No one has a "right" to be ordained. Ordination comes not because a person desires it or craves more distinguished status, but because the church under the leading of the Holy Spirit affirms gifts. If the controversial problem of female ordination had its roots in the fact that some "pushy" women thought they had a right to be ordained, it could have been dismissed long ago because their numbers are too few to make a ripple on the denominational surface. The discussion continues because many members who have nothing to gain personally from the outcome believe that the church should be fully committed to do the right thing—to be fair and just in all its dealings.

But if ordaining women is a matter of justice, does this mean it should be instituted everywhere, regardless of local custom? This is a difficult question, because fairness and justice are required of God's people everywhere, but tact and consideration of community mores are part of representing God's character. However, let us turn the abstract question into a practical one.

In most places in the world field where opposition to the ordination of women prevails, no women are serving as pastors. Of course, if there are no female pastors, then discussion of whether or not to ordain them becomes entirely theoretical and essentially valueless. We can conclude that where there are no women pastors, we should not ordain them. These places might as well withdraw from the discussion with which this chapter is concerned, though an on-going dialog on whether it is biblically proper for a woman to serve as a pastor might be profitable. Although the church has already decided on that one, some are not in agreement with the decision and would like to revisit the subject.

It is also feasible that some women are serving as pastors in societies which would accept a woman as pastor but protest her ordination, though I must confess that I am not personally aware of such places. But if there are areas in today's world where to ordain women who serve as pastors would create community antagonism, hinder the spread of the gospel, and make Adventists look radical and disorderly, it would not be wise to plunge ahead, for God's character would not be glorified. Just as New Testament writers had to bide their time on the question of slavery, so we today must patiently introduce gospel truth, tailoring our approaches to the "readiness" of the prospective hearers.

On the other hand, in the United States and various other places, the equality of the sexes has come to be a given. Government, business, publishing, and television all give at least lip service to gender equality. In this climate a church that discriminates in ordination is widely regarded as unjust and unfair. When inhabitants of these societies discover that our favoritism is based on religious grounds, they turn away in disgust. Our God looks bad. His character is not vindicated in the Great Controversy. How can they find such an unfair God to be appealing?

Conclusion

Some may ask: Are justice and fairness only subjective then? Do they constitute one set of behaviors in one time and place and a different set in another era and location? Is there no objective standard for fairness? Let us remember that the *concept* of justice appeals to morally upright people universally. The *defining details* result from a process of growth and education. Therefore, we should not attempt to push the implementation of these details in areas of the world that are not ready for them. But neither should we deny them in locations where they are readily acknowledged as a part of justice and fairness and thus would enhance the view of God's nature. A scriptural passage that I have found helpful is that in which Jesus unfolds the character of his Father:

> Which of you, if his son asks for bread, will give him a stone? Or if he asks for a fish, will give him a snake? If you, then, though you are evil, know how to give good gifts to your children, how much more will your Father in heaven give good gifts to those who ask him. (Matt 7:9-11)

Some earthly parents might be so cruel and heartless that they would ignore the needs of their children, but the best fathers and mothers would sacrifice everything for the good of their children. Then God must be even more loving and generous, for he always exceeds the highest ideals of humanity.

Personally, I find this to be most persuasive and moving on the subject of our chapter. Of course, Jesus was speaking of answered prayer rather than equality for women. But the principle stated here has a wide application. In its interpretation of v. 11, the *Adventist Bible Commentary* says: "Jesus takes human nature at its best, and then points men to the incomparably greater character of God."[30] Verse 12 states: "So in everything, do to others what you would have them do to you, for this sums up the Law and the Prophets." The Golden Rule is the epitome of justice!

The application made by the *Commentary* provides a great deal of food for thought. Imagine human nature at its best. Are not fairness, justice, and lack of favoritism (Jas 2:1, 4, 9) part of that nature? Then God must be even more so. Where do we imperfect humans get our high ideals anyway? From whence comes the belief that all mortals are created in the image of God and thus deserve to be treated with worth and dignity? Who gave us the lofty vision of impartial consideration for all, regardless of the circumstances of birth such as race or gender? Do we concoct them in our own feeble brains? Do we spin them out of nothing? I do not believe so, for we are not capable of high and noble thoughts apart from our Creator. God himself has planted them in our minds for we were created in his image. He has gradually unfolded these truths to us as he has allowed us glimpses of his character of fairness and justice. "Every gleam of thought, every flash of the intellect, is from the Light of the world."[31]

Therefore, it would seem that when we as Christians live by these principles, we have the opportunity to give the world a clearer glimpse of the character of God. While we would not want to force the ordination of women on any area that is not convinced of its biblical justice, we do believe that in many areas it would be a positive testimony to our faith and a means of breaking down prejudice.

Endnotes

1. Paul K. Jewett, *The Ordination of Women* (Grand Rapids: Eerdmans, 1980), 13-14.

2. While unordained pastors around the world preach, win converts, and administer churches, it is recognized that each world division decides whether they may baptize, solemnize marriages, and celebrate communion. Where unordained ministers obtain permission to perform the last three services, they have usually been ordained as local elders of their congregations and function in that capacity.

3. Not all world divisions have women pastors, so the question of ordaining them does not arise.

4. Ministerial Association of the General Conference of Seventh-day Adventists, *Seventh-day Adventists Believe... A Biblical Exposition of 27 Fundamental Doctrines* (Hagerstown, MD: Review and Herald, 1988), 98, Fundamental Belief 8.

5. Ellen G. White, *Testimonies for the Church*, 5:738.

6. Ellen G. White, *Patriarchs and Prophets*, 68.

7. Ellen G. White, *Christ's Object Lessons*, 415.

8. Ellen G. White, *The Desire of Ages*, 764.

9. Unless otherwise noted, all Scripture references in this chapter are quoted from the New International Version.

10. Stephen C. Mott, "Justice," *Harper's Bible Dictionary*, ed. Paul J. Achtemeier and others (San Francisco: Harper & Row, 1985), 519-520.

11. Ellen G. White, *Acts of the Apostles*, 88.

12. Ibid., 95.

13. The closely related noun appears four times and the verb once.

14. White, *Patriarchs and Prophets*, 42.

15. Ellen G. White, *Ministry of Healing*, 25.

16. White, *Testimonies*, 5:743.

17. Ibid., 6:12.

18. Ministerial Association, 170.

19. Ellen G. White, *The Ellen G. White 1888 Materials*, 1101.

20. Ellen G. White, *Love Unlimited*, 188.

21. See White, *Patriarchs and Prophets*, 41-42.

22. See the chapter by Walter Douglas on the parallels between slavery and the treatment of women.

23. See Walter Douglas' chapter in this book.

24. White, *Testimonies*, 9:224, 223.

25. Meredith B. McGuire, *Religion: The Social Context*, 2d ed. (Belmont, CA: Wadsworth, 1981), 98.

26. White, *Christ's Object Lessons*, 386.

27. "Human Relations—Policy Amendment," *Adventist Review*, 9 January 1997, 26-27. Italics in the original.

28. Ibid., 27.

29. In some world divisions the functions of the unordained pastor might be more restricted by action of the appropriate committee, but the world church has made provision for this wider service, and it is in those areas where male unordained ministers do have such privileges that females are more likely to serve as pastors.

30. "Matthew," *Seventh-day Adventist Bible Commentary*, ed. F. D. Nichol (Washington, DC: Review and Herald, 1953-1957), 5: 356.

31. Ellen G. White, *Education*, 14.

CHAPTER 20

CULTURE AND BIBLICAL UNDERSTANDING IN A WORLD CHURCH

JON L. DYBDAHL

> To the Jew I became like the Jews to win the Jews. To those under the law I became like one under the law (though I myself am not under the law), so as to win those under the law. To those not having the law I became like one not having the law (though I am not free from God's law but am under Christ's law) so as to win those not having the law. To the weak I became weak to win the weak. I have become all things to all men so that by all possible means I might save some. I do all this for the sake of the gospel. (1 Cor. 9:19-23a, NIV)

> Human minds vary: the minds of different education and thought receive different impressions of the same words, and it is difficult for one mind to give to one of a different temperament, education and habits of thought by language exactly the same idea as that which is clear and distinct in his own mind. (Ellen G. White, *Selected Messages*, 1:19)

> The truth a man accepts most willingly is the one he desires.
>
> (Sir Frances Bacon)

Adventism was born in North America. In 1874 the church sent out its first cross-cultural missionary. This small beginning grew into a massive concerted effort to reach out to every "nation, kindred, tongue and people." Today the church is truly international. The combined membership in North America, Australia, and Western Europe is a minority of less than 12 percent of total church membership.[1] By God's grace this multinational, ethnically and culturally diverse body has maintained a remarkable degree of unity.

Some recent events, such as the vote relating to the ordination of women, have put pressure on that unity. This essay is an attempt to promote an understanding of reality in a multicultural situation that will recognize differences but build toward underlying unity.

Traditionally, differences such as women's ordination have been viewed primarily as theological issues. The way to unity was to discuss theology and hope for eventual agreement. While not denying the theological facts, this essay suggests that two other closely related factors play a major role. Our culture and the biblical interpretation related to it to a large extent affect how we position ourselves on important issues.

Worldview and Consciousness

A convenient way to understand these issues is to define worldview and consciousness. Over the last two decades "worldview" has become an increasingly popular term. It has been used to describe the general religious beliefs of people[2] as well as how Christians should "see" or "vision" the world.[3] Students of mission have long been using it to help them in knowing how to communicate the gospel.[4] According to anthropologist/missiologist Paul Hiebert, "a world view provides people with their basic assumptions about reality."[5] Such assumptions are usually unconscious or only vaguely understood. In the course of time other words with similar meaning have come into use. One of these is "consciousness." Missiologist Harvie Conn uses this word to refer to an aspect of worldview that relates to the human understanding of religion and the role of God and science.[6] By "consciousness" Conn and this paper understand that the term refers to a view of life and God, and in particular the way we see ourselves, others, and God (or the Bible) functioning. Consciousness by this definition is not some New-Age idea about "higher consciousness," but a term describing the foundational concepts and attitudes that shape our lives and especially our views of God and belief.

I have deliberately chosen to use the term "consciousness" because what I describe is narrower than worldview, yet has to do with an important and developing basic attitude toward life. In what follows I briefly describe five types of consciousness.

Each consciousness has elements of truth in it. Often people move from one consciousness to another in the order I describe them, but this is not always so. Many times people understand intellectually a certain type of consciousness but do not practice it, choosing to live using a different type of consciousness. Consciousness level is not related to intelligence and may or may not indicate spirituality.

Self Consciousness

In this first type of consciousness the world centers on me and could also be called *ego consciousness*. I recognize myself and though eventually I recognize others, they are useful only as they help or serve me. Children begin here and, unfortunately, without proper training and a knowledge of God, many continue living at this consciousness long after childhood. This stage can be diagramed simply as:

$$P_1$$

P (standing for person) stands alone and is the basic determiner of understanding. Although quite self-centered, this consciousness is important to self-identity and is psychologically a key part of life.

Other Consciousness

This second kind of consciousness arrives when a person seriously takes into account other people; thus it is called *other consciousness*. The "other" could also include God as He reveals Himself in the Bible. Ideally for a Christian these two go together. A person recognizes God's love and authority and learns that she should love other persons. This act of taking God and other people seriously is a change of consciousness. Other Consciousness (for a Christian) can be diagramed in this way:

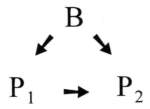

To the P_1 (person standing alone) have been added P_2 (other persons) and B (the Bible, God's Word). The Bible is pictured as above because it is an authority to be followed. P_1 assumes the Bible speaks more or less directly to her (and other people as well) and she is to obey. She is told to love the other person and share with him God's Word. She assumes that she can pass on God's Word directly to others. She (P_1) also assumes that when others (P_2) listen to the Bible, they (P_2) hear from it exactly what she (P_1) has herself heard. The one-way arrows signify mainly one-way, non-dialogic communication.

Historical Consciousness

Historical Consciousness comes with Christian education, either informal or formal. People discover that the Bible was written in a different language from their own, at a different historical time, and within a different cultural context. Missionaries, teachers, and pastors share historical consciousness with believers as a means of helping them apply the Bible and answer their questions about its content. Historical Consciousness deals with issues such as why most Christians today are not obligated to dress as Jesus and the apostles did and literally to greet one another with a "holy kiss" (1 Thess 5:26). Historical Consciousness can be diagrammed like this:

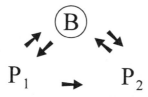

The circle around B (Bible) means that it is now seen to be in a particular cultural/historical context. The two-way arrows between P_1/P_2 and the Bible signify dialogue. While the Bible still is authority, it must now be interpreted. Both P_1 and P_2 dialogue with it, seeking to find reasons and principles behind specific instruction. P_1 and P_2, however, still understand themselves as being without cultural baggage. P_1 assumes that if P_2 is honest, he or she will see the same thing in the Bible as P_1 does.

Theological Consciousness

This fourth kind of consciousness recognizes that P_1 is also living, experiencing, and seeing within a culture. This means that the very way she/he looks at the Bible is affected by his/her background, language, nationality, and history. The movement to live at Theological Consciousness is difficult because the human heart naturally sees its own understanding as valid, clear, and unbiased. While it is easy to see others as culturally conditioned, to see oneself that way demands special grace! Theological Consciousness can be diagrammed as such.

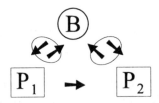

The boxes around both P_1 and P_2 signify that P_1 recognizes that his/her culture affects the interpretation of what the Bible says. The ellipse over the two-way dialogue arrows represents a filter. P_1 recognizes that she/he views Scripture through a filter. Culture is the filter. Note, however, that *both* P_1 and P_2 have a square around them. Their cultures are assumed to be similar. Because they are both human, the cultural differences between them are not seen as significant.

Missiological Consciousness

The final kind of consciousness builds on the earlier consciousness types. The term Missiological Consciousness is used because in this step P_1 recognizes that P_2 is truly different and the same dialogue and same filter which are in place between P_1 and the Bible should be between P_1 and P_2—regardless of whether P_2 is a nonbeliever or a fellow believer. Cultural difference is as important (or even perhaps more important) for true communication between P_1 and P_2 as belief difference. Missiological Consciousness can be diagrammed thus:

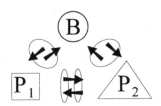

P_2 is now enclosed in a culture but one that is different from P_1. The same dialogue arrows and the filters that were used in biblical interpretation are now in place between P_1 and P_2. The Bible maintains its authority. Both P_1 and P_2 have equal access to the Bible. After seeking to discover God's will in Scripture, while recognizing their own biases, they are now prepared to communicate as equals. They understand clearly that their vision of truth and reality has been affected by who they are.

Remember that the type of consciousness exhibited by a person has little or nothing to do with intellect or commitment. Many who operate at Other Consciousness or Historical Consciousness are more committed to God than some believers who live at Theological Consciousness or Missiological Consciousness. Types of consciousness deal only with understanding and mode of action. However, people at Theological Consciousness and Missiological Consciousness will usually be more effective as cross-cultural missionaries and evangelists than those who manifest Other Consciousness or Historical Consciousness.

Implications

What does all of this suggest? What does it mean to the church in relation to biblical interpretation and theological dialogue?

1. Our cultural context strongly affects our biblical interpretation

By cultural context I mean background, history, language, education, social class, ethnicity, etc. None of us can (or would probably even want to!) escape that context.

Missiologists and some theologians like to say the message of God's word must always be contextualized. That means simply that for eternal truth to be communicated effectively it must be presented in a way that fits the context of both communicator and receptor. Differing cultures make contextualization essential, but doing it faithfully and effectively remains difficult. Much care is needed to be sure that eternal truth is preserved *and* that effective communication takes place.

The simple fact is that *everybody* contextualizes. The difference is that some know it and some do not. People at Other Consciousness and Historical Consciousness usually contextualize unwittingly. Unless they are native speakers of Hebrew or Greek, the message comes to Other Consciousness people in a contextualized form. Translation is a form of contextualization. Theological Consciousness is contextualizing the gospel for people and their culture. That is what theology is. Missiological Consciousness people contextualize the gospel for themselves and then recontextualize it for another culture.

The question, then, is not whether to contextualize or not. It is how *well* we are doing it. The more we understand contextualization and follow correct principles, the closer we are to rightly proclaiming God's eternal word in a way that changes people.

2. Eternal truth is never relative, but our perception of it always is

One objection that some will raise to my suggestions is that they lead to relativism. If the Bible is in a culture and we see things through our culture, then can any truth be sure? Can the Bible be a real authority? Scripture remains the norm, and its authority is not changed. In the diagrams representing consciousness the Bible is always *above* us, showing we are subject to it. Scripture is truth, but our perception of it is culturally affected. The Bible is the standard, but my understanding and application of it are not. I like the way Bernard Adeney expresses it,

> As a Christian I have no doubt that there are absolute values, but an understanding of them is always relative. 'Now we see in a mirror dimly. . . . Now I know only in part' (1 Cor. 13:12). Not only the limitations of our cultural, social and economic background but also the presence of sin in our lives prevents us from absolute understanding.[7]

This viewpoint may seem new to some Adventists, but Bible-believing evangelical Christians have espoused it for a long time. In the Willowbank report, *Gospel and Culture*, published under the auspices of the Lausanne Committee for World Evangelization, the following quotations come from the same page. The first occurs under the heading "Normative Nature of Scripture," and the second under the subject "The Cultural Conditioning of Scripture."

> The Lausanne Covenant declares that Scripture is "without error in all that it affirms" (page 2). This lays upon us the serious exegetical task of discerning exactly what Scripture is affirming.

> We are agreed that some biblical commands . . . refer to cultural customs now obsolete in many parts of the world. Faced with such texts we believe that the right response is neither a slavish literal obedience nor an irresponsible disregard, but rather first a critical discernment of the texts' inner meaning and then a translation of it into our own culture. . . . We are clear that the purpose of such "cultural transposition" is not to avoid obedience but rather to make it contemporary and authentic.[8]

These passages emphasize the need to take Scripture seriously and recognize that it is written in a cultural context. I have quoted extensively to show that such ideas do not come from wild-eyed liberals seeking to undermine scriptural authority, but conservative Christians eager to uphold the Bible and communicate the gospel. These passages clearly affirm the Historical Consciousness and Theological Consciousness perspectives that I have already outlined.

Later passages speak more specifically about the missionary task which I have called Missiological Consciousness.

> No Christian witness can hope to communicate the gospel if he or she ignores the cultural factor. . . . Messengers of the gospel are (at times) guilty of a cultural evangelism which both undermines the local culture unnecessarily and seeks to impose an alien culture instead.[9]

In reality the only extra step I have taken is to say the same principles apply *inside* a multicultured world church like ours. We must not only be sensitive culturally to those *outside* our church; we must as brothers and sisters do the same *inside* the church.

While at first this viewpoint may seem to relativize some things, if properly approached, it leads to a principled moral and theological seriousness that surpasses the old *culturally specific so-called absolutes*. In reality it leads to greater faithfulness with a wider scope of obedience.

An example may be helpful. As were many Adventists of my generation, I was taught that bicycle riding on Sabbath was wrong, as was paying out money such as bus fare. When we served as missionaries in Thailand, some of our poorer church members had no way to get to church but riding bicycles or taking a bus which required a fare. We faced a dilemma. The Bible says nothing directly about bicycles or bus fare. Needless to say, it did not take us too long to realize that what had been a Sabbath-observance rule in 1950s and 1960s America did not apply in 1970s and 1980s Thailand. We rode cars to church; bicycles were an optional pleasure. Some Thais rode bicycles or buses for necessary transport to church; for them riding in a car (which would have to be rented) was an unnecessary Sabbath luxury.

In meeting the issue, we were driven to search for the biblical principles that transcend culture. In doing so, our understanding of and commitment to core biblical truth grew. I believe that the principle of Sabbath observance is *eternal*, but culture does affect how we interpret and apply it. If I accept the fact that the biblical principle has something to say to *all* cultures, then it goes beyond my specific cultural understanding. Scripture is thus *more* widely authoritative rather than less so.

3. Scripture is in many areas polyvalent

By "polyvalent" I mean that more than one meaning can be validly derived from it. This seems rather obvious in relation to biblical stories.

I was taught that the basic meaning of the Joseph story was that, like Joseph, I should stand for truth no matter what the cost, even in situations far from home. Many African and Asian Christians see Joseph primarily as one who in spite of all odds was loyal to and never forgot his family. Careful Bible study reveals that, for Genesis and Israel, the main lesson that Joseph teaches is that in spite of human sin and unfaithfulness (Joseph's brothers), God is faithful to his promises. What is the actual lesson in the story? I believe *all* three are valid. None rules out the other. The Bible is deeper and broader than our cultural reading of it.

Even moral laws that all would agree with—for instance, the seventh commandment forbidding adultery (Exod 20:14)—seem to have been viewed differently. Jews in Old Testament times saw the law as specifically forbidding sex when one or both partners were married or engaged to someone else. Jesus in Matt 5:27-30 taught that male lust for a woman other than one's wife is *heart* adultery. Some consider polygamy to be adultery, while others do not. As long as humanity is diverse in culture and experience, different facets of the command will be emphasized or ignored as application to specific situations is made.

There are certain key basics—the Sabbath, the literal second coming of Jesus, and the nonimmortality of the soul are some examples. They do *not* change. Even these basics, however, are preached and taught somewhat differently from culture to culture. How the Sabbath is kept, what signs of the second coming are emphasized, and the best way to present the state of the dead vary from culture to culture. This *should* be true if we expect to communicate to those who are not like us.

4. The need for the Holy Spirit

When we realize the depth of our own blindness to ourselves and to others, we are driven to God. Then the Spirit of God can lead us into truth. Only the Holy Spirit can take our feeble words and *really* communicate to others the deep truth of God's love in the good news of the gospel.

I believe the Spirit desires to lead us all into a humility of spirit which makes us hesitant to push our interpretations on other people. That humility would teach us to listen carefully to others. If this happened, we would all understand truth better.

5. Often theological conflicts are also cross-cultural conflicts

Some issues are primarily theological. Truth issues do exist. The Sabbath vs. Sunday conflict is, I believe, a theological issue. At the same time, we should realize that people who do not have Sunday as a cultural norm find it easier to accept the Sabbath.

Other issues, though they are treated as theological, have an important cultural component. I believe worship style and music choice fit in that category. Worship and music do have theological bases, but as played out in the church, the issue is often cultural. The issue of women's ordination has major cultural overtones. Again it cannot be denied that theological issues are present, but as played out in the church at Utrecht '95, the issue was also one of cross-cultural conflict. Specific evidence for this will be given in the final section of this chapter where I deal with what these ideas imply for the ordination issue.

What this means is that we should seek resolution of this issue by methods used to solve cross-cultural conflict as much as procedures utilized in theological debate. The issues would also need to be framed so that people can discuss them in ways that deliberately take their cross-cultural overtones into consideration.

Consciousness Change

At this juncture we need to examine how change of consciousness level takes place. Please remember again that level of consciousness does *not* mean spiritual condition or intelligence. It has simply to do with understanding—and hopefully action—in one area of life. It is important, however, because Christians have been given the mandate to share God's message with the whole world. Other Consciousness people can effectively share with their own culture but can be disastrous as cross-cultural missionaries. Consciousness is also crucial to unity and understanding in a world church. The more developed the consciousness level (provided earlier consciousness lessons are not forgotten!), the more biblically and lovingly Christians can relate to both fellow believers and unbelievers of other cultures.

The movement from Self Consciousness to Other Consciousness comes through conversion. Persons living for self come to recognize themselves as children of God, with Jesus as Lord. Evangelism facilitates this change. Some people, who are under the authority of the wrong "other" (false gods/religions), also need a conversion from that false god to the true one.

The movement from Other Consciousness to Historical Consciousness usually comes through religious education. Some educated people already understand this step at their conversion from Self Consciousness. They come to Other Consciousness and Historical Consciousness at roughly the same time. However, as the majority of people study the Bible, especially in a Western educational setting, they develop an understanding of Historical Consciousness and at least practice it to some degree. In-depth religious education and especially theological education usually assume Historical Consciousness and subtly but effectively teach it to students.

The movement from Historical Consciousness to Theological Consciousness and Missiological Consciousness is problematic. Theological Consciousness and Missiological Consciousness require a clear recognition that one's own way of seeing things is incomplete and biased by culture. Some things I may see well, but on other issues even "uneducated people" may have insights that have escaped me. More than likely that realization will call into question some of my cherished viewpoints. Throughout this process of discovery, people are moved out of their comfort zone. It is one thing to admit in Historical Consciousness that the Bible is culturally contextualized, but it comes a lot closer to home when, in Theological Consciousness and Missiological Consciousness, I see the same in myself! Could parts of the Bible that I have ignored because of my culture actually teach important concepts I have been missing? These ideas are not easy to come to terms with! They require not simply a change of consciousness but a humility of heart which is a gift of God.

For a number of years I have worked at the Institute of World Mission, helping prepare SDA missionaries for cross-cultural service. Although it is not stated as such, we have a threefold aim for our intensive training. First, we examine and affirm the call to mission. Second, we confirm and strengthen basic Christian commitment (Other Consciousness). Third, we attempt to move people to Theological Consciousness and Missiological Consciousness. Most who come to us (and in fact a majority in the church) operate at Historical Consciousness.

How do we go about bringing this change in understanding? We have found that teaching sensitivity to and communication with another culture—Missiological Consciousness—often leads to the "aha" experience of self-understanding that is Theological Consciousness. The realization that those with different cultural perspectives have valuable original insights and must be taken seriously can lead to greater self-understanding.

I still vividly remember how Asian friends and colleagues taught me how to deal with differences. My direct Western approach was not effective in Asia. My understanding was that the key issue was hon-esty, which, to my Western way of thinking, implied directness. They schooled me to see that love and harmony were central and that indirectness was a much better way. Honesty did not necessarily mean directness and confrontation. I saw not only what they did in a new light, but I saw my own culture in a changed way. I even became convinced that in most cases their method worked better and was more biblical than mine.

Even intellectually sophisticated people have trouble changing their views because of cultural perspective. Bruce Holbrook worked on his Ph.D. in anthropology at Yale University. His subject was Chinese medical models. During his research he actually came to believe that in some ways the Chinese model of medicine was superior to the Western model he was familiar with. He faced tremendous opposition from faculty advisors back home: he could study Chinese medicine as an object, but to begin to believe it superior to his own culture was "heresy." In the end he wrote two dissertations—one to please his faculty advisors and one to explain what he really felt. His academic advisors were as fundamentalistic and monocultural as any religious zealot living in his or her culture.[10]

Realizing my missionary bias, I nonetheless believe that one of the best ways to come to Theological Consciousness and Missiological Consciousness is to actually live in another culture. Being forced to learn a new language and incarnate oneself into another setting gives a kind of shock treatment that can be conducive to the revolution in thinking that is called for. A brief foray as a tourist will not suffice. Not all missionaries, however, go through the needed change. Some have no education or model to point the way. Others are simply too threatened to take the plunge. Those who do change are never the same. The traditional policy that all General Conference presidents have cross-cultural experience is a good idea. A world church needs a leader with a cross-cultural outlook.

Relation to Women's Ordination

This paper thus far has presented general principles that apply in many situations. Now we must explore how these principles apply to the specific case of women's ordination.

The issue of women's ordination is as much a cross-cultural conflict as it is a theological issue. The cultural lines the vote followed were clear. Conversations with individual delegates indicated that North America, Western Europe, and to some extent Australia were heavily in favor of allowing North America to ordain women. Those from Latin America, Africa, and to a large extent Asia and Eastern Europe were strongly opposed. African Americans and Hispanic Americans, on the other hand, spoke in favor of the measure. It seems obvious that the vote is, then, not really *ethnic* but *cultural*.

Those opposed to the measure spoke of their concerns. They were worried about compromise with the world, decadence, and lax standards. They believed the Bible's authority was threatened by the proposal. They feared that the "liberal" standards they see on television and read in the newspapers (often supposedly originating from America) are on the verge of entering the church. They had visions of militant women's liberationists taking over the church. They were not sure they wanted to see women preaching in churches. In short, the proposal was a threat to who they were culturally and religiously.

Those in favor of the motion shared their concerns. They were worried about fairness and justice to people of different gender and race. They believed that not to ordain women is against the principle of equality in Christ they find in Scripture. They were wondering how they would conform to governmental laws that forbid gender bias. Perhaps most of all, they were afraid of losing a generation of women and young people who heavily favor ordination, and in most cases did not even consider it an issue of debate. In short, not passing the proposal was equally a threat to who they were culturally and religiously.

The concerns of each group are culturally related. Church and societal breakdown and loss of traditional stance are the great fear of ordination opposers. Ordination proponents fear injustice, lack of relevance, and loss of the younger generation. Both types of fear are valid; both are understandable. The fact is that we often forget to recognize how these different fears push us to different theologies and create divisions.

I believe that the most rabid supporters on both sides have simply not listened to and heard the other. They are operating on a Historical Consciousness level and cannot see another viewpoint. I realize that both sides will probably be unhappy with this analysis, but I maintain it to try to raise consciousness, bring healing, and search for a way out of the current impasse.

Let us be honest. There is no clear specific biblical statement on the issue. No verse gives permission to ordain women, and no passage specifically forbids it. Both sides, then, are free to find passages which they seek to apply to the issue by implication or in principle. When this is done, the cultural filter is in full use. People seek to discover what they have been driven to find by their cultural conditioning and preunder-standing.

Both sides use Scripture. In spite of the accusation by antiordination supporters that ordination proponents disregard Scripture, the evidence does not support this charge. When we discover leaders in the Adventist Theological Society (founded specifically to defend a conservative view of inspiration) supporting ordination, the accusation loses credibility.

All this leads us to believe that there is a lot more to this issue than simply theology.

Conclusion—What Can We Do?

In conclusion, what can we say to help us over this rift in our church? What can we as God's people do to begin to bring understanding out of hurt? I suggest four principles or steps.

1. Honestly look at ourselves.

One of the hardest things in the world is to recognize our own biases and inadequacies. Jesus asked, "Why do you look at the speck in your brother's eye and pay no attention to the plank in your own eye?" (Matt 7:3, NIV). The way to begin change is to start with ourselves.

This does not mean that we have to change our actual position. That could perhaps happen, but what needs to take place is the realization that our position on ordination is influenced by all we are. That dawning truth should make us less likely to condemn others whose belief stems from the same source. The way to honest dialogue is then opened.

2. Tell our story and listen to each other's feelings.

Being willing to tell not simply our position but the real story behind it helps clear the way to open communication. We must not only tell our story; we must be willing to carefully listen to the stories of those who disagree with us.

Those who believe in women's ordination need to tell about their daughter who in tears shares how she desires to minister for God but feels discriminated against. They need to discuss the pain of the mature woman who has the same education and experience as her male counterpart but never has received the same recognition. They need to share the agony of the college religion teacher who struggles before a hostile class to defend his church when students feel the government is fairer to women than his beloved community of faith.

Opposers of women's ordination need to express their stories as well. They must share the painful results in their church and society that come from breakdown of order. They must tell how they feel about threats to the full authority of Scripture. They should reveal their agony about the family break-up they see taking place in America and explain how they fear women's ordination may increase and spread it. They should share how in an uncertain world they want the church to stand for meaningful traditions and say no to liberal secular culture.

The truth is that really hearing each other's feelings can begin to make us, as sisters and brothers in the same family, empathize with family members of differing persuasions.

3. Seriously study material that does not support our own view.

Those wanting a full picture should not simply choose to read that which supports how they already feel. Read rational arguments of those who disagree. This book is itself an attempt to be helpful in making the dialogue more like a family council than a battle of opposing armies. That is, in fact, our aim. We do not want to fire shots in a battle but to start a family council. We must create a context in which a world family recognizes that not all see things the same way, but this is natural and we can still be one family. We can remain family so long as we listen to each other and talk to each other under the authority of the Bible in a spirit of love and concern.

4. We must accept the fact that differences need not separate us.

We do not all need to see every issue in exactly the same way. Husbands and wives, as well as siblings, remain in a family relationship even though they differ. The early Adventist Church lived with differences in a healthy way. Cannot we as a church do the same?

If the issue of women's ordination, and other issues as well, could be approached with a humility of spirit that truly listens to others and is willing to evaluate its own understanding; if serious prayer and a dependence on the Holy Spirit were as much in evidence as theological debate, then resolution and unity now only dreamed about could take place in our midst.

Endnotes

1. Projected membership for 2000 by General Conference staff of Archives and Statistics, based on 1960-1988 figures.

2. See, for example, Ninian Smart, *Worldviews: Crosscultural Explanations of Human Beliefs* (New York: Scribners, 1983).

3. See, for example, Brian J. Walsh and J. Richard Middleton, *The Transforming Vision: Shaping a Christian World View* (Downers Grove, IL: InterVarsity, 1984).

4. See, for example, Marguerite G. Kraft, *Worldview and the Communication of the Gospel: A Nigerian Case Study* (South Pasadena, CA: Wm. Carey, 1978).

5. Paul Hiebert, *Cultural Anthropology* (Philadelphia: Lippincott, 1976), 371.

6. Harvie M. Conn, *Eternal Word and Changing Worlds: Theology, Anthropology and Mission in Dialogue* (Grand Rapids: Zondervan, 1984), 46-50, 88.

7. Bernard T. Adeney, *Strange Virtues: Ethics in a Multicultural World* (Downers Grove, IL: InterVarsity, 1995), 20-21.

8. Lausanne Committee for World Evangelization. *The Willowbank Report: Gospel and Culture*, Lausanne Occasional Papers, Lausanne Committee for World Evangelization (Pasadena, CA: Wm. Carey, 1978), 9

9. Ibid., 13-14.

10. Bruce Holbrook, *The Stone Monkey* (New York: William Morrow, 1981), 10-14.

EPILOGUE

So, what did we, the members of the Ad hoc Committee on Hermeneutics and Ordination, learn from our two-year study? Much, in every way! Short reflections on each of the five parts of this book condense our findings.

Our Findings

Ministry in the Bible

After the Fall, worship was directed by the patriarchs, the leaders of families. At the Exodus, God declared that his covenant-keeping people should be a "kingdom of priests" (Exod 19:5-6). He also designated religious leaders for the nation church: physically perfect, male priests, descendants of Aaron. In the New Testament, the Levitical priesthood disappears and Jesus is portrayed as the heavenly High Priest, with all Christians forming part of the royal priesthood of believers. Ministry is no longer in the hands of the few, but there are leaders. The gifts of the Spirit enable those who receive them—regardless of their race, gender, or age—to minister to the church and carry the glad tidings of salvation to the whole world.

Ordination

The word is not used in the Bible, yet ceremonies of installation existed. Hands were laid upon apostles, elders, and deacons by the faithful in preparation for their specific ministries. Within three centuries the pattern changed to the ordination of church leaders by those in higher positions within the church hierarchy; this doctrine in time became known as "apostolic succession." In the mid-nineteenth century, pragmatic Adventism took over to a great extent the ordination patterns of the churches from which its leaders had come. Ellen White viewed ordination as a ceremony by which the church recognized the gifting of the Holy Spirit but which did not add "new grace." She proposed ordination for different types of ministers, both clergy and lay, including women who would spend time in home visitation. A biblical and Adventist view of ordination regards the ceremony as a recognition by the church and a setting apart for ministry, a doorway to service and spiritual leadership rather than to position and prestige.

Women in Ministry and Leadership

Even in the Old Testament, women occupied leadership positions. Sarah, Deborah, Hannah, and Huldah—to mention a few—could hardly be classified as submissive females. Jesus had women disciples; the first proclaimer of the resurrection was a woman. Paul mentions women among his coworkers, and goes so far as to call one an apostle and another a deacon. In Adventism, women have been active in preaching, teaching, healing, and leadership roles from the earliest times, in spite of nineteenth-century prejudices against such activities. Ellen White strongly supported women in ministry, even suggesting that they be paid from the tithe. In the late-nineteenth century, women were active in church leadership and ministry. After 1915 the number in leadership decreased dramatically. The last quarter of this century has seen an increase in the number of women in ministry and leadership; acceptance of these women has not been unanimous, leading at times to debate, centered especially on whether or not these women should receive ordination.

Perceived Impediments to Women in Pastoral Leadership

Arguments often used against ordination are considered and answered. "Headship" belongs to the husband-wife relationship, not to any male preponderance over all females; it is part of God's plan for fallen human beings rather than an original mandate for the sinless world. A study of the whole of Paul's writings, together with a careful exegesis of the specific passages often quoted as prohibiting women in leadership roles, shows that his passages requiring silence in church refer to specific situations and are not to be used as a blanket regulation for all times. However, the principles of order and appropriateness underlying his words do apply. Finally, the use of an Ellen White quotation to affirm that those who support women's ordination might as well abandon the three angels' messages is analyzed and found to refer to the use of the "American costume" and not at all to the question of ordination.

Other Considerations

While these three chapters might appear to be irrelevant to the main argument of this study, the Ad hoc Committee felt they were important and needed to be included. First, a study of the biblical hermeneutics and arguments of nineteenth-century American slaveholders in favor of the permanence and desirability of slavery showed a curious twisting of the Bible. Parallels with the argumentation of those who oppose the ordination of women to pastoral leadership were striking. Especially in the West, nonordination of women who are performing the same tasks as men who are ordained is seen as injustice. And because God is the epitome of justice, this attitude would misrepresent the character of God. Finally, much as we cherish unity in the church, we are constrained to admit that there is diversity in the way we see life, the way we understand Scripture, the way we perceive God. Communication among members of this diverse yet united community demands listening to each other and to the Holy Spirit.

Our Conclusions

Because of Calvary, men and women share equally in a new creation (2 Cor 5:17). While living in the world, they are not of the world (John 17:14). In mutual submission (Eph 5:21) and loving preference of others (Phil 2:3), the old distinctions—Black and White, rich and poor, Jew and Gentile, slave and free, male and female—no longer count (Gal 3:28). The one Head of the church is Christ the Lord.

In this new community, each member of the body is gifted in a special way (Rom 12:4-8; 1 Cor 12:4-11). Paul pointed out that among these gifts were prophets, apostles, and teacher- pastors. Their function was—and is—to equip the saints and build up the body (Eph 4:11, 12), to minister reconciliation (2 Cor 5:18, 19) to those who are far from God, that they may become "citizens" of the kingdom (Eph 2:17-19).

In this body of the redeemed on earth, men and women together are called to exercise their gifts. While there are innate differences between men and women, a woman called and qualified by God to perform pastoral duties, whose labor builds the body, should be recognized as a full-fledged minister. There is no biblical impediment for a woman to minister in any capacity for which she is called and equipped. Neither is there biblical reason for ordination to be withheld because of her gender.

However, the church in all lands may not benefit from having women as pastors. "All things should be done decently and in order" (1 Cor 14:40), with consideration for the opinions of "outsiders" (Col 4:5; 1 Thess 4:12). Above all, care must be taken that tradition not speak louder than the Bible.

Change, although difficult, is possible. What happened at the Jerusalem Council (Acts 15) is instructive. At that time the believers debated vigorously and at length whether it was proper for Gentiles to become Christians without first being circumcised, as had been required for participation in the Old Testament covenant (Gen 17:9-14). God himself had given this sign and failure to circumcise his young son nearly cost Moses his life (Exod 4:24), yet the Jerusalem Council decided to not require circumcision of those who came to faith (Acts 15:19). This change of opinion came after Paul and Barnabas rehearsed the wonders God had performed among the Gentiles. The phrase "it seemed good" appears in vv. 22, 25, and 28 to describe the agreement of apostles, elders, and believers, together with the Holy Spirit, on the new instructions. If circumcision, based on divine mandate, could be changed, how much more could patterns of ministry, which lack a clear "Thus says the Lord," be modified to suit the needs of a growing church?

The Seminary Ad Hoc Committee on Hermeneutics and Ordination has attempted to be faithful to Scripture, allowing the Spirit to lead us and work in us. Our conclusion is that ordination and women can go together, that "women in pastoral leadership" is not an oxymoron, but a manifestation of God's grace in the church. We view our work as a contribution to an ongoing dialog. We trust it will be accepted as such.

CONTRIBUTORS' PROFILES

Daniel A. Augsburger, Professor of Historical Theology, Emeritus.
Writing from retirement, Augsburger brings to his writing a wealth of experience in teaching theology and church history. He holds two doctorates: his Ph.D. dissertation was on religious feeling in the Middle Ages; his Th.D. dissertation dealt with Calvin and the Mosaic Law.

Michael Bernoi, Master of Divinity student at the Theological Seminary.
Before coming to the Seminary, Bernoi worked as a pastor for three years. While a Seminary student, he helped to plant a new Adventist church in Berrien Springs.

Jo Ann Davidson, Assistant Professor of Systematic Theology
Jo Ann Davidson is a wife, mother, and new teacher at the Seminary. She also writes a column discussing theological issues ("Let's Face It") in the journal *Perspective Digest*.

Richard M. Davidson, J. N. Andrews Professor of Old Testament Interpretation.
Chairman of the Old Testament Department at the Seminary, Davidson was elected Teacher of the Year by the Student Forum in 1998. He holds a doctorate in Old Testament from the SDA Theological Seminary. He and Jo Ann are the parents of two lively teenagers.

Raoul Dederen, Professor of Theology, Emeritus.
Dean of Adventist theologians, Dederen has specialized in systematic theology and Roman Catholicism. He writes from an active retirement.

Walter B. T. Douglas, Professor of Church History and History of Religion.
A native of Grenada, Douglas chairs the Church History Department and pastors the All Nations Church in Berrien Springs.

Jacques B. Doukhan, Professor of Hebrew and Old Testament Exegesis
Doukhan holds a doctorate in Hebrew Letters from the University of Strassbourg and a Th.D. from Andrews University, where he currently teaches Hebrew and Old Testament exegesis. He is also the editor of *Shabbaat Shalom* and *L'Olivier*. He has authored many articles and seven books.

Roger L. Dudley, Professor of Church Ministry and Director, Institute of Church Ministry.
Roger Dudley has spent nearly 45 years in the ministry of teaching, preaching, writing, and researching. He has authored 12 books and 160 articles. His interests lie in the intersection of religion and the behavioral sciences.

Jon L. Dybdahl, Professor of World Mission.
Chairman of the World Mission Department at the Theological Seminary, Dybdahl has served as pastor, pioneer missionary in Asia, and college religion teacher. A multi-faceted person, his doctorate is in Old Testament and he teaches spiritual formation for pastors.

J. H. Denis Fortin, Associate Professor of Theology.
A son of French Canada, Fortin pastored for a number of years while completing a degree in theology and church history at Université Laval in Quebec. Besides teaching historical theology, Fortin enjoys family and Pathfindering.

Robert M. Johnston, Professor of New Testament and Christian Origins.
Chairman of the New Testament Department at the Seminary, Johnston has specialized in the study of New Testament backgrounds. A long-time missionary in Korea, Johnston combines New Testament scholarship and all things Oriental. He is the author of two books and numerous articles and papers.

George R. Knight, Professor of Church History.
A well-known writer, Knight has authored 18 books, mostly on Adventist topics. He is currently editor of the Bible Amplifier, a commentary series published by Pacific Press. When he is not preaching around the world, he loves hiking and backpacking.

Keith Mattingly, Associate Professor of Religion.
In 1997 Mattingly wrote his Ph.D. dissertation on laying on of hands. Mattingly teaches religion classes to the undergraduates. His passion is helping to make God "real" to his students.

Jerry Moon, Associate Professor of Church History and Associate Editor *AUSS*.
After 11 years of pastoring, Moon returned to Andrews where he obtained his Ph.D. in Church History and was invited to join the faculty. His area of specialty is Adventist Studies. Moon served as the very efficient secretary of the committee.

W. Larry Richards, Professor of New Testament Exegesis.
Besides teaching exegetical courses, Richards directs the New Testament Greek Manuscript Center at Andrews University, the largest collection in North America of Greek manuscripts on microfilm. His published research on Greek manuscripts puts him among the few specialists in the area of textual criticism.

Russell L. Staples, Professor of Missions, Emeritus.
Retired but still teaching, Staples served in the Department of World Mission for 25 years. Previously he spend 10 years as a pastor in South Africa and 10 years at Solusi College. He has a Ph.D. in Systematic Theology from Princeton Theological Seminary with ancillary studies in anthropology from Princeton University.

Peter M. van Bemmelen, Professor of Theology.
A native of the Netherlands, van Bemmelen was a missionary in Trinidad and Surinam. After completing his Ph.D. at Andrews University, he became a lecturer at Newbold College. From there he returned to Andrews as a professor in 1993.

Nancy Jean Vyhmeister, Professor of World Mission
With 35 years of experience in training young ministers, Vyhmeister has taught Greek and biblical studies, as well as research methods for theology students. Currently she is editor of *Andrews University Seminary Studies*. The wife of a pastor, she has participated in ministry on three continents.

Randal R. Wisbey, Associate Professor of Youth Ministry and Director of the M.A. in Youth Ministry.

Founder of the Center for Youth Evangelism at Andrews University, Wisbey is recognized for his creative work in the areas of youth culture and generational studies. In June of 1998 he became President of Canadian University College.

Alicia A. Worley, Masters in Physical Therapy, M.A. in Anthropology, currently an M.Div. student.

Raised as a missionary's kid in Africa, Worley understands better than most how people are affected by their culture. As she nears completion of her program she looks forward to team pastoring in Ecuador with her new husband Ricardo Palacios.